Psychological research

Psychological Research examines how research is undertaken in psychology and the social sciences where many different and evolving traditions exist together. John Haworth examines how we come to know things in today's world and how we should appraise the results of research in the social sciences and science in general. Implicit in such concerns are fundamental questions concerning the nature of truth and objectivity and the importance of values in making judgements. These questions form the theoretical base from which research strategies and methods are discussed. *Psychological Research* is divided into three sections; survey research, qualitative research and controlled investigations, with contributions from experts in a wide range of research areas. Methods and strategies of research are related to areas such as health behaviour, work psychology and social remembering, offering the reader critical understanding of research in areas at the forefront of psychology. This book will be of direct benefit to all students and professionals undertaking research and to all those concerned with the nature and use of knowledge.

John Haworth is a Lecturer in Psychology at Manchester University with research interests in mental health, work and leisure. His previous books are *Work and Leisure* (1975) and *Community Involvement and Leisure* (1979). He has published extensively in academic journals.

Psychological research

Innovative methods and strategies

Edited by John Haworth

London and New York

First published 1996
by Routledge
11 New Fetter Lane, London EC4P 4EE

Simultaneously published in the USA and Canada
by Routledge
29 West 35th Street, New York, NY 10001

Typeset in Times by
Ponting–Green Publishing Services, Chesham, Bucks
Printed and bound in Great Britain by
Clays Ltd, St Ives plc

British Library Cataloguing in Publication Data
A catalogue record for this book is available from the
British Library

Library of Congress Cataloguing in Publication Data
A catalogue record for this book has been requested

ISBN 0–415–11789–5 (hbk)
ISBN 0–415–11790–9 (pbk)

Contents

Illustrations

Contributors

John Bowers is a Lecturer in the Department of Psychology, University of Manchester, having previously worked at the universities of Oxford, Cambridge and Nottingham. He has been a visiting researcher at Lancaster University, the Sweden Institute for Computer Science and the Royal Institute of Technology, Stockholm. He researches work and interaction using qualitative methods (ethnography, conversation and discourse analysis), in particular focusing on the design and usage of computing technology (especially advanced cooperative systems and virtual reality). His overall aim is to use empirical study to reformulate foundational issues in cognitive science and social organisational theory. Dr Bowers was a founding editor of the journal, *Computer Supported Cooperative Work*. He also writes computer music and has had compositions performed at several concerts in Europe, most recently as part of Membrane, a series of multimedia performances combining dance, music and interactive virtual reality.

Ros Bramwell took her BSc in psychology at Bradford University and her PhD in the School of Management at UMIST. She is a chartered psychologist. She now works in the Department of Psychology at the University of Central Lancashire, and lectures in methodology and statistics and health psychology at undergraduate and postgraduate level. Her research interests include occupational health and reproductive health.

Erica Burman lectures in developmental psychology and women's studies at the Department of Psychology and Speech Pathology, Manchester Metropolitan University. Her previous publications include *Feminists and Psychological Practice* (edited, Sage, 1990), *Discourse Analytic Research* (co-edited, 1993, Routledge) and *Deconstructing Developmental Psychology* (1994, Routledge). She is currently on the editorial board of *Feminism & Psychology* and writes on feminist critiques of and in psychology and development.

Mark Conner is a Lecturer in social psychology at Leeds University. He completed his first degree at Lancaster and his PhD at Birmingham University, both in psychology. He subsequently worked at the Social and Applied

Psychology Unit, University of Sheffield until moving to Leeds University in 1990. His research interests are in attitude theory and social cognitive determinants of health behaviours, with a particular interest in food choice. He teaches courses on research methods and psychometrics to undergraduate and postgraduate psychologists. He also runs third-year option courses for undergraduate psychology students on health psychology and the social psychology of attitudes.

E. Connors is a Lecturer in psychology at the University of Central Lancashire. She graduated in psychology in 1990 and has recently gained her PhD on the social environmental correlates of mastery motivation of infancy. Her research interests are in mother–infant interaction and infant temperament relations, mastery motivation, attachment and exploratory behaviour in infancy.

S.M. Glenn is Professor of Applied Developmental Psychology and Head of Research at the School of Healthcare, Liverpool John Moores University. Her main research interests are in the early development of children with learning disabilities and in family adaptation. She has recent publications on development in Down's Syndrome, contingency awareness in infancy and in children with profound and multiple learning disabilities, and children's drawing. Current projects include: mastery motivation and the home environment in young children and in children with Down's Syndrome; assessment of pain in premature infants and neonates undergoing surgery; emotional expression in infants with disabilities; the environment in the Neonatal Intensive Care Unit and the use of yoga therapy in cardiac rehabilitation.

Robin Goodwin is a Lecturer in social psychology at the University of Bristol. He obtained his degree and PhD from the University of Kent, Canterbury. His main research interests are in the impact of large social transitions on personal relationships, and he has conducted research on this theme in a number of different cultures in Europe and the Far East. He has recently completed a three-year project in the former Soviet Union and is currently working on a project examining the return of Hong Kong to Mainland China. He is also currently directing a project examining Asian marital relationships within the United Kingdom.

J.R. Hanley is a Senior Lecturer in psychology at the University of Liverpool. He has a MA from the University of Dundee and a PhD from the University of Lancaster. He is a regular contributor to leading international neuropsychology journals such as *Neuropsychologia*, and *Cognitive Neuropsychology*. His main research interests include the cognitive neuropsychology of memory, acquired and developmental dyslexia, and disorders of face processing.

James Hartley is Professor of applied psychology at the University of

Keele, Staffordshire. He obtained his first degree and PhD in psychology from the University of Sheffield. His main research interests are in written communication, with especial reference to typography and layout, but he is also well known for his research into teaching and learning in the context of higher education. Professor Hartley is a prolific writer and he has so far published twelve books and over 200 papers. He is a Fellow of both the British and American Psychological Associations.

John Haworth is a Lecturer in psychology at the University of Manchester. He has a BSc from St Andrews University, a M Litt in visual arts from Lancaster University, and a PhD in psychology from Manchester University. His research interests include mental health, work and leisure; the psychology of creativity, and the embodied mind. He has published extensively in international journals. He was co-founder of the Leisure Studies Association, and was founder editor of the international journal *Leisure Studies*. He has been editor of the international journal *Leisure Research*. He has edited two books: *Work and Leisure: An Interdisciplinary Perspective* (1975) and *Community Involvement and Leisure* (1979). He has been a member of several Government Agency Research Commissions on Leisure.

Tim Ingold is Professor and Head of Department in social anthropology at the University of Manchester. He has carried out ethnographic research among Saami and Finnish people in Lapland, and has written extensively on comparative questions of environment, technology and social organisation in the circumpolar North, as well as on evolutionary theory in anthropology, biology and history. His work has also looked at the role of animals in human society, and human ecology. His current research interests are in the anthropology of technology and in aspects of environmental perception. He has edited the *Companion Encyclopedia of Anthropology* (1994) and was editor of *Man* (the journal of the Royal Anthropological Institute) from 1990 to 1992. He has received many awards, including the Rivers Memorial Medal of the Royal Anthropological Institute (1989) and the 1994 prize of the Jean-Marie Delwart Foundation, Royal Belgian Academy of Sciences.

Michelle Meadows graduated with a first class degree in psychology from Hatfield Polytechnic (now the University of Hatfield) and has recently successfully completed a PhD in the Department of Psychology at the University of Manchester on predicting number and type of road traffic crashes from attitudinal and motivational characteristics of car drivers.

Peter R. Meudell is a Professor of psychology at the University of Manchester. His research interests are in normal human memory and in neuropsychology – especially amnesia and related disorders. He has published sixty-five articles and chapters in relation to these topics. He currently holds collaborative Economic and Social Research Council and Wellcome Foundation grants and is a founder member of the Memory Disorders Research Society. Recently he has developed interests in the social aspects of remembering.

Ian Parker is Senior Lecturer in social and abnormal psychology, and co-director of the Discourse Unit in the Department of Psychology and Speech Pathology at The Manchester Metropolitan University. He is author of *The Crisis in Modern Social Psychology* (1989) and *Discourse Dynamics* (1992), and co-author of *Qualitative Methods in Psychology* (1994, P. Banister, E. Burman, M. Taylor and C. Tindall), *Carrying Out Investigations in Psychology* (1995, with J. Foster) and *Deconstructing Psychopathology* (1995, with D. Harper, E. Georgaca, T. McLaughlin and M. Stowell-Smith). He is co-editor of *Deconstructing Social Psychology* (1990, with J. Shotter), *Discourse Analytic Research* (1993, with E. Burman) and *Psychology and Marxism* (1995, with R. Spears).

Rob Ranyard is Reader in psychology at Bolton Institute of Higher Education and an Associate Fellow of the British Psychological Society. He is a member of the Editorial Board of *Acta Psychologica* and his research experience includes process tracing studies of decisions under risk, qualitative studies of financial decision-making and analyses of how important decisions are communicated. He has published more than fifteen research papers on decision-making and economic psychology, including the following: 'Structure and strategy in justifying environmental decisions', *Journal of Environmental Psychology*, 11: 43–57 (1991); 'Estimating the duration of a flexible loan: the effects of supplementary information', *Journal of Economic Psychology*, 14: 317–335 (1993).

Stephen Stradling obtained a first degree and PhD from the University of Newcastle-upon-Tyne and is a Senior Lecturer in the Department of Psychology at the University of Manchester where he runs a modular Masters degree in applied psychology. He is currently undertaking research, with a wide range of collaborators, in areas of applied social psychology such as driver behaviour, occupational and post-traumatic stress, evaluation of therapy, and service encounters in the financial services sector.

Peter Stratton is a Senior Lecturer in the Psychology Department at Leeds University. He is Director of the Leeds Family Therapy and Research Centre which has operated within the department since 1979 providing a base for training family therapists and developing techniques of systemic practice. The research of LFTRC has concentrated on developing techniques based in attribution theory and attachment theory, to analyse family processes and the dynamics of therapy sessions. In 1988 he started an independent company called 'The Psychology Business' to apply qualitative methods from psychology within industry. TPB specialises in providing practical solutions to intractable research problems, and has successfully completed projects for over twenty of Britain's largest companies. His current research includes the form and function of blaming in families and other contexts; child mal-treatment, especially in failure to thrive; family processes around eating, and the effects of advertising on these; the use of intensive qualitative research to provide a basis for surveys of employee and customer opinions, and the use of attributional analysis to record and modify organisational cultures. He is editor of *Human Systems: The Journal of Systemic Consultation and Management*.

Graham F. Wagstaff is Reader in psychology at the University of Liverpool. He has been researching hypnosis for over twenty years and has published widely in most areas of the subject, though he has a particular interest in forensic aspects of hypnosis. He is author of *Hypnosis, Compliance and Belief* (1981), which has become a well-known text on the non-state approach to hypnosis. He is one of the founder members of the British Society of Experimental and Clinical Hypnosis, and is on the editorial boards of *Contemporary Hypnosis*, and *Experimentelle und Klinische Hypnose*. His other research interests include forensic interviewing and the psychology of justice.

Mitch Waterman is a Lecturer in cognitive neuropsychology at Leeds University. His first degree in psychology and biology was completed at Lancaster, with subsequent doctoral research at Keele. His research interests include the cognition and neuropsychology of emotion and memory. His interest in research methods is the result of varied research areas besides those mentioned: music psychology, 'club' culture, stress in the work place. His current involvement is in an ESRC project attempting to identify character-istics of emotion in speech, and in a study assessing the risks of neurological impairment as a result of vascular surgery. He contributes to methods and psychometrics courses, and runs courses in emotion, neuropsychology and neuroscience.

Janis Williamsom is Senior Lecturer in psychology at Bolton Institute of Higher Education. Her doctoral research concentrated on the understanding of maps, and her research interests are still primarily in environmental cognition, and in the development of qualitative research methods for use in this area. She has previously published work on developmental aspects of map understanding, and errors in everyday routefinding. Her current research investigates environmental knowledge in topographically impaired subjects.

Foreword

Psychological research is in turmoil. Perhaps it always has been and always will be, since the discipline has so many different and evolving traditions. In a modern psychology department one can find individuals investigating the brain and collaborating with neurologists, pharmacologists, and computer engineers. Other individuals may be investigating health and well-being, and collaborating with sociologists, educationalists and social policy makers. One set of researchers may be steeped in traditions and methods of enquiry rooted in biological research, while others may be more in tune with methods and insights stemming from research in the humanities. It has been rightly said that many psychologists have a much greater affinity with people in other disciplines than they have amongst themselves. Yet this is only partly the case. It may well be that to conduct a specific piece of research it is more beneficial for a psychologist to associate with members of particular disciplines. Increasingly, however, psychologists as a whole are coming to realise that no one approach to knowledge and understanding, and no particular discipline, is primordinate. A particular approach may be more important in one area than another, but such is the complexity of any area of enquiry that there is always the possibility of psychologists in any field learning something of value from other psychologists about how to conduct research. Recognition of this sort makes the ferment of psychological research, and the community of those undertaking this, a tremendously stimulating and ultimately tolerant milieu. The readers of this volume will, hopefully, experience this and be able to draw on it in their studies and research.

The chapters in this volume are written by experts from a wide range of research areas. The authors are members of a consortium for postgraduate training, given at Manchester University. The volume is divided into three sections: survey research, qualitative research, and controlled investigations. Each section is prefaced by a brief introduction outlining the contributions and pointing to critical issues. These prefaces draw on the content of the research areas tackled by the authors to show how the book gives direct insight into modern psychology and how research is undertaken. A general introduction to the book addresses fundamental issues which cut across the three sections.

The book is dedicated to all the professionals and students undertaking research.

John Haworth
University of Manchester

Chapter 1

Introduction

Contemporary psychological research: visions from positional standpoints

John Haworth

This chapter addresses the topic of contemporary psychological research and the different standpoints from which this is conducted. While much existing literature presents research as being experimental or non-experimental, this introduction examines the similarities in these paradigms, as well as the differences, and shows the potential for multi-method research. The chapter also highlights the debate on the nature of knowledge and how we perceive ourselves and the structures of society.

Psychological research is undertaken for many reasons. An aim can be to gain knowledge and understanding. An objective can be to improve well-being. The meaning of these terms is, of course, open to fierce debate, with different viewpoints and values influencing how research is undertaken (Jahoda 1981). Suppose, however, that one is interested in the effect of a new treatment to improve a certain mental illness. The treatment may be a drug or a form of psychotherapy. By observing the effect of the treatment on a group of patients, we may find that 60 per cent recover. At first sight this may seem to validate the effect of the treatment. But it may be that a certain percentage of patients recover spontaneously without any treatment. If this was 60 per cent, the effect of the treatment could be nil. It is obviously necessary to compare the effect of treatment on one group of patients with the effect of no treatment on a similar group of patients. We could set up two groups of patients who were similar in relation to factors which may influence the effect of the treatment, such as age, gender, occupation, etc., and see if the recovery rates were different in the two groups.

However, as we do not know the spontaneous recovery rate of individual patients, we would not have been able to match the groups on the very variable which could confound our study. It may be that in our assignment of patients to the treatment group we were influenced by some factor, such as the attractiveness of patients, which resulted in spontaneous recovery rate being systematically associated more with the treatment than the non-treatment group. To attempt to control systematic errors due to differences in subjects we would assign each patient by chance, by the toss of a coin, to the treatment or non-treatment group. This random assignment of subjects to the treatment, or 'experimental group', and non-treatment, or 'control group' would mean that the possibility of systematic errors due to differences in subjects was changed into random error, or a chance factor. We would then perform a statistical test to see at what level of probability the result had occurred by chance. Under these conditions, where patients had been randomly assigned to the treatment and non-treatment groups, if we found that there was only a 5 per cent probability (p= .05) that the result had occurred by chance, we could be tempted to accept the validity of the treatment.

Unfortunately, we know that some people will respond to an inert substance, or placebo, when they are told they are being treated, in a similar way to if they had received an active drug. In order to control for spurious treatment effects the patients could be randomly assigned to two groups and one group would receive the active drug, or a specific form of psychotherapy thought to be potent, while the other group would receive the placebo, the inert substance, or a form of psychotherapy similar to the form thought to be potent, but not containing the potent element, if this were possible. The active form of the treatment may then be shown to be greater, at a certain level of probability, than the non-active treatment.

But our problems are still not over. The person administering the treatment may know which is the active form and which is the non-active form, and this knowledge can in some cases influence susceptible people in their reaction to the treatment. These experimenter effects, as they are termed, can in the case of drug treatment be overcome if neither the patient nor the person giving the treatment knows whether the drug being administered is active or inert. This double blind procedure, which is used in clinical trials of certain drugs, is obviously very difficult if not impossible to undertake with certain forms of psychotherapy.

Another objection to this experiment is that it is not ethical to assign patients randomly to treatment and non-treatment groups without their permission, and that the use of volunteer patients for treatment, who may have different characteristics from non-volunteers, could possibly influence an assessment of how efficacious the treatment would be on non-volunteers. The experiment could thus be high on what is termed internal validity: that the administration of treatment, or manipulation of the independent variable, has had a significant real effect on the dependent variable, in this case mental health. However, the experiment could be low on external validity: the extent to which the results of research can be generalised across people, places, times and other measures of a complex variable, such as a form of psychotherapy.

Despite these shortcomings the results could be viewed as encouraging and further research undertaken to see if the results are repeatable on different samples of people under controlled conditions. The validity of the treatment, and more generally the validity of a causal statement that the manipulation of a particular independent variable causes a certain change in a dependent variable, is thus ultimately assessed by our general experience of the relationship. The validity of a causal statement cannot be proven by a single experiment. In fact, as we shall see later, it cannot be proven at all. Instead, all that can be achieved is increasing confidence in the relationship.

CONTROL IN RESEARCH

Carlsmith, Ellsworth and Aronson (1976) define an experiment as 'a study in which the investigator has some control over the independent variables and can assign subjects to conditions at random' (p. 26). They consider that, in general, random assignment is one of the experimenter's most important tools for ruling out the dangers of systematic error, which can typically influence one condition without affecting another and can lead to a spurious finding. This control over potentially confounding subject variables by the ability to randomise is considered to be the critical attribute for defining a study as an experiment. They also point out that while random assignment is essential for eliminating systematic error due to the subjects being in different conditions, it cannot reduce the amount of random error or 'background noise' in the experiment. If the treatment is only one of a large number of factors influencing the subject's behaviour in important ways, its influence may not be strong enough to stand out above the variability introduced by all the other extraneous factors. A common means of controlling random error is, they note, to hold important extraneous variables constant at a single level. This, however, can limit the generality of the conclusions of the experiment to highly specific situations. They also note that 'it is never possible to control all sources of random error, the experimenter must use judgement in deciding which extraneous factors are most likely to produce large fluctuations in the particular variable being measured' (p. 17).

Control and judgement

These are central concerns in research in psychology and the social sciences and are not without significance in other areas of enquiry. Campbell and Stanley (1966) point out that in studying complex phenomena it may be necessary to vary more than one variable at a time in order to study how one independent variable interacts with another to affect the dependent variable. For example, they discuss how a particular type of teacher, e.g. a spontaneous temporiser, may do best with a particular teaching method, e.g. group discussion. They also broaden their discussion of interaction effects to consider the external validity of results and the generalisability of research findings. They note that specific conditions exist at the time of experiments: a certain time of year, barometric pressure, orientation of the stars, gamma radiation level, etc. While these conditions would apply to both the experimental and the control groups, the independent variable may be interacting with one or more of these extraneous variables to produce its effect on the dependent variable. Application of the independent variable at some other time may not have an effect because the associated variables are not present. They note Hume's Truism that 'induction or generalisation is never fully justified logically', and that logically we cannot generalise beyond the specific conditions of the experiment, i.e. that we cannot generalise at all. However, they also note that we do attempt generalisation, and that we learn about the justification of generalisations by our experience, and guessing at what can be disregarded in what circumstances. 'The sources of external invalidity are thus guesses as to general laws in the science of a science: guesses as to what factors lawfully interact with our treatment variables, and, by implication, guesses as to what can be disregarded' (1966: 17).

Campbell and Stanley note that an assumption made in science is one of finite causation: that the great bulk of potentially determining factors can be disregarded, or, in other words, that main effects are more likely than interactions. Related to this is the 'appeal to parsimony', which, while frequently erroneous in specific applications, underlies almost all use of theory in science indicating that, where a common feature can be identified in several sets of differences, this is more likely to be the cause than a series of separate explanations. This, they note, is not deductively justifiable but is rather a general assumption about the nature of the world. Though, one may add, the world they refer to is a modern rather than a postmodern world in which challenges are being made to some of the traditional tenets of science (Gergen 1994). With regard to the ability to generalise results, Campbell and Stanley state: 'Our call for greater external validity will thus be a call for that maximum of similarity of experiments to the conditions of application which is compatible with internal validity' (p. 18). In other words, the experiment should have some ecological validity.

It is apparent that obtaining a significant result in an experiment does not prove that the manipulation of the independent variable has caused a change in the dependent variable, or that a particular hypothesis or theory has been shown to be true. It is not possible to rule out that complex coincidences might have been operating to produce the experimental outcome. While experiments can never prove a particular hypothesis of a relation between variables, they can increase the plausibility of a relationship. Conversely, experiments can also increase the implausibility of other relationships where significant findings are not obtained, in circumstances where the probability is low that the findings are due to poor design or measurement of variables. Campbell and Stanley thus emphasise the importance of the replication of results. 'The more numerous and independent the ways in which the experimental effect is demonstrated, the less numerous and less plausible any singular rival invalidating hypothesis becomes. The appeal is to parsimony.

The "validity" of the experiment becomes one of the relative creditability of rival theories' (p. 36).

Carlsmith *et al.* (1976) consider that while the experiment is an important method of conducting empirical research it is by no means the only method, and that many important and interesting questions are not amenable to experimental research. Kish (1959) also notes that 'much research in the social, biological, and physical sciences – must be based on non-experimental methods' (p. 331). With regard to social research, Kish states that 'Searching for causal factors among survey data is an old, useful sport; and that extraneous and "spurious" correlations have taxed scientists since antiquity and will undoubtedly continue to do so' (p. 329). Investigators can make measurements of variables as they occur in nature and look for relationships between them, or in other words undertake correlational studies. For example, studies have shown that increased aspects of control in daily life are associated with increased aspects of well-being, and a theory of the importance of control has developed. While correlational studies are always subject to 'specification error', that the relationship between two variables is caused by a third unspecified variable, just as experiments cannot fully rule out interaction effects, it is the case as Carlsmith *et al.* note: 'When the measurement of naturally occurring phenomena provides enough evidence which tends to support a theory and none to refute it, causal statements are accepted' (p. 26). This is, however, always a matter of judgement. As Kish (1959) states, 'In considering the larger ends of any scientific research, only part of the total means required for inference can be brought under objective and firm control; another part must be left to more or less vague and subjective – however skillful – judgement' (p. 332).

Control and representation

Kish (1959) notes that the scientist is faced with three basic problems of research – measurement, representation and control – and that in practice one generally cannot solve simultaneously all of these problems, rather one must choose and compromise. In any specific situation one method may be better or more practical than another, but there is no overall superiority in all situations for one method. While Kish is referring to the experimental and correlational methods, arguably this also applies to other methods of investigation, such as observation, critical analysis and interpretation.

Kish states that the experimental method is the scientific method par excellence – when feasible, but that in many situations experiments are not feasible. The experimental method he notes has some shortcomings. First, it is often difficult or impossible to design a properly controlled experiment. Thus, he considers that 'Many of the initial successes reported about mental therapy, which later turn into vain hopes, may be due to the hopeful effects of any new treatment in contrast with the background of neglect' (p. 333).

Second, it is generally difficult to design experiments so as to represent a specified important population. 'Both in theory and practice, experimental research has often neglected the basic truth that causal systems, the distribution of relations – like the distribution of characteristics – exists only within specified universes' (p. 333). Third, contriving a similarity of experiments to the conditions of application is often not feasible. 'Hence, what social experiments give sometimes are clear answers to questions the meaning of which are vague. That is, the artificially contrived experimental variables may have a tenuous relationship to the variables the researcher would like to investigate' (p. 334).

Gergen (1982) broadens this critique of the experimental method to one which embraces the empiricist meta-theory. He claims that the experimental method is embedded in a paradigm with its roots in empiricist philosophy where one typically commences with the assumption of a fundamentally ordered nature to be reflected by scientific theory. He notes that

> When scientists embraced the logical empiricist program for scientific conduct, they simultaneously absorbed the underlying conception of psychological functioning. As a result, relevant disciplines have been significantly limited in the range of their concerns, in the types of behaviour selected for study, in the choice of explanatory constructs, and in their vision of human potential.
>
> (p. 113)

The underlying conceptions of human functioning are rooted in the western intellectual tradition. They are: the dualism of mind and body; the traditional representationist views which conceive the world as being independent of the observer and perception being a representation of pre-given properties of the world where ideal psychological representation occurs when the individual acts as a neutral recording device; and where, through conceptual abstraction, or rational thinking, the individual may draw systematic inferences from a body of sense data and make predictions regarding future events. Emotions, values, desires and motives may serve as a motivational base for seeking knowledge, but once the process has been started they may be viewed as deterrents to proper cognitive functioning, interfering with objectivity. Gergen notes that alternative approaches to knowledge and understanding such as ethnomethodology, where meaning is considered to be context dependent, and arise through ongoing interpretation, rather than being universal and objective, have thus received little attention in psychology.

In emphasising the importance of context, Gergen notes, like Campbell and Stanley (1966) and Kish (1959), that the experimenter does not manipulate a single variable in isolation from the remainder of the stimulus world. Rather, according to Gergen, an event is altered within a context that renders the alteration meaningful, and without which the alteration would be inconsequential. Gergen considers that in psychology the experimenter makes choices of experimental settings, the stimulus material, the experimenter's gender, and that many decisions taken contain a host of assumptions that are unarticulated. Therefore 'From the contextualist standpoint, what passes for knowledge within the discipline may thus rest on an immense number of unstated assumptions and obscured conditions' (p. 130). Bowers, in Chapter 8 in this volume, considers that experimental psychologists trade on an unexplicated and hoped for shared common sense for their instructions and procedures to work.

NEW PARADIGM RESEARCH

Gergen (1994), in the introduction to the second edition of Gergen (1982), argues that several developments in postmodernist theory support his original critique of the empiricist tradition in the social sciences. In particular, he cites developments in ideological, literary–rhetorical, and social critiques of science. Feminist writings, for example, are considered to show how traditional scientific practices are detrimental to the interests of women and to social equality more generally. The 'post-structuralist' movement is viewed as radically altering our conceptions of language, with a movement away from language as representation towards a concern with language as a relatively self-contained system. Social critique presents knowledge as discourse, as socially constituted, and as being constitutive of social patterns and power; and that to question the authority of 'the sciences' is thus to challenge the forms of power relations in the culture. This latter point is one reason Gergen offers as to why

> the empiricist tradition continues to remain stalwart within the social sciences, maintaining a steady grip over the future of the disciplines, shaping decisions regarding educational curricula, journal policy, hiring and firing criteria, the allocation of research funds, and the representation of science to society.
>
> (p. vii)

Gergen is presenting traditional science as 'positioned rationality' and arguing that there are other equally, or even more valuable, ways of looking at the world. This is the view taken by Haraway (1988) who argues that

> Histories of science may be powerfully told as histories of the technologies. These technologies are ways of life, social orders, practices of visualisation. Technologies are skilled practices. How to see? Where to see from? What limits to vision? What to see for? Whom to see with . . .? Positioning is, therefore, the key practice in grounding knowledge.
>
> (p. 587)

Haraway argues that it is precisely in the politics and epistemology of partial perspectives that the possibility of sustained, rational, objective enquiry rests, rather than in a single vision of the world; 'only partial perspective promises objective vision' (p. 583). She argues for 'selected and embodied know-ledges', 'embodied objectivity', 'which is therefore accountable objectivity'. This, she considers, is not fixed location, fixed vision, but about material–semiotic fields of meaning, nodes in fields which change over time.

> Above all, rational knowledge does not pretend to disengagement: to be everywhere and so nowhere, to be free from interpretation. . . . Rational knowledge is a process of ongoing critical interpretation among 'fields' of interpreters and decoders. . . . So science becomes the paradigmatic model, not of closure, but of that which is contestable and contested.
>
> (p. 590)

Thus knowledge becomes situated, context dependent.

In the present volume, in Chapter 7, Ingold, a social anthropologist, also argues that the scientist is practically involved and that, as in any other skilled activity, this shapes understanding unself-consciously. The scientist per-ceives by embodied practice. How we conceive things comes about because we have been embedded in a certain tradition, and this influences what questions we ask, which can restrict one from conceiving alternative ways of viewing the world which may be productive in terms of insights, under-standings, and approaches to problems.

The embodied mind

It can thus be seen that traditional representationist views, which conceive the world as being independent of the observer and perception as being a representation of pre-given properties of the world, much like a camera records a picture of some object, are being challenged. Perception and our knowledge of the world are now considered to be generated by our interaction with the world which takes on a specific form due to the nature of our bodies and our individual and social experiences in the particular culture in which we live.

Varela, Thompson and Rosch (1991) note that one of the most entrenched assumptions of our scientific heritage is that the world is independent of the knower. In challenging this objectivist view of the world they say that the central insight of the non-objectivist orientation is the view that knowledge is the result of an ongoing interpretation. This emerges from our capacities of understanding, which are rooted in the structures of our biological embodiment, but lived and experienced within a domain of consensual action and cultural history. They present cognition as embodied action. They see the central problem of perception, not in elucidating the nature of the information processing problem for recovering pre-given properties of the world, but rather 'to determine the common principles or lawful linkages between sensory and motor systems that explain how action can be guided in a perceiver dependent world'; or in other words 'how the perceiver can guide his actions in his local situation' (p. 173). This approach to perception they see as amongst the central insights of the philosopher, Merleau-Ponty.

Merleau-Ponty (1962), in *Phenomenology of Perception*, argues that our fundamental knowledge of the world comes through our bodies' explorations of it. Primary meaning is reached through co-existing with the world in distinction to intellectual meaning, which is reached through analysis. Primary meaning is brought about mainly by pre-reflexive thought in distinction to reflection. This 'Embodiment Theory' of Merleau-Ponty proposes that the visible unfolds and is concentrated by the body over time. It has a style across time. Perception is seen as a temporal synthesis. This involves structures from the past sensory and affective life of a person sedimented in pre-reflexive thought, and lines of intentionality which trace out at least the style of what is to come; that is, a certain manner of dealing with situations which has issued from perception in distinction to being consciously imposed.

The nature of awareness and the guiding of action is also of considerable interest to psychologists engaged in the study of 'Unintended Thought' (Uleman and Bargh 1989). Posner and Rothbart (1989) note that while considerable advances have been made in studying unintended thought, only rather slowly are cognitive psychologists coming to understand that much of our mental life is structured outside of consciousness and that our intentional control of mental events represents only one, perhaps small, part of the mind.

QUALITATIVE RESEARCH

New paradigm research tends to focus on the use of qualitative data, discourse analysis which treats areas of psychology as processes of discourse between people, and collaborative and action-orientated research. Discourse analysis presents language not so much as representation but more as a system of action and social construction in a particular context for a particular purpose. This is the position taken by Burman in Chapter 11 and Parker in Chapter 12 in this volume. In addition, Parker emphasises the importance of 'discursive complexes' in discourse analysis and focuses on psychoanalytic interpretations.

While critics of discourse analysis argue that results are not reliable and valid in the traditional meanings of the terms, proponents of discourse analysis argue that this is done by persuasive argument, and tests of experience, which is the ultimate way in which much traditional research is justified.

Despite an increase in the use of qualitative research in psychology, Henwood and Pidgeon (1992) consider that, unlike other disciplines in the human sciences, psychology has undervalued the role of qualitative research methods in scientific enquiry. An advantage of qualitative research they emphasise is that theory is generated which is contextually sensitive, persuasive and relevant. In discussing criteria for evaluating the 'goodness' of generative research, where theory emerges in the process of doing research rather than being formulated and then tested, they note that the classical criteria for evaluating research, such as reliability, validity, parsimony, internal consistency and generality, rest on the norm of objectivity which assumes the independence of the knower and the known. They argue that researchers need to acknowledge that the research activity shapes and constitutes the object of enquiry and that this should be revealed in the process of documenting studies: the research process is reflexive. Negative case analysis is also considered important, not only in the traditional sense of falsifying a theory, but for modifying and elaborating a theory where necessary. They note that, while theory may be validated by being recognisable to participants, this is not always the case since people are not always fully aware of the reasons for their actions. In some cases a negotiated reality may be possible. They also consider that the context should be adequately described to make the research transferable in distinction to generalisable so that the findings of a study can be applied in contexts similar to the context in which they were first described. In Henwood and Pidgeon (1995), they point to two considerations deemed to be important in assessing the usefulness of research ideas. The first is generativity: to what extent do they facilitate further issues and questions for research? The second is rhetorical power: how effective is an idea in persuading others to accept your argument? Riessman (1993) also includes the pragmatic usefulness of the research idea as a major consideration.

In their comprehensive sourcebook, *Qualitative Data Analysis*, Miles and Huberman (1994) note that in social anthropology a prime analytic task is to uncover and explicate the ways in which people in particular settings come to understand, account for, take action and otherwise manage their day to day situation; and that this uncovering and explication is typically based on successive observations and interviews which are reviewed analytically to guide the next move in the field. Researchers may begin with a conceptual framework and take it out into the field for testing, refinement and qualification. They note that researchers in life history, grounded theory, ecological psychology, and a wide range of applied studies including education and health care often take this general line.

Coolican (1994) states that for qualitative researchers validity is established through several means:

1 The naturalistic and realistic nature of the data.
2 'Triangulation': the use of several perspectives.
3 Analysis of negative cases.
4 Repetition of the research cycle with participants being reinterviewed.
5 Dialogue with participants in forming conclusions to the research.

Qualitative research can thus involve a feedback process with concepts being open to falsification, as in traditional experimental research. It is also important to recognise that the analysis of qualitative data is influenced by the theoretical models which the researcher is using, the conceptual lenses or positions by which things are viewed. McLeod (1994) notes that a systematic consideration of competing interpretations of the data should be undertaken, and that replication of findings is important.

Not all analysis of qualitative data is new paradigm research. Coolican (1994) notes that for the 'positivist' or traditional researcher, qualitative data can be used to illuminate and give a context to statistical findings; and that it can lead to hypotheses testable in quantitative terms. He considers that to the extent that data are strictly categorised, coded or content analysed, the approach tends to be positivistic rather than new paradigm research, though he notes that there is not a strict dichotomy between the two approaches. This is shown in Chapter 9 and, in particular, in Chapter 10 in this volume. In Chapter 10, the author presents a progressive categorisation and coding scheme used in the context of a new paradigm perspective.

DEMAND CHARACTERISTICS AND THE ETHICS OF RESEARCH

Biased responding may occur in psychological investigations due to respondents attempting to present themselves in the best light and give the answers which they think are required. This responding to the 'demand characteristics' of the situation is an aspect of 'social desirability' effects, and can occur in both field research and experimental situations. The account of research into hypnosis in Chapter 13 in this volume shows that we must be aware of the possibility that the phenomena we are measuring in psychology may be as much a product of our procedures as something measured by them.

In the artificial settings of laboratory experiments, Carlsmith, Ellsworth and Aronson (1976) note that respondents may suspend their 'usual' motivations and produce behaviours which they judge to be consistent with the experimental hypothesis as they see it, making the results meaningless. They note that there are several possible ways of tackling demand characteristics in experimental situations, and that the best is probably the medical placebo model, but that in most social psychological experiments this is difficult to apply. Other approaches suggested, which also apply to non-experimental situations, include giving the respondent false but credible hypotheses as to the purpose of the study. Such deception, however, is now problematic in psychological research. Carlsmith *et al.* (1976) also suggest that it can help to ask respondents for their help in generating accurate data, stressing the seriousness of the task and the importance of honest responses, and reminding respondents of the worthlessness of biased results.

The 'Ethical principles for conducting research with human participants' approved by the British Psychological Society in 1992 and published in *The*

Psychologist (1993) are essentially concerned with the well-being of participants in research. For example, 'The essential principle is that the investigation should be considered from the standpoint of all participants; foreseeable threats to their psychological well-being, health, values or dignity should be eliminated'.

> Intentional deception of participants over the purpose and general nature of the investigation should be avoided whenever possible. Participants should never be deliberately misled without extremely strong scientific or medical justification. Even then there should be strict controls and the disinterested approval of independent advisors. . . . In studies where the participants are aware that they have taken part in an investigation, when the data have been collected, the investigator should provide the participants with any necessary information to complete their understanding of the nature of the research. The investigator should discuss with the participants their experience of the research in order to monitor any unforeseen negative effects or misconceptions.

The ethics of investigations can, however, be more than a consideration for the well-being of the person participating in the research. As Haraway (1988) has indicated, research can include a consideration of the power relations between the respondent and the investigator, and result in a dialogue and not just a consultation.

MULTI-METHOD COLLABORATIVE RESEARCH

In the UK collaborative research is now becoming increasingly important. The Economic and Social Research Council, for example, is funding a multi-million pound research programme into 'The Learning Society' in order to enhance economic competitiveness and quality of life. As part of the remit for the research, the funding agency insists that the research has to have practical utility as well as being important for the development of knowledge. In applying for funds, researchers have to demonstrate how they are discussing and planning the research with the users of the research. In some cases a committee of representative user groups may be involved in the planning, execution, and evaluation of the research, and also with the dissemination of findings. However, such approaches can also create concerns about the efficiency with which research may be undertaken. Some funding bodies are also encouraging the formation of multidisciplinary teams of researchers so that a variety of methods and strategies can be brought to bear on a problem.

Another form of collaborative research which is increasing in popularity is networked seminar activity. One group to which this author belongs is a work process knowledge network consisting of representatives from seven European countries. Members have met on several occasions to share research findings on the acquisition, transmission, support and theorising of knowledge involved in the work process in high technology industries. In all member states of the European Community a gap is perceived between the content of training programmes and the knowledge actually used in the workplace. Most research into training is using traditional models of cognitive science, which sees the operator as an information processor and attempts to model the cognitive structures involved. New models are based on activity theory, embodied practice and embodied mind, which emphasise the importance of situated learning and implicit knowledge. Members of the group include engineers, educationalists, psychologists and sociologists. A wide range of industrial projects are being studied. The network enables the researchers to exchange information and develop practice and theory pertaining to learning and skill development. Advances in communications, such as the Internet, are enhancing such developments.

CONCLUSION

This survey of contemporary psychological research has shown that various perspectives exist and that visions arise from different positional standpoints. The classical, empiricist position aims for control and predictive utility. The non-objectivist position tends to aim more for provisional insight and circumscribed utility in particular situations. While the empiricist position has been taken as *the* scientific approach, new paradigms and strategies are presenting additional viable positional standpoints. A continuing evolution of theoretical groundings, innovative methods and strategies could lead to the use of established methods with a more critical understanding. This would be undertaken alongside the use of new methods, and the development of new perspectives on professional activities. At a broader level the debate on the nature of knowledge and the status of research methods is intimately tied in with our perceptions of ourselves and the structures of society. As such it is critical to developing perspectives on what comes 'after postmodernism' (Simons and Bilig 1994).

REFERENCES

British Psychological Society (1993) 'Ethical principles for conducting research with human participants', *The Psychologist*, 6, 1: 33–35.

Campbell, D.T. and Stanley, J.C. (1966) *Experimental and Quasi-experimental Designs for Research*, Chicago: Rand McNally and Co.

Carlsmith, M.J., Ellsworth, P.C. and Aronson, E. (1976) *Methods of Research in Social Psychology*, London: Addison-Wesley.

Coolican, H. (1994) *Research Methods and Statistics in Psychology*, London: Hodder & Stoughton.

Gergen, K.J. (1982) *Toward Transformation in Social Knowledge*, London: Sage.

Gergen, K.J. (1994) *Toward Transformation in Social Knowledge*, 2nd edn, London: Sage.

Haraway, D. (1988) 'Situated knowledges: the science question in feminism and the privilege of partial perspective', *Feminist Studies*, 14, 3: 575–599.

Henwood, K.L. and Pidgeon, N.K. (1992) 'Qualitative research and psychological theorizing', *British Journal of Psychology*, 83: 97–111.

Henwood, K.L. and Pidgeon, N.K. (1995) 'Grounded theory and psychological research', *The Psychologist*, 8, 3: 115–118.

Jahoda, M. (1981) 'Work, employment and unemployment: values, theories and approaches in social research', *American Psychologist*, 36, 2: 184–191.

Kish, L. (1959) 'Some statistical problems in research design', *American Sociological Review*, 24: 328–338.

McLeod, J. (1994) *Doing Counselling Research*, London: Sage.

Merleau-Ponty, M. (1962) *Phenomenology of Perception*, London: Routledge & Kegan Paul.

Miles, M.B. and Huberman, M.A. (1994) *Qualitative Data Analysis*, London: Sage.

Posner, M.I. and Rothbart, M.K. (1989) 'Intentional chapters on unintended thought', in J.S. Uleman and J.A. Bargh (eds) *Unintended Thought*, London: The Guilford Press.

Riessman, K. (1993) *Narrative Analysis*, London: Sage.

Simons, H.W. and Billig, M. (eds) (1994) *After Post Modernism: Reconstructing Ideology Critique*, London: Sage.

Uleman, J.S. and Bargh, J.A. (eds) (1989) *Unintended Thought*, London: The Guilford Press.

Varela, F.J., Thompson, E. and Rosch, E. (1991) *The Embodied Mind: Cognitive Science and Human Experience*, Cambridge, Mass.: MIT Press.

Part I

Survey research

Preface

This section contains five chapters illustrating a range of field research topics currently undertaken by psychologists. Health and safety features as a major concern. The chapters look at broad issues, such as the importance of linking theory, methods and strategy in research (Chapter 2), the construction of questionnaires and analysis of data in health and driver behaviour (Chapters 3 and 4), advanced multivariate techniques of data analysis (Chapter 5), and issues in cross-cultural research (Chapter 6).

Chapter 2 notes that psychologists from a range of areas are now involved in research into mental health, work and leisure. While research into stress has a long history in psychology, the conditions associated with positive subjective well-being in daily life, including happiness, are increasingly becoming a topic of research. The psychological effects of unemployment and the benefits of work and leisure are receiving attention, producing research of considerable relevance for governments and other policy makers. Besides having practical utility, a characteristic now demanded by agencies which fund research, developments in this area are also of considerable theoretical and methodological significance for psychologists and other social scientists. The chapter illustrates the value of linking theory, method and strategy to produce findings of both specific and general relevance. For example, theoretical models of mental health can have considerable heuristic value, lending themselves to application and development, which may benefit from the use of more than one research method and approach, and by the use of both quantitative and qualitative data. The chapter summarises research using questionnaires and experience sampling methodology, where respondents answer questions in a diary several times a day in response to signals from pre-programmed pagers. It is noted that different methods can be used to see if there is congruence between findings which would give added faith in results, and that at a broader, more strategic level, the use of different methods may juxtapose different 'traditions' of research which could result in valuable new perspectives.

Chapter 3 notes that research into personal health behaviours and their determinants is one of the most rapidly developing fields of psychology. Beliefs and knowledge are considered likely to be two important factors in determining health behaviours; and social cognition models, which emphasise the rationality of human behaviour, are being developed and extensively applied in health psychology. The chapter focuses upon the methodological difficulties in obtaining adequate measures of health-relevant cognitions and behaviours. It illustrates the important link between method and theory in the construction of questionnaires, and emphasises the social nature of the data gathering process. The authors note that responses to questions on the frequency of health-relevant behaviours is in part a construction, rather than a simple recall and counting of instances, and that it is necessary to help respondents to use inferences based upon correct assumptions. In asking questions about attitudes and other cognitions they stress that it is important to have a clear theoretical model of the cognitions and their interactions in order to guide questionnaire construction. Similarly, to reduce bias in questionnaires it is necessary to have a clear conception of what is to be measured which will then often suggest clear ways in which to word questions, which can be tested and developed through preliminary studies. They note that factors which have been found to increase response rate include, amongst others, a short clear letter stating the aims of the study, reassurance that data will be treated confidentially, and obvious personal relevance of the topic area to the respondent – all factors which reflect the social nature of the data gathering process.

Chapter 4 notes that engineering-based safety measures to reduce road accidents are beginning to yield diminishing returns, and that the challenge for psychology is to provide a better understanding of the role of human factors in the causation of road traffic accidents. In reviewing methods of study they consider that each of the four main methods has some drawbacks. Simulated driver studies suffer from lack of ecological validity – the ways in which drivers behave in simulated situations may bear little relation to how they behave in real traffic. Accident statistics may not readily fit the needs of a research project. Observational studies may not be accurate enough. Self-report measures are open to social desirability bias. As the self-report method has the advantage of being comparatively inexpensive and all types of accidents except those fatal to the driver can be canvassed, self-report data is now widely used in the study of driver behaviour. The aim in constructing a questionnaire is to produce a reliable and valid instrument which achieves a high response rate. In general, the likelihood of this is improved if the task is made easy, pleasurable and as hassle-free as possible. Courtesy and consideration towards respondents are important. Having obtained and entered the data it has to be checked for accuracy of input, and the amount and distribution of missing data, as this can bias the data set. Screening of the data for normality is an important step for multivariate analysis. Extreme cases or 'outliers' need identifying. The linear relationship between variables is checked, as is the lack of perfect or near perfect correlations which, if present, can interfere with analysis. Then, as the authors state, 'you are now ready to run sophisticated multivariate analyses of your questionnaire data using a powerful desk top statistical package'.

Chapter 5 illustrates how the use of relatively simple statistical modelling techniques, such as path analysis, can be of great value in giving some assessment of the importance and potential forms of linkage of variables involved in a psychological phenomenon. The author describes in detail how mediated and moderated effects may be investigated using simple multiple regression commands on widely used statistical packages such as SPSS. An example she cites of mediated effects is where age, job status and health may influence absenteeism from work directly, but also through indirect paths. Thus while health may have a direct relationship on absenteeism, job status may have a direct effect on absenteeism and also an indirect effect via its effect on health. Using correlation and multiple regression techniques the relative influence of different variables on health can be investigated as well as different models of the way in which variables may interlink in their effect on absenteeism. Although the use of correlation analysis cannot prove the direction of causal influence, analysis can indicate which of several possible models is likely to be the most important, and whether or not much more explanatory research needs to be done to identify further variables. An important point made is that it is always with reference to existing literature that a decision is made as to whether a particular path model is interesting or useful. Similarly, if the aim of analysis is to 'disprove' an existing theory, the demonstration of the fallibility of a theoretical model by statistical testing may only be a reflection of poor measures of the variables involved. These caveats, however, do not detract from the importance of statistical modelling. Rather, they support a view of scientific endeavour as a process of enquiry which is reliant upon contextual interpretations, such as our current knowledge of a phenomenon.

Chapter 6 shows how research in another culture highlights many points of methodological importance, which also apply to research in general, even though the issues may not be so readily visible. The author points to the concerns about the generalisability and relevance of much psychological work, and the resurgence of interest in the universality of psychological theories and consequently in cross-cultural research. The topic of research is an important consideration. If the issue has little relevance to the people being studied they are unlikely to report or perform seriously on the task in hand. The most valuable psychological work is also likely to involve hypotheses which specify some form of relationship based on theoretical grounds. Participants should also be allowed to be actively involved in the research in order to verify the appropriateness of the questions being posed. Research should be multi-method wherever possible in order to gain a rich under-standing of complex social phenomena. Ethical and social considerations involved in the dissemination of research findings are a significant aspect of the research. These concerns become very real to researchers working in cultures different from their own. They are also repeated by many of the authors in Part II of this volume.

Chapter 2

Mental health, work and leisure

John Haworth

This chapter notes briefly the importance of research into mental health, work and leisure. Some concepts and measures of mental health are summarised, and two related models of situational factors influencing mental health are outlined. Research using these models undertaken at Manchester is reviewed, highlighting methodological considerations. Directions and methods for future work are then discussed. The chapter illustrates the value of linking theory, method and strategy to produce findings of both specific and general relevance.

Psychologists from a range of specialisms are now involved in research into mental health, work and leisure. Extensive research into the effects of unemployment indicates that it impairs mental health, even though the effect is not universal, and a small minority of people show gains in mental health after job loss (Warr 1987: 207). This impairment can include deterioration in affective well-being, and diminished perceived competence and aspiration, with reduced motivation and interest in one's wider surroundings. The conditions associated with positive subjective well-being in daily life, including happiness, are also increasingly a topic of research (Argyle 1987; Csikszentmihalyi and Csikszentmihalyi 1988; Strack, Argyle and Schwarz 1991; Tennen, Suls and Affleck 1991; Haworth 1993). And the psychological and social benefits of work (Jahoda 1982) and leisure (Driver, Brown and Peterson, 1991; Zuzanek and Larson 1993) are receiving increasing attention. These developments have considerable relevance for governments and other policy makers faced with populations increasing in life expectancy, and technology influencing patterns of working life, so that individuals may have to spend as much as half their adult life non-employed. The developments in research are also of considerable theoretical and methodological significance for psychologists and other social scientists, as this chapter will show.

MENTAL HEALTH

Warr (1987) notes that the term mental health is difficult to specify and that no universally accepted definition is available. He proposes five principal components of mental health which he considers would be accepted as important by most western theorists. These are affective well-being, competence, autonomy, aspiration and integrated functioning. Integrated functioning is concerned with the multiple relationships between the other four components and, as yet, does not have questionnaire measures. The most comprehensively investigated measure of Warr's components is affective well-being. This can be measured on three principal axes: the pleasure axis (measuring displeasure to pleasure in context free situations), the anxiety–contentment axis, and the depressed–enthusiasm axis which have been used in the context specific situations of work and leisure (Warr 1989, 1990, 1993). The context specific measures have been more widely used, and have been subject to development (Sevastos, Smith and Cordery 1992; Warr 1992). Warr's emphasis on mental health is on variations in degrees of health and not whether individuals would be identified as ill or not in a medical sense. He views mental health as on a continuum ranging from very good mental health, through conditions considered moderately healthy, to those widely taken to be indicative of moderate and severe illness (Warr 1987: 25). He also rejects a 'passive, contentment' view of mental health, recognising that healthy people often experience strain or anxiety (Warr 1993: 15).

Another related way of conceptualising mental health is to distinguish between the degree of freedom from negative mental health, such as anxiety and depression and negative self-esteem evaluations, and the degree of presence of aspects of positive mental health, such as positive self-esteem, competence, etc. This view, arising from the work of Herzberg (1966), proposes that negative and positive mental health are not on the same continuum, and that different factors may influence each aspect. These two views on mental health have in common the proposition that freedom from negative mental health does not necessarily result in positive mental health, with the implication that mental health should be measured on a range of dimensions. This position is also advocated by Brief, Butcher, George and Link (1993) from their studies of subjective well-being. They state that no longer can it be assumed that if a factor influences one aspect of subjective well-being it will also influence other aspects. The specification of a range of both 'input' and 'output' variables is therefore required in the study of well-being and mental health.

Several questionnaire measures have become established in the study of well-being and mental health, and as such continue to be used regularly. This facilitates comparisons and allows researchers to produce a descriptive profile for their sample to check against others. The general health questionnaire (Goldberg 1972) has several versions, including the twelve item GHQ12. Items cover strain and depression, loss of concentration, sleep, etc. A self-esteem scale (Warr and Jackson 1983) is used to assess respondents' feelings of personal worth. Four items are concerned with negative self-esteem evaluations, and four with positive self-evaluations. Total life satisfaction can be measured by the sum of eleven items of a life satisfaction scale based on Warr, Cook and Wall (1979) where items refer to different aspects of a respondent's everyday life and environment. A twelfth item on the scale asks respondents to rate their life as a whole at the present moment. Scores on this item on a seven point scale ranging from extremely dissatisfied to extremely satisfied provide a measure of an individual's overall life satisfaction. Happiness has often been measured by a single question developed by Bradburn (1969). This asks 'Taking all things together, how would you say things are these days – would you say that you are very happy, pretty happy or not too happy?', respondents having to choose one of these categories. These measures, along with measures of Warr's components of mental health, excluding integrated functioning, have been used in our research at Manchester.

Another approach to the measurement of well-being, used at Manchester, is experience sampling methodology (ESM) which allows the random collection in situ of self-reports about a respondent's subjective well-being and daily experience. First used by Csikszentmihalyi, Larson and Prescott (1977) and Brandstätter (1991), the ESM is regarded as a complementary approach to more traditional rating methods. Brandstätter (1991) considers that traditional questionnaire measures of subjective well-being have several shortcomings. They can require complicated conceptual and judgemental processes to answer some questions. Many people may be tempted to follow social norms rather than reveal sincerely their intimate feelings. They tell us little about the hidden regularities and the interplay between life circumstances and events on the one hand and personality characteristics on the other. Brandstätter considers that time sampling diaries can be designed to overcome some of the flaws and restrictions inherent in traditional rating methods used to measure subjective experience. The advantages of the ESM have also been noted by Hormuth (1986) who states that it is less prone to problems of recall, distortions, and anticipation of report completion than more conventional diary methods. Csikszentmihalyi and Larson (1987) argue that to understand the dynamics of mental health, it is essential to develop measures of the frequency and patterning of mental processes in everyday life situations. They review evidence for the reliability and validity of the ESM, and present studies with both normal and clinical populations to demonstrate the range of issues to which the technique can be applied.

In our studies at Manchester using the ESM, respondents have typically answered a series of short, simple questions in a diary eight times a day for seven consecutive days, in response to signals delivered by either a watch or radio pager programmed to deliver signals randomly within one and a half hour blocks of time. Questions have included the following: 'what was the main thing you were doing?'; 'why were you doing this activity?'. Responses were chosen from a) I had to, b) I wanted to and c) I had nothing else to do. For 'do you wish you had been doing something else?', the answer was given as a rating on a scale ranging from 1, not at all, to 7, very much. The answers from these two questions have been combined to specify which type of motivation is present. For example, if a respondent ticks either 1 or 2 on the question asking 'do you wish you had been doing something else?', and also ticked that they had wanted to do the activity, this can be coded as intrinsic motivation. Extrinsic motivation is indicated by a response 'I had to do the activity' coupled with 6 or 7 on the question 'do you wish you had been doing something else?'. Affective states are measured by questions asking 'how much were you enjoying this activity?', to be answered on a seven point scale ranging from 'not at all' (1) to 'very much' (7), and 'how were you feeling at the time?', answers being rated on two seven point scales, from 'very sad' (1) to 'very happy' (7), and from 'very tense' (1) to 'very relaxed' (7). Questions have also asked 'were you in control of the situation?', and 'how interesting did you find this activity?', answers being required on a seven point scale ranging from 1, 'not at all', to 7, 'very much'; and 'how challenging do you find the situation?', answered on a seven point scale; and whether skills were 'equal to', 'greater than' or 'less than' the challenge, respondents selecting one answer. While the questions only take about two minutes in total to answer at each response signal, considerable commitment is required to complete the diary over seven days. A nominal fee of about £1 a day may partially compensate respondents for their efforts, while not encouraging non-valid completion. In any event, as no research method is without problems, it can be valuable to see if there is some congruence of findings between methods such as standard questionnaire measures of well-being and ESM measures of subjective states, to give added faith in results.

Situation-centred models of mental health

In his categorical, situation-centred model of mental health, Warr (1987) proposes nine principal environmental influences (PEIs), or environmental categories of experience, as having a significant non-linear influence on mental health. These PEIs are: opportunity for control; opportunity for skill use; externally generated goals; variety; environmental clarity; availability of money; physical security; opportunity for interpersonal contact; and valued social position. Warr suggests that, like vitamins, these features have non-linear effects, some improving mental health up to a certain point and then having no further effects, others producing benefits up to a certain level but beyond which increases would be detrimental. These features are proposed as determinants of mental health in all kinds of environments, including work and leisure. They are considered to be properties that an environment has relative to the capabilities and requirements of human beings (Warr 1987: 281). Warr also recognises that individuals can have different enduring characteristics which may moderate the relationship between the principal environmental influences and mental health. The model is thus concerned with processes and person–situation interactions, as well as categorical features.

Warr's model incorporates the environmental categorical model proposed by Jahoda (1982) which indicates that the five categories of experience (time structure, activity, social contact, collective purpose, and social identity or status) are imposed by work and are important for well-being. This model 'emphasises the habitual use people make of social institutions in meeting some psychological need' (Jahoda 1982: 356). Leisure activities from television to sports to self-improvement are considered to be fine in themselves as a complement to employment, but are not considered to be functional alternatives since leisure lacks the compelling manifest function of earning a living. Where deprivation of these categories occurs in unemployment it is considered to give rise to negative psychological symptoms.

Warr indicates that the division of the environment into nine principal categories, which facilitate or constrain personally important processes and activities important for mental health, appears to be appropriately precise for most purposes, but that it is a matter of judgement, partly relating to applications, whether fewer or more categories would be preferable. He considers that 'the evidence proposed for the nine factors is as convincing as that of other models' (p. 283). The strength of his categorical model, he considers, is that it applies to any kind of environment and that it has considerable heuristic value, lending itself to application and development.

Research at Manchester

A study by Evans (1986) used a questionnaire to measure access to the categories of experience (ACE) described by Jahoda, in samples of employed and unemployed young people. The study (also reported in Evans and Haworth 1991) showed that the categories of experience can be obtained by the unemployed and that those with better access had better psychological well-being. However, ACE and psychological well-being was limited when compared to that obtained by the people in the structured situation of employment. This could be because employment provides more money which enables individuals to gain ACE outside of employment. Financial resources are obviously important. Nevertheless, just over half the unemployed sample had a main activity, either work based, leisure based or general social interaction, which gave them a chance to use their abilities and be creative. These individuals had levels of self-esteem similar to the employed sample. However, they had worse affective well-being, life satisfaction and happiness, and less access to the categories of experience of status, social contact and time structure than the employed group. The main activities of the unemployed did not seem to be embedded in informal institutional support systems, and it is an open question as to whether or not this group of people would have had access to all the categories of experience and better psychological well-being if their main activity had been located in a valued social structure. Perhaps if they had been engaged in activities embedded in a social world which was given high status by the community, this would have enhanced psychological well-being and supported the effort necessary to sustain commitment to pursuits.

Another study (Haworth and Ducker 1991) on unemployed young people used questionnaires and experience sampling methodology (ESM). Respondents answered a series of questions in a diary eight times a day for one week in response to signals from an electronic pager. Results showed that a sub-group with higher ACE scores engaged in more work-like and active leisure activities than a sub-group with lower ACE scores who engaged in more passive leisure; and that the higher ACE group had statistically significant better scores on measures of self-esteem, life satisfaction and enjoyment. The results also showed that hope for future (questionnaire measure) and enjoyment (ESM measure) were significantly correlated with scores on the ACE scales.

The results from this study are interesting in that they suggest that respondents with better access to the five categories of experience participate in more positive and engaging activities, or in the terminology of White (1959) more 'competence' serving activities, than the low ACE group. It could thus be expected that the high ACE group would have better self-esteem and general levels of psychological well-being, as was borne out by the results. The finding showing that both enjoyment and hope for the future are significantly associated with Jahoda's categories of experience indicates, perhaps, in line with Fryer and McKenna (1989), that personal agency is an important route into gaining access to these categories of experience. At the same time it may be that the relationship of enjoyment with access to categories of experience represents a dynamic intertwining between the person and the situation. For some situations engagement in activities and other categories of experience could provide enjoyment, whilst at the same time enjoyment could provide the stimulus to continue with engagement in pursuits. Csikszentmihalyi (1982) and Csikszentmihalyi and Csikszentmihalyi (1988) emphasise the pivotal role of enjoyment in psychological well-being. The result from this study of unemployed people may indicate one route by which this pivotal role is achieved.

Further research comparing employed and unemployed samples could be done using the ACE questionnaire as a starting point and undertaking in-depth interviews and obtaining accounts provided by participants of their personal history, daily life and social networks. Csikszentmihalyi and Beattie (1979) and Csikszentmihalyi and Larson (1984) argue that the possession of a life theme is an important organising force in the behaviour of an individual, and that both unconscious and conscious factors operate in the adoption of life goals. The seminal writings of Merleau-Ponty (1962) on the phenomenology of perception stress the importance of lived experience and pre-reflexive thought in how we depict the world. A combination of quantitative and qualitative research should give a clearer picture of the differences between those who cope better and worse with unemployment, particularly if such research could be conducted in relation to enterprises and projects considered valuable by the unemployed and the community. Similar research is also needed on retired people, especially the increasing number of people taking early retirement. Besides having important practical value, such research could be of considerable theoretical importance in elucidating the interplay between personal and situational factors in mental health (Haworth 1986).

Access to categories of experience and enjoyment were also investigated as part of a study of work and leisure in a sample of young employed adults by Haworth and Hill (1992). This study used questionnaires and the experience sampling method over a one week period. ACE was measured separately for work and leisure, and showed interesting results. While there were some correlations between ACE at work and psychological well-being, there was a range of correlations with ACE in leisure. Social contact, collective purpose, status, and a composite measure of the five categories of experience termed 'total access', all correlated significantly with a measure of life satisfaction. Social contact and collective purpose also correlated significantly with happiness in daily life measured by ESM. Status, time structure, and total access all correlated significantly with a measure of self-esteem. Variations in access to categories of experience in the leisure time of employed people thus appear to be important in relation to well-being, contrary to Jahoda's predictions. It may well be that for some people there is not a strict division between the important categories of experience obtained in work and those obtained in leisure.

However, it may be that the mechanisms vary for obtaining ACE in work and leisure. When the seven individuals with the highest and lowest total ACE scores in both work and leisure were compared, the individuals with high ACE in leisure had significantly higher mean enjoyment scores than the individuals with low ACE in leisure, though this was not the case in work. Perhaps ACE at work can be provided to some extent irrespective of enjoyment, as Jahoda (1982) appears to indicate. Whereas perhaps ACE in leisure requires more individual effort, reflected in higher enjoyment scores in leisure.

This line of research exploring the interplay between ACE and enjoyment in different situations is one which unites different traditions of research into well-being. European research has tended to concentrate on questionnaire measures of well-being, but has recognised the importance of social factors in behaviour, even if these are not always investigated adequately. American research using ESM has tended to focus on the importance of person-centred factors in relation to quality of life, including intrinsic motivation, perceived freedom and enjoyment, which perhaps resonate more readily with American values. A marriage of these 'two traditions' could be particularly valuable in future research.

Another study of the importance of ACE in work and leisure for mental health was undertaken on a sample of managers by Haworth and Paterson (1995). The results from multiple regression analysis showed that 'collective purpose' and 'status' in both work and leisure had moderate to large β coefficients, indicative of their potential influence, for a considerable range of measures of mental health covering freedom from negative mental health and positive mental health. 'Activity' and 'social contact' in leisure were also important for aspects of positive mental health. Although the β coefficient (weight) indicates the average standard deviation change in y (mental health measure) with a standard deviation change in x (category of experience measure), the generality of the size of the β weight is restricted to samples with similar variance in the 'predictor' variable (x). The validity of the findings also depends on there being no specification error, such as no relevant independent variables being excluded (Lewis-Beck 1980).

In this study of managers, analysis of a broader range of variables, the principal environmental influences (PEIs), potentially reduced specification error. It also permitted a finer grain analysis. The PEI 'valued social position' incorporates the ACE measures of 'collective purpose' and 'status'. Analysis showed that 'valued social position' remained a significant statistical predictor of a wide range of measures of mental health. Other interesting results from this finer grain analysis showed that 'use of existing skills' in leisure had large β weights associated with total life satisfaction and highly enjoyable flow experiences. 'Social contact' in leisure did not remain significant. Inspection of the regression analysis suggested that the influence of 'social contact' in leisure on mental health in this sample may be through a range of other variables including 'variety', 'control', 'valued social position' and 'skill use'. The use of path analysis (Asher 1976; Chapter 5) would be valuable in investigating these possible indirect influences.

While the statistical association between two variables may reflect bidirectional causal influence, the study has important practical implications. For a company to try and maintain the mental health of managers, it would seem important to reinforce valued social position at work. Equally, time for leisure pursuits in the everyday life of busy managers is not, it would seem, a peripheral consideration, one which can be forfeited without cost.

The final study to be summarised is one focusing on person–situation interactions in a sample of working women, who were primarily office workers (Haworth, Jarman and Lee). The study measured locus of control (Rotter 1966), as a person centred variable, PEIs and mental health, and, using the experience sampling method for one week, activities, enjoyment, interest, motivation and feelings of control. The β weights from multiple regression analysis highlighted the potential importance of 'money' for total life satisfaction and pleasure. 'Valued social position' at work had a large β

weight associated with contentment at work, while 'valued social position' in leisure had large β weights associated with affective well-being and enthusiasm in leisure. However, in this group of working women, in contrast to the group of managers discussed earlier, it was 'clarity' at work which had the greatest number of large β weights associated with a wide range of measures of mental health, namely: total life satisfaction, work affective well-being and enthusiasm at work, leisure affective well-being and enthusiasm in leisure. This indicates that different patterns of PEIs seem to be important for different groups of people in different life situations, with the measures used to measure the PEIs having some discriminant validity.

The study found that locus of control was significantly associated with a wide range of measures of well-being, with 'internals' having more favourable scores. Respondents were divided into two groups on the basis of the locus of control scores. Analysis showed the more 'internal' locus of control group to have significantly better scores on several PEIs including 'clarity' in both work and leisure. Conceivably, while locus of control could have a direct influence on well-being, through feelings of control, internals, who have a greater learned expectancy for reinforcements to be contingent upon their own behaviour than externals, could have better well-being through the indirect path of greater access to principal environmental influences. While path analysis gave some indication of this being the case, it did not hold for each measure of well-being. However, further research is needed using larger samples.

Analysis of the ESM data showed that 'internals' had greater levels of enjoyment, interest and control for the week of the study, which is congruent with results from the questionnaire measures of well-being. 'Internals' also reported more of their activities as intrinsically motivated than the 'external' locus of control group. Leisure, in comparison to work, provided significantly greater levels of enjoyment and feelings of control, but not interest. In leisure, social interaction, spectating, reading, hobbies, shopping and self-maintenance had above average levels of enjoyment, with many of these activities also showing above average levels of interest and control. Chores and domestic activities, including washing, cooking and general housework, were also high on the positive experience of control, even though below average on enjoyment and interest. Work also provided several areas where control was high, and also some of the most enjoyable activities.

Rotter (1966, 1990) emphasises that locus of control is a learned expectancy. Spector (1982) points to an interactive relationship between locus of control and experience, in that locus of control may affect behaviour and the consequences of behaviour may in turn affect locus of control. Parkes (1984) notes that internal locus of control is reciprocally related to skill use at work. The results from the present study of working women suggest the possibility of positive subjective states in leisure being reciprocally related to internal locus of control. Enjoyment and feelings of control in leisure may enhance internal locus of control, which in turn may lead to enhanced mental health either directly, or indirectly through greater access to principal environmental influences, in work or leisure. Further studies using questionnaires and the ESM on larger samples of working women are required.

Future research

Warr (1987) notes that the strength of his model is that it applies to any kind of environment and that it has considerable heuristic value, lending itself to application and development. In order to tease out the relative importance of different principal environmental influences for people with different enduring characteristics, Warr stresses the necessity for large-scale survey research including longitudinal studies and multivariate analysis. The model emphasises the importance of studying the processes involved in person–situation interactions important for mental health, for which questionnaire research using causal modelling will be important.

Warr also notes that 'more descriptive and interpretive research is now required, which can elucidate the processes whereby particular sets of environmental features work together to have their environmental effects' (p. 290), and also that it is 'essential that we study the interaction defined in a processual sense, seeking to deepen our understanding of the models of person–situation interactions across time' (p. 291).

The research summarised in this chapter shows that the categorical models of Warr and Jahoda are useful in studying focused samples where the aim is to get information of practical value for a particular type of group in a particular situation. Such information could help managers and policy makers concerned with work and leisure in their understanding of factors associated with well-being and health. Although the specific findings from focused samples are only relevant in a 'predictive' sense to samples with similar characteristics, the utility of such research can be greater if 'findings' are used as 'insights' which policy makers and managers use as a guide. The strategy of using focused samples can be further enhanced by studying the processes and dynamics underpinning person–situation interactions, which may help in the construction of general theory concerning mental health, work and leisure. Warr's model provides one overall perspective from which to develop this research.

Equally, other variables, methods and perspectives could be used in conjunction with questionnaire studies of Warr's model. The importance of enjoyment has been highlighted in the present research. Enjoyment may play a pivotal role in gaining access to categories of experience, either through the direct effects of rewards, or through enhancing internal locus of control. Rotter (1982) has pointed to the importance of studying 'enhancement behaviours'. These are 'specific cognitive activities that are used to enhance and maintain good feelings' which may help to explain why 'there are people who are happy, content and in a good mood much of the time, and that the objective circumstances of such people may not differ markedly from those of others who are mildly unhappy, discontented, or worried about bad things that might happen' (p. 339). In what Warr (1987: 138) has termed the complex interweaving of simultaneous interactions between the person and the environment, the role of enjoyable activity in well-being may involve both conscious and subconscious processes. Uleman and Bargh (1989) have reviewed research into the importance of 'unintended thought' in the experience of stress. Future research could investigate the role of 'unintended thought', and similar constructs such as 'pre-reflexive thought' (Haworth 1986), in positive mental health. In investigating these complex areas, the long-term success of research which attempts to have both practical and theoretical value will depend on the innovative marriage of theory, method and strategy.

REFERENCES

Argyle, M. (1987) *The Psychology of Happiness*, London: Metheun.

Asher, B.H. (1976) *Causal Modelling*, London: Sage.

Bradburn, N.M. (1969) *The Structure of Psychological Well-being*, Chicago: Aldine Publishing.

Brandstätter, H. (1991) 'Emotions in everyday life situations. Time sampling of subjective experience', in F. Strack, M. Argyle and N. Schwarz (eds) *Subjective Well-being: An interdisciplinary perspective*, Oxford: Pergamon Press.

Brief, A.P., Butcher, A.H., George, J.M. and Link, K.E. (1993) 'Integrating bottom-up and top-down theories of subjective well-being: the case of health', *Journal of Personality and Social Psychology*, 64, 4: 646–653.

Csikszentmihalyi, M. (1982) 'Towards a psychology of optimal experience', in L. Wheeler (ed.) *Review of Personality and Social Psychology* (vol. 2), Beverly Hills, Calif.: Sage.

Csikszentmihalyi, M. and Beattie, O. (1979) 'Life themes: a theoretical and empirical explanation of their origins and effects', *Journal of Humanistic Psychology*, 19: 45–63.

Csikszentmihalyi, M. and Larson, R. (1984) 'Validity and reliability of the experience-sampling method', *The Journal of Nervous and Mental Disease*, 175, 9: 526–536.

Csikszentmihalyi, M. and Csikszentmihalyi, I.S. (1988) *Optimal Experience*, Cambridge: Cambridge University Press.

Csikszentmihalyi, M., Larson, R. and Prescott, S. (1977) 'The ecology of adolescent activity and experience', *Journal of Youth and Adolescence*, 6: 281–294.

Driver, B.L., Brown, P.J. and Peterson, G.L. (eds) (1991) *Benefits of Leisure*, Pennsylvania: Venture Publishing.

Evans, S.T. (1986) 'Variations in activity and psychological well-being in unemployed young adults', unpublished PhD thesis, University of Manchester.

Evans, S.T. and Haworth, J.T. (1991) 'Variations in personal activity, access to categories of experience and psychological well-being in unemployed young adults', *Leisure Studies*, 10: 249–264.

Fryer, D. and McKenna, S. (1989) 'Redundant skills: temporary unemployment and mental health', in M. Patrickson (ed.) *Readings in Organisational Behaviour*, New South Wales: Harper & Row.

Goldberg, D.P. (1972) *The Detection of Psychiatric Illness by Questionnaire*, Oxford: Oxford University Press.

Haworth, J.T. (1986) 'Meaningful activity and psychological models of non-employment', *Leisure Studies*, 5: 281–297.

Haworth, J.T. (1993) 'Skill-challenge relationships and psychological well-being in everyday life', *Society and Leisure*, 16, 1: 115–128.

Haworth, J.T. and Ducker, J. (1991) 'Psychological well-being and access to categories of experience in unemployed young adults', *Leisure Studies*, 10: 265–274.

Haworth, J.T. and Hill, S. (1992) 'Work, leisure and psychological well-being in a sample of young adults', *Journal of Community and Applied Social Psychology*, 2: 147–160.

Haworth, J.T. and Paterson, F. (1995) 'Access to categories of experience and mental health in a sample of managers', revised version submitted to *Journal of Applied Social Psychology*, 25, 8: 712–724.

Haworth, J.T., Jarman, M. and Lee, S. (forthcoming) 'Positive subjective states in the daily life of a sample of working women', paper in preparation.

Herzberg, F. (1966) *Work and the Nature of Man*, Chicago: World Publishing Co.

Hormuth, S.E. (1986) 'The sampling of experience in situ', *Journal of Personality*, 54, 1: 262–293.

Jahoda, M. (1982) *Employment and Unemployment: A Social Psychological Analysis*, Cambridge: Cambridge University Press.

Lewis-Beck, M.S. (1980) *Applied Regression: An Introduction*, London: Sage.

Merleau-Ponty, M. (1962) *Phenomenology of Perception*, London: Routledge & Kegan Paul.

Parkes, K.R. (1984) 'Locus of control, cognitive appraisal and coping in stressful episodes', *Journal of Personality and Social Psychology*, 46, 3: 655–668.

Rotter, J.B. (1966) 'Generalised expectancies for internal versus external control of reinforcement', *Psychological Monographs*, 80 (whole no.) 609.

Rotter, J.B. (1982) *The Development and Applications of Social Learning Theory*, New York: Praeger.

Rotter, J.B. (1990) 'Internal versus external locus of control of reinforcement: A case history of a variable', *American Psychologist*, 45, 4: 489–493.

Sevastos, P., Smith, L. and Cordery, J.L. (1992) 'Evidence on the reliability and construct validity of Warr's (1990) well-being and mental health measures', *Journal of Occupational and Organisational Psychology*, 65: 33–49.

Spector, P. (1982) 'Behaviour in organisations as a function of employee's locus of control', *Psychological Bulletin*, 91: 482–497.

Strack, F., Argyle, M. and Schwarz, N. (eds) (1991) *Subjective Well-being: An Interdisciplinary Perspective*, Oxford: Pergamon Press.

Tennen, H., Suls, J. and Affleck, G. (1991) 'Personality and daily experience: the promise and the challenge', *Journal of Personality*, 59, 3: 313–337.

Uleman, J.S. and Bargh, J.A. (eds) (1989) *Unintended Thought*, New York: The Guilford Press.

Warr, P. (1987) *Work, Unemployment and Mental Health*, Oxford: Clarendon Press.

Warr, P. (1989) 'The measurement of well-being and other aspects of mental health', MRC/ESRC Social and Applied Psychology Unit, memo. University of Sheffield, Sheffield, UK.

Warr, P. (1990) 'The measurement of well-being and other aspects of mental health', *Journal of Occupational Psychology*, 63: 193–210.

Warr, P. (1992) 'A measure of two axes of affective well-being', MRC/ESRC Social and Applied Psychology Unit, memo 1392. University of Sheffield, Sheffield, UK.

Warr, P. (1993) 'Work and mental health, a general model', in F. La Ferla and L. Levi (eds) *A Healthier Work Environment*, Copenhagen: World Health Organisation.

Warr, P.B. and Jackson, P.R. (1983) 'Self-esteem and unemployment among young workers', *Le Travail Humain*, 46: 355–366.

Warr, P., Cook, J. and Wall, T. (1979) 'Scales for the measurement of some work attitudes and aspects of psychological well-being', *Journal of Occupational Psychology*, 52: 129–148.

White, R.W. (1959) 'Motivation reconsidered: the concept of competence', *Psychological Review*, 66: 297–333.

Zuzanek, J. and Larson, R. (eds) (1993) 'Leisure in the context of everyday life', *Society and Leisure*, 16, 1: Whole issue.

Chapter 3

Questionnaire measures of health-relevant cognitions and behaviours

Mark Conner and Mitch Waterman

INTRODUCTION

The significance of behaviour and lifestyle for health and well-being is now widely acknowledged. For instance, studies in Alameda County, USA identified seven features of lifestyle – not smoking, moderate alcohol intake, sleeping 7–8 hours per night, exercising regularly, maintaining a desirable body weight, avoiding snacks, and eating breakfast regularly were together associated with morbidity and subsequent long-term survival (Belloc and Breslow 1972; Breslow and Enstrom 1980). And such results have been replicated in a number of samples (Metzner, Carman and House 1983; Brock, Haefner and Noble 1988). These behaviours have been referred to as health behaviours. With health behaviour being defined as 'Any activity undertaken by a person believing himself to be healthy for the purpose of preventing disease or detecting it at an asymptomatic stage' (Kasl and Cobb 1966). Such behaviours are now the target of major health promotion campaigns and health promotion advice given through primary health care contacts (*The Health of the Nation* 1992). Research into personal health behaviours and their determinants is one of the most rapidly developing fields of psychology (Rodin and Salovey, 1989).

Information concerning health behaviours is vital to the planning of health education and primary prevention programmes. Health behaviours have been monitored in several large-scale surveys in the US, including the National Survey of Personal Health Practices and Health Consequences. In the UK, similar surveys have been carried out such as the health and lifestyle survey by Blaxter (1990). Such studies have revealed the difficulty of obtaining accurate measures regarding those who perform such behaviours. Psychologists are uniquely placed to provide advice about how such information might most accurately be assessed. This chapter gathers together a number of important findings concerning questionnaire measures of health-related behaviours and cognitions.

Much effort has gone into understanding the determinants of health behaviours. A greater understanding of such determinants may be one way in which health behaviours and ultimately individual health might be improved. A variety of factors are thought to underlie differences between those who perform health behaviours and those who do not. These include economic considerations and cultural factors. But individual cognitions have particularly attracted the attention of psychologists. For instance, knowledge about behaviour–health links (or risk awareness) is an essential factor in an informed choice concerning a healthy lifestyle. The reduction of smoking over the past twenty years in the Western world can be largely attributed to a growing awareness of the serious health risks posed by tobacco use brought about by widespread publicity. However, the fact that tobacco continues to be widely used amongst lower socio-economic status groups, and the growing uptake of smoking among adolescent girls in some countries, illustrate the fact that knowledge of health risks is not a sufficient condition for avoidance of smoking. Similarly, few adults in the UK can be unaware that sweets promote caries, or that high fat consumption can increase the risk of heart disease; nevertheless, sugar and fat consumption over the past decade have scarcely shown any change (*The Health of the Nation* 1992).

Yet another cognitive factor which is closely allied with risk awareness is belief or attitude. Many accounts of health behaviours incorporate some concept which addresses the individual's belief that the behaviour will lead to valued outcomes. And many studies find a relationship between aspects of evaluation of a behaviour and frequency of performing that behaviour. However, it is also true that a single set of beliefs are unlikely to underlie the full range of healthy behaviours. Rather each health behaviour is likely to be determined by a different set of beliefs. And indeed for each behaviour, performance is likely to be based upon differing factors as well as beliefs, e.g. habits, social support, etc.

Hence both beliefs and knowledge are likely to be two important factors in determining health behaviours. Beliefs about the importance of carrying out a range of different activities for health maintenance in general are likely to be important in determining behaviour. Health knowledge is also an important factor in health behaviours, and associations between the two are commonly reported for diet (Charny and Lewis 1987), smoking, alcohol intake, exercise and breast self-examination (Dean 1989). Many health education programmes aim to provide accurate information concerning the relevance of personal habits to health maintenance, in the interests of influencing risk appraisal and ultimately behaviour (Catford and Nutbeam 1984).

There are also likely to be a range of other cognitions which may determine health behaviours. Commonly studied variables include perceptions of health threat, barriers to performance of the behaviour, the value placed upon health, health locus of control, perceived social pressure, self-efficacy and emotional reactions. Each of these have been found to have some predictive power in explaining the performance of health behaviours. Several models relating attitudes, beliefs and emotions to health behaviours have been developed and extensively applied in health psychology. These are commonly referred to as social cognition models. Most social cognition models emphasise the rationality of human behaviour. The health behaviours to be predicted are considered to be the end result of a rational decision-making process. Most assume that behaviour and decisions are based upon elaborate, but subjective, cost/benefit analysis of the outcomes of differing courses of action. As such they have roots going back to expectancy-value theory (Peak 1955). Essentially the idea is that the expected outcomes of behaving in a particular way have differing (subjective) probabilities of occurring and are of differing value to individuals. Comparison of the expected outcomes of differing behaviours in terms of costs and benefits leads to the choice of that behaviour with the greatest benefits and fewest costs. The social cognition models commonly used in relation to health behaviours include the Health Belief Model (HBM; e.g. Becker 1974; Janz and Becker 1984), the Theory of Reasoned Action/Theory of Planned Behaviour (TRA/TPB; e.g. Ajzen and Fishbein 1980; Ajzen 1991), Social Cognitive Theory approaches (SCT; e.g. Bandura 1991; Schwarzer 1992), and Protection Motivation Theory (PMT; Maddux and Rogers 1983; van der Velde and van der Pligt 1991).

Given the apparent acceptance of the importance of cognitively based accounts of the performance of health behaviours, it is also possible to envisage research based upon more general models of behaviour being applied to the issues of health. For example, the Drive, and Expectancy Theories of Hull (1943) and Vroom (1964) can be seen as relevant precursors not only to the social cognition models cited above, but also to more behaviourally oriented models such as that of Binswanger (1986), and Locke and Latham (1990). These models clearly focus upon the interaction of goals in the individual's behaviour (usually in the workplace), and as such might have an intuitive appeal to researchers in the health field. Furthermore, with the contemporary interest in the cognitive psychology of emotion, it is also readily apparent that cognitive emotion theories might also be of future value in health research (e.g. Ortony, Clore and Collins 1988; Oatley 1992).

However, rather than considering models that have been applied to health in detail here, which is done elsewhere (e.g. Conner and Norman 1994), or making explicit the potential of more general models, we will focus upon the methodological difficulties in ensuring we obtain adequate measures of health-relevant cognitions and behaviours. The rest of this chapter considers first general issues of questionnaire contents focused on facts, behaviours and cognitions. Problems of bias in questionnaires is considered next along with procedures for minimising such biases. The final section considers practical difficulties in developing and initially assessing a questionnaire along with suggestions for important things to check at each stage.

The content of this chapter considers self-reports. In many ways individuals are uniquely placed to observe and report their own health-relevant behaviours and cognitions. In the case of cognitions this argument is particularly strong as it is not possible to directly observe others' cognitions. Throughout the history of psychology there has been considerable debate over the individual's ability to accurately introspect and report their own thoughts and feelings. However, many modern views assume that individuals possess the ability to perform such a task (e.g. Ryan 1970). For behaviours, it is frequently possible to use observational methods to obtain objective measures. However, this becomes problematic when studying large groups or complex behaviours. Hence, it is common for self-report measures to be used. The research discussed here focuses on the factors thought to enhance accurate self-reports of cognitions and behaviour.

THE CONTENTS OF QUESTIONNAIRES

The content of a questionnaire will be driven by the particular research question. This will include not only the issues covered by the questions, but also the relative number of questions devoted to each topic and the ordering of the topics. This section considers some general issues concerned with writing items on different topics.

The number of questions on a topic will be partly determined by its importance to the overall research question. There is a need to strike a balance between time pressures and need for detailed information (i.e. multiple questions for reliable and valid scales). It is also often necessary to put answers in a context; for example, is the opinion specific to one, or more health behaviours – and is that specificity clear to the respondent? Remember that the research may be focusing upon a complex issue, and thus you may require several questions rather than just a single item. Perhaps the relative importance of the complex issues may need to be ascertained. But while trying to do these things one must also minimise the number of questions.

Sensitivity or level of threat posed by a question or group of questions is another issue to consider early on. If the response might be viewed as private or personal by the respondent, special precautions in wording can be applied to maximise the chance of obtaining a valid answer instead of misinformation or refusals to answer. Indeed, the researcher should be aware that validity of question responses regarding a topic that is sensitive must be assumed only with caution. Some suggestions for improving validity in this sense include putting sensitive questions at the end, making the context and relevance of such questions clear to topic of interest, and using anonymous postal questionnaires or skilled interviewers to administer the questionnaires (Kidder and Judd 1986). Questions of validity of responses, if seriously doubted, might lead the researcher to consider an alternative research methodology (e.g. qualitative methods).

Aside from these very general considerations there are a number of issues concerned with the types of questions being asked. Questionnaire contents can be split into items about what respondents know (factual questions), what they think, expect, feel or prefer (cognition questions) or what they have done (behaviour questions). In many ways similar issues arise when writing factual and behaviour questions and so these will be considered together. Somewhat different issues arise when writing cognition questions and so these will be considered separately.

Questions aimed at assessing facts and behaviours

These appear to be the simplest type of questions to write but are often not so simple as might be first expected. Whilst we expect people to know a whole range of facts about themselves (e.g. age, education, religion, income, marital status, frequency of brushing teeth, etc.) there is the possibility of error. It is important to allow the respondent to say they don't know if they do not. These errors arise from memory problems or from response biases of various forms, e.g. respondents may overstate their income in order to impress the inter- viewer with their importance, or understate it if they think a true statement may have a financial penalty.

Considerable advances in our understanding of the processes by which respondents answer questions and their importance for obtaining accurate measurement have been achieved through collaboration between survey re- searchers and cognitive psychologists (e.g. Hippler *et al.* 1987; Tanur 1992). For example, answering a quantitative autobiographical question about frequency of taking exercise requires that the respondent undertake several tasks:

1 The respondent must understand the referent in question (i.e. exercise).
2 Relevant instances must be recalled or reconstructed from memory.
3 The respondent must then decide if these instances occurred during the reference period.
4 A report of the number of instances must be mapped onto the researcher's response categories.

Let us look at these stages in a little more detail.

The apparently simple stage of understanding the referent in the question can provide a number of problems, with significant mismatches between the researcher and respondent over the meaning given to terms in the question (e.g. Belson 1968). For example, let us take a concrete example:

How frequently did you take physical exercise in the past month?
Never   Once or twice   3–5 times   6–10 times   More than 10 times

In this example, the term physical exercise may be given a range of meanings from walking to work through to prolonged engagement in vigorous sports such as squash. The frequency reports are likely to vary dramatically depending upon the meaning assumed by the respondent. This is particularly likely to be a problem where the respondent finds the question difficult to answer. In such cases the respondent is likely to interpret the referent more broadly than intended and respond to the gist of the question rather than to its exact wording (Schwarz 1990).

Once the respondent has formed an impression of what the question refers to, relevant information needs to be retrieved from memory. The traditional assumption is that the respondent uses a recall and count model, whereby all relevant instances that match the target behaviour that occurred during the reference period are recalled and counted. However, this is unlikely to be the strategy the respondent applies except for very rare and important behaviours. A body of memory research indicates that respondents are unlikely to have detailed representations of numerous individual instances of a behaviour stored in memory (see Schwarz 1990). Hence, in answering questions such as our example, respondents are likely to use fragmentary recall and inference rules to compute a frequency estimate. A common strategy amongst survey researchers is therefore to use appropriate cues to simplify the respondent's task. So, in relation to our example, the use of specific exemplars (e.g. vigorous walking, squash) and common situations (e.g. on the way to work, at weekends) is likely to provide more accurate recall. In general, it is suggested that global questions be broken down into several more specific ones and short rather than long reference periods be used to improve recall. This links to the third task of the respondent – deciding whether the behaviour occurred during the reference period. Here it has been found that periods defined in terms of several weeks or months are frequently misinterpreted. In relation to our example, it may be that some respondents interpret this as the previous calendar month (e.g. May), exclude the current week, or use a four week period finishing some days previously. The use of specific dates is also not particularly helpful as these are unlikely to be encoded in memory in any relevant way. Salient personal or public events (referred to as landmark dates), such as Christmas or New Year's Eve, have been found to be useful by some (e.g. Loftus and Marburger 1983). However, the general advice is to keep such reference periods short, clearly defined and temporally close to the present.

The above research demonstrates that respondents are unlikely to use a recall and count model in answering questions requesting information about the frequency of performing health-relevant behaviours. Rather inference processes will play a major role, with respondents using any information available to them in order to generate a reasonable response (Bradburn *et al.* 1987). For example, the availability heuristic (Tversky and Kahneman 1973) relies on the ease with which specific instances come to mind. Rare and vivid events are more likely to come easily to mind and their frequency of occurrence will tend to be overestimated, while mundane and pallid events are more likely to be difficult to recall and be underestimated. A particularly common strategy used by respondents is the decomposition strategy. This is where a respondent recalls a limited period, uses the recall and count model for this period, and then multiplies up to obtain an estimate for the relevant period. In our example, a respondent may consider how frequently they exercise on a typical week (even split this into weekdays and weekends), with the final estimate obtained by multiplying this value by the appropriate amounts. Such a strategy can easily lead to serious errors.

Another important source of information upon which inference processes used in answering questions are based is the response alternatives provided by the researcher. The range of categories for responses may be interpreted by the respondent as reflecting the researcher's knowledge or expectation about how common is the behaviour. Hence, in our example, the range provided may be interpreted as reflecting the range of usual responses. Therefore, in producing a reply the respondent may use this range as a frame of reference (Schwarz 1990), and rather than using a recall and report model may use a comparison model. For instance, if you believe that you tend to take rather less exercise than 'average' you may take the middle responses as representing average and select a lower frequency. Indeed such a strategy could lead to fairly accurate reporting provided the response categories do indeed reflect the distribution in the population and the comparison process is accurate. However, individuals may differ greatly in the groups against whom comparisons are made, leading to significant biases in the responses. Practical advice to avoid such biases is somewhat limited. The information in the response categories appears to be particularly used where other sources of information are limited and the task is vague or difficult. Hence, one strategy is to use short simple questions that are not difficult for the respondent and provide relevant retrieval cues. Linked to this idea is the notion that the response categories provided should where possible be clearly linked to the distribution in the population so that any comparison inferences are thus based upon correct assumptions about the response categories.

Hence, research in this area demonstrates the fact that responding to questions asking about the frequency of performing health-relevant behaviours is likely to be based upon inference processes more than recall and count models. In effect, the response, though deemed appropriate by the individual, is, at least in part, a construction. As such it is necessary to aid the respondent to use inferences based upon correct assumptions. Most attempts to do this focus on the need to simplify the response task and avoid memory errors where possible. There are dangers here, however. For example, the researcher must be aware of which assumptions are appropriate, and which are not – aiding a respondent in her responses by allowing inferences based upon incorrect assumptions might provide responses that are even less reliable than those that might have arisen without such aid intervention. Of course, these issues are most relevant for distant memories; most memory 'failures' are likely to be for events in the distant past or for trivial or routine items. Structuring of the task may ease the respondent's difficulties in remembering the facts, e.g. temporally related events to the ones of interest may aid recall of the desired facts.

Reinterviews also aid the recall of sought-after details, though the period between interviews should be a consideration. Waterman (1994) reports an apparent transition from explicit memory to implicit memory if this period is extreme (e.g. a year) – the result being a satisfying similarity of response across time, but a difference in the self-reported reasoning underlying the response.

Questions aimed at cognitions

There has been much written about the development of reliable and valid measures of a variety of psychological constructs including cognitions such as attitudes. Particularly good texts include Cronbach (1990), DeVellis (1991), Kline (1992), and Oppenheim (1992). However, here the focus will be upon the writing of individual items to assess internal knowledge representations (i.e. cognitions) such as attitudes and beliefs. For the moment, we will exclude questions regarding feelings from this discussion, even though many theorists would argue that they are as much cognitive as attitudes and beliefs (e.g. Oatley and Johnson-Laird 1987).

Questions about cognitions are probably the most difficult to write for several reasons. First, there is always the possibility that respondents may not have an attitude, belief, etc. because they never thought about the issue until asked about it. You cannot count on the respondent saying 'I do not know' in these situations. Second, their attitude may be only slightly valenced – the issue is not of great import to the respondent. Indeed Schuman and Presser (1981) have shown that many people simply respond with a 'doorstep opinion' which is simply not well thought through and may not represent what they would say had they the chance to think it through. Of course, this need not inherently be undesired; sometimes the research actually requires that the respondent refrain from careful thought about the topic (e.g. with sensitive issues). In laboratory experiments, Russell Fazio (1990) has shown that you can distinguish people who have and have not formed an opinion by their speed of answer. However, this is at present of little use in most questionnaires except perhaps those conducted via the telephone.

A second problem is that cognitions are often complex. Attitudes, for example, are often complex and multidimensional. So a person may not have a single overall attitude towards a complex issue (e.g. vegetarianism), but may favour it in some complex circumstances and reject it in others, e.g. medical versus moral considerations. The difficulties arise due to the complex interaction of several 'types' of cognition (e.g. standards, attitudes, goals), and their dissociation for the purpose of a question response may well be artificial. Thus to address an attitude in detail you may need to take in a whole series of issues. For this reason it is important to have a clear theoretical model of the cognitions and potentially their interactions being examined in order to guide questionnaire construction. Some of the social cognition models may be particularly relevant here. It may be necessary to assess the dimension of intensity in assessing attitudes. Some people feel very strongly about an issue one way or another, while, as noted above, others feel very little. Intensity differences can be attributed to a number of influences, such as unexpectedness or reality (Ortony *et al.* 1988), and it might be of value to consider why an attitude might be firmly held by one individual, and not so by another. Questionnaires usually try to assess this strength of feeling. The theoretical model should also guide the type and content of questions to ask. For instance, it might guide which component of attitude to ask about or the way questions should be asked.

As a consequence of these types of factors, reported cognitions are dependent on the details of question wording, question sequence, and any interviewer-effects to a much greater degree than are responses involving facts or behaviours. Opinion polls offer an obvious example. There is much research now showing the effects of these factors. Indeed public acknowledgement has led to the publishing of actual question wordings used in opinion surveys.

BIAS IN QUESTIONNAIRES: ITEM WORDING AND ITEM ORDERING

Questionnaires can be biased in a number of ways. If respondents are not well motivated to complete your questionnaire carefully and accurately, it is unlikely that the results will be useful. Hence, motivating respondents to report accurately is an important prerequisite for valid survey-type research. However, even well-motivated respondents can produce invalid or biased responses. Bias can be assessed in a number of ways (examination of responses across the sample, for example), and can be addressed, at least in part, by carefully constructing and ordering questions. Unfortunately, responses that are not valid are far more difficult to identify. The respondent may have purposefully answered inaccurately, may have misunderstood, may have responded with an inappropriate category – there are numerous possible causes. These issues have generally been tackled in two ways. First, in terms of question wording and second, in terms of question ordering.

Question wording

This is perhaps the most difficult, but most important task in questionnaire construction. One essential prerequisite is a clear conceptual idea of what content is to be measured. Then it is important to pre-test the questions to revise and improve them. Decisions about question content will provide some outline to the wordings to be used and this must be clear enough to provide specific guidance. Essentially it is a question of conceptual clarity – clear conceptions of what you wish to measure will often suggest clear ways in which to word questions. We have already examined research on the way in which respondents interpret questions which can give further guidance to their effective writing. However, a number of other issues should be considered.

Terminology

The choice of terms to convey the question concepts is perhaps the most difficult part of question wordings. Generally, terms should be exact, simple, avoid ambiguous or vague words (e.g. quantifying words such as *frequently* are not as preferable as specific number ranges), and avoid biased words (e.g. avoid terms which produce powerful emotional responses, such as *bureaucrats*). Careful selection of terminology can be a powerful tool in discouraging response biases; this is especially so when the content topic is sensitive or controversial.

Question structure

Use short, simple questions, with the key idea in the question last, in order to avoid respondents formulating answers prematurely. As we noted earlier, questions should simplify the respondent's task. For example, if we wanted the percentage of income spent on food, it is simpler and more accurate to ask the respondent for income, average food bill, and frequency of shopping all separately.

Expressing all alternatives

Questions should make all the alternative responses clear in the question or the response categories. Pilot work may be necessary in order to identify these alternatives. Schuman and Presser's (1981) work indicates that giving forced choices in questions produces less bias than agree–disagree responses, probably because it cuts down on acquiescence bias (i.e. the tendency to agree response bias, which lie scales or social desirability scales are designed to identify).

Avoid unwarranted assumptions

Certain questions make assumptions which mean that not all respondents can report correctly (e.g. What is your occupation? Have you stopped beating your wife?). This is solved by asking the obvious preliminary questions, and then only asking the respondent to complete additional questions where appropriate. Also avoid double-barrelled questions in order to avoid this same problem.

Response categories

Open-ended questions allow the respondent to answer in a relatively unconstrained way. The response is then coded in some way by the researcher, if you are to perform quantitative analyses. They allow respondents to convey fine shades of opinion to their own satisfaction, they can be used when the researcher does not know the full range of opinion. They can provide information that the most carefully worded or ordered question might inadvertently bias. They are also costly and difficult to code, often self-contradictory, incomprehensible or irrelevant and defy categorisation. They are also a function of possibly irrelevant factors such as educational level or fluency. Closed-ended questions are easy to code and produce meaningful results for analysis. The categories often provide clarification of the issue, or aid memory. But they may oversimplify matters. The two sorts of response categories can be combined in questions by using an open category as a response – but this sort of question is principally useful in identifying important categories which have been missed. Perhaps the best combination is to use open-ended questions in a small pre-test and then construct the closed-ended questions on the basis of the responses (Schuman and Presser 1981).

With closed-ended questions further decisions remain – such as the number and type of categories. There is a need to balance vagueness and overprecision and the precise categories used should be determined partly by the use to which the responses are to be put. However, it is clear from the research we examined earlier that the response categories provided will be used by the respondent in order to guide their choice of response. Perhaps the most useful advice that can be provided is to carry out adequate pilot work to assess the range of responses typically reported and use a set of categories which adequately cover this range. Even with this precaution, however, researchers should not be surprised to find unexpected categories arising in their responses.

Another issue in providing response categories concerns respondents' use of differing categories. Some respondents have a tendency to use only one part of the response format (e.g. tending to agree with all items or tending to use only one portion of the response format). While the responses of such respondents are unlikely to be useful in answering the research question, their effects upon the results can at least be minimised by reversing half the items. A related form of bias in self-report questionnaires are social desirability effects. This is where the respondent completes the questionnaire with self-presentation considerations foremost in their mind rather than accurate reporting. While clear questionnaire instructions should minimise such effects, they can never be totally eliminated. It is with sensitive topics, where social-desirability can be a source of difficulty, that researchers desire responses that are not overly considered – allowing a respondent time for thought may well encourage thoughts of self-presentation to take precedence. A common response to such problems is to incorporate lie or social desirability scales (e.g. I have never told a lie). These are not generally to be recommended because of the time taken to construct, the problem of what to do with individuals who score highly on such a scale, and perhaps most importantly their potentially distracting or off-putting nature.

Question ordering

The ordering of the questions presented in a questionnaire influences the ease of questionnaire completion and helps to avoid biases in responses. It is generally recommended that questionnaires should begin with a few relatively easy and unchallenging questions to put the respondent at ease. These questions should also be interesting and relevant to the study in order to get the respondent's attention. These should be followed by the main body of questions, with demographic questions at the end (Kidder and Judd 1986). Also, it is generally useful to keep topically related questions together. Each topic should show clear links with the purpose of the study, making clear to the respondent their relevance if necessary. Within a topic area it is common to apply the 'funnel principle' – general questions first, followed by specific, detailed questions at the end. This has greater face validity to respondents and is generally considered to produce less bias. Another problem concerns the interrelatedness of questions and is somewhat more difficult to take account of.

Cognitive social psychologists have made advances in understanding the processes involved in answering items within questionnaires and how such responses are interrelated. This research has involved examination of the way in which individuals process the information in questions and formulate their answers. Tourangeau and Rasinski (1988) argue that answering an attitude question is the product of a four-stage process:

1 The question is first interpreted to determine which attitude is being referred to.
2 Relevant beliefs and feelings are then retrieved.
3 These beliefs and feelings are then combined in some way to form a judgement.
4 Finally the judgement is used to select an appropriate response.

Each of these stages can be influenced by prior questionnaire items. Prior items may provide a context for interpreting later questions. They can also prime some beliefs and make them more accessible to retrieval. Finally, prior items can suggest a standard of comparison and encourage the respondent to answer in a manner that is consistent with responses to earlier items, but that may also be artificial. This complexity of possible effects makes the impact of prior items often difficult to predict and advice on how to avoid context effects difficult to give.

Thus, it is important to be aware of how earlier questions can affect later responses (Schuman and Presser 1981; Gaskell *et al.* 1993). Again adequate pilot work should identify any major problems. With these recommendations in mind, however, we must advise a note of caution; the priming of responses by earlier items on a questionnaire is likely to be a function of item interrelatedness, and therefore grouping questions relevant to a particular topic together is likely to influence responses to some of those questions. Furthermore, the magnitude of this influence will be unknown and uncontrolled. Some measure can be taken against these types of effects by careful word ordering, and reversal of question valence. However, caution is particularly necessary when items are removed following pilot study. Questions that remain will then be free of the influence of those removed. Therefore, responses to those questions remaining may differ from responses obtained at the earlier pilot stage. Of course, one obvious control against these 'priming' effects would be to randomly order questions – and better still, to present different random orders to each respondent. However, this is almost always impractical, and, as Budd (1987) and more recently Sheeran and Orbell (in press) have shown, such measures are likely to result in dramatic reductions in the ease of data interpretation. Perhaps the best advice is to be aware of potential interactions between questions, and to separate those that the researcher feels are likely to interrelate.

THE MECHANICS OF QUESTIONNAIRE PREPARATION

In this section we move on to consider some of the general practical issues involved in the differing stages of developing a questionnaire.

Preparing the questionnaire

Once you have gathered all your questions together which you wish to ask there is still the stage of preparing the actual questionnaire. With advanced wordprocessing packages it is now possible to prepare very professional looking questionnaires which can simply be photocopied rather than going to the extra expense of typesetting. In addition to the considerations we have already discussed it is necessary to give some thought to the layout of the questionnaire. This can have effects upon the way the questionnaire is filled in and particularly upon response rates. Principally you need to give thought to questionnaire size and layout. Size will be determined by the number of questions you wish to ask. However, remember that there is a trade-off between having too many/too few pages and how well-spaced the questions are. Essentially you want to make the respondent's job of filling in the questionnaire as easy as possible. This means ensuring that instructions are clearly marked and questions are set out on the page in a way that makes for easy completion. For instance, distinguishing the response from the question is a good idea. Giving respondents a place to make comments upon the questionnaire or survey is also advisable. It makes it clear to them that you are interested in their views and often gives you valuable information that can be used in interpreting the results or in designing future surveys.

Some general comments on pilot studies

Once you have your finalised questionnaire it is advisable to carry out a pilot study with a few individuals to ascertain:

1 if all questions are understandable;
2 if individuals are likely to make mistakes;
3 how long it will take to complete.

Some of these things can be achieved by giving it to colleagues, but others require that you give the questionnaire to individuals representative of the group of interest. Their reactions to your questionnaire are often a very enlightening experience!

Samples and response rates

Sampling techniques are more than adequately dealt with elsewhere (e.g. Kalton 1983). Here we deal with considerations of sample selection and the ensuring of high response rates. A variety of techniques are available. Nonprobability sampling involves approaching samples that are easy to gain access to, and usually involves getting responses from everyone in the group. For instance, approaching every motorist using a garage. Probability sampling involves selecting individuals from a larger group or population, usually by a random selection method.

General purpose samples can be obtained from the electoral register. Approximately 7 per cent of people were not included on the register in 1981. Only names and addresses are included, so surveys appropriate to particular groups need to set up an initial screening in order to reach the appropriate group. Other sources of samples will vary depending upon the population of interest (Kidder and Judd 1986; Moser and Kalton 1971).

Once the source of the sample has been selected the actual numbers to be surveyed need to be determined. The actual sample size to use will depend upon the analyses which are planned and the expected response rate. There are now computer packages available to assist in the selection of an appropriate sample size and the calculations are relatively simple (e.g. Lipsey 1990). Important in such calculations are estimates of the likely response rates – both in the general sense, and in terms of response rates from particular groups of interest within the research sample (i.e. subsamples). A variety of factors influence likely response rates. For example, in a mail survey, reminders and reply paid or stamped envelopes are essential. The usual practice is to send two reminders (each with questionnaires and reply envelopes). As a rough guide about half the final response will be obtained without sending any reminder, and another third from one reminder (Cartwright 1989). Clearly, in order to send reminders it is essential to be able to identify the people who have replied and those who have not. A serial number is one way to do this – it does not make the replies anonymous but does give some sense of confidentiality to the respondent. Reminders should be sent when replies virtually stop coming in, usually two to three weeks.

A large number of factors have been shown not to affect response rates (sometimes surprisingly). These include:

- first versus second class mailings;
- personalised letters or not;
- precise form of address (Ms vs Mrs);
- signature by hand or stamp; and
- signatory of letter accompanying questionnaire being junior or senior;
- number of questions.

However, it seems advisable to present your respondent with an appropriate 'questionnaire package', and, therefore, taking note of several of these factors may be worthwhile. As noted, even length of questionnaire seems not to have dramatic effects on response rates: 35, 50, 65 and 110 questions are reported to give similar response rates (Cartwright 1989). But the topic and sample will have an effect, as will the design of the questionnaire, i.e. careful layout, logical ordering of questions, clear phrasing, attractive presentation.

Cartwright (1989) reports the following factors to influence response rates:

- attitude questionnaires tend to get lower response rates than factual or behaviour questionnaires;
- asking for future help or for a telephone contact reduces the response rate;
- if the source of questionnaire is an organisation known and relevant to the respondent, response rate tends to be higher.

Some factors which *have* been found to increase the response rate include:

- a short clear letter stating the study aims;
- how the person was chosen;
- reassurance that data will be treated confidentially (and what that means);
- details of the organisation carrying out the study;
- obvious personal relevance of the topic area to the respondent.

Questionnaire analysis

If a questionnaire has been adequately designed, this stage is relatively straightforward. If the data are to be statistically analysed it will usually be necessary to code the data and enter them into a computer package. With closed-ended questions this is relatively simple. With open-ended questions it may be necessary to design appropriate coding schemes first and ensure their reliability (e.g. via inter-rater reliability measures). Once the data are entered onto a computer it is usually worth considerable effort to ensure that the data have been correctly entered. Both authors have experienced the misery of distraught researchers upon their realisation that data had not been correctly entered – and that possibly large quantities of data might require re-entry. Perhaps the most sophisticated form of such checking is independent entry of the complete set of data to two separate files with cross checking between files to isolate errors. Clearly, however, this is a time-consuming and repetitive task; less effortful methods involve checking the range and number of entries for each variable. Once this is complete the data can be analysed in relation to the research question.

CONCLUSIONS

Questionnaires have long been used by psychologists to investigate a range of issues. Carefully designed questionnaires provide a powerful tool for examining a number of important research questions. Designing a useful, reliable and valid questionnaire measure of health-relevant cognitions and behaviours is, of course, in many ways similar to developing any other questionnaire.

A number of the important considerations in designing such measures have been presented here along with suggestions for good practice. Awareness of the dangers and cautionary notes presented should, we hope, allow the design and administration of valuable, reliable, and valid instruments.

REFERENCES

Ajzen, I. (1991) 'The theory of planned behavior', *Organisational Behavior and Human Decision Processes*, 50: 179–211.

Ajzen, I. and Fishbein, M. (1980) *Understanding Attitudes and Predicting Social Behavior*, Englewood Cliffs, N.J.: Prentice-Hall.

Bandura, A. (1991) 'Self-efficacy mechanism in physiological activation and health-promoting behavior', in J. Madden (ed.) *Neurobiology of Learning, Emotion and Affect*, New York: Raven Press.

Becker, M.H. (1974) 'The health belief model and sick role behavior', *Health Education Monographs*, 2: 409–419.

Belloc, N.B. and Breslow, L. (1972) 'Relationship of physical health status and health practices', *Preventative Medicine*, 9: 421–469.

Belson, W.A. (1968) 'Respondent understanding of survey questions', *Polls*, 3: 1–13.

Binswanger, H. (1986) 'The goal-directedness of living action', *The Objectivist Forum*, 7, 4: 1–10.

Blaxter, M. (1990) *Health and Lifestyles*, London: Tavistock.

Bradburn, N.M., Rips, L.J. and Shevell, S.K. (1987) 'Answering autobiographical questions: the impact of memory and inference on surveys', *Science*, 236: 157–161.

Breslow, L. and Enstrom, J.E. (1980) 'Persistence of health habits and their relationship to mortality', *Preventative Medicine*, 9: 469–483.

Brock, B.M., Haefner, D.P. and Noble, D.S. (1988) 'Alameda County Redux: replication in Michigan', *Preventative Medicine*, 17: 483–495.

Budd, R.J. (1987) 'Response bias and the theory of reasoned action', *Social Cognition*, 5: 95–107.

Cartwright, A. (1989) *User Surveys of General Practice*, London: Institute for Social Studies in Medical Care.

Catford, J.C. and Nutbeam, D. (1984) 'Towards a definition of health education and health promotion', *Health Education Journal*, 43: 2–3.

Charny, M. and Lewis, P.A. (1987) 'Does health knowledge affect eating habits?', *Health Education Journal*, 46: 172–176.

Conner, M.T. and Norman, N. (1994) 'Comparing the health belief model and the theory of planned behaviour in health screening', in D.R. Rutter and L. Quine (eds) *Social Psychology and Health: European Perspectives*, 1–24, Aldershot: Avebury.

Cronbach, L.J. (1990) *Essentials of Psychological Testing*, New York: HarperCollins.

Dean, K. (1989) 'Self-care components of lifestyles: the importance of gender, attitudes and the social situation', *Social Science and Medicine*, 29: 137–152.

DeVellis, R.F. (1991) *Scale Development: Theory and applications*, London: Sage.

Fazio, R.H. (1990) 'A practical guide to the use of response latency in social psychological research', in C. Hendrick and M.S. Clark (eds) *Research Methods in Social and Applied Psychology*, London: Sage.

Gaskell, G., Wright, D. and O'Muircheartaigh, C. (1993) 'Reliability of surveys', *The Psychologist*, 2: 500–503.

Hippler, H.J., Schwarz, N. and Sudman, S. (1987) *Social Information Processing and Survey Methodology*, London: Springer-Verlag.

Hull, C.L. (1943) *Principles of Behavior*, New York: Appleton-Century-Crofts.

Janz, N.K. and Becker, M.H. (1984) 'The health belief model: a decade later', *Health Education Quarterly*, 11: 1–47.

Kalton, G. (1983) *Introduction to Survey Sampling*, London: Sage.

Kasl, S.V. and Cobb, S. (1966) 'Health behaviour, illness behaviour and sick role behaviour', *Archives of Environmental Health*, 12: 246–266.

Kidder, L.H. and Judd, C.M. (1986) *Research Methods in Social Relations*, New York: Holt.

Kline, P. (1992) *The Handbook of Psychological Testing*, London: Routledge.

Lipsey, M.W. (1990) *Design Sensitivity: Statistical power for experimental research*, London: Sage.

Locke, E.A. and Latham, G.P. (1990) *A Theory of Goal Setting and Task Performance*, Englewood Cliffs, New Jersey: Prentice-Hall.

Loftus, E.F. and Marburger, W. (1983) 'Since the eruption of Mt. St. Helens, has anyone beaten you up?', *Memory and Cognition*, 11: 114–120.

Maddux, J.E. and Rogers, R.W. (1983) 'Protection motivation and self-efficacy: a revised theory of fear appeals and attitude change', *Journal of Experimental Social Psychology*, 19: 469–479.

Metzner, H.L., Carman, W.J. and House, J. (1983) 'Health practices, risk factors and chronic disease in Tecumeseh', *Preventative Medicine*, 12: 491–507.

Moser, C.A. and Kalton, G. (1971) *Survey Methods in Social Investigation*, Aldershot: Gower.

Oatley, K. (1992) *Best Laid Schemes – The Psychology of Emotions*, New York: Cambridge University Press.

Oatley, K. and Johnson-Laird, P.N. (1987) 'Towards a cognitive theory of emotions', *Cognition and Emotion*, 1, 1: 29–50.

Oppenheim, A.N. (1992) *Questionnaire Design, Interviewing and Attitude Measurement*, London: Pinter.

Ortony, A., Clore, G.C. and Collins, A. (1988) *The Cognitive Structure of Emotions*, New York: Cambridge University Press.

Peak, H. (1955) 'Attitude and motivation', in M.R. Jones (ed.) *Nebraska Symposium on Motivation* (3,: 149–188), Lincoln: University of Nebraska Press.

Rodin, J. and Salovey, P. (1989) 'Health psychology', *Annual Review of Psychology*, 40: 533–579.

Ryan, T.A. (1970) *Intentional Behavior*, New York: Ronald Press.

Schuman, H. and Presser, S. (1981) *Questions and Answers in Attitude Surveys*, New York: Academic.

Schwarz, N. (1990) 'Assessing frequency reports of mundane behaviors: contributions of cognitive psychology to questionnaire construction', in C. Hendrick and M.S. Clark (eds) *Research Methods in Social and Applied Psychology*, London: Sage.

Schwarzer, R. (1992) 'Self-efficacy in the adoption and maintenance of health behaviors: theoretical approaches and a new model', in R. Schwarzer (ed.) *Self-efficacy: Thought control of action*, London: Hemisphere.

Sheeran, P. and Orbell, S. (in press) 'How confidently can we infer health beliefs from questionnaire responses?', *Psychology and Health*.

Tanur, J.M. (1992) *Questions about Questions: Inquiries into the cognitive bases of surveys*, London: Sage.

The Health of the Nation (1992), London: HMSO.

Tourangeau, R. and Rasinski, K.A. (1988) 'Cognitive processes underlying context effects in attitude measurement', *Psychological Bulletin*, 103: 299–314.

Tversky, A. and Kahneman, D. (1973) 'Availability: a heuristic for judging frequency and probability', *Cognitive Psychology*, 5: 207–232.

van der Velde, W. and van der Pligt, J. (1991) 'AIDS-related behavior: coping, protection motivation, and previous behavior', *Journal of Behavioral Medicine*, 14: 429–451.

Vroom, V. (1964) *Work and Motivation*, New York: Wiley.

Waterman, M.G. (1994) 'Emotional responses to music: implicit and explicit effects in listeners and performers', paper presented at the 3rd International Conference on Music Perception and Cognition, 23–27 July 1994, Liège, Belgium.

Chapter 4

Large-scale questionnaire research on drivers

Michelle Meadows and Stephen Stradling

THE IMPORTANCE OF STUDYING DRIVER BEHAVIOUR

Traffic accidents are a major public health problem in the UK, the US and most other motorised societies. In 1993, for example, 3,814 people were killed and 302,206 injured on roads in the UK. The economic cost of these accidents was estimated at £10.8 billion (Department of Transport 1994). In 1987 the Department of Transport outlined an objective to reduce road casualties by one-third by the year 2000 (Department of Transport 1987). In order to reach this target and prolong accident reductions beyond the year 2000, new road safety campaigns need to be introduced.

The improvement of the road and traffic environment has achieved considerable accident reduction in recent years. However, there is a growing feeling that these engineering-based safety measures are beginning to yield diminishing returns. There is a general consensus that new road safety campaigns need to be directed at changing road user behaviour. This consensus is partly due to a number of studies which illustrate the predominant role played by 'human factors' in traffic accidents. For example, in a four-year study of accident causation in Great Britain, Sabey and Taylor (1980) concluded that driver and pedestrian error and impairment were the sole or main contributory factors in 95 per cent of the 2,130 accidents they examined. Hence, the challenge for psychology is to provide a better understanding of the role of human factors in the causation of road traffic accidents.

METHODS USED IN THE STUDY OF DRIVER BEHAVIOUR

Four main methods have been used to study driver behaviour and its role in crash causation. Each method has its difficulties and its advantages.

Simulated driving situations

Here the driver is typically placed in front of a screen showing a range of more or less realistic road situations. Various measures can be taken regarding time to react to hazards, judgements of one kind or another, or other indices thought to be relevant to the driving situation. Such studies have revealed a great deal relating to accident involvement. For example, Quimby *et al.* (1986) used a driving simulator to examine the relationship between hazard perception and accident frequency. They found that slower detection of hazards in a driving simulator was associated with higher accident rates, independently of a driver's age and experience (calibrated by annual mileage driven).

However, this method of studying driver behaviour may be criticised for lacking ecological validity (specifically 'treatment by setting interaction' – Neale and Liebert 1986) thereby limiting generalisation to driving and to crash causation on the road. Simulators lack realism and the social and motivational context of driving is completely removed (for example: 'What is the purpose of your journey?'; 'Are you under time pressure to get there in a hurry?'; 'Who do you have in the car with you?'). A key problem with this approach is the expense involved in constructing a simulator complex enough to imitate the real driving environment. Further, in a simulator the consequences of risky driving are lacking. Risky driving on the road may result in a near miss or an actual accident. However, there is no realistic way of simulating these consequences. The ways in which drivers behave in a simulated situation may bear little relation to how they behave in real traffic. It is important to study not how the driver *can* drive but how the driver *does* drive (the competence vs performance distinction which afflicts so many areas of psychology). Another shortcoming of this approach is that the range of possible explanations for different driving styles and accident involvement that can be studied is significantly restricted. For example, this methodology alone could not provide a feasible way of examining the possible association between personality and accident frequency.

Accident statistics

Accident statistics are a major source of data. Some careful and detailed analyses have revealed a great deal about the relative accident involvement of drivers of different age and sex, as well as the effects of time of day and of week. For example, from examination of accident statistics, Broughton (1988) found that one of the most common types of accident for young drivers was the single vehicle accident. More male drivers aged 17 to 20 were injured in this type of accident than in any other. Broughton also showed that the male casualty rates for single vehicle accidents were over twice the female rates.

Official records of drivers' accident involvement may be more objective than self-reports in that they are less subject to the biases and errors resulting from idiosyncrasies of drivers' memories or reporting styles, and they will include accidents in which the driver dies. However, because they have been collected primarily for reasons other than research, the way in which the accident details are recorded may not readily fit the needs of a research project. In the UK the type of information held in the national accident database is inadequate for research purposes. No information is available on exposure to risk – the number of miles travelled per year, the types of roads used and so on – and although the national accident records include the age of the driver, the number of years of driving experience is not included. Accident histories of individual drivers cannot be obtained and, because these records include injury only accidents reported to the police, the average frequency of such accidents is very small. Maycock, Lockwood and Lester (1991) argue that this frequency – of the order of 0.01 accidents per driver per year – is too low to enable multivariate statistical techniques to be used satisfactorily.

The data sets available to insurance companies are not made available to outsiders for commercial reasons and, even if they were, they would only cover those accidents involving a claim. Hence, in many countries the most widely used database on road accidents is the police accident file. It is generally computerised and contains numerous data items on road traffic, driver and vehicle characteristics associated with the accident. Because accident statistics mainly rely on the data collected through police accident files they are restricted to those accidents which the police attend. Even assuming that all police officers complete the forms precisely and uniformly, it is clear that not all accidents are included in this data set, and there will be some accidents where the relevant information cannot be obtained.

Moreover, there is evidence of inaccuracies and discrepancies in police reports of accidents. A number of studies have compared the contents of police records with other, not always independent, data sources. The most frequently used comparative data source is the detailed police file or notebook. Hakkert and Hauer (1988) quote work by Shinar *et al.* (1983) in which a random sample of police records were compared with detailed information collected on those cases by multi-disciplinary accident investigation teams. One hundred and twenty-four accidents, involving 207 drivers were investigated. Police data were most reliable for the following variables: location, day of week, and numbers of drivers, passengers and vehicles involved. The least reliable variables included accident severity and road surface. Relatively large misclassification errors were found in driver age (11.6 per cent) and vehicle model year (5.3 per cent) with model year not stated for a further 9.7 per cent.

Fatality data tend to be more complete than data on injuries at other levels, and the definition of fatality involves less uncertainty than for any other type of loss. However, fatality data is still not free from errors. Hutchinson (1987) demonstrated differences in the total numbers of fatalities indicated in death certificates and in police records in most countries. Not all deaths are necessarily known to those responsible for the data sets, and missing data can be especially abundant in less economically developed countries.

Observational studies

Studies have been conducted where drivers are observed driving either their own vehicles, or specially instrumented vehicles provided by the research team. For example, several observational studies have associated younger drivers with faster speeds (Galin 1981; Wilde and Ackersviller 1982; Rolls *et al*. 1991).

The observational method is considerably more realistic than some of the others employed, but still suffers from some validity problems. These include the possible effects of altered behaviour as a result of being watched by others, as well as the effects of studying a process outside of its 'natural habitat'. Findings may not be generalisable to performance in the driver's own car and/or to a different, more familiar, route.

A few studies have used on-the-road observation, in which drivers are observed without knowing it (e.g. Baxter *et al*. 1990). Whilst this avoids the reactive effects of being studied and the behaviour is still within its natural habitat, the lack of tight control over the situation makes the data somewhat 'noisy'. Estimates of, for instance, the age of the driver need to be made from some distance away. For example, Baxter *et al*. could only attempt to distinguish between 'younger' (less than 30 years old) and 'older' (more than 30 years old) drivers. Moreover, linking variables with accidents in this way would require a huge investment of time and money, accidents being infrequent and unpredictable.

Self-report measures

A number of studies have been conducted using questionnaires, either to investigate personality, attitudes, risk perception or other aspects which might point to differences between accident involved and non-accident involved drivers, or to obtain information on driving styles. For example, Reason *et al*. (1991) reported a major series of studies on the role of self-reported driving errors, lapses and violations in accident rates. They found that violations but not errors or lapses were associated with higher accident rates after taking account of age, sex and mileage.

Self-report measures, however, are open to social desirability bias, the imposition of response formats, and potential ambiguity of wording. They are also removed from the real situation, can be criticised as being unreliable, and rely completely upon respondents' willingness and ability to produce meaningful responses. Obviously accidents in which the driver is killed cannot be studied in this way.

Studies in which driver-reported and state-reported accident data have been compared suggest substantial under-reporting of accidents by drivers (Harano *et al.* 1975; Owsley *et al.* 1991). Accidents may be deliberately concealed or drivers may vary in what they consider constitutes a reportable accident. There is also evidence that accidents are forgotten. Maycock *et al.* (1991) found that when asked to report accidents going back over a three year period, drivers tended to report fewer accidents in the first year than the second, and fewer in the second than the third, most recent year. This difference could not be accounted for by age or maturation or general decreases over time in traffic safety. They concluded that the most likely explanation was forgetting. The rate of forgetting was approximately 30 per cent per year.

On the other hand, there is evidence that self-report measures correlate with observational measures of driver behaviours. West *et al.* (1993) examined the relationships between self-reports of driver behaviour and observer's reports. The results indicated that self-reports of certain aspects of driver behaviour could be used as substitutes for observational measures although there would be some loss of accuracy. For example, observed speed on the motorway was found to correlate well with self-reports of normal driving speed. The same was true for ratings of calmness, and observer ratings of attentiveness and carefulness correlated significantly with self-reports of deviant driving behaviour. Further, Reason *et al.* (1991) and Parker *et al.* (1995) have reported that self-reported commission of violations predicted *frequency* of accident involvement, and *type* of accident involvement has recently been shown to be predicted by self-reported violations (Parker *et al.* 1995b) and, independently, by both violations and thrill-seeking in driving style (Meadows 1994). In all these studies, self-reports of manner of driving were found to be systematically related to actual events on the road.

The self-report method has the advantage of being comparatively inexpensive and all types of accidents except those fatal to the driver can be canvassed. Thus minor, damage-only accidents can be included which are not included in the official statistics. Also details of accidents and driver characteristics relevant to the research project can be obtained, which is not always possible when official statistics are used. For these reasons self-report data is now widely used in the study of driver behaviour.

The collection and analysis of self-report, questionnaire data will now be discussed. There are several main issues to be considered: the construction of the questionnaire; sampling procedures; administering the questionnaire; and screening the data for univariate and multivariate analysis.

CONSTRUCTION OF THE QUESTIONNAIRE

There are a number of points to bear in mind whilst devising questionnaires. First, the questions should be written clearly in standard English. In particular the use of double negatives should be avoided because they are not easy to not misunderstand! The questions should be concrete and close to the respondents' experience. Questions should be short, embodying a single idea. Items that are very similar should not be included – they may confuse the statistical analysis, as well as the respondents. Only necessary questions should be asked and they should not be crowded together. The questionnaire should allow respondents enough room to write and each question should be set apart from the next. Words, names and views that might automatically bias the responses for or against your hypotheses should be avoided. To avoid reporting bias refrain from asking very personal questions, for example frequency of convictions for traffic offences.

The length of the questionnaire will depend on how much information is required. However, short questionnaires are more likely to be completed by subjects. Further, subjects are more likely to complete the latter parts of the questionnaire correctly if the questionnaire is short. However, the questionnaire must contain enough items to make the data analysis credible.

The responses to the questions may be open- or closed-ended. The responses to closed-ended questions can take the form of yes/no answers, check lists or rating scales. Rating scales may be graphic, but often they ask respondents to make comparisons in the form of ranks (e.g. 1 = top, 10 = bottom) or along a continuous scale (e.g. from 1 = definitely agree to 5 = definitely disagree). The numerical values assigned to rating scales can be classified as nominal, ordinal, interval or ratio level of measurement. Each has characteristics that must be considered when the results of the survey are analysed. Powerful multivariate statistics prefer interval or ratio variables.

Closed-ended items with several choices are easier to score than are open-ended questions. Open-ended questions allow respondents to state a position in their own words – unfortunately these words may be difficult to interpret and will require coding. However, such a format does – sometimes – generate quotable quotes which may enliven the final report of the study.

Pilot testing helps get survey methods into shape. It allows the 'debugging' of many potential errors. A trial run will help determine if the questions elicit the information that is needed, that the subjects understand the questions, and so on.

The goal is a reliable and valid questionnaire which achieves a high response rate. One way of ensuring the reliability and the validity of the questionnaire is to base it on one that someone else has developed, tested and reported on in the literature. Before using another researcher's questionnaire check that it has proven reliability and validity. In general, the likelihood of a good response rate is improved if the questionnaire compiler takes pains to make it as easy, pleasurable and hassle-free as possible for the (right) respondents to provide you with the information you need for analysis. This aim is assisted by attention to presentation and detail at this stage and in the administration of the questionnaire (see below).

SAMPLING PROCEDURES

There are two basic methods of sampling – probability and non-probability sampling. A probability sample is one in which each person in the population of interest has an equal chance of being selected. The resulting sample is then thought likely to be representative of the population from which it was taken. In simple random sampling subjects are selected at random. This is un-complicated, but if the sample contains certain sub-groups that might influence the results, stratified random sampling is required to ensure that the structure of the sample mirrors that of the population. Another form of sampling is cluster sampling where groups are selected randomly rather than individuals. This form of sampling is mainly used when sampling individuals is unethical or administratively difficult. In systematic sampling every nth case may be selected from a list. However, if the list of potential subjects has a pattern, bias is introduced since not all cases have an equal chance of being selected. Non-probability samples include those acquired by accident or opportunity, and purposive samples in which subjects are chosen on the basis of some attribute, for example, because they know the most or are the most typical.

To send the questionnaire to the subjects, their names and addresses are normally required. Hence, current and accurate lists of names and addresses are needed. Before using a list of potential subjects it is necessary to check that you have a right to use the list for survey purposes. Ethical con-siderations protect individuals' rights to privacy or anonymity. Large polling organisations have issued statements of ethical conduct that are worth considering.

The response rate to the questionnaire should be as high as possible. Losing subjects introduces bias into the results as there is no way of knowing whether the subjects who dropped out are the same as the ones who responded in terms of important factors such as age, sex, or accident rate. This is likely, since those most educated and most interested in the topic of the questionnaire are most likely to respond. Consider giving incentives to encourage people to respond. However, this may substantially increase the cost of the survey. Be prepared to follow up or to send reminders. These should be brief and to the point. It often helps to send another copy of the questionnaire with a reminder. Money and time must be budgeted for these additional mailings.

ADMINISTERING THE QUESTIONNAIRE

Preparation, piloting, printing, collation, addressing and packaging of mailed questionnaires for a large-scale survey always takes longer than you think. Before the questionnaire is sent out it may be a good idea to send the subjects a letter outlining the purpose of the questionnaire. This informs them that the survey is coming, explains why they should answer the questions, and tells them who is being surveyed. A short, formal letter should also accompany the questionnaire. If a pre-letter has been sent, this one should be very concise. It should describe the survey, its aims and participants. Consider offering to send the respondents a summary of the findings so that they can see how the data are used. If this offer is made it will have to be budgeted for. If there are questions that may be taken as personal – such as accident rate, speed preference or police contact – explain why they are required. It is best to keep the questionnaire procedures simple. Provide stamped self-addressed envelopes for the subjects to return the questionnaire in. Keep page folding to a minimum so that respondents do not feel that they are involved in complicated procedures. Courtesy and consideration towards persons who are spending their time for your benefit, plus good housekeeping, should enhance the success of the venture.

It is helpful to keep records of when questionnaires are sent out and which are returned so that it is possible to ascertain which subjects have not responded. To do this it is necessary to number the questionnaires in some way. This may lead subjects to question the confidentiality of their responses. It may therefore be necessary to conceal the identification number. This will allow reminders to be sent to the non-respondents. It is typical to allow approximately three weeks before reminders are sent. However, at holiday times, for example Christmas, it is advisable to leave longer. Indeed in general it is best to avoid sending questionnaires out during these times as subjects are likely to put them to one side and either forget them or lose them. It is also best to avoid sending out questionnaires following severe accidents that have been covered by the media or in the middle of a high profile road safety campaign as it is possible that this could systematically bias the findings. Keeping a record of those subjects who have not responded will allow assessment of the response rate. It is also advisable to keep a record of any questionnaires that are returned uncompleted because the subject has moved, passed away or no longer drives. This enables the researcher not to bother the individual again.

When questionnaires are returned they should be designated a subject identification number. This identification number is entered along with the subject's responses into a data file. This allows the case in the data file to be traced back to the original questionnaire.

Before the data is analysed there are a number of issues to be considered. These issues are relevant to most analyses. However, they are not all applicable to all analyses all the time. Further, some analyses have assumptions not mentioned here. In addition there are differences in data screening for grouped and ungrouped data. These variations in procedures are not covered here but a complete review can be found in Tabachnick and Fidell (1989).

SCREENING DATA PRIOR TO ANALYSIS

Inspection of univariate statistics for accuracy of input

First the accuracy with which the data have been entered into the data file must be assessed. To do this one must check if the values on all the variables are within range; if the means and standard deviations are plausible; and if the codes for any missing variables are accurately entered.

Once it has been established that the data are accurately entered, the coefficient of variation (standard deviation divided by the mean) should be calculated for each continuous variable. When means are very large and standard deviations very small, the values in correlation matrices are also sometimes too small. Statistical programs often encode the first several digits of a very large number and then round the rest off. If the variability is in the digits that are dropped, the correlations between the variables and other variables are inaccurately computed. The coefficient of variation serves as an indicator of this problem.

Evaluation of the amount and distribution of missing data

Next, the amount and distribution of missing data is examined. If only a few data points are missing in a random pattern from a large data set, the problems are not usually serious and most procedures for handling them yield similar results. If, however, a lot of data are missing from a small to moderate sized data set, the problems can be serious. It is the pattern of the missing data that is vital. Non-randomly missing values are important because they affect the generalisability of the results. Refusal to answer questions may be related to important variables. For example, drivers who fail to report their age may be older rather than younger. Examination of the missing data, through the creation of dummy 'missing' versus 'non-missing' variables, reveals any pattern. If there is no pattern, decisions about how to handle missing data are not so critical. However, if there is a pattern, there are a number of strategies that you should consider.

One procedure for handling missing values is simply to drop any cases with them. If only a few cases have missing data and they seem to be a random sub-sample of the whole sample, deletion is a good method. Listwise deletion of cases with missing values is the default option for most statistical programs.

If missing values are concentrated in a few variables and they are not critical to the analysis, or are highly correlated with other variables for which you have complete data, the variables with missing cases are profitably dropped. But if missing values are scattered throughout cases and variables, deletion of cases can mean substantial loss of data. Another option is to estimate missing values and then use the estimates during data analysis. This can be done using prior knowledge, that is making an educated guess; by inserting group or ipsative mean values calculated from available data; or by using regression to predict the missing value from available data. Another method of dealing with missing data involves the analysis of a missing data correlation matrix. In this option all available pairs of values are used to calculate each of the correlations (casewise deletion). For example, a variable with five missing values has all its correlations with other variables based upon five fewer pairs of cases. If some of the other variables also have missing values, but in different cases, the number of complete pairs of variables is further reduced. Thus each correlation can be based on a different number and a different subset of cases, depending on the pattern of missing values. This can mean that some correlations are less stable than others in the same correlation matrix. But that is not the only problem. In a correlation matrix based on complete data, the sizes of some correlations place constraints on the sizes of others. If, however, the correlations are based upon different subsets of cases, correlations can go out of range. The statistics derived under these conditions are very likely to be distorted.

Missing data may be treated as data. It is possible that failure to respond to a question is itself a good predictor of the behaviour of interest. A dummy variable may be created where cases with complete data are, for example, assigned 0 and cases with missing data 1. This dummy variable may then be used as another variable in the analysis.

If you use some method of estimating missing values or a missing data correlation matrix, consider repeating your analyses using only complete cases. If the results are similar you can have confidence in them. If they are different, however, you need to investigate reasons for change, and evaluate which result may more nearly approximate the true state of affairs.

Identification of non-normal variables

Screening for normality is an important step in almost every multivariate analysis. Normality of variables may be assessed by either statistical or graphical methods. Statistically there are two components to normality, skewness and kurtosis. Skewness has to do with the symmetry of the distribution. Kurtosis has to do with the peakedness of a distribution. When a distribution is normal the values of skewness and kurtosis are zero. If there is positive skewness there is a pile up of cases to the left and the right-hand tail is too long. Kurtosis values that are above zero indicate a distribution that is too peaked. Kurtosis values that are below zero indicate a distribution that is too flat.

Frequency histograms are a useful way of assessing normality, especially with a normal distribution overlay. Even more useful are expected normal probability plots and detrended expected normal probability plots. In these plots the scores are ranked and sorted, then an expected normal value is computed and compared with the actual normal value for each case. If nonnormality is found transformation of variables should be considered. Variables differ in the amount they diverge from normal. If the distribution differs moderately from normal, a square root transformation is tried first. If the distribution differs substantially a log transformation is tried first. If the distribution differs severely the inverse is tried. Finally if the departure from normality is severe and no transformation seems to help, you may wish to dichotomise the variable. The direction of the deviation is also important. If there is negative skewness, first reflect the variable and then apply the appropriate transformation for positive skewness. To reflect the variable find the largest score in the distribution and add one to it to form a constant that is larger than any score in the distribution. Then create a new variable by subtracting each score from this constant. It is important to check that the variable is normally or near-normally distributed after transformation. Often you may need to try first one transformation and then another until you find the transformation that produces skewness or kurtosis values below unity, or the fewest outliers.

Identification of outliers

Outliers, both univariate and multivariate, *must* be dealt with because analyses both of differences and of relationship may be unduly influenced by them. Univariate outliers are cases with an extreme value on one variable. Multivariate outliers are cases with an unusual combination of two or more scores. Outliers among dichotomous variables are those with very uneven splits between two categories. Rummel (1970) suggests deleting dichotomous variables with 90–10 splits between categories because the correlation coefficients between these variables and others are truncated and the scores in the category with 10 per cent of the cases are more influential than those in the category with 90 per cent of the cases. However, when your main variable of interest is a relatively rare event, such as a road traffic crash, and its deletion would obviate the whole study, it may be possible to employ multivariate statistics (e.g. regression) based on the Poisson rather than on the normal distribution.

Among continuous variables univariate outliers are cases with very large standardised (z) scores on one or more variables. Cases with standardised scores greater than $z = \pm 3.00$ are potential outliers. As an alternative or in addition to inspection of z scores there are graphical methods for finding univariate outliers. Helpful plots are histograms, box plots, normal probability plots or detrended normal probability plots. Once potential univariate outliers are located, the search for multivariate outliers may begin. These are cases with an unusual pattern of scores. Their standardised scores on variables considered singly are sometimes within expected ranges. They can be detected by the computation of Mahalanobis distance for each case. This is the distance of the case from the centroid of the remaining cases where the centroid is the point created by the means of all the variables. Multivariate outliers can also be detected through graphical methods. These are available through regression programs which plot results of residuals analysis. Outliers are cases which produce points that are distant from those of other cases in the plots. Often outliers hide behind other outliers. If a few cases identified as outliers are deleted, other cases are then extreme with respect to the central tendency of the group. Hence, it is a good idea to screen for multivariate outliers several times until no new outliers are identified.

Once multivariate outliers are identified, you want to know why the cases are extreme. It is important to identify the variables on which the cases are deviant for two reasons. First, it provides an indication of the kinds of case to which your results do not generalise. Second, if you are going to modify scores instead of deleting cases, you have to know which scores to modify. To examine the outliers create a dummy grouping variable where the outlier(s) have a value of 1 and the rest of the cases a value of zero. The dummy variable is then used as the grouping variable in discriminant function analysis or the dependent variable in regression.

Once the outliers have been identified there are several strategies for reducing their influence. First, however, check the data file to make sure the value has been entered correctly! If one variable is responsible for most of the outliers also consider deleting that variable if it is not critical to the analysis. If the outliers are not part of the population you intended to sample they can be deleted. However, if they are part of the intended population steps can be taken to reduce their influence. Variables can be transformed or scores changed. Variable transformation (as described above) may be undertaken to change the shape of the distribution to one that is more nearly normal. Cases that were outliers are still on the tails of the transformed distribution, but their impact is reduced. A second option is to change the score(s) on the important variable(s) for the outlying case(s) so that they are deviant but not as deviant as they were. For instance assign the outlying case(s) a raw score on the offending variable(s) that is one unit larger (or smaller) than the next most extreme score in the distribution.

Identification of non-linearity and homoscedasticity

The assumption of linearity is that there is a straight line relationship between two variables. Linearity is fundamental to multivariate statistics because solutions are based upon the general linear model. Further, the assumption of multivariate normality implies that there is linearity between all pairs of variables and linearity is important in the practical sense because only the linear relationships between variables are being analysed. Non-linearity can be diagnosed either from residuals plots or from bivariate scatterplots between pairs of variables. If both variables are normally distributed and linearly related a scatterplot will appear oval shaped. If the overall shape of the scatterplot is not oval, the variables are not linearly related. Some pairs of variables are known to be non-linearly related, e.g. anxiety and performance. If this is the case the variable can be recoded or a non-linear analytic strategy can be used. If there are a number of pairs of variables, screening all possible pairs can be burdensome. You may use statistics on skewness and kurtosis to screen only pairs which are likely to depart from linearity.

The assumption of homoscedasticity is that the variability in scores for one variable is roughly the same at all values of the other variable. This assumption is related to that of normality because when the assumption of multivariate normality is met the relationships between variables are homoscedastic. Homoscedasticity is evaluated through bivariate scatterplots. The bivariate scatterplots between two variables or residuals should be of roughly the same width all over. Heteroscedasticity can be corrected by transformation of variables.

Identification of multicollinearity and singularity

Finally, perfect or near-perfect correlations among potential predictor variables can threaten a multivariate analysis by rendering unstable the matrix inversion required in many analyses. With multicollinearity the variables are very highly correlated (.90 and above). With singularity the variables are perfectly correlated and one of the variables is a combination of one or more of the other variables. Either bivariate or multivariate correlations can create multicollinearity or singularity. If a bivariate correlation is too high, it shows up in a correlation matrix as a correlation of above .90. After deletion of one of the two redundant variables the problem is solved. Too high multivariate correlations are more difficult to detect. Most programs protect against multicollinearity and singularity by calculating squared multiple correlations (SMCs) for variables. If the SMC is high there is multicollinearity, the variable is highly related to others in the set. If the SMC is 1 there is singularity, the variable is perfectly related to the other variables in the set. Screening for multicollinearity or singularity is routine with most programs. If there is a problem the system will abort when you try to run your main analyses.

You are now ready to run sophisticated multivariate analyses of your questionnaire data using a powerful desktop statistical package. Description of these inferential procedures is beyond the scope of this chapter, but very helpful advice is provided in a number of recent texts: on getting started with SPSSPC+ and SPSS for Windows (Foster 1993); on running and interpreting more advanced analyses (West 1991); on ensuring your data meet the assumptions for advanced statistical analysis (Tabachnick and Fidell 1989); and on choosing appropriately among these techniques (Tabachnick and Fidell 1989: 30–31).

REFERENCES

Baxter, J.S., Manstead, A.S.R., Stradling, S.G., Campbell, K., Reason, J.T. and Parker, D. (1990) 'Social facilitation and driver behaviour', *British Journal of Psychology*, 81: 351–360.

Broughton, J. (1988) *The Variation of Car Drivers' Accident Risk with Age*, Transport and Road Research Laboratory Contractor Report RR135, Crowthorne: TRRL.

Department of Transport (1987) *Road Safety: The Next Steps*, London: HMSO.

Department of Transport (1991) *Road Accidents in Great Britain: 1990. The Casualty Report*, London: HMSO.

Department of Transport (1994) *Road Accidents in Great Britain: 1993. The Casualty Report*, London: HMSO.

Foster, J.J. (1993) *Starting SPSS/PC+ and SPSS for Windows: A Beginner's Guide to Data Analysis*, 2nd edn, Wilmslow: Sigma Press.

Galin, D. (1981) 'Speeds on two-lane rural roads: a multiple regression analysis', *Traffic Engineering and Control*, August–September: 433–460.

Hakkert, S. and Hauer, E. (1988) 'The extent and implications of incomplete and inaccurate road accident reporting', in J.A. Rothengatter and R.A. de Bruin (eds) *Road User Behaviour: Theory and Research*, Assen/Maastricht NL: Van Gorcum.

Harano, R.M., Peck, R.C. and McBride, R.S. (1975) 'Prediction of accident liability through bibliographic data and psychometric tests', *Journal of Safety Research*, 7: 15–52.

Hutchinson, T.P. (1987) *Road Accident Statistics*, Australia: Rumsby Scientific Publishing.

Maycock, G., Lockwood, C.R. and Lester, J.F. (1991) 'The accident liability of car drivers', Transport and Road Research Laboratory Research Report 315, Crowthorne: TRRL.

Meadows, M.L. (1994) 'The psychological correlates of road crash types', unpublished PhD thesis, University of Manchester, 2 volumes: 1–512.

Neale, J.M. and Liebert, R.M. (1986) *Science and Behavior: An introduction to methods of research*, 3rd edn, New Jersey: Prentice-Hall.

Owsley, C., Ball, K., Sloane, M.E., Roenker, D.L. and Bruni, J.R. (1991) 'Visual/cognitive correlates of vehicle accidents in older drivers', *Psychology and Ageing*, 6: 403–415.

Parker, D., Reason, J.T., Manstead, A.S.R. and Stradling, S.G. (1995a) 'Driving errors, driving violations and accident involvement', *Ergonomics*, 38, 5: 1036–1048.

Parker, D., West, R., Stradling, S.G. and Manstead, A.S.R. (1995b) 'Behavioural characteristics and involvement in different types of traffic accident', *Accident Analysis and Prevention* 27(4) 571–581.

Quimby, A.R., Maycock, G., Carter, I.D., Dixon, R. and Wall, J.G. (1986) 'Perceptual abilities of accident involved drivers', Transport and Road Research Laboratory Contractor Report RR27, Crowthorne: TRRL.

Reason, J.T., Manstead, A.S.R., Stradling, S.G., Parker, D. and Baxter, J.S. (1991) 'The social and cognitive determinants of aberrant driving behaviour', Transport and Road Research Laboratory Contractor Report 253, Crowthorne: TRRL.

Rolls, G.W.P., Hall, R.D., Ingham, R. and McDonald, M. (1991) 'Accident risk and behavioural patterns of younger drivers', Basingstoke: A.A. Foundation for Road Safety Research.

Rummel, R.J. (1970) *Applied Factor Analysis*, Evanston, Ill.: Northwestern University Press.

Sabey, B.E. and Taylor, H. (1980) 'The known risks we run: the highway',

Transport and Road Research Laboratory Supplementary Report 567, Crowthorne: TRRL.

Shinar, D., Treat, J.R. and McDonald, S.T. (1983) 'The validity of police reported accident data', *Accident Analysis and Prevention*, 15, 3: 175–191.

Tabachnick, B.G. and Fidell, L.S. (1989) *Using Multivariate Statistics*, 2nd edn, London: Harper & Row.

West, R. (1991) *Computing for Psychologists: Statistical Analysis Using SPSS and Minitab*, London: Harwood.

West, R., French, D., Kemp, R. and Elander, J. (1993) 'Direct observation of driving, self reports of driver behaviour and accident involvement', *Ergonomics*, 35: 557–567.

Wilde, G.J.S. and Ackersviller, J. (1982) 'The effect of posting observed driver behaviour upon subsequent driver response: the case of moving speed', *Queen's University, Studies of Safety in Transport*. Report prepared for Transport Canada, Traffic Safety, July 1982 (54 pages). Kingston, Ontario: Queen's University.

Chapter 5

Advanced uses of multiple regression
Modelling mediated and moderated effects

Ros Bramwell

Undergraduate psychology students are often dismayed by the apparently simplistic view of human behaviour which seems implied by experimental-style research designs incorporating the use of univariate statistics. These statistics are, of course, very often appropriate tools for the exploration of vital and fascinating aspects of behaviour, but an implication that this is 'all' quantitative analysis has to offer may lead to disillusionment, and the misconception that more complex psychological models can only be formulated within 'qualitative' approaches.

Breakwell (1994) introduces very persuasively the fascinating possibilities of statistically modelling behaviour. She points out that statistically modelling the specific interrelationships between variables 'is a very different approach from saying that some lists of factors are important', but that we have been slow to adopt the use of such modelling techniques.

That such modelling techniques have been underused may give us the hint that there are some perceived drawbacks to their use. Certainly, larger sample sizes are required, and longitudinal data may be desirable, both of which add to the cost of the research. It is commonly assumed that the use of complex statistical procedures and specialist software is also necessary. This, however, is not the case, and this chapter explains how investigation of two particular types of model, those involving moderated and mediated effects, may be investigated using simple multiple regression commands available on widely-used statistical packages such as SPSS. Example printouts are taken from the SPSS for Windows package, but 'rival' packages such as that produced by BMDP are also entirely suitable for these sorts of analyses. A basic understanding of multiple regression is assumed in this chapter. Anyone who is unsure of any of the terms and concepts associated with multiple regression which are used should refresh their memory with one of the more readable texts such as Tabachnik and Fidell (1989). Such texts also give the limitations on multiple regression techniques, such as the levels of measurement and ratio of cases to independent variables required, and these guidelines should be followed in deciding on the type of data and sample size required to investigate mediated and moderated effects using multiple regression.

MEDIATED EFFECTS

In many areas of psychology a causal chain of effects is assumed. The simplest instance of this is shown in model 1.

Model 1 $B \rightarrow C \rightarrow D$

where B has a causal impact on D, but only through the impact of B on C. In other words, B is causally prior to C, which in turn is causally prior to D. Let us imagine a situation where reported job pressure had been shown, among a particular occupational sample, to be related to the number of days being taken off sick. It is suggested, however, that this effect is entirely due to heavier drinking amongst those reporting greater pressure, and that it is the drinking which is the direct cause of the absenteeism. In other words, following model 1, job pressure (B) leads to more heavy drinking (C) which in turn leads to more absenteeism (D). The situation is, of course, rarely this simple. Very soon, we start to want more complex models. We may wish to add more links into the chain, as in model 2.

Model 2 $A \rightarrow B \rightarrow C \rightarrow D$

Going back to our imagined example above, we may wish to suggest that the increase in reported job pressure (B) begins with longer working hours (A). It is, however, quite likely that models will include a mixture of both direct and indirect effects, as in model 3.

Model 3 $C \rightarrow D$
 $\uparrow \; \nearrow$
 B

Model 3 could represent the situation where job pressure (B) was assumed to have both a direct effect on absenteeism (D), and an indirect effect through heavy drinking (C).

Through a technique known as 'Path Analysis' we are able to trace such models using just the ordinary correlation and multiple regression techniques available on widely used packages such as SPSS. It is important to remember what such techniques cannot do. They cannot provide 'proof' that the direction of causality is that which we predict. We are here relying on correlational techniques, rather than the manipulation of cause and effect in an experimental, or even quasi-experimental, way. We can, however, look at how well our model fits the data by looking at the prediction of variance achieved. We might also test competing models to see which provides the best fit to our data. Another important use is to test the relative strengths of different paths between variables. So, in our example, we might ask whether the direct effect of job pressure on absenteeism is stronger or weaker than the indirect effect via the effects of drinking. An answer to this question might be of considerable practical benefit in planning a health promotion pro- gramme motivated by the need to reduce sickness absence, and might influence the choice to adopt an alcohol awareness campaign.

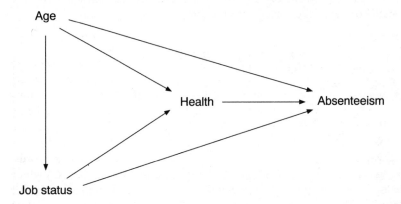

Figure 5.1 Hypothetical model for the relationship between age, job status, health and absenteeism

   To demonstrate this technique, let us consider the following (fictional) example. Figure 5.1 shows a hypothetical model for the relationship between age, 'job status' (i.e. positioning on the job status and pay scale within the company from 1, machine operator level, to 6, top management level), health (measured on a standardised well-being questionnaire such that a maximum score of 60 indicates an extreme of poor health), and absenteeism (the number of days taken off sick within the previous six months). The actual data is cross- sectional (i.e. it was all gathered at one point in time, using a questionnaire and company personnel records), but we are hypothesising the causal rela- tionships shown in Figure 5.1. Health has a direct relationship on absenteeism, but job status has both a direct effect, and an indirect effect via its effect on health. The relationship between age and absenteeism is even more complex: There is a direct effect of age on absenteeism, an indirect effect via health, and further indirect effects via job status. In this example, we have not, at this stage, made any hypothesis about the direction of these effects.

   Figure 5.1 is an example of a path diagram, and follows certain conven- tions. For instance, causally prior variables are placed on the left of the diagram, so that we follow the direction of effects left to right across the page. Single-headed arrows are used to indicate the causal relationships within the model. Note that in this example, all relationships are assumed to be causal. Some models contain variables which are assumed to be related but neither variable is assumed to be causally prior to another, and such relationships are indicated by a double-headed curved arrow in path diagrams.

The first step is to determine the path coefficients, which give the relative strength of relationships between variables. These values are, in fact, the standardised beta coefficients obtained from multiple regressions, and we therefore need to perform several multiple regression analyses in order to obtain path coefficients to insert into the diagram.

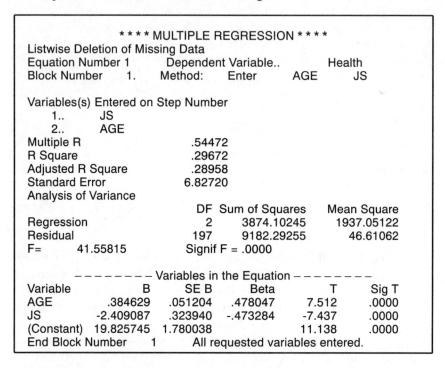

Figure 5.2 SPSS printout for the regression of health onto age and job status

In this example, the first regression performed would be of health onto age and job status. A 'standard' multiple regression is used (SPSS method 'Enter'). This produced the printout shown in Figure 5.2. Looking at the bottom of the printout, under 'Variables in the Equation', we find the beta weighting of .48 and −.47 for age and job status respectively (rounded to two significant figures). These figures can then be entered in the path diagram on the relevant paths: So .48 is entered on the arrow from age to health and −.47 is entered on the arrow from job status to health. Next, absenteeism is regressed onto age, health and job status, and the relevant beta weight-ings are entered into the diagram. The coefficient for the path from age to job status is easiest to obtain, being simply the (Pearson) correlation coefficient (.34).

How are these numbers to be interpreted? The coefficient for the path from, for instance, age to health, indicates the strength of the relationship between age and health when job status is held constant. The size of the beta coefficient indicates the strength of the relationship between variables, whilst the sign of the coefficient indicates the direction of the relationship. The beta coefficient of .48 indicates that an increase in age is associated with an increase in the health score (when job status is held constant). Similarly, the path coefficient of –.47 indicates that an increase in job status is associated with a decrease (indicated by the minus sign) in health score (when age is held constant). Higher job status is associated with a better (lower) score on the health questionnaire. The strength of these relationships is very similar, as indicated by the absolute size of the coefficients. It is worth remembering that the sign of a coefficient will depend on the direction of the measure used. In this case, a measure which gave a high score for good health would have produced path coefficients of the opposite sign.

An indication of the success of the model may be obtained by looking at how much of the variance in the variables which make up the model remains unexplained. Looking at the printout in Figure 5.2, we can see that R^2 is .29672. To calculate the error term, e, associated with the health variable in this model we take the square root of $1 - R^2$, which in this case is .84 (to 2 significant figures). This process is repeated for absenteeism and job status (here, obviously, we use the square of the Pearson correlation coefficient).

Figure 5.3 shows the path diagram with all path coefficients and error terms included. Looking at this, we are able to assess the relative strength of direct and indirect pathways. Each indirect pathway is traced forward along the arrows, passing along each arrow and through each variable only once. The path coefficients are multiplied to compute the strength of an indirect pathway between two variables. So the indirect effect of age on absenteeism via an effect on health in this example is equal to .48 × –.09 = –.04.

There are actually four pathways from age to absenteeism in this example. If all paths are traced then the effects may be summed to give the total direct and indirect effects of age on absenteeism – which is equal to the simple correlation between these two variables (apparent minor discrepancies may result from 'rounding error' in computer printouts). An interesting point to note is the way in which the simple relationship between two variables can be made up of a mixture of positive and negative direct and indirect effects. For instance, there is a moderate, positive direct relationship between age and health (.48), and a weak, negative path from age to health via job status (.34 × –.47 = –.16), which added together make up the correlation coefficient of .32.

How can we assess the success of the model overall? An important point is to look at the error variance in the model. It is immediately obvious that error variance in this model is high – above .8 in all cases, and especially high for absenteeism. Of course, several causes of error variance are being 'lumped together' in these e values. The error includes measurement error,

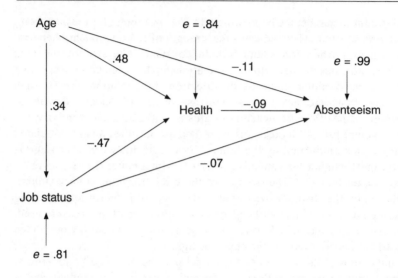

Figure 5.3 Path diagram for the relationship between age, job status, health and absenteeism showing path coefficients and error terms

as well as errors in the model. Model error may arise both from the omission of important relevant variables, and a mis-ordering of elements within the model.

In this imaginary example we might, for instance, be concerned about the psychometric properties of our measure of 'health', and how well the scheme for assigning status to particular job titles had worked. Collecting the data cross-sectionally may also be a cause of some measurement error. Questionnaire responses at the time of the study are being taken as an indication of well-being over the previous six months, the period for which absenteeism data has been collated, and there are obvious problems with this procedure. It also seems likely that important causal variables have been omitted from the model. These results suggest that absenteeism in this particular working population cannot be well predicted by age, job status and health, however, and this indicates that some more exploratory work needs to be undertaken before an absenteeism problem can be tackled, perhaps looking more at issues such as motivation and morale in the workplace.

In cases such as this where a model shows poor fitting to the data, the researcher may wish to see whether an alternative arrangement of elements within the model would produce better results. Whilst this may indeed produce some interesting exploratory results, the researcher must beware of making generalisations from a model generated from one data set. Overfitting to the particular data set is a real possibility. In other words, it is possible to produce a model which fits that particular sample very well, but which does not generalise to other samples, and the model should be re-tested subsequently on a new data set. Researchers may, if the data set is sufficiently large, choose to perform exploratory analyses on a randomly chosen sub-set (say 50 per cent) of subjects, and then confirm a final model on the remainder of subjects.

When can the researcher be satisfied with the model produced? Of course, the answer is probably 'never' in the sense that it seems to be in the nature of researchers to want to go on and do more research! As is often the case in multivariate analysis, we are not aiming towards a simple goal of 'significance'. As Tabachnik and Fidell (1989) say, if the guidelines concerning ratio of cases to independent variables have been observed, the F test of our multiple regression equation should always achieve significance even when, as in this example, error variances are unacceptably high. Similarly, beta coefficients may be significant, but it may still be clear that a particular path adds little or nothing to the model. It is always with reference to the existing literature that we can decide whether a particular path model is interesting or useful.

The aim of the analysis may, of course, be to 'disprove' an existing theory. To demonstrate the fallibility of a theoretical model, however, we have to be sure that the fault lies with the model rather than, for instance, the measures used when path coefficients are low and errors high. It is probable that evidence against a theoretical model is best produced by showing that an alternative model gives a better fit to the data.

MODERATED EFFECTS

Many current models within health and occupational psychology emphasise the way in which variables interact with each other. For instance, it is often suggested that individual differences, such as 'hardiness', or coping mechanisms, such as social support, may buffer the individual from the effect of stressful situations on well-being . Authors refer to situational variables being moderated by individual differences, coping strategies, etc. Psychologists are all familiar with the concept of interaction between variables as exemplified by analysis of variance (ANOVA). This technique allows us to test for the effect of interaction of categorical independent variables on an interval-level dependent variable, but often the predictor variables of interest are measured on scales which produce 'scores' which are at least ordinal level, usually approximating to interval level data. Of course, data can always be 'downgraded': a set of Locus of Control scale scores could be converted to classify individuals as 'externals' and 'internals', for instance. Converting predictor variables in this way would allow the researcher to use analysis of variance to test for interactive effects.

The researcher may, of course, be loath to lose the power associated with the greater refinement of measurement achieved by their test score. Let us consider the example of a researcher looking at perceived job pressure from role ambiguity, Type A behaviour pattern (the 'coronary prone' behaviour pattern which is characterised by free-floating hostility and excessive time-urgency), and job (dis)satisfaction. The researcher has hypothesised that Type As are much more affected by role ambiguity than type Bs, and has collected data from 300 individuals using scalar measures of each of these variables. This hypothesis could be investigated by classifying individuals as reporting either 'low' or 'high' role ambiguity, and as Type A or B, and then performing a two way analysis of variance using these as the independent variables, and job satisfaction as the dependent variable. In doing this, however, the power associated with a scalar measure of job role ambiguity would be lost. Moreover, the researcher may be convinced that role ambiguity truly represents a continuum of experience.

One option is to divide the sample into Type As and Type Bs. The hypothesis predicts that the impact of role ambiguity on job satisfaction will be much greater amongst the Type As than the Type Bs. The researcher might choose to look at the relative strength of the correlation coefficients, but a comparison of the slope of a simple regression line might be much more informative.

In choosing this option, the Type A measure has, of course, still had to be downgraded and there are some potential problems with this type of data conversion. The first consists in the possibilities for missing effects due to misclassification of individuals. A frequent procedure when classifying individuals as, for example, extrovert vs introvert or Type A vs Type B, is to divide the sample at the median; another option is to split the sample at the 'population' mean as presented in normative data tables. It will be clear on reflection, however, that the reliability of such measures is such that a very small score difference in an individual at the centre of the distribution, well within test error, can lead to them being classified as either Type A or B, and clearly such misclassifications can 'muddy' the results. One strategy to avoid this problem is to drop cases in the middle third of the range – the loss of sample size being considered less important than achieving a clear division of cases.

The decision to divide the sample may also depend on theoretical concerns. In this example, the researcher may consider that Types A and B are truly discrete categories, so that it is entirely appropriate to divide the sample in this way. Others, however, may take the view that Type A–B properly represents a continuum, and that the above method of analysis would still involve an undesirable downgrading of data, to which the loss of a third of cases would represent injury added to insult. The method open to the researcher then would be to make use of an interactive or moderator term in a multiple regression analysis. This procedure allows one to make use of all the data, and to use it as interval level data, although the technique is slightly more complicated.

The procedure is basically this, the researcher computes an 'interactive term' by multiplying together the role ambiguity and Type A score for each case (this is quite simply performed using the 'compute' option for data transformation in SPSS). Then, a hierarchical multiple regression is performed with job satisfaction as the dependent variable. The 'simple' role ambiguity and Type A scores are entered at step 1, and the interactive term at step 2. If there is an interaction between role ambiguity and Type A, as predicted, then there will be an (significant) increase in R^2 between step 1 and step 2 – in other words, the interactive term will increase prediction of job satisfaction.

Let us consider the example in detail. Imagine that pressure from role ambiguity (PRESS) has been measured on a scale which scores from 6 (low role ambiguity) to 24 (high role ambiguity); Type A (TABP) on a scale from 10 (extreme Type B) to 40 (extreme Type A); and job satisfaction (JS) on a scale from 5 (extremely satisfied) to 30 (extremely dissatisfied). The interactive or moderator term (MODER), when computed, will be such that a Type B with low role ambiguity will have a low score, and a Type A with high role ambiguity will have a high score. Furthermore, we are predicting a positive relationship between the interactive term and the job dissatisfaction measure. I would recommend that you always aim to have all scales running in the same 'direction' (as in this case all scales run from low 'good' to high 'bad'), reversing directions using data transformation functions if necessary, otherwise it is very easy to get totally confused! It also helps to make a clear note of the direction of all scales, and the direction of relationship expected.

Figure 5.4 shows the printout produced when this procedure was applied to some fabricated data for this example. We see that at step 1 TABP and PRESS were entered into the equation. Both showed a significant, positive association with job (dis)satisfaction, with 78 per cent of the variance in job satisfaction explained. Is there, then, any interactive effect? The next step suggests that indeed there is. The variance in job satisfaction predicted increases to over 89 per cent (and note that the sign of the beta weighting confirms that the relationship is a positive one). This suggests that the effect of role ambiguity pressures on job satisfaction is indeed greater when individuals are more Type A.

The last step is to check that the increase in R^2 is indeed significant. This is done using the equation:

$$F = \frac{(R_2^2 - R_1^2)/(K_2 - K_1)}{(1 - R_2^2)/(N - K_2 - 1)}$$

where R_1^2 is the R^2 for step 1 and R_2^2 is the R^2 for step 2, K_1 is the number of independent variables in step 1 (in this case 2), K_2 is the number of independent variables in step 2 (in this case, 3) and N is the sample size (in this case 300).

```
* * * * Multiple Regression * * * *
Listwise Deletion of Missing Data
Equation Number 1        Dependent Variable..    JS
Block Number    1     Method:    Enter    PRESS      TABP
Variable(s) Entered on Step Number
      1..       TABP
      2..       PRESS


Multiple R                .88465
R Square                  .78261
Adjusted R Square         .78115
Standard Error           3.57752
Analysis of Variance
                         DF  Sum of Squares    Mean Square
Regression                2    13684.35823     6842.17912
Residual                297     3801.18843       12.79861
F =      534.60312        Signif F =   .0000

– – – – – – – Variables in the Equation – – – – – – –
Variable         B        SE B       Beta           T       Sig T
PRESS      1.133083    .035922    .862035       31.543      .0000
TABP        .108437    .026625    .111304        4.073      .0001
(Constant) -1.457421   .852038                  -1.711      .0882

– – – – – – – Variables not in the Equation – – – – – – –
Variable       Beta In    Partial   Min Toler        T       Sig T
MODER        1.487732    .722950    .051334      18.003      .0000
End Block Number    1     All requested variables entered.


Block Number    2     Method:    Enter      MODER
Variable(s) Entered on Step Number
      3..       MODER


Multiple R                .94669
R Square                  .89623
Adjusted R Square         .89518
Standard Error           2.47588
Analysis of Variance
                         DF  Sum of Squares    Mean Square
Regression                3    15671.07268     5223.69089
Residual                296     1814.47399        6.12998
F =      852.15468        Signif F =   .0000

– – – – – – – – Variables in the Equation – – – – – – –
Variable         B        SE B       Beta           T       Sig T
PRESS      -.237014    .080062    -.180317       -2.960      .0033
TABP       -.739172    .050560    -.758714      -14.620      .0000
MODER       .058793    .003266   1.487732       18.003      .0000
(Constant) 17.843745  1.223585                  14.583      .0000
```

Figure 5.4 SPSS printout for the multiple regression including an interactive (or moderator) term

Substituting values from the printout in the equation gives us an F of 321.62. The degrees of freedom associated with this F are $K_2 - K_1$ and $N - K_2 - 1$, in this case 1 and 296. Tables for looking up values of F can be found in the back of most statistics texts – and in this example, the F is indeed significant.

It will be clear that this technique offers the opportunity to study subtle and complex interactive relationships between, for instance, situational and individual difference variables such as are often suggested by theories in many areas of psychology. Indeed, once aware of the existence of such techniques, it becomes surprising that they are so seldom used, and that papers all too often introduce the possibility that interactions exist between variables measured, but never go on to test for such effects.

Nevertheless, the technique does have its pitfalls. The researcher must always remember that regression looks at linear relationships between variables, and that some moderator effects, such as 'threshold' effects, may be underestimated or missed entirely by the use of moderator terms. In contrast, if the bivariate relationship between the 'simple' independent and dependent variables is in fact non-linear, then the analysis may produce an apparent interactive effect which is in fact simply a reflection of the better estimation of the non-linear relationship given by the interactive term than the original variable. The moral so often ignored is, of course, to inspect the data in simple scatterplots etc. as a first step in the analysis.

In conclusion, theoretical writings which posit more complex relationships between variables can and should be explicitly tested, and the means to accomplish this by advanced use of multiple regression are available to the majority of psychological researchers through well-known commercial packages. This process encourages the production and testing of true models of psychological phenomena, rather than mere 'shopping lists' of variables which are presumed to be interrelated in some unspecified way.

REFERENCES

Breakwell, G. (1994) 'The echo of power: A framework for social psychological research', *The Psychologist*, 7, 2: 65–72.

Tabachnik, B.G. and Fidell, L.S. (1989) *Using Multivariate Statistics*, New York: HarperCollins.

Chapter 6

A brief guide to cross-cultural psychological research

Robin Goodwin

ABSTRACT

Despite a recent increase in interest in issues of cross-cultural general-isability, cross-cultural psychological research is still predominantly atheor-etical and unsystematic. In this chapter, I discuss some of the complexities of doing cross-cultural research by proposing a five-stage guideline for conducting such work, which moves from the generation of broad research questions, through the use of appropriate methods and data analysis tech-niques, to the sensitive reporting of obtained results. This guideline aims to help the unfamiliar researcher to apply their own theories across cultures, and by emphasising the role of the participant and the complex ethical and political questions involved in such research, aims to challenge some traditional 'mainstream' assumptions about inter-cultural investigations.

INTRODUCTION

Since the late 1920s, psychologists have been pointing to a 'crisis' in their field, a crisis sparked originally by questions of methodology and ethics and, more recently, by wider issues concerning the generalisability and relevance of much psychological work (e.g. Parker 1989). These more recent concerns have stimulated a resurgence of interest in the *universality* of psychological theories and consequently in cross-cultural variation in both the content and processes of human interaction. Such work can serve a number of purposes. First, it can help answer important questions concerning the way in which individual personality factors interact with wider societal forces (Gudykunst and Ting-Toomey 1988; Huston and Levinger 1978). Second, it can be used to test apparently 'universal' and competing theories under particularly stringent conditions – those where there is considerable cultural variation. Third, cross-cultural work allows us to learn directly from other cultures, particularly where an undesirable social activity (such as relationship violence) is less prevalent (see Levinson 1989, for details on the case of relationship violence). Finally, acculturation processes in new or changing societies have important implica-tions for a range of social behaviours (Furnham and Bochner 1986).

Yet despite all of these valuable characteristics of cross-cultural work, a recent survey of psychological texts failed to find a single chapter that dealt primarily with 'cross-cultural' issues (Tedeschi 1988). Smith and Bond (1993) note how that even when texts are written by non-American authors (e.g. Pandey's 1981 survey of Indian social psychology), citations of North American literature still predominate. Whilst much of this is undoubtedly due to the sheer quantity of North American research (Rosenzweig 1992 estimates that some 64 per cent of the world's research psychologists are North American), it probably also has much to do with the *status* and *prestige* associated with North American (and to some extent Australasian and West European) research. Unfortunately, this is not helped by the failure of many cross-cultural researchers to promote their own case. Much of the research that does reach the established journals appears to result from 'one-off' empirical 'fishing expeditions', aiming to find simple 'cultural differences' (Leung 1989; Sharon and Amir 1988). Such research offers little in the way of organising theory or insight into the generality and cultural applicability of our psychological 'laws' (Bond 1988a; Fletcher and Ward 1988; Zebrowitz-McArthur 1988). In many instances, methods are haphazard, with participant groups frequently chosen more on the availability of collaborators rather than on theoretical criteria (and hence students are the main group of study). Furthermore, in the great majority of cases, materials and procedures are simply 'imported' Western designs (Rosenblatt and Anderson 1981), with even basic translation guidelines often ignored.

In this chapter, I want to suggest five stages of research that form an introductory guideline for those hoping to carry out cross-cultural investigations. These stages should be seen as one researcher's attempt to 'make sense' of the complex dilemmas involved in cross-cultural research, and is drawn from his own experiences (primarily in Eastern and Central Europe, but also in South America) as well as the pertinent literature. In particular, these stages are aimed at those wanting to apply their own theories in other cultures, and thus conduct what is usually termed 'etic' research (Berry 1989) involving direct access to others through techniques such as interviews, questionnaires and the like. This is in contrast to 'emic' research (e.g. Heelas and Locke 1981) which involves the development of culturally specific, indigenous theories. Given the space available, my discussion of the topics raised is far from exhaustive, and at the end of the chapter I suggest some possible sources suitable for those seeking a more comprehensive coverage of the topics discussed.

STAGE 1: THE GENERATION OF CENTRAL RESEARCH QUESTIONS

The first stage is to define clearly which *cultures* and *topics* are to be investigated. Defining exactly what a 'culture' is can be very problematic (see the special edition of the *Journal of Cross-Cultural Psychology, 15, 2,* for a protracted discussion). The norm is to use geographical units as the basis, and in so far as the researcher recognises the problems associated with this (for example, which groups in a population should not be classified as part of that 'culture') this can be a reasonable basis for procedure. Despite the frequent temptation to do otherwise, the practical rule is usually to 'think small'. For example, defining all people of Chinese origin (Hong Kong, Taiwan, Mainland Chinese, Singaporean Chinese, Overseas Chinese, etc.) as a 'Chinese cultural group', and treating all data from this group as one homogeneous sample, is often more problematic than focusing on one particular section of this population (e.g. Hong Kong). If we ignore this, we risk enveloping highly variable populations into one data set, potentially confounding this data.

Defining exactly which topics are suitable for study across the cultures of interest provides an interesting challenge. Such topics should be applicable to all the cultures under investigation – even if the manner of examination and the terminology used will vary culturally. The researcher who spends his or her life working on a small, obscure psychological thesis, and then attempts to replicate this in other countries, often faces a serious problem. If the issue under investigation is so far removed from the indigenous concerns and practices that it has little relevance to those countries being compared, it raises not only ethical issues about why the research is being done at all (Warwick 1980), but means that the researcher is unlikely to engage the interest of participant groups involved. This will often mean that getting respondents to participate will be difficult, and even then they are unlikely to report or perform seriously on the tasks in hand.

This does *not* mean that focusing on rather mundane human activities is necessarily inappropriate: for example, we might expect individuals to talk about different things with different people, and this might be a just topic for research (e.g. Goodwin and Lee 1994). Other topics might be broader in scope, such as a cross-cultural analysis of leadership styles (e.g. Smith and Tayeb 1988). Although the terms 'leadership' and 'conversation' may need a culturally specific definition, we may make progress in our research so long as people talk to others, or there are leaders in all the societies we are studying. However, we must be more wary when tackling areas where the concept itself is problematic. Thus comparing people on their pitch scale for tones may be relatively easy, but comparing groups on 'intelligence' ratios is likely to be very difficult (Poortinga 1989). Unless incredibly flexible in their definition of the terms (and hence immediately open to criticism) cross-cultural researches are unlikely to make any meaningful progress in these more contentious areas.

To avoid the restrictions associated with data 'fishing expeditions' these broad questions should be explicitly formulated on *theoretical grounds* (Amir and Sharon 1987). The most valuable psychological work is likely to involve hypotheses which specify some form of relationship between broad social structural variables (e.g. socioeconomic status) and individual behaviour, cognition or affect (House and Mortimer 1990). Here the researcher might turn to one or more of the systems of cultural variation which act as mediating predictors for the interaction of societal influence and individual behaviour.

The most widely-used of these is that of individualism–collectivism, which is derived from the work of Hsu (e.g. Hsu 1971) and Hofstede (e.g. Hofstede 1980). In the *individualist* culture, the emphasis is on the 'I want to', 'This interests me' approach to life: the 'I' dominates (Yang 1981). In these cultures, the stress is on an individual's goals, and individuals tend to prefer a loosely-knit social framework. In *collectivist* cultures, the group is all important, the preference is for a tightly-knit social framework, and one or more primary groups have a substantial impact on the individual's life (Hui and Triandis 1986; Triandis 1990). Here the individual is encouraged to follow authority ('I owe this', 'my parents will be pleased', etc.): it is the 'we' that dominates. Western Europe, Australia and North America have been traditionally viewed as mainly 'individualist' cultures, the Far East as stereotypically 'collectivist' (Hofstede 1980).

The individualism–collectivism divide has generated an enormous quantity of research (see Triandis 1990, for a review), and it is probably fair to say that this concept now dominates most cross-cultural comparisons. Other researchers have generated other value dimensions that also allow us to 'divide up' cultures. The Chinese Culture Connection (1987) tried to assess the universality of Chinese values across twenty-three cultures, identifying four values (integration, human-heartedness, the Confucian work dynamic and moral discipline) as central to Chinese culture. Schwartz (e.g. Schwartz 1992) identified ten value types from a wide-ranging study of countries across the world. Finally, Douglas' 'cultural theory' (e.g. Douglas 1978) specifies two important divides termed 'grid' (how important rules and regulations are within a society) and 'group' orientation (similar to the collectivism dimension).

Whilst this work has been important in allowing the beginnings of a theory-based and more systematic basis for comparative research, it has not been without its problems. Most obvious is the overlap between the various divides, with a number of commentators (e.g. Smith and Bond 1993) noting how, for example, the Chinese Culture Connection's 'integration' overlaps with the notion of collectivism, as do Schwartz's values of security, traditionality and conformity, and Douglas' concept of 'group'. A second issue concerns the independence of the dimensions used: individualist and collectivist values, for example, are not necessarily opposed to one another (Dion and Dion 1988; Schwartz 1990), with some societies showing a mixed collectivist–individualist pattern (e.g. Italy). Furthermore, the origins of these value dimensions, and the rationale and motivational factors that underpin change along the divide, remain uncertain (cf. Schwartz 1990 on individualism–collectivism). Finally, the divides can be used in a rather ethnocentric manner, with many models implying that the 'individualist' pole is the most desirable (Adamopoulos and Smith 1990). Nevertheless, as long as the researcher is clear about the meaning of the cultural divides he/she is using, and honest in stating what would (and would not) validate the use of their theory (and not too keen to argue that an uncomfortable finding can simply invoke a new, not-included 'cultural dimension') there is the potential here for valuable cross-cultural work.

STAGE 2: ENSURING YOUR QUESTIONS ARE SUITABLE

Once we have focused in on a reasonable subject for cross-cultural enquiry, we should then ensure that they are relevant to the culture(s) being explored. At the very least, this is likely to involve the researcher consulting widely with colleagues from the culture(s) under examination. In larger projects, it is advisable to form a broad panel of critics with the job of identifying political or cultural biases (Warwick 1980). Whilst it is unlikely that a cross-culturalist involved in large multi-cultural studies will manage to immerse him/herself in *every* culture under investigation, at least some interest in the culture(s) under study, and honest and serious conversation with researchers working in that culture, are important if the research is to be viable. Such an interest does not merely mean visiting the country in hand (although this is likely to be the most fruitful form of experience): it can also mean immersing yourself in the literature of the land, as well as following details about changes in political and economic structures in the countries under investigation as covered in the more 'respectable' media (Kukla 1988). Needless to say, this should not be an uncritical exercise, and the media projection that a culture (or power elite) seeks to project is often an interesting research topic in itself.

A further important complementary approach is to allow the participants in the country(ies) under investigation to become 'an active participant in the research' (Mamali 1982) and thus to verify the appropriateness of the questions being posed. A number of open-ended methods exist for encouraging participant-centred designs. Mamali (1982), for example, asks participants to produce their own questions within the constraints of a broad theme, and then proceeds to work with these throughout the data collection (see also the handbook of methods edited by Reason and Rowan 1981). Mamali (1991) uses the broad concept 'problems of youth today' in stimulating his respondents to list what they believe to be the most pertinent problems. There are then a variety of things one can do with this data including asking participants to actually write the precise questions that should be asked, and then getting them to answer the questions, as well as the more conventional approach of using the topics listed as a guide and developing one's own questions from there.

One important issue is the translation of the questions. Whilst it is of course essential that this is done well, researchers should be warned that this can be a lengthy, and sometimes expensive, procedure (there are, for example, at least four major languages in the Bombay region of India). There are a variety of degrees of translation, ranging from broad pragmatic translations to a more specific aesthetic-poetic interpretation, involving translation of affect, emotion and feelings of the first language (Brislin 1980). Brislin's excellent chapter suggests a number of rules for maximising 'translateability' (e.g. the careful contextualisation of language), as well as a number of approaches to how translation might be operationalised, and is an excellent source for translation procedures.

Probably the most widely used systematic approach is back-translation (Brislin 1970, 1980). Here a researcher prepares material in one language, a first translator translates it into the target language and a second one back into the researcher's original language, at which point the quality of the translation can be judged. Thus any poorly translated (or translatable) terms can be modified through this back-translation process. My personal experience, from having worked in a number of cultures, is that excellent translators are usually available, although it is not always best to use the 'official' mandarins 'recommended' by those in authority (although obviously sometimes this is essential for good relations). Where the translators meet your respondents, such 'officials', apart from often showing a striking family resemblance to those in 'authority', may also be associated with regimes or power-structures which may dissuade your participants from full and open co-operation, or could significantly affect their responses.

STAGE 3: PILOTING THE RESEARCH QUESTIONS

This can be a relatively short procedure, but is nevertheless essential. This 'refinement' involves the 'trying out' of your translated research questions, or research procedures, usually through open-ended interviews with pilot samples similar to those from the target sample, and always taken from the same culture. Schuman (1966) describes a valuable 'random-probe' technique particularly useful for researchers using questionnaire methods. Here, random items from a questionnaire are posed to pilot samples selected to be as similar to the actual target participant group as possible. These participants are then challenged on the *meaning* of their answers to ensure complete comprehension. This allows the often misleadingly-elegant translations obtained by expert translators to be modified where appropriate.

It is also usually a good idea at this stage to attempt to assess some of the 'situational'/ 'ideological' factors that might affect the distribution of your inventory, or the running of your experiment. It is a good idea to ask your pilot participants to write down, anonymously and as honestly as possible, what was going through their minds when you (the researcher) arrived and asked them to participate. Again, personal experience has revealed a number

answers to this question, ranging from 'let's make everything
d up these wealthy Western academics' to 'are my responses
e put on official file and used against me?' An awareness of these
ts' can both help you alter the procedures of the real data collection,
a.   e you important insight when interpreting your data (!).

STAGE 4: THE ACTUAL COLLECTION OF DATA

The first important issue is sample selection (Brislin and Baumgardner 1971). Because 'students' are usually seen to be equivalent across cultures (they are usually wealthy, of at least average intelligence, young, etc., i.e. un-representative of their cultures) then they are the normal participant group in most psychological research. However, as Smith and Bond (1993) point out, despite these criteria there are still important variables on which university students may differ across cultures (e.g. on religion). Thus it is necessary to look at the actual background of participants, and try to partial out con-founding variables. The careful researcher must also be careful to clearly specify the *boundaries* of their defined participant group (Rohner 1984). It is easy to think of examples even within the relatively small world of British academia where the differences between 'part-time' students, full-time 'mature' students and 'direct entry' students (i.e. those aged 18) may significantly affect the results of a number of research projects.

Related to this is the issue of what to do with groups that might reside within your cultural grouping (perhaps a nation-state, if this is how you define your culture), but are visiting from abroad, are only first-generation members of that state, and so on. Whilst it might be wise to exclude a group such as first-generation British Chinese in a study of British social values, the extent to which you exclude a population on the basis of ancestry is not only a very sensitive issue, but may actually lead to misleading comparisons. Thus, for example, some nations (e.g. Australia) are notable for their cultural mix, and to include only participants from 'ancestral Australian stock' would involve only including the aboriginal population. This returns us to a central theme running through this chapter. Your choice of theory, cultures for comparison and participants within that culture must be closely related to your topic of research. It is this topic which must then dictate the sampling procedures you follow.

A general rule for much psychological research (Fielding and Fielding 1986), and one gaining in prominence in many of the literatures, is the notion that research should be multi-method wherever possible. Culture is such a complex phenomenon (and cultural differences so easily misinterpreted) that this guidance may be particularly pertinent to cross-cultural research (Brislin 1980; Cartwright 1979; McGuire 1976; Sharon and Amir 1988; Triandis 1976). Whilst the marrying of results from different techniques may often be difficult, the richness of analysis and understanding that a multi-method perspective affords makes this a price well worth paying. Thus in the author's own research into intimacy and disclosure in Russia (Goodwin 1995; Goodwin and Emelyanova 1995) analyses of structured questionnaires revealed that respondents from a variety of different occupational groups disclosed approximately the same *amount*. However, an analysis of more open-ended descriptions of *what* they would and would not discuss revealed marked occupational differences in the nature of their taboo topics. A final analysis of indepth interviews (Goodwin, in preparation) showed how these disclosure patterns were part of a rich tapestry of changing social relations.

Quantitative analyses dominate the cross-cultural literature, and a large literature now exists on the establishment of cultural equivalence (e.g. Bond and Forgas 1984; Leung 1989; Watkins 1989). Factor analyses are the most widely used methods of cross-cultural data analysis (Poortinga 1989; Watkins 1989), and can, within limits, be used to establish the relevance of the question schedules devised in other cultures (Tedeschi 1988). Researchers, however, must be aware of at least two pitfalls. One concerns scaling: response sets (such as a tendency to acquiesce) may confound results (Smith and Bond 1993), and researchers are advised to use one of the established procedures for overcoming this problem (e.g. Bond 1988b). Second, researchers must be particularly wary when using exploratory multivariate methods, as any cross-cultural data is probably open to a plethora of interpretations. For example, a 'map' of items resulting from a multi-dimensional scaling analysis may indicate (theoretically convenient) associations which are quite untenable in one or more of the cultures under investigation. The rule here is for researchers to be modest and honest about their predictions, to openly discuss interpretations of their results with collaborating colleagues in different cultures, and where possible to compare their data with competing models, through such techniques as LISREL (Watkins 1989).

One enduring question is the relationship between individual personality and cultural variants, with researchers often confronted with an almost impossible 'chicken and egg' situation of what came first, the personality or the cultural influences. Unfortunately, researchers are still at the early stages in developing an appropriate range of statistical techniques for unpacking the independent effects of cultural and individual variables. For some of the most promising developments, readers are recommended to consult the work of Leung (1989; Leung and Bond 1989), who has shown that multi-level analysis *is* possible through the careful use of within culture standardisation and the inclusion of relevant antecedent variables.

A range of valuable qualitative techniques also exist that are suitable for cross-cultural investigations (Trimble 1988). Apart from the traditional open-ended interviews, these include the analysis of folktales and the use of more exploratory techniques such as free-association tests (Brislin 1980). Also available are a variety of semi-structured devices such as Wheeler's Rochester Interaction Recorder (e.g. Wheeler and Nezlek 1977) and Duck's Iowa Communication Record (Duck 1991), as well as the vast (but underutilised) anthropological resource available at the Human Relations Area Files (which contain ethnographic source materials on more than 300 cultural 'units' throughout the world: Barry 1980). Such techniques should not, however, be seen as 'the easy way out' for those less keen on statistical analysis. Such analyses are subject to explicit rules and procedures which pay careful attention to sampling of items, coding, reliability and validity (e.g. Brislin 1980: see also Dey 1993 for a useful but broader discussion of qualitative research techniques).

STAGE 5: THE 'WRITING UP' AND DISSEMINATION OF FINDINGS

An unfortunate fact of much psychological research is that even the most dedicated researcher, who perpetrates his or her work with unbending theoretical vigour and the most careful attention to detail, will rarely pay much heed to the way in which research results are disseminated. Yet for the cross-cultural researcher, the ethical and social considerations involved in the dissemination of research findings are rarely simple, although they potentially form one of the most significant aspects of his/her work (Mamali 1982; Warwick 1980).

One issue is the extent to which the process of being researched is itself a transforming process (Mamali 1991). This may sound trivial to the practised Western researcher raised on the diet of undergraduate laboratory work, but when you ask a participant in a racist, divided society the meaning of belonging to a minority group, you are asking them to reflect on something far deeper and far more personal than whether it was a letter 'S' or 'T' that just flashed across the screen. In some, more repressive regimes, participation in a study conducted by nationals from another culture may raise suspicions from authority about these participants. Furthermore, the researcher's treatment of his/her participants may also have long-lasting effects on the attitudes towards other researchers entering this culture for the first time. An insensitive approach to key figures can obviously limit future access. Equally, however, a too sycophantic approach to institutions of authority can restrict the honesty of your participants, and have particularly unfortunate consequences if that authority should fall from grace. As a young, rather naive researcher entering Romania shortly after the fall of Ceausescu, I was amazed to hear that all social psychologists were seen as right-wing agent provocateurs, dedicated to the reduction of workers' rights and a variety of other, illiberal agendas. This was quite a different picture of my own stereotype of the British social psychologist!

Another, important concern when writing up reports is the utility of the findings for the people under investigation. In a more sinister vein, we also need to be wary of those who aim at a simple, and usually derogatory, summary of a culture. The 'IQ' debate, for example, has been awash with criticisms of racism (Rose, Lewontin and Kamin 1984). Research on the multi-million dollar 'Camelot' project on social change and conflict was explicitly aimed at providing the army with ways of combating 'insurgency' in developing nations (Warwick 1980). Sometimes, however, the (mis)use of psychological research is more subtle. Some work, for example, has tried to correlate national economic development, such as individualism, with a set of psychological values (Hofstede 1980). Yet here we cannot be sure of the direction of causality (which came first, the development or the value?). Thus to naively assume that a particular (usually 'Western') value system will lead to a particular product in very difficult cultures grossly underplays the complexities of cultural variation, and can have potentially damaging consequences for the culture(s) in question (Goodwin 1995; Goodwin and Emelyanova 1995).

Perhaps the main message from all this is the need to be honest in writing up cross-cultural work. Rather optimistically, Andre (1981) suggests that write-ups should include a section entitled 'Research Process', which includes details about the researchers and their working relationships (including discussion of disagreements that arose, etc.), and details about who is funding the research and why. In thus going beyond the 'squeaky-clean' interpretations normally found in methodological reports, researchers may enable future workers to become aware of these issues and thus warn them of certain difficulties. Such honesty in 'writing up' may also help readers interpret the reported findings in the light of these issues.

CONCLUSIONS

Two particular themes run across these stages. First is the importance of the link between the topic of interest and the method of investigation. In practice, this means that there are times where conventional sampling techniques are essential, and others where convenience and accessibility are enough to provide insight. It also means that sometimes standard quantitative techniques are desirable, at other times literature, common myths, media reports and so on are all valid ways of generating data. The one enduring question must be 'do these techniques provide me with insight into this culture?', and, where appropriate, 'do they allow me to meaningfully compare this culture with others?'

A second, enduring theme is that of ethics. In the words of Warwick 'all cross-cultural research . . . raises both ethical and political issues . . . almost any project, no matter how well intentioned, honestly conceived, and carefully designed, can become explosive if it ventures into the right minefield' (1980: 391, 333). As has been noted, ethical concerns are rarely discussed in cross-cultural research, and a purview of a long list of leading cross-cultural texts revealed only the one chapter on the subject, by Warwick (1980). Yet the researcher must ask him/herself several important questions when conducting cross-cultural work. These include: 'Why am I doing this particular topic?' (and not one of a number of other possible cross-cultural projects, which might be more useful); Why am I being funded to do this, and is there a hidden agenda?; Why am I being *allowed* to do this in culture '*x*'?; Why are my participants taking part, and will participation have any effect on them afterwards (do I now owe some 'duty of care' towards these individuals?)?; What should I report as my 'findings' (simple statistical differences, points of commonality, notes on the political relevance of certain questions?)?; How will my results be used, both by my sponsoring organisation and authorities in the cultures under investigation? These questions should not be seen as merely the musings of privileged Western academics, but have the potential to provide important insights into both the minds of our participants (who are likely to be asking similar questions themselves) as well as indicating the wider social realm in which our investigations take place. As such, they should be at the forefront of cross-cultural research design.

Cross-cultural research has many benefits. Apart from the theoretical advantages listed in the introduction to the paper, there are practical advantages too, with at least two former editors of the prestigious *Journal of Personality and Social Psychology* claiming that cross-cultural work is actually easier to publish (Wheeler and Reis 1988). Cross-cultural work at its most challenging requires flexibility accompanied by strict methodological purity, elaborate planning accompanied by considerable luck, and dogmatic determination accompanied by a perverse sense of humour. In my own experience, however, it is worth it. Cross-cultural work can also bring immense personal satisfaction, allowing the researcher the privileged opportunity to work with psychologists from very different perspectives, whose freshness and originality provides insight not only into how other people live and perform, but has the potential to challenge and undermine our own, most treasured assumptions.

SOME SUGGESTED FURTHER READING

There is a steadily growing market in social psychological texts, aimed at the postgraduate audience.

A good general text for those interested in methodological issues, as well as social and personality research, is Bond, M. (1988) *The Cross-Cultural Challenge to Social Psychology*, Newbury Park: Sage.

More general texts are:

Smith, P. and Bond, M. (1993) *Social Psychology Across Cultures*, New York: Harvester Wheatsheaf.

and the 'rival':

Moghaddam, F., Taylor, D. and Wright, S. (1993) *Social Psychology in Cross-Cultural Perspective*, New York: Freeman.

Useful source books include the six volumes in Triandis' edited *Handbook of Cross-Cultural Psychology* (1980, 1981, a new edition is in preparation) and the expanding 'Cross-cultural Research and Methodology Series' (Sage).

REFERENCES

Adamapoulos, J. and Smith, C. (1990) 'The emergence of individualism and collectivism as cultural patterns of interpersonal behaviour', paper presented at the conference on Individualism and Collectivism: Psychocultural perspectives from East and West, Seoul, Korea

Amir, Y. and Sharon, I. (1987) 'Are social-psychological laws cross-culturally valid?', *Journal of Cross-Cultural Psychology*, 18: 383–470.

Andre, R. (1981) 'Multi-cultural research: developing a participative methodology for cross-cultural psychology', *International Journal of Psychology*, 16: 249–256.

Barry, H. (1980) 'Description and uses of the human relations area files', in H. Triandis and J. Berry (eds) *Handbook of Cross-Cultural Psychology Vol. 2*, Boston: Allyn & Bacon.

Berry, J. (1989) 'Imposed etics-emics-derived etics: the operationalization of a compelling idea', *International Journal of Psychology*, 24: 721–735.

Bond, M. (1988a) *The Cross-Cultural Challenge to Social Psychology*, Newbury Park: Sage.

Bond, M. (1988b) 'Finding universal dimensions of individual variation in multi-cultural studies of values: the Rokeach and Chinese value surveys', *Journal of Personality and Social Psychology*, 55: 1009–1015.

Bond, M. and Forgas, J. (1984) 'Linking person perception to behaviour intention across cultures: the role of cultural collectivism', *Journal of Cross-Cultural Psychology*, 15: 337–352.

Brislin, R. (1970) 'Back-translation for cross-cultural research', *Journal of Cross-Cultural Psychology*, 1: 185–216.

Brislin, R. (1980) 'Translation and content analysis of oral and written materials', in H. Triandis and J. Berry (eds) *Handbook of Cross-Cultural Psychology, Vol 2*, Boston: Allyn & Bacon.

Brislin, R. and Baumgardner, S. (1971) 'Non-random sampling of individuals in cross-cultural research', *Journal of Cross-Cultural Psychology*, 2: 397–400.

Cartwright, D. (1979) 'Contemporary social psychology in historical perspective', *Social Psychology Quarterly*, 42: 82–93.

Dey, I. (1993) *Qualitative Data Analysis: A user-friendly guide for social scientists*, London: Routledge.

Dion, K. and Dion, K. (1988) 'Romantic love: individual and cultural perspectives', in R. Sternberg and M. Barnes (eds) *The Psychology of Love*, New Haven: Yale University Press.

Douglas, M. (1978) *Cultural Bias*, London: Royal Anthropological Institute Occasional Paper, No. 34.

Duck, S. (1991) 'Diaries and logs', in B. Montgomery and S. Duck (eds) *Studying Social Interaction*, New York: Guilford.

Fielding, N. and Fielding, J. (1986) *Linking Data*, London: Sage.

Fissell, M. (1991) 'Kinship and culture', paper presented at the Inter-disciplinary Workshop on 'Approaching Culture', University of Manchester.

Fletcher, G. and Ward, C. (1988) 'Attribution theory and processes: a cross-cultural perspective', in M. Bond (ed.) *The Cross-Cultural Challenge to Social Psychology*, Newbury Park: Sage.

Furnham, A. and Bochner, A. (1986) *Culture Shock: Psychological reactions to unfamiliar environments*, London: Methuen.

Goodwin, R. (1995) 'The privatisation of the personal? I: Intimate disclosure in modern-day Russia', *Journal of Social and Personal Relationships*, 12, 21–31.

Goodwin, R. and Lee, I. (1994) 'Taboo topics amongst Chinese and British friends: a cross-cultural comparison', *Journal of Cross-Cultural Psychology*, 25: 325–338.

Goodwin, R. and Emelyanova, T. (1995) 'The privatisation of the personal? II: Attitudes to the family and child-rearing values in modern-day Russia', *Journal of Social and Personal Relationships*, 12, 32–40.

Gudykunst, W. and Ting-Toomey, S. (1988) *Culture and Interpersonal Communication*, Newbury Park: Sage.

Heelas, P. and Locke, A. (eds) (1981) *Indigenous Psychologies: The anthropology of the self*, Lancaster: Academic Press.

Hofstede, G. (1980) *Culture's Consequences: International differences in work-related values*, Beverly Hills: Sage.

House, J. and Mortimer, J. (1990) 'Social structure and the individual: emerging themes and new directions', *Social Psychology Quarterly*, 53: 71–80.

Hsu, F. (1971) 'Eros, affect and Pao', in F. Hsu (ed.) *Kinship and Culture*, Chicago: Aldine.

Hui, C. and Triandis, H. (1986) 'Individualism–collectivism: a study of cross-cultural researchers', *Journal of Cross-cultural Psychology*, 17: 225–248.

Huston, T. and Levinger, H. (1978) 'Interpersonal attraction and relationships', *Annual Review of Psychology* 29: 115–156.

Kukla, A. (1988) 'Cross-cultural psychology in a post-empiricist era', in M. Bond (ed.) *The Cross-Cultural Challenge to Social Psychology*, Newbury Park: Sage.

Leung, K. (1989) 'Cross-cultural differences: individual-level vs. cultural-level analysis', *International Journal of Psychology*, 24: 703–719.

Leung, K. and Bond, M. (1989) 'On the empirical identification of dimensions for cross-cultural comparisons', *Journal of Cross-Cultural Psychology*, 20: 133–151.

Levinson, D. (1989) *Family Values in Cross-cultural Perspective*, Newbury Park: Sage.

McGuire, W. (1976) 'Historical comparisons: testing psychological hypotheses with cross-cultural data', *International Journal of Psychology*, 11: 161–173.

Mamali, C. (1982) 'Democratization of social research', in P. Stringer (ed.) *Confronting Social Issues: Applications of Social Psychology (2)*, London: Academic Press.

Mamali, C. (1991) 'The technique of directed self-inquiry and the status of the subject', unpublished paper, University of Bucharest.

Pandey, J. (1981) *Perspectives on Experimental Social Psychology in India*, New Delhi: Concept.

Parker, I. (1989) *The Crisis in Social Psychology – and How to End it*, London: Routledge.

Poortinga, Y. (1989) 'Equivalence of cross-cultural data: an overview of basic issues', *International Journal of Psychology*, 24: 737–756.

Reason, P. and Rowan, J. (1981) *Human Inquiry: A sourcebook of new paradigm research*, Chichester: John Wiley.

Rohner, R. (1984) 'Towards a conception of culture for cross-cultural psychology', *Journal of Cross-Cultural Psychology*, 15: 111–138.

Rose, S., Lewontin, R. and Kamin, L. (1984) *Not in our Genes: Biology, ideology and human nature*, Harmondsworth: Penguin.

Rosenblatt, P. and Anderson, R. (1981) 'Human sexuality in cross-cultural perspective', in M. Cook (ed.) *The Bases of Human Sexual Attraction*, London: Academic Press.

Rosenzweig, M. (1992) *International Psychological Science: Progress, problems and prospects*, Washington D.C.: American Psychological Association.

Schuman, H. (1966) 'The random probe technique: a technique for evaluating the quality of closed questions', *American Sociological Review*, 31: 218–222.

Schwartz, S. (1990) 'Individualism–collectivism: Critique and proposed refinements', *Journal of Cross-Cultural Psychology*, 21: 139–157.

Schwartz, S. (1992) 'The universal content and structure of values: theoretical advances and empirical tests in 20 countries', in U. Kim, H. Triandis and G. Yoon (eds) *Individualism and Collectivism: Theoretical and methodological issues*, Newbury Park: Sage.

Sharon, I. and Amir, Y. (1988) 'Cross-cultural replications: a prerequisite for the validation of social psychological laws', in M. Bond (ed.) *The Cross-Cultural Challenge to Social Psychology*, Newbury Park: Sage.

Smith, P. and Bond, M. (1993) *Social Psychology Across Cultures*, New York: Harvester Wheatsheaf.

Smith, P. and Tayeb, M. (1988) *Leadership, Organizations and Culture*, London: Sage.

Tedeschi, J. (1988) 'How does one describe a platypus? An outsider's questions for cross-cultural psychology', in M. Bond (ed.) *The Cross-Cultural Challenge to Social Psychology*, Newbury Park: Sage.

The Chinese Culture Connection (1987) 'Chinese values and the search for culture-free dimensions of culture', *Journal of Cross-Cultural Psychology*, 18: 143–164.

Triandis, H. (1976) 'Methodological problems of comparative research', *International Journal of Psychology*, 11: 155–159.

Triandis, H. (1990) 'Cross-cultural studies of individualism and collectivism', in J. Berman (ed.) *Nebraska Symposium on Motivation, 1989*, Lincoln: Nebraska University Press.

Trimble, J. (1988) 'Putting the etic to work: applying social psychological principles in cross-cultural settings', in M. Bond (ed.) *The Cross-Cultural Challenge to Social Psychology*, Newbury Park: Sage.

Warwick, D. (1980) 'The politics and ethics of cross-cultural research', in H. Triandis (ed.) *Handbook of Cross-cultural Psychology, Vol 1*, Boston: Allyn & Bacon.

Watkins, D. (1989) 'The role of confirmatory factor analysis in cross-cultural research', *International Journal of Psychology*, 24: 686–701.

Wheeler, L. and Nezlek, J. (1977) 'Sex differences in social participation', *Journal of Personality and Social Psychology*, 35: 742–754.

Wheeler, L. and Reis, H. (1988) 'On titles, citations and outlets: what do mainstreamers want?', in M. Bond (ed.) *The Cross-Cultural Challenge to Social Psychology*, Newbury Park: Sage.

Yang, K. (1981) 'Social orientation and individual modernity among Chinese students in Taiwan', *Journal of Social Psychology*, 113: 159–170.

Zebrowitz-McArthur, L. (1988) 'Person perception in cross-cultural perspective', in M. Bond (ed.) *The Cross-Cultural Challenge to Social Psychology*, Newbury Park: Sage.

Part II

Qualitative research

Preface

The chapters in this section show how qualitative research can be undertaken in the contexts of traditional empiricist enquiry and new paradigm research. They illustrate the diversity of qualitative methods and include ethno-methodological studies of the introduction of technology into the workplace; observation of mother–infant interactions; categorisation, coding and content analysis of interview data; and discourse analysis. The section commences with a chapter on the nature of research and the paradigms which underpin this.

Chapter 7 on 'Culture, perception and cognition' asks why two people from different backgrounds placed in the same situation are likely to differ in what they make of it. The attempts to answer this question have, the author considers, resulted in anthropologists coming up against some of the most contested issues in the psychology of perception and cognition. The chapter shows how they have dealt with these issues and examines approaches drawn from cognitive science, ecological psychology and phenomenology. It illustrates that how we conceive things influences what questions we ask. The author notes, for example, that some of the neatly ordered taxonomies in cognitive anthropology resulted from the particular methods used by the anthropologists rather than having any counterpart in the cognitive organisation of the people studied. Conversely, the traditional method in anthropology of participant observation operates for reasons which are fundamentally different from the axioms of traditional science. Instead of ordering sensory data or impressions of the world by representations or concepts – the Cartesian dualism of mind and nature – in order to achieve a common understanding, the author argues that communion of experience comes about by the body acting in similar ways, through common practical activity, which may then be interpreted according to one's own custom. Scientists in general, the author notes, are practically involved, and as in other skilled activity this shapes understanding unself-consciously. The scientist perceives by embodied practice. The author concludes that the future will bring a radical realignment of the interface between anthropology and psychology, and that this will come from the application of ethnographic understanding in the delivery of a resounding critique of the foundations of contemporary academic psychology.

Chapter 8 on 'ethnography' points to the participant observation tradition of this 'people writing' form of research, and notes that there are disputes within ethnography about the aims of research, the role of the researcher, the relationship between ethnography and other orientations, but that disputes of this sort should characterise any approach that is alive and self-reflexive. The author considers that, in line with the premises of symbolic interactionism social scientists too construct meanings on the basis of their encounters with the world, and dynamically change them as experience and interaction with the world unfold. The author has studied the introduction of computing technology into organisations and how this is experienced and what consequences occur for work. The chapter discusses several substantive methodological issues which arise from the practice of enthnography, including, amongst others, ethnography's emphasis on the relationship between meaning and practical action; the role of the ethnographer in the field; and ethnography and theory development. It is noted that while empathy is important for understanding, a carefully measured 'distance' can also aid understanding of a field site so as to report not just what members of the organisation feel and take for granted but also how these ways of making sense of the world work in practice. The author makes clear that ethnography is not merely a method for doing social and psychological research but that it also involves commitments which challenge some dominant values, especially in experimental psychology. It is emphasised that all theory construction involves measures of insight, guesswork, good luck, powerful rhetoric and bravado. While recognising the utility of combining ethnography with experimentation, it is claimed that experimental psychologists trade on an unexplicated and hoped for shared common sense with subjects for their instructions and procedures to work.

Chapter 9 on 'Observing mother–infant interactions in natural settings' advocates the necessity for a degree of control in qualitative studies, with observations being conducted systematically so as to increase the generalisability of the data. The authors advise that where lengthy observations are not possible the context of observation should be controlled in naturalistic studies, and that reactivity to observation may be minimised by the investigators becoming acquainted with participants and allowing them to become familiar with the procedure before commencing observations. They add, however, that in order to gain an understanding of everyday patterns of interaction, free observation in the natural environment remains the preferred method. The chapter also discusses in some detail practical aspects of observational research and makes a number of points. Preliminary studies are needed to get some feel for the behavioural characteristics of the population and to consider what data recording techniques could be used. Defining and producing clear and reliable categories of behaviour can take considerable time. Recording behaviour can be done by computerised event recorders which can also sort data ready for analysis. However, this may not always be possible for observations of complex behaviour made over a relatively long period. For such cases various methods of time sampling events need to be considered. While video cameras are useful for collecting and analysing complex data they can be intrusive and produce excessively large quantities of data. Inter-observer reliability needs to be assessed in different contexts and over time. In longitudinal studies predictive behaviours should be assessed by independent observers to eliminate experimenter bias.

Chapter 10 on 'Systemic interviewing and attributional analysis applied to international broadcasting' includes a detailed rationale for understanding qualitative research in this area and advocates a comprehensive categorisation and coding process for the analysis of data. The author notes that new paradigm research and associated approaches lead towards the idea that research is a process creating meaning rather than uncovering findings; and that qualitative research should not be judged by the same criteria as hypothetico-deductive research, with quantifications of validity and generalisability, but that it does need to lead to usable results. The approach described in this chapter uses interviews or group discussions to create verbal accounts which can then be intensively analysed. A major problem identified with qualitative research is that the data are so rich, and the methods of analysis can be so hidden, that it becomes difficult to judge whether the analysis accurately reflects the major themes of the data. The approach to analysis described in this chapter is one which attempts to avoid reliance on simple description or simple computer generated categorisation, but instead uses repetitive procedures for processing the data, generating and testing hypotheses, and coalescing the coding into progressively higher order concepts. The author considers that this kind of qualitative research can provide sound and usable findings in its own right and also be a secure foundation for quantitative surveys. The chapter illustrates the process involved by a study of international broadcasting.

Chapter 11 on 'Constructing and deconstructing childhood' points to the values, assumptions, approaches and practices underlying much of child psychology. The psychological models on offer, the author notes, recycle and scientise culturally gendered stereotypes. Discourse analysis can open a window into the tissue of meanings associated with an area which we may normally not consider. Before analysing texts a necessary analytic step is to consider the context in which the text is generated, what conditions prompts its emergence, and what is the field of possible alternatives. The author reflects on the process of generalising meaning from texts, and the status and limits of the analysis. For example, discourse analysts need to be aware of the ways the verbal and visual material they analyse gains new life from such activity. The analyst has to participate in the practices commented upon, and be a culturally competent member in order to identify and interpret discourses. The text needs to be analysed in the context of its production. Knowledge is thus grounded and situated. The author notes that the commitment to Western psychological models of childhood inadvertently imposes them on Third World children, families and cultures, and that dominant constructions of childhood emerge as far from innocent in the production and reproduction of prevailing structures of authority.

Chapter 12 on 'Discursive complexes in material culture' elaborates a discourse analytic reading of an item of material culture (a toothpaste ad) using psychoanalytic notions to elaborate 'discursive complexes'. The chapter reflects on the role of method in this version of discourse analysis which deconstructs the link between language and power in 'common sense' and shows that what seems trivial can be seen as symptomatic of patterns of regulation. The author examines three assumptions about the nature of discourse. The first is variation: the assumption of multiple meanings inhabiting a given space and being conveyed to the reader at a non-conscious level, where specific psychoanalytic notions of representation are required to account for how the meanings operate alongside and against one another. The second assumption concerns function and the way the text produces certain effects upon a reader, who is situated in multiple subject positions which can be contradictory and which can be revealed by psychoanalytic discourse analysis. The third assumption concerns the construction of the meaning in the text which is influenced by the discursive complexes or patterns of meaning that systematically form objects and subjects and which help to relay meaning and specify subject positions. Amongst these discursive complexes are psychoanalytic notions which circulate as elements of self-understanding in Western culture. A psychoanalytic discourse reading looks to the way in which texts reproduce such categories, and reproduce subjects who can make sense of the texts and hold on to them. This is undertaken on the toothpaste ad. The point is made that an essential part of discourse analysis is the production of a 'critical distance' between the reader and the text so that one is able to ask what collections of relationships and theories of self must obtain for this material to make sense. At the same time the analytic device of the 'discursive complex' is used to provide an embedded notion of subject position. 'The engagement with any text is always an engagement from within discourse, and the task of a discourse analytic reading is to engage in a way that lays bare the work of ideology and the plays of power, the unravelling of ideology and the spaces of resistance.'

Chapter 7

Culture, perception and cognition

Tim Ingold

I am by trade a social anthropologist, not a psychologist. Let me begin, therefore, with the question that, perhaps more than any other, motivates anthropological enquiry. Take two people from different backgrounds and place them in the same situation; they are likely to differ in what they make of it. Indeed such difference is something that every anthropologist experiences in the initial phases of fieldwork. But why should this be so? How do we account for it? In their attempts to answer these questions, anthropologists have come up against some of the most contested issues in the psychology of perception and cognition. My task in this chapter is to show how they have dealt with these issues. The chapter is divided into two parts. In the first part I trace something of the history of the problem over the past century of anthropological thought. In the second, I go on to assess the relevance for anthropological understanding of alternative approaches drawn from cognitive science, ecological psychology and phenomenology. This is a considerable agenda, and in the space of a short chapter I can do no more than touch on the many questions raised.

I
SOCIAL ANTHROPOLOGY

In British social anthropology (as distinct from American cultural anthropology) thinking about perception and cognition goes back to the classic work of Emile Durkheim, himself one of the founding fathers of what was then the new science of sociology. In his manifesto for the new discipline, *The Rules of Sociological Method* (first published in 1895), Durkheim adamantly opposed all attempts to explain social phenomena in terms of the psychological properties of individuals. As he famously declared, 'every time a social phenomenon is directly explained by a psychological phenomenon, we may rest assured that the explanation is false' (1982[1895]: 129). If sociology is a kind of psychology, Durkheim thought, its object of study must be the mind of society, not of the individual. This mind, the consciousness of the collectivity, was supposed to have emergent properties of its own, in no way reducible to the given properties of individuals as inscribed in human nature. But it was not until the concluding chapter of his greatest work, *The Elementary Forms of the Religious Life*, that Durkheim explicitly spelled out the relation between the consciousness of the individual and that of the collectivity – 'the highest form of the psychic life' (1976[1915]: 444). He did so in terms of a thoroughgoing distinction between sensation and representation.

The distinction was made on two grounds. The first lies in the contrast between the ephemerality of sensations and the durability of representations. Every sensation, Durkheim argued, is tied to a particular moment that will never recur, for even if – at a subsequent point in time – the thing perceived has not changed, the perceiver will no longer be the same. We are nevertheless able to represent our experience, and so to know what we have perceived, by catching perceptual images that would otherwise float by on the stream of consciousness within the mesh of a system of concepts which remains somehow aloof from this sensory agitation (in a 'different portion of the mind', Durkheim suggested, which is more calm and serene). Like language, which is the medium in which concepts are expressed ('for every word translates a concept'), the conceptual system has a kind of stability: it endures, whilst the stream of consciousness flows on (Durkheim 1976[1915]: 433).

Second, whereas sensations are private and individual, representations are public and social. Since sensations consist in the reactions of the organism to particular external stimuli, there is no way in which a sensation can be made to pass directly from one individual consciousness to another. If people are to share their experiences they must talk about them, and to do that these experiences must be represented by means of concepts, which in turn may be expressed in words whose meanings are established within a community of speakers by verbal convention. Thus collective representations serve as a kind of bridge between individual consciousnesses that are otherwise closed to each other, furnishing them with a means of mutual understanding: 'the concept is an essentially impersonal representation; it is through it that human intelligences communicate' (Durkheim 1976[1915]: 433–4).

Following Durkheim's lead, British social anthropologists carried on with the comparative study of collective representations – otherwise known as 'social structures' – without paying much attention to the psychological premises on which such study rested. Fifty years later, two of the most influential social anthropologists of the day, Edmund Leach and Mary Douglas, could still pose the problem of perception and cognition in very much the same terms. Given that the world of our immediate, sensory experience is a formless and continuous flux in which nothing is the same from one moment to the next, how can we know what we perceive? To recognise specific objects and events in the external world, Leach claimed, the flux has to be cut up into bounded chunks. Thus thought fragments the continuum of life as it is lived, and the diversity of culture lies precisely in the manifold ways in which the continuum can be cut. Leach's first explicit statement of this theory of perception and cognition was presented in an article on 'Anthropological aspects of language', published in 1964. Here he argued that the categories of language provide the 'discriminating grid' which, laid over the continuous substrate of raw experience, enables the speaker to tell one thing from another, and so to see the world 'as being composed of a large number of separate things, each labelled with a name' (1964: 34). As the child learns its mother-tongue, thereby taking on board a conventional system of named categories, so its environment literally takes shape before its very eyes.

Two years later, Mary Douglas published her seminal study, *Purity and Danger*. Here, too, we find the same basic idea: that in perception the world is constructed to a certain order, through the imposition of culturally transmitted form upon the flux of experience.

> As perceivers we select from all the stimuli falling on our senses only those that interest us, and our interests are governed by a pattern-making tendency ... In a chaos of shifting impressions, each of us constructs a world in which objects have recognisable shapes, are located in depth, and have permanence.
>
> (1966: 36)

As with Leach, the roots of Douglas's thinking lie in Durkheim's theory of knowledge. This theory, as we have seen, effectively divides the human subject into two mutually exclusive parts. One part, fully immersed in the sensate, physical world, is continually bombarded by stimuli which are registered in consciousness as a 'chaos of shifting impressions'. The other part, however, stands aside from this engagement, and is untouched by it. Here are located the conceptual categories that sort the sensory input, discarding or suppressing some elements of it while fitting the remainder into a pre-existing, socially approved schema. Crucially, then, perception is a two-stage phenomenon: the first involves the receipt, by the individual human organism, of ephemeral and meaningless sense data; the second consists in the organisation of these data into collectively held and enduring representations.

CULTURAL ANTHROPOLOGY

The rigid distinction between social and psychological phenomena that British social anthropology took from Durkheim was not matched by the parallel, North American tradition of cultural anthropology. The founder of this latter tradition, Franz Boas, consistently adopted the position that the patterned integration of culture, as a system of habits, beliefs and dispositions, is achieved on the level of the individual rather than having its source in some overarching collectivity, and is therefore essentially psychological in nature. Accordingly, American cultural anthropologists of the mid-twentieth century paid a great deal of attention to the way in which the individual personality is fashioned out of the cultural materials available to it. Yet the outcome was a view of perception and cognition not greatly different from that espoused by British writers. Already in the writings of Kluckhohn (1949: 32) and Kroeber and Kluckhohn (1952: 114) we find a stress on culture as an internalised system of rules and meanings *as distinct* from manifest patterns of behaviour and their products (such as artefacts). And in 1957, Ward Goodenough pronounced that 'A society's culture consists in whatever it is one has to know or believe in order to operate in a manner acceptable to its members' (cited in D'Andrade 1984: 89). This view of culture, as knowledge rather than manifest behaviour, was taken considerably further in an influential article by Clifford Geertz, originally published in 1966, on 'The impact of the concept of culture on the concept of man' (Geertz 1973: 33–54).

Culture, Geertz argued, 'is best seen not as complexes of concrete behaviour patterns – customs, usages, traditions, habit clusters – . . . but as a set of control mechanisms – plans, recipes, rules, instructions (what computer engineers call "programs") – for the governing of behaviour'. These control mechanisms, however, are not to be found locked up inside the heads of individuals. Their domain is the public and intersubjective space of social interaction – 'the house yard, the marketplace, and the town square' – whence they are 'used to impose meaning upon experience' (1973: 44–5). For any one individual, the range of symbolic meanings which can be drawn upon is more or less given by what is current in the community into which he or she is born. But without the guidance provided by cultural symbols, human beings would be hopelessly lost, unable to establish their bearings in the world – for unlike other creatures whose activities are more closely controlled by innate response mechanisms, humans depend on a substantial input of additional information, learned rather than innate, in order to function adequately in their normal environments. 'Undirected by culture patterns – organized systems of significant symbols – man's behaviour would be virtually ungovernable, a mere chaos of pointless acts and exploding emotions, his experience virtually shapeless' (Geertz 1973: 46).

Despite their different intellectual backgrounds, in American cultural anthropology and British social anthropology respectively, Geertz and Douglas came up with strikingly similar conclusions. At root, the similarity lies in the assumption that culture consists in a framework of symbolic meanings, common to a community and relatively impervious to the passage of time and generations, which gives shape to the raw material of experience, and direction to human feeling and action. People, in short, are supposed to construct the world, or what for them is 'reality', by organising the data of sensory perception in terms of received and culturally specific conceptual schemata (Berger and Luckmann 1966). And to return to our original question: if two individuals from different backgrounds, placed in the same environment, perceive different 'realities', the reason would be that in their construction, each has brought a different cultural schema to bear in organising the same material of sensation. Granted, then, that every community has its own particular system for the cognitive organisation of experience, anthropological attention naturally came to focus on cultural variation in the organisational principles involved. The result was the emergence, in the late 1960s, of a field of enquiry known rather generally as 'cognitive anthropology', though in a narrower and more restricted form as 'ethnoscience' (Tyler 1969).

COGNITIVE ANTHROPOLOGY

The problem for the cognitive anthropologist, Tyler explains, 'is to discover how other people create order out of what appears to him to be utter chaos' (1969: 6). They do so, it is supposed, by grouping the infinitely variable phenomena of the experienced world into a finite set of named, hierarchically ordered classes. This is done by attending only to those perceptual cues that differentiate things as belonging to one class rather than another, while ignoring those that would indicate the uniqueness of every member of a class. But the ordering principles that govern this process of selective attention are given in the mind, not in the world: 'there is nothing', Tyler asserts, 'in the external world which demands that certain things go together and others do not' (1969: 7). In other words, the principles of classification are arbitrary and subjective with regard to the world whose phenomena are to be classified. They are to be discovered through the formal analysis of responses provided by native informants to a series of questions of the form 'is this thing here a kind of X?', 'what other kinds of X are there?', 'is X a kind of Y?', and so on, all of which are designed by the investigator to elicit precisely the distinctions he or she is looking for.

Despite early promise, the project of cognitive anthropology soon ran into difficulties. An enormous amount of effort was put into mapping out rather limited semantic domains – for example of kinship terms, plant and animal taxonomies or colour classifications – without bringing any comparable advance in understanding how people actually negotiate their relationships with one another, and with their non-human environments, in the usual course of everyday life. It became apparent that the key to such negotiation lay in a certain flexibility in the use of concepts and a sensitivity to context that was disregarded by formal semantic analysis. The neatly ordered paradigms and taxonomies yielded by this method of analysis seemed to be artefacts of the anthropologists' techniques of controlled elicitation rather than having any counterpart in the cognitive organisation of the people studied. The special-ised tasks of naming and discrimination that the latter were expected to perform were not, after all, ones that they would have ordinarily encountered. Indeed the ability to name things correctly is but a small and relatively insignificant part of what a person needs to know in order to get by in the world, so that the greater part of cultural knowledge had still to be uncovered. Above all, cognitive anthropology was unable to grasp the source of human motives: one learned no more from an analysis, say, of kinship terminology about people's feelings for one another than one might learn from a grammar of a language about why its speakers say the things they do.

In recent years, and partly in response to these objections, cognitive anthropology has resurfaced in a new guise, as the investigation of what are now called 'cultural models'. Introducing a seminal volume of essays on *Cultural Models in Language and Thought*, Quinn and Holland define such models as 'presupposed, taken-for-granted models of the world that are widely shared . . . by the members of a society and that play an enormous role in their understanding of that world and their behaviour in it' (1987: 4). They differ from the classificatory schemas identified by earlier cognitive anthropologists in three major ways. First, rather than dividing up the continuum of experience into named categories, cultural models offer a description of the world framed in terms of networks of interconnected images or propositions, in which objects, events and situations take on regular, prototypical forms. Actual experience in the real world is then organised by matching it to the prototypical scenarios built into the simplified worlds of the cultural models, and these, in turn, furnish conventional guidelines for action. Second, although linguistic data provide important clues to underlying cultural knowledge, it cannot be assumed that word meanings stand for components of the cultural model in a simple relation of one-to-one correspondence. The relation is rather complex and indirect, and can only be grasped through an analysis of the richly textured material of ordinary discourse. Third, cultural models – to the extent that they are fully internalised – do not merely describe or represent the world, they also shape people's feelings and desires. That is to say, they can have 'motivational force' (D'Andrade 1992: 28). As Strauss argues, in her introduction to a recent volume dedicated to the demonstration of this point, the realm of cognition is inseparable from the realm of affect; thus cultural models should be understood as 'learned, internalised patterns of thought-feeling' (Strauss 1992: 3).

Despite these fairly radical revisions, the programme of cognitive anthropology remains basically unchanged. Starting from the premiss that culture consists in a corpus of intergenerationally transmissible knowledge, as distinct from the ways in which it is put to use in practical contexts of perception and action, the objective is to discover how this knowledge is organised. Moreover the assumptions on which the programme rests are much as they were in Durkheim's day. They are that cognition consists of a process of matching sensory experience to stable conceptual schemata, that much if not all of the order that people claim to perceive in the world – and especially the social world – is imposed by the mind rather than given in experience, that people are able to understand one another to the extent that their cultural orderings are founded on consensus (such that the limits of consensus define the boundaries of society), and that the acquisition of such orderings involves a process of internalisation. These assumptions have not, however, gone unchallenged – indeed there is a powerful movement within contemporary anthropology that would reject them altogether. One of the most influential figures in this movement has been Pierre Bourdieu, who in a series of works has attempted to show how cultural knowledge, rather than being imported by the mind into contexts of experience, is itself generated within these contexts in the course of people's involvement with others in the practical business of life. Through such involvement, people acquire the specific dispositions and sensibilities that lead them to orient themselves in relation to their environment and to attend to its features in the particular ways that they do. These dispositions and sensibilities add up to what Bourdieu calls the *habitus* (1990: 52–65).[1]

THE THEORY OF PRACTICE

Like the 'cultural model' of cognitive anthropology, the *habitus* of Bourdieu's theory of practice could be described as a pattern of thought-feeling. The similarity ends there, however. For thinking and feeling, in Bourdieu's account, do not go on in an interior subjective (or intersubjective) space of images and representations but in the space of people's actual engagement in the settings of practical activity. Whereas cultural models are supposed to exist independently of, and prior to, their application in particular situations of use – such as in doing things or making things, or in the interpretation of experience – the *habitus* exists only as it is instantiated in the activity itself. In other words, the *habitus* is not expressed in practice, it rather *subsists in it*. What Bourdieu has in mind is the kind of practical mastery that we associate with skill – a mastery that we carry in our bodies and that is refractory to formulation in terms of any system of mental rules and representations. Such skill is acquired not through formal instruction, but by routinely carrying out specific tasks involving characteristic postures and gestures, or what Bourdieu calls a particular body *hexis*. 'A way of walking, a tilt of the head, facial expressions, ways of sitting and of using implements' – all of these, and more, comprise what it takes to be an accomplished practitioner, and together they furnish a person with his or her bearings in the world (Bourdieu 1977: 87). And if people from different backgrounds orient themselves in different ways, this is not because they are interpreting the same sensory experience in terms of alternative cultural models or cognitive schemata, but because, due to their previous bodily training, their senses are differentially attuned to the environment.

In the anthropological study of cognition this kind of approach is perhaps best represented in the work of Jean Lave. Her recent book, *Cognition in Practice* (1988), is a manifesto for an 'outdoor psychology' – that is, a psychology that would take as its unit of analysis 'the whole person in action, acting within the settings of that activity' (1988: 17). Cognition, in Lave's view, is not a process that goes on 'inside the head', whose products are representations that bear some complex relation to the world outside, but rather a social activity that is situated in the nexus of ongoing relations between persons and the world, and that plays its part in their mutual constitution. It is a process wherein both persons, as knowledgeable social agents, and the settings in which they act, continually come into being, each in relation to the other. Thus thinking is inseparable from doing, thought is 'embodied and enacted', and cognition is 'seamlessly distributed across persons, activity and setting' (1988: 171). To study cognition is to focus on the *modus operandi* not of the mind, in organising the bodily data of sense, but of the whole body-person – conceived as an undivided centre of agency and awareness – in the business of dwelling in the world.

The implications of this approach for the concept of culture, as conventionally understood in cognitive studies, are profound. According to this conventional understanding, culture consists in an ever-accumulating stock of knowledge – or what D'Andrade (1981: 179) calls '"pass it along" type information' – which is available for transmission, in symbolically encoded form, independently of the practical contexts of its application. Lave repudiates the view that cultural knowledge exists in such a context-free form, and with it the orthodox account of learning as a process of internalisation involving the literal transplantation of information from one mind to another (1988: 7–9). For although the novice of course listens to what other people say and watches what they do, words and deeds do not carry meaning into contexts of interaction but rather gather their meanings from the settings in which they are 'in play'. Thus what each generation contributes to the next are the specific contexts of development in which successors, growing up in a social world, acquire their own embodied skills and dispositions. And if knowledge is shared it is because people work together, through their joint immersion in the settings of activity, in the process of its formation.

What, then, becomes of the models and schemata of the cognitive anthropologists? Are they merely artefacts of analytic abstraction, products of attempts by anthropological observers to represent manifest behaviour as the output of formal programmes? Or do they, to the contrary, offer clues to basic truths about the way the human mind works? The answers to these questions hinge on more fundamental differences of approach which divide psychologists as much as anthropologists. Roughly speaking, the division is between advocates of cognitive science on the one hand, and their critics on the other, who find inspiration in an ecological or phenomenological perspective on perception and cognition. These differences of approach, and some of their implications for anthropology, are reviewed in the next part of this chapter.

II
COGNITIVE SCIENCE

In the field of psychology, cognitive science emerged as an alternative to behaviourism in the 1950s, alongside the development of the digital computer. Its founding axioms are that people come to know what is 'out there' in the world by representing it in the mind, in the form of 'mental models', and that such representations are the result of a computational process working upon information received by the senses. The functioning of the mind, then, can be compared to the operation of a computer programme, and the relation between mind and brain to that between the programme and the 'hardware' in which it is installed (Johnson-Laird 1988). But the computing analogy also found its way into cognitive anthropology – I have already referred to Geertz's (1973: 44) likening of cultural control mechanisms to computer software – where it was similarly supposed that the mind is equipped with programmes that construct internal representations of the environment from the data of sensation, and deliver appropriate plans for action (D'Andrade 1984: 88–9). Whereas cognitive scientists, however, have by and large been concerned to discover universals of human cognition, which are attributed to innate structures established in the course of evolution under natural selection, cognitive anthropologists have sought to account for human perception and action in terms of acquired schemata or programmes that differ from one culture to another.

How, then, should we view the relation between these two projects? Are they contradictory or mutually compatible? D'Andrade (1981: 181–2) tackles this question by considering the fit between *programmes* and *processors*. By programmes he means the informational content of transmitted culture – what is 'passed along' from generation to generation. By processors he means the apparatus of acquisition that makes such transmission possible, an apparatus that is assumed to be common to all human minds. According to this division, cognitive anthropology is concerned with the diversity of cultural content, and with the way in which its organisation is constrained by invariant properties of the processing devices that govern its acquisition, while cognitive psychology is concerned with the structure and functioning of the devices themselves, and the way in which they work on all kinds of information (including cultural information). This formulation, however, obscures a critical difficulty. For if mental representations are the products of a processing of information by acquired cultural programmes, and if the latter are in turn products of a processing apparatus that is already in place prior to the acquisition of culture, then whence came the programmes that specify the structure and operation of the apparatus itself? As Johnson-Laird points out, 'programs cannot be constructed out of thin air . . . . A program that learns may itself have been learned – you can learn to learn, but then that learning would depend on another program, and so on. Ultimately, learning must depend on innate programs that make programs' (1988: 133). In short, any theory which supposes that all human cognition is grounded in culturally specific schemata must also presuppose that human beings come universally pre-equipped with the structures necessary to enable these schemata to be acquired in the first place.

This is precisely the conclusion reached by Sperber (1985), in the context of his critique of cultural relativism – the doctrine, long ascendant in anthropology, that people in different cultures inhabit different cognitive (or rather, cognisable) worlds, each with its own criteria of rationality and judgement. Relativists argue that just as every non-human animal species, depending on its evolved cognitive organisation, can only know the world in its own particular way, so also every human culture is locked into the cognitive framework of a unique worldview. But whereas species differences have a genetic basis, cultural differences are assumed to be entirely independent of genetic constraint. Thus cultural relativists tend to suppose that theirs is a position opposed to an innatist view of the human mind, and that evidence for the diversity of incommensurate worldviews only goes to prove that the underlying structures of human cognition are genetically underdetermined and malleable to the effects of experience.

Yet in this, Sperber shows, they are mistaken. Relativists, he contends, have failed to attend to the psychological implications of their assumption that human behaviour is rooted in tradition rather than heredity. Had they done so, they would have realised that a creature capable of taking on not just one form of life but *any one* of a very large number of possible alternative forms would require more rather than less by way of innate programming. On the basis of a formal logical argument, Sperber concludes that 'the greater the diversity of the cultures that humans are capable of acquiring, the greater the complexity of the innate learning abilities involved' (1985: 43). Thus the relativists' appeal to human cultural diversity is not at all contrary to the universalist claims of cognitive science; rather it depends upon them.

Though the logic of Sperber's argument may be impeccable, it rests on a foundation that is far from secure – namely, that cultural knowledge takes the propositional (or semi-propositional) form of *beliefs*, 'representations acquired through social communication and accepted on the ground of social affiliation' (1985: 59). Underlying the commonsense understanding of the culturally competent actor is supposed to lie a huge database of such representations, which provide all the information necessary to generate appropriate responses under any given environmental circumstances. Yet as many critics of cognitive science have pointed out, and as the failure of attempts to replicate human skills in the design of expert systems has amply demonstrated (Dreyfus and Dreyfus 1987), even the simplest and most routine of everyday tasks are refractory to codification in propositional form. By and large, these tasks are not represented (save in the notebooks of observers), nor are such representations communicated in learning situations. Most cultural learning takes place through trial-and-error and practice, albeit in socially structured situations, and although beginners may need to follow rules, these rules structure the situation of learning and do not themselves form any part of the content of what is learned. For the skilled practitioner consults the world, rather than representations (rules, propositions, beliefs) inside his or her head, for guidance on what to do next. As Chapman (1991: 20) puts it: 'If you want to find out something about the world that will affect how you should act, you usually just look and see . . . . You don't need to maintain a world model; the world is its own best representation.'

Faced with the evident artificiality of depicting cultural knowledge in algorithmised form as a set of programmes, acquired by means of a processing device that is somehow constituted in advance of ontogenetic development, cognitive science has come up with an alternative model of the way the mind works. Instead of positing one giant processor with a massive capacity for information storage and retrieval, it is suggested that the mind consists of a very large number of small, simple processors, massively interconnected, all operating in parallel, and receiving inputs and delivering outputs to each other along the countless pathways linking them. Crucially, a system so constituted can learn from experience, not by taking on new informational content, but by adjustments to the differential strengths of the connections among processing units. In other words, knowledge is acquired through the establishment of particular patterns of connection: any processor may therefore be involved in the representation of diverse experiences; conversely the representation of any experience may be distributed across many processors (Johnson-Laird 1988: 174). This so-called 'connectionist' model of the mind has a certain anthropological appeal – thus cognitive anthropologists such as D'Andrade (1990: 98–9) have noted that the proper-ties of cultural models are precisely what would be expected from the operation of parallel processing networks, while Bloch (1991) has recently suggested that the acquisition of practical skills may best be understood in terms of the development of tightly connected networks dedicated to particu-lar domains of cognition.

Despite its greater realism, connectionism remains open to much the same criticisms that have been levelled against earlier versions of artificial intelligence (Dreyfus 1992). For ultimately, it is still grounded in the Cartesian ontology that is basic to the entire project of cognitive science – an ontology that divorces the activity of the mind from that of the body in the world, as though the latter were no more than a recipient of information to be 'processed' by the former and played no part in cognition itself. Indeed as Reed (1987: 144–5) has pointed out, modern cognitive psychology does not dispute the founding assumptions of the behaviourist theory that it claims to have overthrown, namely that perception is based on discrete bodily sensations touched off by external stimuli, and that action is based on the corresponding bodily responses. The objection to behaviourism was that, as a theory, it was incomplete: the simple linkage of stimulus and response was considered insufficient to account for the knowledgeability of actors or the productivity of their actions. To complete the picture, cognitive scientists posited a mental processing device that would convert the stimulus input into knowledge, and generate plans for the delivery of meaningful responses.

There is, however, another way out of behaviourism, and this is to treat the perceiving organism not as a passive recipient of stimuli but as an active agent who purposively seeks out information that would specify the meaningful properties of his or her environment. This was the path taken by James Gibson in his pioneering studies of visual perception, and in doing so he laid the foundations for an approach, known as 'ecological psychology', which is radically opposed, in almost every respect, to the project of cognitive science.

ECOLOGICAL PSYCHOLOGY

The point of departure for ecological psychology is the proposition that perceptual activity consists not in the operation of the mind upon the bodily data of sense, but in the intentional movement of the whole being (indissolubly body and mind) in its environment. The emphasis on movement is critical. Cognitive science assumes a static perceiver who has nothing to go on but transient patterns of sensory excitation that are, in themselves, quite insufficient to specify the objects and events that gave rise to them. Thus the problem of perception, for the cognitive scientist, is to show how these ephemeral and fragmentary sense data are reconstructed, in terms of pre-existing schemata or representations, into a coherent picture of the world. But for Gibson, sensations do not, as such, constitute the data for perception (Gibson 1979: 55). Rather, what the perceiver looks for are constancies underlying the continuous modulations of the sensory array as one moves from place to place. In visual perception, for example, we do not see patterns of light but objects in our environment. We do so because, as we move about, the pattern of light reaching the eyes from reflecting surfaces in the environment (that is, the 'optic array') undergoes a gradual transformation. It is the invariants that underlie this transformation, and not the momentary patterns of stimulation themselves, that specify what we see. Indeed it is Gibson's contention that the invariant relations that structure the modulations of an optic array for a moving observer contain all the information necessary to specify the environment. Perception, then, is a matter of extracting these invariants. The perceiver has no need to reconstruct the world in the mind if it can be accessed directly in this way.

Certain implications follow. First, if perception entails movement, then it must be a mode of action rather than a prerequisite for action. For Gibson, perception is an active and exploratory process of information pickup; far from working on sensations already received, it involves the continual movement, adjustment and reorientation of the receptor organs themselves. What is important, he argues, 'is the looking, listening, touching and sniffing that goes on when the perceptual systems are at work' (1982[1976]: 397–8). Second, if perception is a mode of action, then what we perceive must be a direct function of how we act. Depending on the kind of activity in which we are engaged, we will be attuned to picking up particular kinds of information. The knowledge obtained through direct perception is thus *practical*, it is knowledge about what an environment offers for the pursuance of the action in which the perceiver is currently engaged. In other words, to perceive an object or event is to perceive what it *affords*. Perhaps the most fundamental contribution of Gibson's approach to perception lay in his insight that the information picked up by an agent in the context of practical activity specifies what are called the 'affordances' of objects and events in the environment (Gibson 1979: 127–43).

Third, the information that is potentially available to an agent is inexhaustible: there is no limit to what can be perceived. Throughout life one can keep on seeing new things in an otherwise permanent world, not by constructing the same sense data according to novel conceptual schemata, but by a sensitisation or 'fine-tuning' of the perceptual system to new kinds of information. Novel perceptions arise from creative acts of discovery rather than imagining, and the information on which they are based is available to anyone attuned to pick it up. Finally, and following from the above, one learns to perceive in the manner appropriate to a culture, not by acquiring programmes or conceptual schemata for organising sensory data into higher-order representations, but by 'hands-on' training in everyday tasks whose successful fulfilment requires a practised ability to notice and to respond fluently to salient aspects of the environment. In short, learning is not a transmission of information but – in Gibson's (1979: 254) words – an 'education of attention'. As such, it is inseparable from a person's life in the world, and indeed continues for as long as he or she lives.

There are clear parallels between the ecological critique, in the field of psychology, of cognitive science and the critique by 'practice theorists' of cognitive anthropology, which I reviewed in the first part of this chapter. Both Gibson's ecological psychology and Bourdieu's theory of practice set out to re-embed perception and cognition within the practical contexts of people's ongoing engagement with their environments in the ordinary course of life. And both seek to escape from the sterile Cartesian dualisms of mind and nature, subject and object, intellection and sensation, and so on. Yet while the impact of Bourdieu's work in social and cultural anthropology has been immense, the relevance of Gibsonian ecological psychology to anthropological theory has been little explored. An obvious reason for the discrepancy lies in the fact that Gibson himself devoted scant attention to the specifically social and cultural dimensions of human life, preferring – if anything – to downplay the significance of the distinction between human beings and other animals. In developing his theory of affordances, Gibson did devote a brief section to 'other persons and animals' in the environment of the perceiver, noting that they have the peculiar capacity to 'act back' or, literally, to *interact* with the perceiver. Thus 'behavior affords behavior, and the whole subject matter of psychology and of the social sciences can be thought of as an elaboration of this basic fact' (Gibson 1979: 135). But beyond suggesting that the perception of mutual affordances in social life involves the same principles of information pickup as are involved in the perception of inanimate objects, Gibson did not pursue further the implications of this rather sweeping statement.

A recent attempt to develop this neglected aspect of the Gibsonian programme has been made by Reed (1988). The crux of his argument is that social agents can not only directly perceive their mutual affordances for one another, but can also *share* their direct perception of other constituents of the environment. Attuned through prior training and experience to attending to similar invariants, and moving in the same environment in the pursuit of joint activities, they will pick up the same information (Reed 1988: 119–20, see Gibson 1982[1967]: 412). Thus, contrary to the axioms of cognitive anthropology, the awareness of living in a common world – the communion of experience that lies at the heart of sociality – does not depend on the organisation of sensory data, initially private to each perceiver, in terms of an objective system of collective representations. Rather, sociality is given from the start, *prior* to the objectification of experience in cultural categories – or in Bourdieu's (1977: 2) phrase, 'on the hither side of words or concepts', in the direct, perceptual involvement of fellow participants in a shared environment (Ingold 1993: 222–3). This, indeed, is what makes anthropological fieldwork possible, for it allows the fieldworker and local people to inhabit a common ground of experience, even though each may bring to bear a radically different conceptual frame to the task of its interpretation. As Jackson notes, 'by using one's body in the same way as others in the same environment one finds oneself informed by an understanding which may then be interpreted according to one's own custom or bent, yet which remains grounded in a field of practical activity and thereby remains consonant with the experience of those among whom one has lived' (1989: 135).

The environment of joint practical activity should not, however, be confused with the physical world of 'nature' (Gibson 1979: 8). For the world can appear in this latter guise only to a creature that can disengage itself – or imagine itself to be disengaged – from the processes of its own material life. But the world we inhabit does not confront us, it surrounds us. This does not mean that it is any less real; the environment, however, is reality constituted in *relation* to the beings whose environment it is. As I have argued elsewhere (Ingold 1992), Gibsonian psychology offers a way of thinking about human–environmental relations that dispenses with the conventional dichotomy between naturally given and culturally constructed worlds. According to convention, it is necessary to distinguish between the 'real' environment, as it is presented to detached, scientific observation, and the 'perceived' environment as it is built up through a selective response to stimuli (Brookfield 1969: 53). In anthropology, the distinction is commonly expressed by means of a contrast between the 'etic' level of objective description and the 'emic' level on which the environment is made meaningful by cultural subjects.[2] Yet from a Gibsonian perspective, it is apparent that the world becomes a meaningful place for people through being *lived in*, rather than through having been constructed along the lines of some formal design. Meanings are not attached by the mind to objects in the world, rather these objects take on their significance – or in Gibson's terms, they afford what they do – by virtue of their incorporation into a characteristic pattern of day-to-day activities. In short, far from being inscribed upon the bedrock of physical reality, meaning is immanent in the relational contexts of people's practical engagement with their lived-in environments.

PHENOMENOLOGY

It is at this point that ecological psychology makes contact with an older, Continental European tradition of philosophical enquiry, broadly characterised as phenomenological, and represented above all in the works of Heidegger and Merleau-Ponty. Just as the point of departure, for Gibson, had been the perceiver-in-his/her-environment, so likewise these philosophers set out from the premiss that every person is, before all else, a being-in-the-world. And their intellectual agenda, like that of Gibson, was fundamentally antagonistic to the kind of rationalism whose contemporary manifestation, in the field of psychology, is cognitive science. Yet in some ways they went even further. For all his emphasis on perception as a process that is continually going on, Gibson assumed that the world which the perceiver moves around in and explores is relatively fixed and permanent, somehow pre-prepared with all its affordances ready and waiting to be taken up by whatever creatures arrive to inhabit it. From a phenomenological standpoint, by contrast, the world emerges with its properties alongside the emergence of the perceiver in person, against the background of involved activity. Since the person is a being-in-the-world, the coming-into-being of the person is part and parcel of the process of coming-into-being of the world.

Consider, for example, Heidegger's critique of Cartesianism (reviewed in Dreyfus 1991: 109–27). Heidegger begins by distinguishing two ways in which the world may 'show up' to a being who is active within it: availableness and occurrentness. The former is evident in our everyday use of the most familiar things around us, which, absorbed into the current of our activity (as indeed, we are ourselves), become in a sense transparent, wholly subordinate to the 'in-order-to' of the task at hand. The latter refers to the way in which things are revealed in their essential nature to an observer who self-consciously stands back from the action, assuming a stance of con- templative detachment or disinterested reflection. Now Cartesian ontology, which takes as its starting point the self-contained subject confronting a domain of isolable objects, assumes that things are initially encountered in their pure occurrentness, or brute facticity. The perceiver has first to make sense of these occurrent entities – to render them intelligible – by categorising them, and assigning to them meanings or functions, before they can be made available for use. Heidegger, however, reverses this order of priority. For a being whose primary condition of existence is that of dwelling in the world, things are initially encountered in their availableness, as already integrated into a set of practices for 'coping' or getting by. To reveal their occurrent properties, things have to be rendered *un*intelligible by stripping away the significance they derive from contexts of ordinary use. This, of course, is the explicit project of natural science, which seeks to describe and explain a world which the rest of us are preoccupied with living in. Yet the scientist, like everyone else, is a being-in-the-world, and scientific practice, as any other skilled activity, draws unselfconsciously upon the available. Thus even science, however detached and theoretical it may be, takes place against a background of involved activity. The total disengagement of the subject from the world, from which Cartesianism charts a process of building up from the occurrent to the available, is therefore a pure fiction which can only be reached by extrapolating to the point of absurdity a progressive reduction from the available to the occurrent.

If, as Heidegger seems to suggest, self and world merge in the activity of dwelling, so that one cannot say where one ends and the other begins, it surely follows that the intentional presence of the perceiving agent, as a being-in- the-world, must also be an *embodied* presence. This was the principal contention of Merleau-Ponty in his massive treatise, dating from 1945, on the *Phenomenology of Perception*. 'The body', Merleau-Ponty wrote, 'is the vehicle of being in the world, and having a body is, for a living creature, to be involved in a definite environment, to identify oneself with certain projects and be continually committed to them' (1962: 82). Like Heidegger, Merleau- Ponty was concerned to reverse the ontological priorities of Cartesian rationalism. Just as for Heidegger, the available is the ground upon which we may seek to reveal the properties of the occurrent, so for Merleau-Ponty our knowledge of the body as a physical thing – as a mere conduit or target of the mind's attention – is grounded in a more fundamental awareness, pre- objective and pre-conscious, which is given by the existential condition of our total bodily immersion, from the start, in an environment. Only because we are thus immersed in the world can we imagine ourselves as existing separately from it. The problem of perception lies in understanding the nature of this immediate pre-objective experience, itself a precondition for objective thought. Accordingly, Merleau-Ponty sought to uncover 'underneath the objective and detached knowledge of the body that other knowledge which we have of it by virtue of its always being with us and of the fact that *we are our body*' (1962: 206; my emphasis). In this latter sense, the body is neither object nor instrument, it is rather the *subject* of perception.

In recent years, albeit somewhat belatedly, many anthropologists have begun to read Merleau-Ponty with renewed interest. Though there is nothing particularly novel about anthropological concerns with the body and its symbolism, much work in this field is marked by a tendency to treat body praxis as a mere vehicle for the outward expression of meanings issuing from a superior source in culture or society. This is true, for example, of the writings of Mary Douglas. In line with her general thesis, reviewed in the first part of this chapter, of the cultural construction of experience, Douglas holds that the body is a medium whose forms – whether adopted in movement or repose – 'express social pressures in manifold ways' (1970: 93). As Michael Jackson has eloquently shown, this 'subjugation of the bodily to the semantic' diminishes the body and its experience in two ways. First, body movements – postures and gestures – are reduced to the status of signs which direct the analyst in search of what they stand for, namely *extra*-somatic cultural meanings. Second, the body is rendered passive and inert, while the active role of mobilising it, putting it to use and charging it with significance, is delegated to a knowing subject which is both detached from the body and reified as 'society' (Jackson 1989: 122–3). The first reduction fails to recognise that gestures, whatever they might be held to symbolise, delineate their own meanings through their embeddedness in social and material contexts of action. As Merleau-Ponty notes, your angry gesture '*does not make me think* of anger, it is anger itself' (1962: 184; original emphasis). The second reduction ignores a consideration that is absolutely pivotal to Merleau-Ponty's phenomenology: that the body is given in movement, and that bodily movement carries its own immanent intentionality. Indeed it is because of this intentionality that the subject's action is, at one and the same time, a movement of perception (1962: 110–11).[3]

Drawing inspiration from Merleau-Ponty, Jackson (1989) calls for studies that would take as their focus the 'body subject' in its dealings with the world. In similar vein, and linking Merleau-Ponty's concerns with perception to Bourdieu's with practice, Csordas (1990) puts the case for the establishment of a 'paradigm of embodiment' in anthropological enquiry. Far from treating the body as an *object* of study, this paradigm would be launched from the postulate that 'the body is to be considered as the *subject* of culture, or in other words as the existential (as opposed to the cognitive) ground of culture' (1990: 5). In its promise to collapse the Cartesian dualities between mind and body, subject and object, the paradigm holds a certain appeal for many anthropologists whose familiarity with indigenous, non-Western understandings – which are not generally concordant with such dualities –

predisposes them to adopt a critical attitude towards the foundational assumptions of Western thought and science. Not everyone has been won over, however, as is evident from the continuing strength of cognitive anthropology, and from the pronouncements of anthropologists such as D'Andrade, Sperber and Bloch who see a role for anthropology in an interdisciplinary alliance with cognitive science. Moreover there remain two major obstacles to the further development of the phenomenological approach.

The first has to do with the problematic status of biology. Even anthropologists who would readily accept the idea of embodiment as a paradigm for the study of culture, and who denounce the mind/body distinction, tend to balk at attempts to soften the conventional dichotomy between culture and biology (e.g. Csordas 1990: 36). Yet it is difficult to see how the 'body subject' can be distinguished from the human organism, or the process of embodiment from the development of the organism in its environment, without falling back on a Cartesian subject/object dichotomy. Indeed to posit some kind of biological residuum that exists prior to, and independently of, the culturally constituted body is to resort to the very objectivism that the paradigm of embodiment claims to repudiate. Second, even if it is agreed that a phenomenological approach offers a richer and more 'experience-near' (Geertz 1984: 124) account of human life in the world than do the more formal, 'experience-distant' concepts of cognitive science, the problem remains of translating this approach into a programme of research that would give us a more accurate idea than we presently have of how people routinely succeed, in their everyday, skilful 'coping', in performing with ease actions that are far beyond the capabilities of any machine yet devised. It is easy to pour scorn on the efforts of researchers in artificial intelligence to replicate the processes at work in the human brain, but as Dreyfus admits (1992: xliv), no one knows how the brain does it, nor are philosophers in any way equipped to provide the answers.

What we can say, however, is that the effect of taking the agent-in-an-environment rather than the isolated, self-contained individual as our point of departure is to collapse not only the venerable Durkheimian distinction between the individual and society, but also the division – which has traditionally rested on this distinction – between the two disciplines of anthropology and psychology. As a result, topics previously reserved for psychological study – perception, cognition, emotion, learning, memory, consciousness and the unconscious – have rapidly risen to the top of the anthropological agenda. There is no doubt that the future will bring a radical realignment of anthropology's interface with psychology. And it will come, I predict, not so much from the application of established principles of psychology to the analysis of ethnographic material, as from the application of ethnographic understanding in the delivery of a resounding critique of the foundations of contemporary academic psychology.

NOTES

1 The concept of *habitus* is not original to Bourdieu. It was introduced to anthropology by Marcel Mauss in his study, dating from 1934, of techniques of the body, to refer to the repertoire of culturally patterned postures and gestures to be found in any particular society (Mauss 1979: 101).

2 The contrasting terms are drawn, by analogy, from 'phonetics' and 'phonemics' in linguistics.

3 The affinity, here, between the approaches to perception and action of Merleau-Ponty and Gibson is striking – all the more so because they came from such different intellectual backgrounds. They were one in insisting upon the centrality of movement to visual perception. As Merleau-Ponty asks, rhetorically,

> What would vision be without movement? And how could the movement of the eyes bring things together if the movement were blind? If it were only a reflex? If it did not have its antennae, its clairvoyance? If vision were not prefigured in it?
>
> (1964: 162)

Moreover with Gibson, Merleau-Ponty rejected outright the representation-alistic account of visual perception, of the kind that would treat it as 'an operation of thought that would set up before the mind a picture or a representation of the world' (*loc. cit.*).

Gibson never referred to Merleau-Ponty's work, but there is anecdotal evidence that he had read the *Phenomenology of Perception*, and that he approved of it (Heij and Tamboer, n.d.).

REFERENCES

Berger, P. and Luckmann, T. (1966) *The Social Construction of Reality*, Harmonds-worth: Penguin.

Bloch, M. (1991) 'Language, anthropology and cognitive science', *Man* (N.S.), 26: 183–198.

Bourdieu, P. (1977) *Outline of a Theory of Practice*, Cambridge: Cambridge University Press.

Bourdieu, P. (1990) *The Logic of Practice*, Oxford: Polity Press.

Brookfield, H. C. (1969) 'On the environment as perceived', *Progress in Geography*, 1: 53–80.

Chapman, D. (1991) *Vision, Instruction and Action*, Cambridge, Mass.: MIT Press.

Csordas, T. A. (1990) 'Embodiment as a paradigm for anthropology', *Ethos*, 18: 5–47.

D'Andrade, R. G. (1981) 'The cultural part of cognition', *Cognitive Science*, 5: 179–195.

D'Andrade, R. G. (1984) 'Cultural meaning systems', in R. A. Shweder and R. A. LeVine (eds) *Culture Theory: Essays on mind, self and emotion*, Cambridge: Cambridge University Press.

D'Andrade, R. G. (1990) 'Some propositions about the relations between culture and human cognition', in J. W. Stigler, R. A. Shweder and G. Herdt (eds) *Cultural Psychology: Essays on comparative human development*, Cambridge: Cambridge University Press.

D'Andrade, R. G. (1992) 'Schemas and motivation', in R. G. D'Andrade and C. Strauss (eds) *Human Motives and Cultural Models*, Cambridge: Cambridge University Press.

Douglas, M. (1966) *Purity and Danger*, London: Routledge & Kegan Paul.

Douglas, M. (1970) *Natural Symbols: Explorations in cosmology*, Harmondsworth: Penguin.

Dreyfus, H. L. (1991) *Being-in-the-world: A commentary on Heidegger's Being and Time, Division I*, Cambridge, Mass.: MIT Press.

Dreyfus, H. L. (1992) Introduction to the MIT Press edition, in *What Computers Still Can't Do*, Cambridge, Mass.: MIT Press.

Dreyfus, H. L. and Dreyfus, S. E. (1987) 'The mistaken psychological assumptions underlying the belief in expert systems', in A. Costall and A. Still (eds) *Cognitive Psychology in Question*, Brighton: Harvester Press.

Durkheim, E. (1976) [1915] *The Elementary Forms of the Religious Life*, trans. J. W. Swain, London: Allen & Unwin.

Durkheim, E. (1982) [1895] *The Rules of Sociological Method and Selected Texts on Sociology and its Method*, S. Lukes (ed.), trans. W. D. Halls, London: Macmillan.

Geertz, C. (1973) *The Interpretation of Cultures*, New York: Basic Books.

Geertz, C. (1984) '"From the native's point of view": on the nature of anthropological understanding', in R. A. Shweder and R. A. LeVine (eds) *Culture Theory: Essays on mind, self and emotion*, Cambridge: Cambridge University Press.

Gibson, J. J. (1979) *The Ecological Approach to Visual Perception*, Boston: Houghton Mifflin.

Gibson, J. J. (1982) *Reasons for Realism: Selected essays of James J. Gibson*, E. Reed and R. Jones (eds), Hillsdale, New Jersey: Lawrence Erlbaum.

Heij, P. and Tamboer, J. (n.d.) 'Embodied intentionality: the significance of Merleau-Ponty's embodied intentionality for the foundations of Gibson's ecological psychology', paper presented at the Workshop on Situated Action, International Society for Ecological Psychology, Manchester, UK, 23–24 September 1991.

Ingold, T. (1992) 'Culture and the perception of the environment', in E. Croll and D. Parkin (eds) *Bush Base: Forest Farm. Culture, environment and development*, London: Routledge.

Ingold, T. (1993) 'The art of translation in a continuous world', in G. Pálsson (ed.) *Beyond Boundaries: Understanding, translation and anthropological discourse*, Oxford: Berg.

Jackson, M. (1989) *Paths Toward a Clearing: Radical empiricism and ethnographic inquiry*, Bloomington: Indiana University Press.

Johnson-Laird, D. N. (1988) *The Computer and the Mind: An introduction to cognitive science*, London: Fontana.

Kluckhohn, C. (1949) *Mirror for Man*, New York: McGraw-Hill.

Kroeber, A. L. and Kluckhohn, C. (1952) *Culture: A critical review of concepts and definitions*, papers of the Peabody Museum of American Archaeology and Ethnology, Harvard University, vol. XLVII, no. 1. Cambridge, Mass.

Lave, J. (1988) *Cognition in Practice*, Cambridge: Cambridge University Press.

Leach, E. R. (1964) 'Anthropological aspects of language: animal categories and verbal abuse', in E. H. Lennenberg (ed.) *New Directions in the Study of Language*, Cambridge, Mass.: MIT Press.

Mauss, M. (1979) 'Body techniques', in *Sociology and Psychology: essays by Marcel Mauss*, trans. B. Brewster, London: Routledge & Kegan Paul.

Merleau-Ponty, M. (1962) *Phenomenology of Perception*, London: Routledge & Kegan Paul.

Merleau-Ponty, M. (1964) *The Primacy of Perception, and Other Essays on Phenomenological Psychology, the Philosophy of Art, History and Politics*, Evanston, Illinois: Northwestern University Press.

Quinn, N. and Holland, D. (1987) 'Culture and cognition', in D. Holland and N. Quinn (eds) *Cultural Models in Language and Thought*, Cambridge: Cambridge University Press.

Reed, E. (1987) 'James Gibson's ecological approach to cognition', in A. Costall and A. Still (eds) *Cognitive Psychology in Question*, Brighton: Harvester Press.

Reed, E. (1988) 'The affordances of the animate environment: social science from the ecological point of view', in T. Ingold (ed.) *What is an Animal?*, London: Unwin Hyman.

Sperber, D. (1985) *On Anthropological Knowledge*, Cambridge: Cambridge University Press.

Strauss, C. (1992) 'Models and motives', in R. G. D'Andrade and C. Strauss (eds) *Human Motives and Cultural Models*, Cambridge: Cambridge University Press.

Tyler, S. A. (1969) 'Introduction', in S. A. Tyler (ed.) *Cognitive Anthropology*, New York: Holt, Rinehart & Winston.

Chapter 8

Hanging around and making something of it: ethnography[1]

John Bowers

INTRODUCTION: WHAT IS ETHNOGRAPHY?

Ethnography is an orientation to research which emphasises detailed pro-tracted observation of people in naturally occurring settings, a close involve-ment of the researcher with those researched, and qualitative or interpretative data analysis. Ethnography is in short 'ethno-graphy': people-writing. I shall treat 'participant-observation' as a cognate phrase which is preferred in some research traditions and which emphasises well the dual standing of the researcher with respect to the 'field site': as observer to be sure but also as someone who partakes in the daily life of the field site as well.

So much for definitions, for – like many research orientations – there are almost as many ethnographies as ethnographers. There is a diversity of opinion as to the nature and role of ethnographic research. For some writers, ethnography is essentially a descriptive enterprise geared towards giving richly detailed (or 'thick') descriptions of some culture, social group or activity of interest. For others, ethnography should be inextricably bound up with theory development and testing (Glaser and Strauss 1967), where the terms and character of the theory under development are 'grounded' in detailed and extended observation. Naturally, there are disputes within ethnography about the aims of research, the role of the researcher, the relationship between ethnography and other orientations, whether ethno-graphy can be deemed a 'method' in any strict sense, and so forth. I say 'naturally' because disputes of this sort should characterise any approach to research that is alive and self-reflective. Ethnography is not a 'dead method' nor a 'black box' which can be mechanically applied to yield results.

Accordingly, this chapter cannot introduce its subject matter by offering an 'algorithmic', how-to-do-it, step-by-step guide to ethnography. This seems especially inappropriate as – for some ethnographers – it is precisely the desire to escape these kinds of methodological strictures that makes them ethnographers (rather than experimentalists or survey researchers) in the first place. Ethnography is not a 'technique'.[2] Furthermore, anything I offer will necessarily be a partial view: *a version* of ethnography, its history and practice. However, this is not to say I'll be offering you any old version. What I want to do is to suggest some of the appeal that lies in turning to ethnography and some of the objections that often arise to ethnographic research. Several of these points I shall illustrate with examples taken from my own fieldwork.

I am also conscious of the fact that this chapter appears in a book written with psychologists in mind. This raises some interesting and particular issues because ethnography is a very minor player in that discipline, more marginalised than in sociology for example (where – even so – survey and questionnaire techniques dominate). Accordingly, I want to pay particular attention to the appeal ethnography might have for psychologists and the kinds of worries potential ethnographers from that disciplinary background might have.

Ultimately though, this will lead me to make some remarks about the old methodological squabbles which exist in psychology over the status of the laboratory experiment and its alternatives. However, I shall do this at the *end* of this chapter because it is not always particularly fruitful to *set up* ethnography in an 'either–or' contest in opposition to experimentalism. For one thing, even though ethnography and experimentalism remain quite different research orientations, there are researchers who have attempted to combine the two systematically. Also, I think it is misleading to present ethnography as The Answer to researchers' dissatisfactions with laboratory work. Not only is ethnography itself problematic in its turn, it has its own traditions, its own schools of thought, its own in-fights. All of these might be ignored if we merely set up ethnography as the latest anti-experimentalist fad, appealing though this may be for some psychologists. In methodology there are no easy answers. To believe otherwise suggests a failure of nerve!

THE ORIGINS OF ETHNOGRAPHY, BRIEFLY

Ethnography has its origins in anthropology. Indeed, as has been often pointed out, the ethnographic approach is practically obligatory for anthropologists introducing themselves to people whose language, customs and forms of life are almost wholly unknown and who have no written records available for analysis. To find out about such peoples, one has to (in some sense) *live* with them over a protracted period and attempt to find out about their world *from the inside*. There's scarcely any other option than to be a participant observer![3] While field experimentation has become a method of choice for some anthropologists in recent times, this really only becomes possible through there *already existing* a basic and fundamental acquaintance that anthropologists have of the people under study – an acquaintance founded on maybe over a century of *ethnographic* encounters by earlier researchers.[4] It is hard to imagine how one might find out about a social world *for the first time* by experiment alone.

In sociology, ethnography came to prominence first in the research conducted in the 1920s and 1930s in the Sociology Department of the University of Chicago. While the 'Chicago School' coined the term 'participant observation' to describe their activities (first in Lindeman 1924), the ethnographic concern to study activities and social groups *in vivo*, in naturally occurring settings, over protracted periods of observation is clearly manifested in their various studies of slums, hoboes, gangs, dance halls, rooming house districts, delinquent and immigrant groups and so forth (see inter alia Anderson 1923/1961; Cressey 1932).

As historians of the Chicago School (e.g. Bulmer 1984) often point out, the social changes in metropolises like Chicago itself constituted a major impetus and opportunity for their research. The expansion of Chicago as an industrial and manufacturing centre saw the migration of many thousands to the city both from other parts of America and from abroad. The nature of and the relations between these groups were urgent matters not only for social research but also for public policy. In this context, the Chicago School developed a disdain for grand and formalised theories in favour of practically useful, empirically grounded knowledge.

Furthermore, the School was strongly influenced by American liberal political thinking. A theme of this thinking is often the celebration of the small community as a 'natural' form of social organisation where distinctive social identities can flourish unhindered by the intervention of state regulation and external control through, for example, centralised urban planning. Accordingly, the Chicago School ethnographies often focus on marginal groups and have a concern to explicate their distinctive moral and social organisation, rather than to treat them as mere instances of 'universal' phenomena or as lacking in any coherent organisation, moral or otherwise. This characteristic 'concern for the underdog' (as it is sometimes expressed) is a feature of many ethnographies and accounts for some of the moral and political appeal of the ethnographic tradition and method.

In the post-war period, ethnography and participant observation became more systematically developed as *methods* for social science and their similarities and difference with other approaches began to be topics for debate. In addition, ethnography began to develop a close association with a particular style of theorising in the social sciences – symbolic interactionism. Symbolic interactionism draws extensively on the writings of George Herbert Mead who argued for an intimate link between the sociality of human beings and their mental life in their development of a sense of self and others. It is possible to isolate (cf. Denzin 1970) three foundational principles for symbolic interactionism:

- human beings act toward things on the basis of the meanings that these things have for them;
- meanings arise in the context of behaviour, in particular in the context of social interaction;

- meanings are deployed and dynamically modified through interpreting the world as it is encountered in everyday life.

Symbolic interactionism presents a view of human beings as active social agents constructing social worlds and meaning itself. Overall social structure on this view dynamically emerges as the result of multiple symbolic interactions. Clearly, this emphasis on an active, dynamic, processual and constructive form of social agency did much to counter the behaviouristic conceptions which were abroad in sociology much as they were in psychology at the time.

However, for our purposes, it is important to note also the emphasis on the everyday-world-as-encountered in interactionist theory and how this motivates studying the social world ethnographically. The relationship between meaning and actual concrete social situations which interactionism insists on mandates the study of everyday life *in situ*. Furthermore, the principle that meanings are dynamically modified commends one to study social actors *over the long term* lest what is true of a momentary 'snapshot' gets mistaken for being a fixed, never changing or universal feature.

Finally (and most significantly), interactionists wish principles like Bulmer's to be understood in a self-consistent or reflexive way, that is, not merely as pronouncements about the relationship of meaning to everyday social interaction for those studied but as true for those doing the studying too. Social scientists too construct meanings on the basis of their encounters with world, dynamically change them as experience and interaction with the world unfold and so forth (see Denzin 1970; and the criticisms of mis-statements of such reflexive principles in Silverman 1985: 101 *et seq.*; and Hammersley and Atkinson 1983: 234–235). Ethnography, for symbolic interactionists then, is close to being the *only* feasible method as it alone emphasises the same features that interactionists claim are true of all social knowledge. Rock (1979: 187) puts this forcibly: 'Interactionism espouses participant observation because it is based on an epistemology that describes immediate experience as an irreducible reality.' If immediate experience is irreducible in this sense, it cannot and must not (for interactionists) be 'reduced' by quantitative and statistical analysis as (inevitably) quantification and categorisation involve the loss of unique detail, nor can social life be clarified through surrogates (like the experiment) which are not only 'non-immediate' but also reductions in the name of simplicity and experimental control.

Symbolic interactionism remains an influential strand of thought in social theory. However, on the contemporary scene, no one theoretical orientation can be said to hold a monopoly on ethnographic method. There are feminist, Marxist, poststructuralist, postmodernist, hermeneutic and phenomenological ethnographers. I cannot here review (or even define!) all these trends of thought and what each one takes ethnography to be. Rather, I shall try and draw out a series of threads which many approaches have in common and which we have already seen exemplified in the more 'traditional' ethnographic work discussed so far.

ETHNOGRAPHIC ORIENTATIONS

As I remarked in the introduction, it is impossible to offer a neutral view when ethnography is itself in dispute. Accordingly, this section also offers some critical observations where I think they are called for. Also as remarked in the introduction, it is ill-advised to offer a how-to-do-it manual for ethnography. Accordingly, this section discusses some more substantive methodological issues which arise from the practice of ethnography. These focus on:

- ethnography's concern to study naturally occurring phenomena in actual settings;
- ethnography's occasional concern for 'taking the actors' point of view';
- how ethnography can study the accomplishment or production of social order, not merely assume that social order exists or provide an abstract theoretical account of it;
- ethnography's emphasis on the relationship between meaning and practical action;
- the questions surrounding the role of the ethnographer in the field (the ethnographer as stranger, guest or 'acting undercover');
- ethnography and theory development.

This is not of course a complete list of issues raised by ethnography but it'll certainly suffice for now!

Naturally occurring settings

Clearly, ethnography is concerned with the description of human action and interaction in naturally occurring settings. What is meant by 'natural' here should be something like 'a setting which pre-existed its encounter with the ethnographer and has to (in some sense) continue its existence in spite of his or her presence in it'. 'Natural' should not be taken as denoting some unsophisticated 'state of nature' which humans exist in or should exist in. This kind of romantic and sentimental thread can be found in some of the ethnographies of the Chicago School as remarked above. But it is a confusion of the aims of ethnography in my view to conflate the two senses. Ethnographers should avoid the artificial production of phenomena or the imposition of some strange setting or technique onto the phenomenon which is under investigation. Ethnographers should also avoid transporting the phenomenon to some foreign location like the laboratory. Phenomena should be studied both *in vivo* and *in situ*. None of this means that we need have a sentimental attachment to the world as it is.

Defining ethnography in terms of its connection to 'naturally occurring settings' can sometimes arouse criticism.[5] Can there be such 'natural settings'? Do ethnographers not come to settings with their own pre-suppositions so that they can hardly be deemed to be encountering 'nature' as if for the first time? Is not observation a 'constructive' affair such that people (ethnographers included) are always going beyond what is given to them and making more of it? How can an ethnographer, then, be said to be encountering something 'natural' with all the connotations of naive observation that this can suggest?

These are important and often heard objections. There is truth in them but not – I feel – a truth that would cause us to give up ethnographic work or spend the rest of our research careers in guilt-ridden introspection. A few clarifications are in order. *Of course*, every ethnographer comes to a setting with their commonsensical pre-suppositions and *of course* they will make of the setting something which is influenced by their concerns. In other words, no observer can be completely detached and 'neutral'. But this does not mean that it is always within the ethnographer's power to conjure phenomena in the setting out of nothing by their mere presence alone. Nor does this argument excuse forcing *theoretical* pre-suppositions (i.e. assumptions derived from a pre-existing body of academic theory) onto the interpretation of a field site.

For example, there exist quite a battery of ethnographic studies of the work of control room operators in settings such as Air Traffic Control (ATC) or the control rooms of the London Underground (Harper and Hughes 1993; Heath and Luff 1992). While these ethnographers have particular orientations to the study of control room activity, it is far fetched to argue that their very presence constitutes new phenomena in the control room. After all ATC or underground traffic control still have to go on whether there's an ethnographer present or not! And they have to continue to go on in an ordered and intelligible way for their work to be possible at all. It is far-fetched to object (as some do) to ethnographic studies on the grounds of the disruption that ethnographers must cause or because of some Heisenberg-like perturbation that the very act of observing brings about. Not only does this objection ignore just how routine 'being observed' is in many contemporary forms of life,[6] it gives an arrogantly inflated power to the ethnographer's eye![7]

However, in all this, I do not want to be heard as arguing that there are never problems about how the ethnographer should act in the field setting. Far from it. Indeed, I shall discuss some of these issues below. Rather, I am insisting that there is no knock-down argument against ethnographic studies to be had by merely pointing out the constructive nature of observation. One can grant this point without it entailing that what the ethnographer observes are 'mere fictions' or bespoke productions for the ethnographer's benefit or that the ethnographer will necessarily disrupt the setting through observation alone. In a sense, a carefully done ethnography can contain its own 'monitoring mechanism'. Provided the relationship with the field site has been set up and maintained in the right way, if you are being disruptive, making it all up or forcing your pre-existing prejudices onto a context where they do not fit, *people will tell you!*

Taking the actors' point of view

A major theme of ethnographic work since the Chicago School has been to 'take the actors' (or participants' or members') point of view'. What does this phrase mean? In some ways, it is an injunction to take a natural and not an overly theoretical attitude to what one finds in field settings, at least in the first instance. Rather than foist the categories, terminology and procedures of some academic *theoretical* stance, one takes the stance of the actors in that setting themselves. The aim on this precept, then, is to understand the setting less through the eyes of a sociologist or a psychologist or an anthropologist (or any other professional academic viewpoint) but through the eyes of traffic controllers, hoboes, migrant workers or whoever.

While the aim of resisting the premature imposition of theoretical categories is a good one,[8] there can be some problems with the injunction to take the point of view of the actors themselves as a methodological principle. First, as we have noted before, understanding the concepts, practices and ways of life of the participants is not necessarily the same as siding with them in a moral or political sense, though the liberalism of some ethnographers has often permitted that conflation to be made. Second, merely to be told to take the members' point of view underspecifies what the ethnographer might do in practice. What does this actually consist in? Whose point of view do we follow if there are alive disputes within the field setting? Objections like these lead Dingwall (1981) to castigate principles such as taking the actors' point of view (and allied symbolic interactionist recommendations that the researcher should have 'empathy' with those studied) as 'woolly'.

Accomplishing social order: ethnomethodological ethnography

Drawing on Garfinkel (1967), Dingwall (1981; and see also Silverman 1985) works out a programme for what he calls ethnomethodological ethnography. I do not have space here to give a satisfactory exposition of ethnomethodology and its relation to orthodox theorisations in the social and psychological sciences (for this, see Heritage 1984, and Button 1991). Suffice it to say that a major preoccupation with ethnomethodologists is their aim to explicate the details of ordinary, everyday social life so as to reveal how the orderliness of everyday action and perception are accomplished. This involves taking the 'taken-for-granted' as an object of study but penetrating beyond it to uncover just how everyday, commonsensical knowledge is deployed in its situations of use. While mainstream psychology might debate the accuracy or otherwise of common sense, ethnomethodologists would be concerned to explicate (i.e. make clear) what common sense consists of and how it is practically deployed. While mainstream sociology might debate the nature of social order (is society founded upon consensus, class- or gender- or ethnicity-based conflict, or by some other means?), ethnomethodologists would be concerned to show the means by which social order comes to be practically produced in whatever form it does so happen to take. It is comparatively easy to demonstrate *that* some setting under study is socially organised but to show *how* is another matter. Ethnomethodologists are concerned to show how people produce through practical action the order that their everyday world has.

Taking an ethnomethodological orientation to ethnography (as commended by Dingwall 1981) would enable us to cast the traditional stipulation to take the perspective of the actors into a critical light. Actors themselves (air traffic controllers, hoboes and the rest) rarely have cause to reflect upon *how* they perceive the world in the way that they do or *how* they act in it as the kinds of social actors they are. To identify with the actors' perspective, then, would be to disqualify us from asking about how the actors' everyday means for acting in their world comes to be constructed, maintained and deployed. We would find ourselves taking that for granted in much the same way as the actors themselves do. We would find ourselves documenting the *what* of their point of view while ignoring the *how*. This is one reason why (lesser) ethnographic accounts are sometimes criticised as mere journalism. Ethnographies often make for exciting reading precisely because they tell 'news' about some new and exotic form of life. But *telling how* this form of life has the form it does and how that form is maintained involves analysis beyond merely *reporting that* the form of life exists.

Meaning and practical action

The previous section developed the argument that the traditional symbolic interactionist injunction to take the point of view of the actors themselves, while it may seem to liberate research from the strictures of, say, laboratory or questionnaire methods, actually might lead the researcher into a restricted view of the field setting in turn. Let me exemplify some of these points with an example from my own research.

Since 1989 I have been conducting field research in a number of UK central government organisations (see Bowers and Rodden 1993; Bowers 1994). In particular, I have been looking at the introduction of computing technology to such organisations, how computing technology is experienced by them and what consequences for the traditional work of civil servants computerisation might have. This is part of a general interest in the relationship between organisations, technology and work. One group of people I studied were introducing a local area computer network connecting together about twenty computers spread across several floors of a central London building. The introduction of these computers was itself a deliberate experiment within the organisation to see how networking and running advanced communications software might impact upon their work. On this brief description, it might seem that I already had the same perspective, interests and point of view that this organisation (or at least those who sanctioned the project) did: we all seemed to be interested in the relationship between technology, organisation and work. If one naively followed the principle of adopting the actors' point of view, it would look like my fieldwork already had success ensured!

However, it soon became apparent that terms like 'experimental' had a very different sense for this organisation's members than they did for me coming from an academic social science background. For example, the organisation in question had a policy of using IBM-compatible PCs in its work. However, for this investigation into local area networking and advanced communications software, Apple Macintosh computers had been purchased. The reason for this was that those responsible for the planning of the project argued that only using these machines could they procure the right kind of software to make the study possible. However, to convince the senior management of the organisation that this departure from normal procurement policies was justified, the project was depicted as 'an experiment'. In this way, the temporary suspension of normal practice could be justified. Purchasing the Macintoshes was part of an experiment and in no way a subtle means for overturning existing organisational practice.

My point with this example is that what 'experiment' meant to members of the organisation I studied was very different to what one might have expected without unpacking the concept and falling back on my own taken-for-granted understanding of the term. 'Experiment' for these folk had little to do with control groups, independent measures and external validity. It had everything to do with justifying an atypical course of action without showing disrespect to existing organisational standards. It is at moments like this, perhaps, where there is a suspiciously fortuitous similarity between 'points of view', that one is most likely to be misled by attempts at 'empathy' with those one studies.

Rather than empathy and adopting indigenous points of view I prefer the more prosaic slogan: *explicate member categories and practices*. That is, one should attend to the categories (as manifested in linguistic terms, notations, depictions, etc.) that members themselves use and explicate the patterning of their usage in their everyday activities in terms that members themselves use and understand. In approaching how people were planning and discussing a computer network in terms of its 'experimental' status in this spirit, I felt I was able to uncover the importance of organisational standards to the people I was studying but also their felt ability to suspend them if necessary. This may lead one to suspect that the 'success' or 'failure' of their 'experiment' with the new computers might hinge not only on whether people did indeed think that the new machines helped their work but whether this was *a legitimate departure from organisational standards for this group of people in the first place.*

Indeed, in the latter stages of 'the experiment', I heard some people referring to it as a failure because using non-standard machines reflected badly on an organisation devoted to formulating and following standards, even though many acknowledged that the new machines and their software had indeed been useful to them. If I had not analysed members' own ways of talking about 'the experiment', I would have either systematically ignored such remarks or 'ironised' them (cf. Garfinkel 1967). I may have said: 'These people have a successful use of computer technology on their hands but they can't see it because of silly organisational reasons.' Doubtless, this may have been the conclusion that a researcher who had little concern for organisational affairs or who was not willing to explicate the members' own ways of seeing technology might have come to. But, I would suggest, such a researcher would have developed a false, overly optimistic view of how computer technologies can be introduced to organisations.

These examples demonstrate I believe another point: meaning has to be understood in relation to practical action. The civil servants I studied had the practical problems on their hands of securing permission for installing a new computer network and after that managing its use. It is in relation to these practical problems (and the others which come their way, like remaining consistent with what they take the organisation as a whole to be doing) that we should understand the meaning of their discourse and the sense and significance of their actions. In contrast, many psychologists would be tempted to take an abstract, formalised approach to meaning and action and *then* see how it is instantiated in specific settings. The ethnographic orientation, I would argue, entails exactly the opposite: work out meaning and action in relation to the practical activities of actual people in specific settings and *only then* (and on the consideration of many such cases) see if there is some abstraction ready to hand to capture them all. Naturally, these remarks raise the whole question of theory development in ethnography which I shall return to later. For the time being, though, I merely want to emphasise the point that meaning should be understood in relation to the specificities of practice.

Anthropological strangeness

Often, of course, important member categories are more noticeable for the ethnographer than subtle and interestingly different uses of terms familiar to him or her (like 'experiment' in the example above). Analysing local slang and other vernaculars can often be a useful way in to understanding what's going on in a field site. These are the kinds of things which are likely to appear immediately strange to an ethnographer. Indeed, much of the early periods on site can often be devoted to trying to work out what on earth people are talking about.

To the extent that indigenous ways of talking embody a great deal of taken-for-granted knowledge, the status of the ethnographer as a *stranger* can often be of analytic utility and *not* (as one might first think) a barrier to field work. Strangers do not and cannot take for granted the same things as members do. This is precisely what makes them strangers! So, far from 'empathy', sometimes a carefully measured 'distance' can aid understanding a field site – especially if the aim of the ethnography is to go beyond documenting what members take for granted towards *telling how* their taken-for-granted ways of making sense of the world work in practice.

Early in my fieldwork with the central government organisation mentioned above, I engaged in a round of interviews with a number of personnel. It is commonplace for ethnographers to start up their research with interviews,[9] though these interviews typically have a very different character from those research interviews which are little more than an oral presentation of a questionnaire (Hammersley and Atkinson 1983). My early interviews were geared towards asking people to describe in their terms (and in their time, these interviews were open-ended) the nature of their work, their organisation and (because it was the specific occasion of my study) their usage of computing technology and their thoughts about the new network. Early interviews like these are an opportunity for gaining an initial impression of the field site, one that can be deepened and revised with later observational work, and of the categories which are important for members in understanding their world. They are also occasions where the ethnographer's naivety is most on display.

At one moment in an interview, after the interviewee had given me a lengthy account of the different ways in which the new network could be made secure, I remarked with a view to closing down the topic that 'We'll just have to wait and see what measures are adopted.' Hearing my remark as a way of dismissing the topic, the interviewee insisted: 'You ought to be more concerned with security issues than that. Security could close down this project.' This moment – initially painfully – revealed to me the importance of security, a topic which I hadn't investigated deeply until that moment. Indeed, it turned out that a whole section of the organisation were dedicated to ensuring that their computing technology was secure from outsiders or misuse from within. It also turned out that these people were harder to appease with the characterisation of the network as 'an experiment'. In short, finding out about how security questions impacted upon the computer network and were experienced in this organisation became an important item on my own research agenda. All of this stemmed from a moment when I was heard (accurately!) as being naive and uninterested in such crucial issues. My strangeness at once let me down while also revealing issues to me which were salient for members.

Dingwall (1981: 136) argues that it is often important for an ethnographer to deliberately stand 'on the margins' of the field site so as to 'interchange cultural frames'. Indeed, this is the traditional and inevitable position for the anthropological ethnographer who cannot help but be on the margins much like many of us would be should we wish to study air traffic control, brain surgery, concert pianists or – indeed – highly skilled factory workers.

Access, covert and overt ethnography

In some quarters in the ethnographic literature, there is much debate as to the correctness (ethical and otherwise) of overt versus covert ethnography. Should the researchers be explicit about their identity or should they attempt to pass themselves off as members, hiding the fact that they have research interests? To me, this is a question which should first be addressed on practical grounds. There are some field sites which it might only be possible to study covertly (e.g. some secure institutions). Under these circumstances, the researcher has the difficult task of weighing up the merits that the research might ultimately have against the possible wrongs involved in deception. Covert ethnography depends upon the anticipated benefits of the study and the risks one is prepared to take. In contrast, there are some field sites where it is impossible to be covert. For example, one might be collaborating (e.g. as part of a jointly funded research project) with the organisation where the fieldwork is being done, or one might be a consultant to it. While there may be problems weighing up one's responsibilities as a collaborator or a consultant with one's responsibilities as an independent researcher, it should not be thought that these problems are too odious or destructive for the research. Covert ethnography may have its advantages under some circumstances. But, as I have argued, the position of the 'marginal stranger' (which can be most readily fostered by being overt from the start) has its analytic advantages too.

Hughes, King, Randall and Sharrock (1993: 10) put some of these points with a refreshing practicality:

> Much of ethnographic practice, certainly while in the field, is about presenting oneself as a reasonable, courteous and unthreatening human being who is interested in what people do because s/he is interested in them and respects them. It involves very prosaic abilities, though not everyone has them, including an ability to listen to others, encourage them rather than compete with them, show an interest in what they do and what they have to say, possess immense patience and tolerance, and show that you will respect the subjects sufficiently so as not to gossip, report what they say to management, or otherwise jeopardise their interests and reputation.

In short: act like a polite guest should do! I argued above that a well crafted ethnography can contain its own 'monitoring mechanism' whereby the researcher can try out his or her emerging understanding by folding it back to members for their appraisal. It is the experience of many ethnographers that comporting oneself in the field site in just the kind of way Hughes *et al.* suggest is the key element for this. Anyway, the *last* thing one should do is to come on like a know-it-all social scientist, even if one's ignorance in the face of a novel field setting can sometimes tempt this form of panic!

Validation, generalisation and theory development

Throughout I have emphasised that ethnography should resist premature theorising, understand member categories and practices in terms which are recognisable for members themselves, attend to the specific detail of the site under study and not force academic theoretical categories onto what is observed. This gives some critics of ethnography the impression that ethnography is the enemy of theory, that it is impossible to develop theory under such strictures. I think this is a false argument based on a false notion of what theory consists of.

First of all, it is a familiar argument in the philosophy of science that a single contrary case can cause difficulties (if not refute) a theoretical generalisation. On this view, a single ethnographic case could certainly contribute to theory testing by offering potential falsifying instances. Every social scientist or psychologist who looks to Karl Popper (e.g. 1972) for a philosophy of science based on bold conjectures and refutations need not be disappointed by ethnography!

Equally, though, many writers have been at pains to point out that ethnographic work can aid in *theory development*. I take a theory to be a set of statements which together account for a phenomenon or class of phenomena. Ethnographic work can ensure that the phenomena are appropriately identified and characterised. It can provide evidence that there *are* indeed such phenomena to be accounted for as the theory maintains. It can provide (based on member categorisations) descriptions under which phenomena should be ordered and theoretical terms formulated. In short, ethnography is only the enemy of groundless or premature theory – theory without basis in everyday, worldly affairs.[10]

CONCLUSION: REFORMULATING THE SUBJECT MATTER OF PSYCHOLOGY

It should be clear by now that ethnography as I've characterised it is not merely a method for doing social and psychological research, it also involves commitments which challenge some dominant views, especially in experimental psychology. This is particularly clear in the work of many symbolic interactionists which contains not only a headlong critique of laboratory based, experimental and quantitative work but also an entire competing theoretical edifice for psychology and sociology to consider. The challenge of ethnography is also apparent in the writings of ethnomethodological ethnographers who have a conception of social scientific enquiry which is completely at odds with orthodox theory development and empiricism. In its most developed forms, ethnography is not mere method. If ethnography is to be taken seriously, both psychology's methods *and* subject matter will have to be reconsidered.[11]

However, especially as the overall intent of this chapter is to introduce ethnography to psychologists, I feel that it is important to conclude by getting the measure of ethnography's challenge to experimentalism, as this is doubtless a concern for many practising psychologists given the dominance of experimentalist thinking in the discipline. First of all, I want to dispel two ways by which an abrupt distinction between ethnography and experimentalism might be made by both critics and advocates. It is wrong – I insist – to criticise (or defend) ethnography on the grounds that it is a qualitative (and not a quantitative) method and, furthermore, it is equally false to criticise (or defend) ethnography on the grounds that it is a subjective (and not an objective) method.

Hammersley (1992) has done much recently to argue against crude ways of marking out the methodological distinctiveness of ethnography. For example, although it is true that quantification and calculation reduce much of the unique detail of an event (as emphasised by the symbolic interactionists), this is also true about the ethnographic report. It too cannot help but be a selection and reduction of all that the ethnographer has been witness to which itself of course is a further selection and reduction of what occurs in the field site. This is not to say that the report should be cursory in its documentation of phenomena. Far from it. Merely that there cannot be a fully complete presentation of all phenomena: an 'et cetera' is always involved – a point which goes for qualitative and quantitative work both.[12]

Equally, Hammersley argues that one must be careful not to endorse crude versions of the subjective/objective distinction. To be sure, ethnography is an interpretative orientation to research and is in that sense 'subjective'. But *all* scientific activity irrespective of method employed is interpretative. Philosophers of science for many decades have taught us that data underdetermine theory. No data set no matter how large will uniquely point to just one theory. *All* theory construction involves measures of insight, guesswork, good luck, powerful rhetoric and bravado. This is not to say that scientific theory involves *only* guesswork and the rest: there is also the hard work of designing and implementing experiments (or whatever) too. But in ethnography, there is also the hard work of observation and data collection. In psychology especially, it is important not to be led into arguments with experimentalists which are founded on false subjective/objective distinctions.

If one is to capture the specific flavour of ethnographic research, I think we have to look to considerations which are much more closely related to the *practice* of ethnography and experimentation (see also Bowers 1991). These include:

- The *location* of the research encounter. In ethnography, this tends to be on the terrain of those researched. The ethnographer plays 'away from home'. In laboratory based experimentation, the reverse is the case.
- The *time scale* of the research encounter. In ethnography, this follows the indigenous rhythms of those studied. If they work shifts, so do you (as Hughes *et al.* 1993, put it). In laboratory based experimentation, the time scale is often to the practical convenience of the researcher or because the researcher's pre-existing theory treats time as an important 'variable'.
- The *'grain' of the topic* under investigation and the *'grain' of the explanatory resource*. In laboratory based experimentalism, a deliberately narrow topic is selected, just one activity or just one alleged mental capacity. Explanations tend to be couched in terms of individual functions and processes. Ethnographic work has to start out with an agnosticism about what will turn out to be the 'size' of the topic under investigation. One has to be open to the possibility that one will end up studying (even) a whole socio-techno-ecology which does not come 'ready-sliced' into phenomena of any fixed or anticipated 'grain-size' to suit the investigator.
- The *status and time of theory*. Well-crafted laboratory experiments (or so we are told) test prior theories or hypotheses. Ethnographic research resists premature theorising and hypothesis testing by (at least initially) accepting and following the members' terms and topics.
- The *involvement* of the participants in research and the *involvement* of the researcher in the setting. Well-crafted laboratory experiments (again so we are told) minimise the mutual influence experimenters and subjects have on each other. Their interaction is minimised to the point of experimental 'procedures' and 'instructions'. On the contrary, ethnographers might live, eat, sleep and breathe with the participants in their research.
- The *control* of the encounter. Well-crafted laboratory experiments (so we are told yet again) minimise the number of variable factors and place all that do vary under experimenter control. Ethnographic research involves relinquishing this kind of control. Indeed, it allows the study of something which experimental control necessarily rules out: just how do actors themselves practically manage (and in that sense control) the multiple considerations which may be varying in their setting?[13]

Clearly, there are profound differences between experimentation and ethnography. However, this does not for me (quite) constitute an irresistible argument against their combination in a research programme – especially combining ethnography with *field* experimentation (where the subjects 'play at home'). For example, Jean Lave (1988), in her studies of everyday mathematics, conducted ethnographic work with shoppers and weight-watchers, looking at how they worked out (respectively) best value buys and food quantities within a dietary regime. On the basis of this, she conducted field experiments in which she presented ratio calculations to people either as, say, shopping problems (which is better value: so many ounces of beans at this price or so many at that price?) or as abstract mathematical ratios (which is the greater: 17/8 or 35/17?). Lave found that people were much better at solving the ratio problems when they were presented in an everyday form than if the computationally identical problems were presented in mathematical terms.

On the basis of such findings and further consideration of her ethnographic work, Lave develops a theory of everyday mathematical competence in terms of *people-acting-in-settings*. Interestingly, in this theory, the abstract mathematics of the classroom becomes just that: a form of mathematics tied to a particular set of settings (the classroom, the lecture theatre, the research journals). It has no analytic priority over any other form of mathematics-in-practice. Lave goes on from this observation to criticise much of the ideology of mathematics teaching which not only presents a particular form of mathematics (schoolroom mathematics) as the only form (with everyday reckoning practices being deviant or degenerate) but also elevates mathematics to be the acme of the human intellect.

Importantly for our purposes, although Lave combines ethnography and experimentation, she does ultimately accord a priority to the ethnographic encounter. Without that, she would not have been able to select pertinent phenomena (e.g. those involving ratio comparisons) for more detailed study and would not have been able to develop theoretical accounts relevant to the world outside the field experiments. I agree with Lave that any attempt to combine ethnography and (field) experimentalism must begin and end with the former for the latter depends upon it.[14]

Indeed, I would want to put this point more generally and strongly: *any experiment depends upon an (often) implicit and unexplicated 'ethnographic' knowledge that experimenters have acquired through being informal 'participant-observers' in forms of everyday life they believe they share with their subjects.* To the extent that the commonsensical assumptions experimenters build into experiments (in the form of instructions, procedures, the presentation of factors at different levels and so forth) are indeed shared with subjects, the edifice may yet stay intact (indeed, may be self-reinforcing). To the extent that this is not fulfilled, experimental programmes may grind to a halt or make much celebrated, 'counter-intuitive' discoveries! Whatever. Just as a contemporary anthropologist conducting a field experiment trades on the basis of generations of ethnographic work, so does an experimental psychologist trade on an unexplicated and often hoped-for common sense. It is time to make clear those commonsensical assumptions while introducing a requisite modesty to experimental programmes.

Ethnography is just such a way to explicate those senses both common and uncommon that are abroad in the world.

NOTES

1 This chapter owes a great deal to discussions of questions of method and theory which I have conducted over a number of years with Graham Button, John Hughes, Dave Randall, Wes Sharrock and Susan Leigh Star.

2 This does not, however, stop some ethnographers trying to codify their practice in some way or another. The most successful how-to-do-it guide that I know of is Hammersley and Atkinson's (1983) textbook. However, it is 'successful' for me in the largely ironic sense of giving you *so much* advice about the contingencies of fieldwork that you ultimately come to realise the truth of the matter: you are all on your own! Some ethnographers (e.g. Hughes *et al.* 1993) go so far as making one of their points of advice: Do not read textbooks! While I am tempted to suggest that the reader should not read this chapter, I think it is too early just yet for this advice!

3 Of course, I do not want to give the impression that ethnography is unproblematic in anthropology. Several writers have pointed out, for example, that the *involvement* of the early anthropologists with the people they studied was rather curtailed. Some anthropologists rarely 'came down from the verandah'. Equally, it is important to note that early anthropological ethnography was made possible through the expansionist desires of colonial powers and that the ethnographies (as they gave knowledge of people about to be colonised) were themselves active resources for further expansion. For a subtle discussion of these issues and the relationship between ethnography and anthropological knowledge, see Fabian (1983).

4 I shall return to this question of the possible dependence of experiment on (sometime presupposed) ethnography below.

5 The next few paragraphs is a digest of a number of ongoing debates within ethnography together with a brief rendering of my own position. More details of these debates can be found in Hammersley and Atkinson (1983), Hammersley (1992) and Atkinson (1990).

6 Many of the people I have studied are quite used to having people around to follow their work – British Standards inspectors, people from Head Office, students, people on courses, in-house trainees etc. etc. My point is that being observed is not always such a strange and mysterious thing for people in settings. At least, not so strange that you can make a decisive objection against ethnographic research on its basis.

7 As if one glance would make 'planes drop out of the sky!

8 And – as noted above – one cannot avoid the use of *common sense* presuppositions: ethnographers recruit those just as anyone else would have to in encountering a new setting.

9 It is also commonplace (and a practice I follow) to finish off one's contact with a site with a round of interviews. These serve not merely a debriefing function. They also enable the ethnographer's overall understanding to be tested out with the members themselves. It is also very important not to leave a field site without saying goodbye. Summative presentations are often also useful in this regard. If at all possible, I try to cycle between a number of rounds of open-ended field interview and observation, trying to systematically link the two by looking out for things which I have been alerted to in interview, and folding back my emerging understanding of the field site to members in interview. Throughout, tape and video recordings are taken whenever I have permission, copies of documents are obtained in confidence, and copious notes are taken as I sit in on meetings, discussions or observe activities being engaged in. Hold on! Didn't you say that

you were going to avoid a how-to-do-it approach? Well, it is only a footnote and I haven't wasted too much of your time. Besides, it's the best I can do!

10 To name just a few, Strauss (1987), Silverman (1985) and Hammersley and Atkinson (1983) provide much more detailed examinations of how ethnography can contribute to theory testing and development. In particular, Strauss offers a systematisation of how one can ground theory in ethnographic observation. He also offers many examples of the collaborative analysis of ethnographic materials by groups of researchers working with him. In my own practice, I have tended to find that – while Strauss' examples and the spirit of 'grounded theory' (see also Henwood and Pidgeon 1992) are useful – his systematisation didn't touch on my fieldwork experience and it took me quite a while to convince myself that I wasn't necessarily doing anything wrong! So much again for how-to-do-it guides.

11 I do not have space here to examine in full the ramifications of an ethnographic turn for psychology. For example, to take seriously ethnography's concern to explicate member categories and practices would involve abandoning the assumption that member categories and practices will be only and strictly 'psychological'. In my own fieldwork (Bowers 1994), I make the point that members often have to deal with a whole array of heterogeneous problems in their everyday life (organisational, economic, political, moral ones, etc.), not just ones which they express in psychological discourse (e.g. in terms of beliefs, desires, knowledge or individual intention). If one is concerned to explicate *their* problems and practices, we have to abandon *our* disciplinary purity. In short, there is no such thing for me any more as a (purely) psychological issue. Bowers (1991) contains some further arguments concerning the relation between ethnography and experimental practice as part of an overall critique of cognitive science/ psychology.

12 Arguments like these do have an especial import for ethnographers though. Many writers argue (as we have noted) that ethnography should be (in some sense) a reflexive enterprise. This has the implication that ethnographers must consider ways of making their readers aware of the principles which govern the selection of the data and the characterisation of the phenomena within their research reports. Atkinson (1990) critically analyses much of the ethnographic tradition for the devices it has used which precisely have the effect of suppressing how ethnographic writing is as selective and as constructive as any other form, devices which have given ethnographic reports a 'reality effect' through textual means alone.

13 Actually, this observation – coupled with the argument in the next two paragraphs – is my key objection to orthodox experimentation as one's only research method. Orthodox experimentation rules out of court the examination of precisely the question of how the orderliness of settings can be accomplished. In the experimental setting, the experimentalist (or so we are told) guarantees the orderliness of the setting through experimental control. How actors accomplish this control themselves cannot be studied, therefore, experimentally – at least not without trivialising the issue or inviting circular argument.

14 In a sense which *isn't* true the other way round: ethnography can survive without experimentalism.

REFERENCES

Anderson, N. (1923/1961) *The Hobo*, 2nd edn, Chicago: Chicago University Press.

Atkinson, P. (1990) *The Ethnographic Imagination: Textual constructions of reality*, London: Routledge.

Bowers, J. (1991) 'Time, representation and power/knowledge: towards a critique of cognitive science as a knowledge producing practice'. *Theory and Psychology*, 1: 543–569 (special issue on 'Cognitivism and its Discontents').

Bowers, J. (1994) 'The work to make a network work: studying CSCW in action', in *CSCW '94 – Proceedings of the fifth conference on Computer Supported Cooperative Work, November 1994, Chapel Hill, North Carolina, USA*, New York: Association of Computing Machinery.

Bowers, J. and Rodden, T. (1993) 'Exploding the interface: experiences of a CSCW network', in *InterCHI '93:Bridges Between Worlds – Proceedings of InterCHI '93, April 1993, Amsterdam, The Netherlands*, New York: Association of Computing Machinery.

Bulmer, M. (1984) *The Chicago School of Social Research: Institutionalization, diversity and rise of sociological research*, Chicago: Chicago University Press.

Button, G. (1991) *Ethnomethodology and the Human Sciences*, Cambridge: Cambridge University Press.

Cressey, P. (1932) *The Taxi Dance Hall*, Chicago: Chicago University Press.

Denzin, N. K. (1970) *The Research Act in Sociology*, London: Butterworth.

Dingwall, R. (1981) 'The ethnomethodological movement', in G. Payne, R. Dingwall, J. Payne and M. Carter (eds) *Sociology and Social Research*, London: Croom Helm.

Fabian, J. (1983) *Time and The Other: How anthropology makes its object*, New York: Columbia University Press.

Garfinkel, H. (1967) *Studies in Ethnomethodology*, Englewood Cliffs, N.J.: Prentice-Hall.

Glaser, B. and Strauss, A. (1967) *The Discovery of Grounded Theory*, Chicago: Aldine.

Hammersley, M. (1992) *What's Wrong With Ethnography?*, London: Routledge.

Hammersley, M. and Atkinson, P. (1983) *Ethnography: Principles in practice*, London: Routledge & Kegan Paul.

Harper, R. and Hughes, J. (1993) 'What a F-ing system! Send 'em all to the same place and then expect us to stop 'em hitting: Making technology work in Air Traffic Control', in G. Button (ed.) *Technology in Working Order: Studies of work, interaction and technology*, Cambridge: Cambridge University Press.

Heath, C. and Luff, P. (1992) 'Collaboration and control: crisis management and multimedia technology in London Underground Line Control Rooms', *Computer Supported Cooperative Work*, 1: 69–94.

Henwood, K. and Pidgeon, N. (1992) 'Qualitative research and psychological theorizing', *British Journal of Psychology*, 83: 97–111.

Heritage, J. (1984) *Garfinkel and Ethnomethodology*, Cambridge: Polity.

Hughes, J., King, V., Randall, D. and Sharrock, W. (1993) *Ethnography for System Design: A guide*, COMIC ESPRIT project report (LANCS-2–4), Lancaster University.

Lave, J. (1988) *Cognition in Practice*, Cambridge: Cambridge University Press.

Lindeman, E. (1924) *Social Discovery*, New York: Republic.

Popper, K. (1972) *The Logic of Scientific Discovery*, London: Hutchinson.

Rock, P. (1979) *The Making of Symbolic Interactionism*, London: Macmillan.

Silverman, D. (1985) *Qualitative Methodology and Sociology*, Aldershot: Gower.

Strauss, A. (1987) *Qualitative Analysis for Social Scientists*, Cambridge: Cambridge University Press.

Chapter 9

Methodological considerations in observing mother–infant interactions in natural settings

E. Connors and S. M. Glenn

INTRODUCTION

Naturalistic observations of mother–infant interaction have become widespread in developmental research. For example, they have been used to identify possible predictors of adaptive and maladaptive functioning, to assess the effectiveness of intervention programmes, and to study interactive behaviour when either the mother or infant is suffering from some physical or psychological dysfunction. This chapter addresses methodological considerations which confront researchers in this area. The research used to exemplify these issues is a study carried out by the authors to identify conditions in the natural environment that influence infant learning and motivation to master the environment. This research arose out of a previous laboratory project which studied the effects of contingent and non-contingent stimulation (activation of a musical mobile) on the kicking responses of 3½ month old infants, with and without disabilities (O'Brien 1991). This work established negative effects of both non-contingency and changing contingency on rates of responding and emotional expression in both groups of infants. Thus, support was provided for the possibility of 'learned helplessness' (Seligman, 1975) developing in infants whose environments provided low (less consistent) levels of consistent contingent experiences.

However, such experimental demonstrations do no more than establish infants' abilities. Naturalistic studies are also necessary if we are to understand what experiences infants have in their daily lives, and how these affect their development. Consequently, a research project was undertaken to determine whether and how contingent experiences in the first year of life, mediated by the caregiver, relate to the development of motivation to master the environment. Results of this study (Connors, Glenn and Service 1994) showed that infants who experienced high levels of maternal contingent responding exhibited greater motivation in free-play. These infants focused more intently on the play materials, explored the play set more thoroughly and displayed higher levels of competence accompanied by positive affect.

Thus, through naturalistic observation, we were able to generalise the earlier laboratory findings to the everyday lives of infants.

The chapter is divided into two broad sections. The first is devoted to methodological concerns that must be addressed in naturalistic observations in order to maximise the generalisability of data. Two important issues are discussed: the effect of interaction context on interactive behaviour (which has implications for the amount of behaviour to observe), and the effects of observer presence on participants' behaviour. In the second part of the chapter, some useful pointers are offered for developing a coding scheme, choosing a recording method and making behavioural observations.

I OBSERVATIONS IN THE NATURAL ENVIRONMENT: METHODOLOGICAL ISSUES

Where the aim of the research is to gain a broad understanding of the everyday experiences of infants, it is essential that observations be carried out in the home. Here mothers and infants are able to move around freely, engaging in familiar activities so that behaviour is likely to be more spontaneous than that observed in a laboratory. For our own research, we were interested in rates of naturally occurring contingent and non-contingent maternal reponses to infant behaviours. It was therefore, necessary to conduct a home-base study. However, naturalistic observations are not without problems, one major concern is how much behaviour to observe in order to obtain a true representation of everyday experience. Second, there is the problem that participants' behaviour may be altered due to the presence of an observer or video equipment. It was necessary for us to carefully consider both of these important issues in order to carry out our research. Here, we shall discuss the research evidence relating to both of these issues and our approach to dealing with them.

Effects of interaction context on behaviour

Unfortunately, time constraints, as well as concerns for the privacy of individuals under investigation, make it impracticable for most researchers to be able to make lengthy and continuous observations. Consequently, many studies sample a relatively small amount of interactive behaviour, for example one or two hours. Yet it is important to consider whether such limited periods of observation can give a truly representative picture of naturally occurring patterns of interactive behaviour. Recent research findings suggest that studies which sample only a limited range of interactive situations may compromise generalisability and make it difficult to discern individual differences in everyday interaction. Several investigations have revealed significant variations in interactive behaviours dependent upon the context in which mother–infant interaction is observed. For example,

O'Brien, Johnson and Anderson-Guetz (1989) found that higher ratings of verbal stimulation and positive emotion were given to mothers in face-to-face play than during 'normal routine' behaviour in the home. In another study, Pett, Wampold, Vaughan-Cole and East (1992) found that both mothers and pre-schoolers were significantly more controlling during mealtime than during structured block-play in the home. Finally, Seifer, Sameroff, Anagnostopolau and Elias (1992) examined four naturalistic interaction contexts: close interaction, caretaking, feeding and distant interaction, and found differences in behaviour across all of these. Mothers of 4 month olds were more interactive during caretaking and least interactive during feeding. In contrast, infants were significantly more spontaneous during close interaction and most responsive during feeding. With 12 month olds, virtually across the board there was significantly more social interaction on the part of both mother and infant during play interaction than during caretaking. Additionally, in this latter study, context of interaction accounted for more variation in behaviour than did such theoretically important characteristics as sex of child, social status of family and maternal mental illness.

These findings show how studies which sample relatively brief periods of everyday interaction and, consequently, a narrow range of interaction contexts may have limited generalisability. It would seem advisable for researchers to attempt to sample as wide a variety of contexts as possible. However, no definite answers can be given to the question of how much observation is necessary in order to achieve this. Epstein and O'Brien (1985) have suggested aggregating data from observations made over several occasions and situations. However, as Pett et al. (1992) argue, collecting and coding data from multiple, naturalistic observations over lengthy periods of time would be extremely costly in terms of time and money. They propose an alternative strategy of aggregating smaller samples of multiple observations. We would suggest that where only relatively brief periods of observation are possible (as in our own study), researchers may be advised to calculate rates of interactive behaviour for each context observed. In our case, behaviour rates were calculated for each of three different contexts: play, caretaking and 'mother otherwise occupied' (i.e. not involving her infant). This allowed us to make direct comparisons across subjects. In addition, we asked mothers to keep diaries of their normal everyday routines so that individual differences in time spent in different contexts could be estimated and variations controlled for in statistical analysis.

Another, more subtle contextual variable was highlighted by Kindermann and Skinner (1988). They studied mother–infant interactions during central or non-central developmental tasks: learning to walk, self-feed and dress at 9, 12 and 21 months. (For example, learning to walk is central for most 9–12 month olds, whereas learning to dress is not.) Patterns of contingent maternal responding to infant initiations were both more homogeneous and more sensitive during the learning phase of a developmental task than during pre-

and post-task phases. Thus, developmental stage is perhaps another factor which should be taken into account especially if the researcher is investigating types of maternal responding.

Observer influences on behaviour

A frequent criticism of naturalistic observations is that behaviour is likely to be affected in some way due to participants' awareness of being observed, an effect which is commonly referred to as subject reactivity.

Attempts have been made to determine the extent to which behaviour may be affected by direct observation. However, this is not a subject which lends itself easily to empirical investigation for, in order for evidence of reactivity to be found, investigators must look for changes in behaviour across two conditions; (a) when participants know they are under observation compared to (b) when they believe they are not. This poses a problem in that observation is, by necessity, required in each of these two conditions. Methods of dealing with this difficulty have been to compare periods of obtrusive and unobtrusive observation, or to compare periods where individuals are aware of being observed with periods in which observation is carried out without their knowledge. Obviously, there are ethical concerns associated with the latter method. A third approach is to look for evidence of habituation to the observation situation, with the assumption that behaviours that have initially been altered due to the novelty of being observed will gradually return to normal as people become accustomed to the situation.

Results of such studies have been mixed. For example, Zegiob, Arnold and Forehand (1975) observed mothers in the laboratory with and without their awareness. Significant increases in positive maternal behaviours, play interaction and structuring of child behaviour were found in the former condition. No apparent changes in maternal negative behaviour occurred across the two conditions. However, Johnson and Bolstad (1975) observed family interacive behaviour surrounding an evening mealtime over a six-day period. On alternate days, either the observer plus a tape recorder were present, or the family activated the tape recorder themselves. No difference in rates of deviant child behaviours were found across the two conditions, nor was there evidence of habituation throughout the period of the investigation.

Firm conclusions concerning reactivity are difficult to draw from such research findings. There appears to be some evidence of increased task oriented and socially desirable behaviours, and withholding of negative behaviours, when subjects are under observation. It has been suggested that the presence of negative behaviours such as scolding and reprimanding may indicate that subjects are no longer inhibited by the presence of an observer. However, few beatings have ever been recorded even in more severely disturbed families (Lytton 1971). Methodological problems surrounding this research make the findings difficult to interpret. For example, no differences in target behaviours between obtrusive and unobtrusive conditions could mean either that subjects are not influenced by being observed in either condition, or that both conditions affect behaviour equally. Lack of evidence of habituation could be similarly explained. Until further evidence is available, it would seem advisable to attempt to reduce the impact of the observer as much as possible.

Some attempts have been made to devise unobtrusive methods of observation. For example, Johnson, Christensen and Bellamy (1976) used radio assisted audio-recording. Children were 'bugged' at both random and pre-selected times and behaviour compared across conditions. In another study, Christensen and Hazzard (1983) set up tape recorders in inconspicuous locations within participants' homes. These were activated at random during peak interaction periods over a two-week period. In addition, a condition was included in which families were led to believe that the equipment had broken down so that they were no longer under observation. There was little evidence of behavioural changes across conditions or over time. In this study, families were fully debriefed and given the opportunity to withdraw from the investigation if they wished. Nonetheless, ethical concerns remain about designs involving deception.

The problems inherent in attempting to reduce the potential impact of observer presence are apparent from the above research. However, a more ethical and practical solution that we would endorse is to allow participants to accustom themselves to the procedure prior to the study proper. In addition, it is important to spend time becoming acquainted with families before commencing the observations (Russell, Russell and Midwinter 1992) and to provide a clear explanation of the procedure in order to alleviate any anxieties (Jacob, Tennenbaum and Krahn 1987).

It is worth bearing in mind also that the presence of an observer may affect family members differently. Russell et al. (1992) conducted naturalistic observations of mothers and fathers interacting with their children. Of the mothers and fathers, 66 per cent reported that they had experienced little or no effect of being observed. Comparisons were made of the observed behaviour of fathers and mothers who said they had been influenced by the observer and those who had not. Few differences in behaviour were found for mothers whereas fathers who had been influenced showed more stereotypic 'fatherly' behaviour (possibly indicative of a social desirability effect) than fathers reporting no influence. In addition, there were more child initiated interactions when parents reported having been influenced.

It is interesting that in Russell et al.'s (1992) investigation two-thirds of subjects reported having experienced little or no influence of being observed. Such reports are characteristic of many investigators' experiences, especially where time has been taken to develop a good rapport between the researcher and participants prior to commencement of the investigation. Parents often say they are simply too busy to be affected by the observations (Dunn, Plomin and Nettles 1985; Jacob *et al.* 1987).

Summary

We have outlined two important factors that must be considered in designing naturalistic observations of mother–infant interaction: (a) the effects of interaction context; and (b) the presence of an observer on the behaviour of participants. We concluded, first, that where lengthy observations are not possible, context of observation should be controlled for in naturalistic observations. Second, we suggested that reactivity to observation may be minimised by becoming acquainted with participants and allowing them to become familiar with the procedure before commencing observations.

In our investigation we were studying only mothers and infants in families where the mother was the primary caregiver. We recruited single child families or families in which mothers spent time alone with their infants on a regular basis. In other circumstances, researchers may need to consider the influences of having other family members present during observations. As we have pointed out, there is research evidence to suggest that the behaviour of target subjects may be affected as a result of having other family members present during direct observation (Russell *et al.*, 1992). (See Lamb (1979) for a more detailed discussion on social context effects.)

Finally, free observation may not always be the most appropriate method of observing interactive behaviour. Where only specific behaviours are of interest, it may be more appropriate to structure the observation, selecting the most suitable interaction context to ensure that the behaviour of interest will occur. For example, if maternal control strategies were the focus of the investigation, it may be more productive to focus the observation on the family mealtime where more maternal controlling behaviour is likely to occur (Pett *et al.*, 1992) than to spend an hour or two in general observation. However, in order to gain an understanding of everyday patterns of inter-action, free observation in the natural environment remains the preferred method.

II CONDUCTING BEHAVIOURAL OBSERVATIONS

The second part of this chapter is devoted to more practical aspects of observational research. Again we will refer to our own research experience as a means of highlighting some of the decisions that must be made in devising a method by which to observe and record mother–infant interactive behaviour.

Piloting

Before behavioural categories are finally selected and defined it is important to spend time observing mothers and infants of the appropriate age to determine what behaviours are characteristic of this population. In our own project, it was necessary to develop a coding scheme that could be used to measure interaction between mothers and infants of 3½, 8 and 14 months. The behavioural repertoire of the infant increases dramatically over this period: for example, whereas the social behaviour of the 3½ month old may involve simply looking, smiling, vocalising and fussing, by 14 months it may also include going to, following, giving objects to the mother and gesturing requests. The final behavioural categories needed to be broad enough to encompass all these behaviours.

A piloting period is also valuable for practising data recording techniques before deciding upon the most suitable method. If time-sampling is to be used, then piloting is essential in order to determine behaviour frequencies and durations before deciding upon the length of sampling interval to be used. Finally, piloting will allow the researcher to become acquainted with the observation setting and to identify any practical problems that are likely to occur prior to commencing data collection.

Defining behaviours

Discrete categories

The next stage is to define key behaviours in such a way that they can be easily discriminated by independent observers. Category definitions should, therefore, be as clear, comprehensive and unambiguous as possible. Martin and Bateson (1993) offer the following general guidelines. There should be sufficient categories to describe behaviour in the detail necessary to answer the research questions and perhaps provide some further background information. Definitions should be precise and independent (rather than different ways of measuring the same thing). Finally, categories should be homogeneous in the sense that all aspects of the same category share the same properties.

It is necessary at this stage to decide on the level of behavioural analysis to be used. Is a more molecular or a more molar analysis better suited to answering the research question? Bakeman and Gottman (1986) advise defining categories at a slightly more molecular level than is actually necessary. Molecular (specific) categories require less inference on the part of observers and are, therefore, more likely to be reliable. In addition, they may provide unexpected information regarding behaviour which may be useful to the investigation. Categories may easily be combined later for the purpose of analysis.

Behaviour ratings

Infant outcomes have been found to be affected not by the contingency of maternal responding per se but also by the quality and appropriateness of those responses (Ainsworth, Blehar, Waters and Wall 1978). We, therefore, considered it important in our own study to make ratings of the warmth and sensitivity of maternal responses to infants. Measures of quality, such as these, are more difficult to define than more discrete behaviour categories because they depend, to some extent, on subjective judgements of observers. Generally, as a reflection of this difficulty, interobserver agreement for qualitative ratings has a tendency to be lower than for discrete behaviour categories (Schaefer 1989). However, we were able to develop a 3 point rating scale for sensitivity and a 5 point scale for warmth which were sufficiently objective to enable high levels of interobserver reliability to be achieved.

Arriving at a reliable set of behaviour categories can be an extremely lengthy process, taking around about a year in our case. However, it is worth spending time at this stage to ensure reliability and validity of the coding scheme.

Choosing a recording method

Having decided upon behaviour categories and definitions it is necessary to select a method of recording those behaviours. The outcome measures required from the study will influence the choice of recording method to be used. Common outcome measures are frequencies, rates, durations and ratings of behaviours and sequential information.

In our study, we were concerned with the contingency of maternal reponses to infant behaviour, which implies the *sequencing* of responses as well as the *rate* at which interactive behaviours occurred. In addition we wanted to have qualitative *ratings* of sensitivity and warmth and, in the assessment of mastery motivation, we were interested in the *duration* of infant exploratory behaviour with individual toys. Thus, it was necessary to find a recording method capable of providing all these outcome measures. Two methods were considered: continuous recording using a computerised event recorder and time-sampling.

Continuous recording using a computerised event recorder

Computerised event recording involves the use of a computer program to record behaviours that are represented by individual keys on the computer keyboard. These programs produce a continuous record of events as they occur which are logged against the time they occurred. Programs may also sort the data ready for analysis. There are several such event recorders commercially available (see Donat 1991).

Advantages of this method are that it is neat and efficient and that it deals well with frequency, duration and sequential data. However, there are limitations. The most important of these is the difficulty in coding more than a few behaviour categories at a time, especially when behaviours occur rapidly and concurrently. Difficulties are exacerbated when durations of behaviours need to be recorded as it is also necessary to remember to activate the onset and offset keys. However, this problem may be eliminated if mutually exclusive categories are used so that the onset of one behaviour signals the offset of another. Extensive training may be required in order to obtain acceptable levels of interobserver reliability. Finally, this method requires a great deal of concentration if errors are to be avoided, as these may not easily be corrected or may go undetected. This is a severe drawback when observations of complex behaviour are to be made over a relatively long period. Because of the quantity and complexity of behaviours we were observing, this method was found to be inappropriate for our needs and we decided to consider the time-sampling method.

Time sampling

This method involves dividing the period of observation into equal time intervals and then noting at the end of each interval whether or not behaviours of interest either: (a) are occurring at the end of the interval (instantaneous sampling); or (b) have occurred during the interval (one-zero sampling). Instantaneous sampling is the preferred method for recording behavioural states of long duration, whist one-zero sampling is better suited to recording discrete behaviours of relatively short duration. Interval lengths are determined by the particular behaviours to be observed. If these are relatively infrequent, then a fairly long interval may be used, whereas more frequent behaviours will require a shorter interval. If intervals are short relative to the duration of behaviour, time sampling will produce similar results to continuous recording. Because we were mostly interested in recording rates of discrete behaviours, we opted for the use of the one-zero method, and, after extensive piloting, decided upon an interval length of 15 seconds. Behaviours tended not to occur more than once per 15 seconds except in very intense bouts of interaction, for example in face-to-face play, and this context was relatively infrequent.

It has been argued that one-zero sampling is unsuitable for recording sequences (Parke 1989). As noted earlier, we were interested in recording the contingent responses of mothers, and so sequence of behaviour was important. However, we were able to deal with this within the one-zero method by recording maternal responses for each interval, and then using the 3 point sensitivity rating scale concurrently to indicate the extent to which responses were appropriate as well as contingent. Warmth ratings were made in the same way: for each 15 second interval mothers were rated on a 5 point scale as to the warmth of her involvement with her infant during that interval. It is quite feasible to make one-zero and instantaneous recordings concurrently where both frequencies and durations of behaviours are required. In the few instances in our own study where duration of behaviours were required, instantaneous recordings were made every 15 seconds along with the one-zero recordings. Thus, we were able to use time sampling to effectively produce all the outcome measures of interest.

There is some controversy over the use of the one-zero time sampling method. Several authors (Altmann 1974; Mann, Tann-Have, Plunkett and Meisels 1991) have argued against its use because it tends to underestimate frequencies and overestimate durations. Smith (1985) believes these criticisms are misguided. He stresses that event frequency or duration are not the only valid measures of behaviour. In fact, frequency and duration do not necessarily correlate with one another – each provides a different measure of 'amount' of behaviour, and may mean different things. One-zero sampling, on the other hand, provides an index combining both frequency and duration, and is not necessarily less valid than each on its own. Smith presents data showing that one-zero sampling scores correlate more highly with frequency and duration scores than the latter with one another. It is our view that unless there are compelling theoretical reasons why actual frequencies or durations of behaviour are important, then one-zero sampling can be used. It can provide more data on more complex categories more reliably than other methods. Furthermore, when sampling short duration behaviours (typical when detailed studies of mother–infant interaction are of interest) it provides statistically independent frequency counts.

The use of video cameras in naturalistic observation

Often, the use of a video camera is essential in order to be able to collect all the data of interest. Larger quantities and more complex data may be collected and recorded on video tape allowing a more detailed behavioural analysis to be made at a later date. This was important in our own study. Other advantages of video recordings are that they enable higher levels of inter-observer reliability to be achieved, and a permanent record of behaviour to be made which may be referred back to as further research questions arise.

However, there are two possible drawbacks to the use of video cameras. First, they may present too much of an intrusion and thereby affect the behaviour that is being observed (although there is evidence to suggest that filming is no more intrusive than simply having an observer present). Dunn et al. (1985) video-recorded mothers interacting with their 12 month old infants. When interviewed afterwards, mothers reported that the camera had little effect on their own or their infants' behaviour because the situations were too engrossing, and because there was a good rapport between mothers and infants and the observer. In our own study, mothers indicated that they were only aware of the camera in situations where there was little activity, but that in general they were too involved with their infants to notice. Nevertheless, it should be noted that in recruitment, several potential subjects declined to take part in the study because they felt they would be too embarrassed by the camera, and so perhaps an element of sample bias may be introduced where a video camera is to be used. Second, there is a cost in time when using this approach. Recording data to be coded at a later date more than doubles the workload. In our case it took approximately four hours to code each hour of video-recorded data. It is far quicker to collect live data but this may reduce both the quality of the data and the ability to record more complex behaviour. Finally, where video recordings are to be made access to editing facilities is also necessary.

Interobserver reliability

In order to assess the reliability of the behavioural coding scheme and to reduce subjective bias in observations, interobserver reliability must be assessed. When observations are to continue over a considerable period of time, reliability both within and between observers should be monitored at regular intervals to prevent 'observer drift'. Several methods of assessing interobserver reliability may be encountered in the research literature. However, selection of a particular method warrants careful consideration. The two most popular reliability statistics are probably percentage agreement and the Pearson correlation coefficient.

Percentage agreement is the easiest to compute and is, therefore, particularly useful during the development of a coding scheme when repeated assessments of interobserver reliability are required. However, percentage agreement may be spuriously inflated when occurrences or non-occurrences of behaviour are frequent. It has been suggested that in these instances effective percentage agreement be calculated on either: (a) non-occurrences of a code when the occurrences are frequent; or (b) occurrences when non-occurrences are frequent (Jackson, Della-Piana and Sloane 1978). The *Pearson correlation coefficient* is often preferred over percentage agreement since, unlike percentage agreement, the metric properties of the correlation coefficient are well known. It is important to note, however, that high correlations between observers may not represent good agreement between pairs of coders. It is quite possible that one observer may consistently code more instances of a behaviour than a second observer. Nevertheless, high correlations will be achieved if the observers' scores follow a similar pattern. In addition, the more categories there are in a coding scheme, the greater the likelihood of obtaining high correlations between observers (Hollenbeck 1978). A serious limitation to the use of both percentage agreement and the Pearson correlation coefficient is that they do not correct for chance agreements between observers. We, therefore, prefer the use of a third alternative, Cohen's *kappa* (Cohen 1968) which shares some of the advantages of the correlation coefficient and does control for chance agreement between observers.

There are additional points to consider in calculating interobserver reliabilities. First, Hartmann (1982a) points out that reliabilities may vary across contexts and experimental conditions and that reliability calculations should involve samples of data from each of these dimensions. We would advise that, in longitudinal studies of mother–infant interaction, data samples from each stage of the study be included in calculations, as interactive behaviours can vary enormously from stage to stage due to the rapid rate of infant development. Also, as rates of interactive behaviour do vary across interaction contexts (O'Brien *et al.*, 1989; Seifer *et al.*, 1992), it is important that a range of contexts are included in assessments of interobserver reliability. Second, interobserver reliabilities should be reported for each variable that is to be subjected to statistical analysis. Where variables are combined for statistical analysis, interobserver reliability should be reported on the composite of these variables (Hartmann 1982a; Jacob *et al.*, 1987). Finally, in longitudinal studies where predictions regarding the influence of earlier stage behaviour on later behaviour are being made, independent observers should be used at each stage to eliminate experimenter bias.

Conclusion

The aim of this chapter has been to outline some of the key methodological concerns surrounding observational studies of mother–infant interaction. The most important point to emphasise is that, in conducting observational studies, researchers should aim to maximise the generalisability of the resulting data. We have attempted to draw attention to factors which may limit generalisability, and to provide some useful suggestions as to how to overcome these problems. We have also provided an account of the decision-making process involved in the development of a coding scheme to record interactive behaviour, highlighting some of the pros and cons of alternative approaches. Through our own naturalistic observations of mothers and infants, in which careful consideration was given to the methodological issues discussed here, we were able to find support for previous laboratory findings concerning the effects of contingent experience on infant motivation for learning. In relating to our own research experiences, we hope to have provided a practical and illustrative approach to these issues. Further accounts of observational methods may be obtained from the following sources: Bakeman and Gottman (1986); Hartmann (1982b); Jacob *et al.* (1987); Martin and Bateson (1993); and Sackett (1978).

REFERENCES

Ainsworth, M., Blehar, M., Waters, E. and Wall, S. (1978) *Patterns of Attachment*, Hillsdale, N.J.: Lawrence Erlbaum Associates.

Altmann, J. (1974) 'Observational study of behaviour: sampling methods', *Behaviour*, 49: 227–267.

Bakeman, R. and Gottman, J.M. (1986) *Observing Interaction: An introduction to sequential analysis*, Cambridge: Cambridge University Press.

Christensen, A. and Hazzard, A. (1983) 'Reactive effects during naturalistic observation of families', *Behavioural Assessment*, 5: 349–362.

Cohen, J. (1968) 'Weighted kappa: nominal scale agreement with provision for scaled agreement', *Psychological Bulletin*, 70: 213–220.

Connors, E., Glenn, S. M. and Service, V. (1994) 'Social environmental correlates of infant exploratory and mastery motivation. Poster presentation', *International Society for Infant Studies. IXth Biennial Meeting*, Paris, June 1994.

Donat, P. (1991) 'Measuring behaviour: the tools and the strategies', *Neuroscience and Biobehavioural Reviews*, 15: 447–454.

Dunn, J. F., Plomin, R. and Nettles, M. (1985) 'Consistency of mothers' behaviour toward infant siblings', *Developmental Psychology*, 21: 1188–1195.

Epstein, S. and O'Brien, E. J. (1985) 'The person–situation debate in historical and current perspective', *Psychological Bulletin*, 98: 513–537.

Hartmann, D. P. (1982a) 'Assessing the dependability of observational data', in D. P. Hartmann (ed.) *Using Observers to Study Behaviour*, San Francisco: Jossey-Bass Inc.

Hartmann, D. P. (1982b) *Using Observers to Study Behaviour*, San Francisco: Jossey-Bass Inc.

Hollenbeck, A. R. (1978) 'Problems of reliability in observational research', in G. P. Sackett (ed.) *Observing Behaviour (Vol. 2): Data collection and analysis methods*, Baltimore: University Park Press.

Jackson, D. A., Della-Piana, G. M. and Sloane, H. N. (1978) *How to Establish a Behaviour Observation System*, Englewood Cliffs, N.J.: Education Technology Publications.

Jacob, T., Tennenbaum, P. L. and Krahn, G. (1987) 'Factors influencing the reliability and validity of observational data', in T. Jacob (ed.) *Family Interaction and Psychopathology*, New York: Plenum Press.

Johnson, S. M. and Bolstad, O. D. (1975) 'Reactivity to home observation: a comparison of audio-recorded behaviour with observers present or absent', *Journal of Applied Behaviour Analysis*, 8: 181–185.

Johnson, S. M., Christensen, A. and Bellamy, G. T. (1976) 'Evaluation of family intervention through unobtrusive audio-recordings: experiences in "bugging" children', *Journal of Applied Behaviour Analysis*, 9: 213–219.

Kindermann, T. and Skinner, E. A. (1988) 'Developmental tasks as organisers of children's ecologies: mothers' contingencies as children learn to walk, eat and dress', in J. Valsiner (ed.) *Child Development within Culturally Structured Environments. Vol. 2. Social Construction and Environmental Guidance in Development*, Norwood, N.J.: Ablex.

Lamb, M. E. (1979) 'The effects of social context on dyadic social interaction', in M. E. Lamb, S. J. Suomi and G. R. Stephenson (eds) *Social Interaction Analysis: Methodological Issues*, Madison, WI: University of Wisconsin Press.

Lytton, H. (1971) 'Observation studies of parent–child interaction: a methodological review', *Child Development*, 42: 651–684.

Mann, J., Tann-Have, T. T., Plunkett, J. W. and Meisels, S. J. (1991) 'Time-sampling: a methodological critique', *Child Development*, 62: 227–241.

Martin, P. and Bateson, P. (1993) *Measuring Behaviour: An introductory guide*, 2nd edn, Cambridge: Cambridge University Press.

O'Brien, M., Johnson, J. M. and Anderson-Guetz, D. (1989) 'Evaluating quality in mother–infant interaction: situational effects', *Infant Behaviour and Development*, 12: 451–464.

O'Brien, Y. (1991) *Reactions to response-contingent and non-contingent stimulation by non-handicapped infants and infants with multiple learning difficulties*, unpublished PhD thesis, Lancashire Polytechnic.

Parke, R. D. (1989) 'Social development in infancy: a 25 year perspective', *Advances in Child Development and Behaviour*, 21: 1–48.

Pett, M. A., Wampold, B. E., Vaughan-Cole, B. and East, T. D. (1992) 'Consistency of behaviours within a natural setting: an examination of the impact of context and repeated observations on mother–child interactions', *Behavioural Assessment*, 14: 367–385.

Russell, A., Russell, G. and Midwinter, D. (1992) 'Observer influences on mothers and fathers: self reported influence during home observation', *Merrill Palmer Quarterly*, 38: 263–283.

Sackett, G. P. (ed.) (1978) *Observing Behaviour (vol. 2): Data Collection and Analysis Methods*, Baltimore: University Park Press.

Schaefer, E. S. (1989) 'Dimensions of mother–infant interaction: measurement, stability and predictive validity', *Infant Behaviour and Development*, 12: 379–393.

Seifer, R., Sameroff, A. J., Anagnostopolau, R. and Elias, P. L. (1992) 'Mother–infant interaction during the first year: effects of situation, maternal mental illness and demographic factors', *Infant Behaviour and Development*, 15: 405–426.

Seligman, M. (1975) *Helplessness*, San Francisco, CA: W. H. Freeman.

Smith, P. K. (1985) 'The reliability and validity of one-zero sampling: misconceived criticisms and unacknowledged assumptions', *British Educational Research Journal*, 11: 215–220.

Zegiob, L. E., Arnold, S. and Forehand, R. (1975) 'An examination of observer effects in parent–child interactions', *Child Development*, 46: 509–512.

Chapter 10

Systemic interviewing and attributional analysis applied to international broadcasting*

Peter Stratton

This chapter reports a research technology which is intrinsically qualitative but which goes beyond the usual limits. It not only creates an analysis of the cognitive structures underlying people's evaluations and decisions: it enables estimates to be made of the relative importance of different components of their thinking, and can provide a framework for subsequent quantitative research. Because the techniques offer new possibilities they have found extensive use in both basic and applied research. The rationale of the method is described, then it is illustrated through its application in constructing a performance indicator for the BBC World Service. The illustration provides a step-by-step account of the process of such research, but necessarily in a summary form. The account may be used either as a framework for researchers to create similar processes for their own needs, or as a way of judging the potential usefulness of the approach before following up the sources in more detail.

Like most research techniques, the methods described in this chapter can be used for a variety of purposes and within a variety of conceptual frameworks. But like any other method, the approach is strongly influenced by its origins, and will be understood and used more effectively if those origins are known. I therefore start with a very brief overview of the trends which have made this kind of research possible.

Qualitative research has tended to be seen, both within psychology and in practical areas such as market research, as more limited, and less scientific, than quantitative methods. Experimental methodologies in particular have been almost exclusively quantitative. A number of recent developments within psychology have opened up the possibility of extending the rigour and applicability of qualitative methods. One strand is an increasing application of system theory (von Bertalanffy 1962) which is helping people to break away from studying the isolated individual and towards understanding people within their contexts. Then we have a series of developments in conceptualising research which have moved away from attempting to imitate the positivistic physics that was so successful seventy years ago. One label for this movement is of 'new paradigm research' (Reason and Rowan 1981); another is 'the new physics' (Ryan 1986).

A related movement is that of social constructionism which does not see meaning as inherent in the object being studied, or even in the psychologist doing the studying. Meaning is constructed between people and so exists through communication (Gergen 1992). This leads to the final component to be mentioned, which is an enriched view of human language. With its roots in Wittgenstein and systems-based studies such as that of Watzlawick *et al.* (1967), the movement has led writers such as Pearce (1989) to place language as the core phenomenon that must be understood in order to understand important aspects of human functioning.

All of these movements lead towards the idea that research is a process of creating meanings (rather than uncovering 'findings') and that research on humans (when conducted by humans) is a process of negotiating or co-creating phenomena which must then be reported and interpreted.

One of the dominant methodologies, discourse analysis (Potter and Wetherell 1987), takes the account offered as the phenomenon to be examined and described. This avoids the problems of making claims about what the person thinks are the sources of their action, but is correspondingly limited in any claims it may make about the general significance of its findings. The issue of going beyond description to provide explanations is a difficult one in qualitative research at present. Qualitative research should not be judged by the same criteria as hypothetico-deductive research, with quantifications of validity and generalisability, but it does need to lead to usable results. Perhaps the best solution at present is provided by Lincoln and Guba's (1985) concept of 'transferability'. A well-grounded piece of qualitative research will produce results which can be accurately understood and interpreted, such that it is possible to make a judgement about where, when and in what ways the implications transfer to other contexts.

The various trends converge on the notion of research as being 'reflexive'. The whole process needs to be informed by the recognition that the participants in the research will be continually formulating hypotheses about what the others are doing and that this will influence their actions (Steier 1991). The approach described in this chapter uses interviews or group discussions to create verbal accounts which can then be intensively analysed. When planning such research it is essential to specify all aspects of the interview with a clear concept of how it will be interpreted and acted on by the interviewee. The place and time of the interview, the information given during recruitment, the explanation given at the start of the interview about the objectives of the research, the engagement or warm-up procedures early in the interview, and the schedule itself will all have significant effects on the course of the interview. Then it is necessary to plan how the responses elicited will influence the interviewer. Anything from preparing probes for unresponsive interviewees, through to dealing with emotional reactions to certain kinds of responses, must be considered.

THE CONTEXT

The BBC's World Service broadcasts in both English and local languages around the world. It is funded by the Foreign Office and has been required to develop independent measures of its performance. One aspect of performance, which poses particular challenges, is the judgement that the audience makes as to the quality of the product it receives. This judgement may differ considerably from the assumptions of broadcasters or of politicians. But if the framework of thinking and motivation with which the audience approaches and judges broadcasting is not understood in its own right, we miss an important component of the effects of the medium. Relevant issues include the effects of the station on the knowledge, political awareness and cultural interests of the audience, the extent to which its activities transport the values of the originating country and the effect on the audience's evaluation of that country. Also relevant, of course, is the question of whether and why people choose to listen.

For answers to be useful, such questions must be answered from the perspective of the audience. For a full answer it is necessary to acquire a detailed analysis of the components of perceived quality and to determine how these components relate to the audience's evaluation of the broadcaster and to their decisions about whether and when to tune in.

When the pattern of listener values is unknown, qualitative methods are essential either in their own right or as a precursor to quantitative research. The problem with qualitative research has been that the data are so rich, and the methods of analysis so hidden, that it becomes difficult to judge whether the analysis accurately reflects the major themes of the data.

THE PROBLEM WITH QUALITATIVE RESEARCH

There are two alternative ways of attempting to deal with the richness of qualitative data. The first is to use the extraordinary capacity of the human cognitive system to identify patterns in complex stimuli. The researcher needs to immerse themselves in the data and use their full range of understanding to identify the significant aspects and underlying structures. There is no question that we have a great capacity to carry out such tasks successfully, but on its own this approach leaves the results difficult to evaluate. All of the usual influences on selective perception are likely to operate: motivational factors, expectations, familiarity, avoidance of discomfort. These may all have free play because in the complexity of the task we cannot easily monitor our own processes. The result is that the product of the analysis may be strongly influenced by personal factors. This would not matter if the analysis was repeated independently by a number of researchers who all came to the same conclusions, but such replication is not usually possible.

The alternative is to try to use computers to provide a detailed analysis of the material. This has seemed like a tempting option particularly with verbal material which can easily be stored in a computer and then processed repeatedly. However, once it is attempted the limitations become rapidly apparent. People do not express themselves coherently and grammatically in normal circumstances. Much is taken for granted and so left unsaid, and individual words have various meanings and nuances that are difficult for computers to recognise. A specific example relevant to attributions is the relatively low frequency with which people use connectives like 'because' when making attributional statements. A computer search would identify less than 40 per cent of attributions from the constructions that people use (Rae 1993). Johnson (1989) subtitled a review of this issue 'cybernetic nirvana or information graveyard' and inclined to the conclusion that reliance on computer processing of interview material has more of the graveyard about it at present. However, Dey (1993) does provide a coherent and positive account of the uses of computers in qualitative data analysis. This more recent work suggests that using computers to assist meaning-based explorations of data will become increasingly viable.

These two approaches can be viewed as extremes of a continuum of ways of dealing with qualitative data. The approach described in this chapter has been to develop a set of techniques which combines the strengths of both while avoiding slipping into simple description at one end, or simple-minded positivism at the other.

Grounded theory and constructivism

A coherent approach to a full qualitative methodology at present is provided by grounded theory (Strauss and Corbin 1990). This method specifies that qualitative data should be processed in great detail without imposing any theoretical framework, so that the theory that finally emerges is grounded in the data. Strauss and Corbin give detailed procedures for coding data and grouping the codings into 'categories'. An important feature of the method is that hypotheses derived from the data are followed up through repeated interviews. Henwood and Pidgeon (1992) give a useful account of the application of grounded theory in psychology, while Costain Schou and Hewison (1994) provide an extensive analysis and critique of grounded theory (and particularly of Henwood and Pidgeon's position) which is illustrated through its application to cancer patients.

Our method has much in common with grounded theory, but differs because we do not believe that it is possible to avoid theoretical assumptions when constructing an interview, nor in deciding how to code data. The most 'unstructured' interview will have to indicate to the respondent what the interviewer is interested in hearing about, and any process of coding will be influenced by the epistemology of the researcher. Our approach has been to make our theoretical base explicit, and to construct the interview and the coding on this base (Stratton 1992). However, we still avoid building in assumptions about the phenomena we are studying, and the descriptions in grounded theory will be useful for any researcher applying attributional analysis. The repetitive procedures for processing the data, generating and testing hypotheses, and coalescing the coding into progressively higher-order concepts can be seen in the description of the research project which follows.

Grounded theory is based in a constructivist paradigm. In a basic form, also called an interpretivist framework, this position recognises that meaning is not something inherent in a reality 'out there' but is constructed by the individual (Segal 1986). The job of qualitative research must then be thought of in terms of describing the meanings that lie behind the accounts that people give during interviews and other data gathering exercises. There are two problems with this approach: it allows meaning to be described as personal and possibly non-sharable, whereas we are doing research in order to make meanings public; the people who pay for research, and researchers them-selves, may not be satisfied simply with descriptions – they want explanations that they can use to bring about change.

The approach developed by The Psychology Business started with an attempt to understand the processes operating in troubled families. Within the context of a family therapy clinic (the Leeds Family Therapy and Research Centre, LFTRC), we constructed a form of research using the causal statements made during the therapy sessions. Subsequently we have extended the methodology to a variety of applied contexts.

A synthesis: attributional analysis

The multidisciplinary family team brought perspectives from developmental psychology, systems theory, psychoanalysis and clinical psychology. While systems theory provided a framework for combining these perspectives, we also wanted to focus on a psychological process which would be fundamental to the functioning of families. Eventually we fixed on a concept that was in fact being studied outside of any of these areas, in social psychology. We identified the perceptions that people have of each other and of events in their lives, and particularly the beliefs held about why things happen as they do, as a core phenomenon in determining how people react to events.

The methodology most suited to analysing these perceptions was at the time (and is still) being provided by attribution theory. Appropriately, attribution theory owes its origins to Heider (1958) whose work originated in the attempt to take seriously the 'everyday psychology' by which ordinary people (i.e. non-psychologists) operate. Today attributional analysis has been shown to be an extremely powerful technique for predicting behaviour, having the potential to avoid the limitations of traditional attitude studies and of attempts to predict behaviour from hypothesised structural characteristics (traits or personalities) of individuals.

The LFTRC research group took the basic structure of attribution theory but then found it necessary to spend several years developing and refining a set of techniques which would enable attributional beliefs, as expressed in any verbatim material, to be identified and comprehensively analysed. The system (Stratton *et al.* 1986) is still the only properly validated and tested procedure to do this within either the clinical or the social psychological fields. The technique is a form of content analysis and has taken account of the advances made in various areas of discourse analysis (Potter and Wetherell 1987) with specific inputs from script theory (Schank and Abelson 1977). It is however unique in providing a comprehensive account of all of the important and more-or-less coherently expressed beliefs made during interviews, and converting essential aspects of these to a numerical coding which can then be processed statistically. At the core of the method is the claim that whenever people are confronted by a significant phenomenon they search for reasons, causes, or explanations. In an appropriately structured interview, respondents will provide the richest supply of causal attributions for the issues that most concern them. A technique for identifying and coding causal beliefs such as the Leeds Attributional Coding System (Stratton *et al.*, 1988) will convert the output of an open interview into a structured data set that can be subjected to detailed processing.

Having sketched the rationale and background of this kind of research it is now possible to use the BBC study to illustrate the stages involved. A more detailed account of some of the procedures, illustrated through a different research study, is provided by Stratton (1995).

THE RESEARCH

Interviewing

For the purpose of developing a measure of audience perception of quality, we conducted group discussions in six countries: India (Delhi); Poland (Warsaw); Turkey (Ankara); Nigeria (Sokoto); Ivory Coast (Abidjan); and Kenya (Nairobi). In all, some 400 listeners to international radio broadcasting provided over 120 hours of recorded interview. A major advantage of the technique is that the interviews, which were all conducted by trained interviewers in their first language, can be processed through the first stages of the coding before being translated. This ensures that as far as possible the cultural assumptions of the original are not lost by translation at an early stage. The training in systemic interviewing was designed to ensure the maximum scope for the respondents' views to be expressed and covered issues such as how to avoid showing your own position through to dealing with dominant or silent group members. The interview schedule was carefully constructed to move progressively from broad and non-specific issues such as the uses made of different media through to highly focused questions by the end of the interview dealing with comparisons of different types of programme.

Groups of six to eight international broadcast listeners participated in group discussions run according to a schedule of topics by an interviewer who had been trained in constructionist techniques. All of the fieldwork was supervised either by staff of TPB or from the BBC.

Extracting the attributions

The recorded discussions were processed to identify the attributional beliefs expressed during the discussions. For this kind of research an attribution is defined as:

Any statement in which an outcome is indicated as having happened, or being present, because of some identified event or condition.

As an example of the process of extracting attributions, consider the following brief extract from a group discussion in Nairobi:

Moderator: *How did you get started on international broadcasting?*
Respondent: *Well, I can say it was that urge of wanting to have international news: news from the other side of the border. After listening to BBC you will always want to hear more from outside. I started listening when I was in school, I remember my dad used to tell me to tune into Deutsche Welle. I can say my dad is the one who introduced me.*

This snatch of verbatim contains no fewer than five attributions, each of which has a cause and an outcome:

Cause: *Wanting to have international news*
Outcome: (*I got started on international broadcasting*)

Cause: *Wanting . . . news from the other side of the border*
Outcome: (*I got started on international broadcasting*)

Cause: *After listening to BBC*
Outcome: *You will always want to hear more from outside*

Cause: *My dad used to tell me to tune into Deutsche Welle*
Outcome: *I started listening when I was in school*

Cause: *My dad used to tell me to tune into Deutsche Welle*
Outcome: *I can say my dad is the one who introduced me*

Coding the attributions

Once the attributions have been extracted, each statement is coded. Here is a statement from a group discussion in Delhi:

I prefer to listen to BBC because VOA comes on very late at night

Details of the coding system have been described in detail in the *Leeds Attributional Coding System (LACS) Manual* (Stratton *et al.*, 1988). For the purposes of this illustration, we can say that the system first breaks the statement down into its two component parts – the cause ('VOA comes on late at night') and the outcome ('I prefer to listen to the BBC'). The next step is to construct a coding of personnel which can be used to identify the speaker (when appropriate), the person responsible in the cause (whom we call the agent) and the person who the outcome most affected (the target). The coding then identifies the agent of the cause (an international broadcaster) and the target of the outcome (the speaker).

For each attributional statement the coding identifies the attributional dimensions which apply. The cause is both *stable* and *global* – VOA always comes on late at night and there are no grounds for supposing that this will be different in future (*stable*) and in the context of international broadcasting this is a significant consideration (*global*). For the speaker and the BBC, the cause is produced by *external* circumstances (VOA being on late at night) which are *universal* and could happen to anyone (the experience would be the same for any listener) but the outcome is under the speaker's *control* (he may choose whether to listen or not). For VOA, the cause is *internal* and originates within the organisation (VOA chooses to broadcast late at night), is *personal/unique* (other stations don't broadcast late at night), and is *uncontrollable* (VOA could not change the situation without a radical change in the way it operates).

Each of these coding decisions is recorded as a number, so that each statement eventually has some twenty numerical codings attached to it. These are not scores, but labels in a form that facilitates computer exploration. The analysis consists of searching for dominant patterns, exploring them through varying relationships within the data, defining paradigm criteria for the hypothesised phenomena and then using the codings to identify core statements, which can then be listed and examined for the final stage of interpreting the tendencies.

The application of these codings follows a detailed set of rules covering definitions of the dimensions: which part of the statement is to be coded; whose perspective is to be taken; and resolution of difficult cases. Summary definitions of the dimensions follow, and these have been found to be viable as a basis for research. However, potential users are encouraged to write for a copy of the *LACS Manual* which contains far more detailed instruction than can be given in this context.

Stable [1] / Unstable [2]
Will the cause apply in future? Attribution to stable causes implies an expectation that whatever caused this event will continue to be a causal factor in future events.

Global [1] / Specific [0]
Does the cause have a significant range of consequences? The choice of global causes means that events of this kind are tied to a wide range of significant possible consequences.

Internal [1] / External [0]
Did the cause originate within the person, or was it an external circumstance? When people attribute internally they see the cause arising from themselves or their actions rather than being caused by people or events outside.

Personal [1] / Universal [0]
Did the event happen because this particular person was involved or would it have been true for anybody? People who attribute personally have a belief that they are especially likely to experience these events.

Controllable [1] / Uncontrollable [0]
Could the person have exerted a significant amount of influence over the outcome? Complete control is not necessary, and control may be exerted other than through the specified cause.

These definitions are sufficient to undertake a basic coding of attributional statements. The fundamental rule is to keep in mind how the coding will be interpreted. For example, when deciding whether an outcome is controllable, remember that a coding of control will contribute to an interpretation that this person sees themselves as able to influence outcomes. In any particular piece of research it will usually not be necessary to code all five dimensions. You should decide on theoretical grounds which are most likely to be important, and just code these. The present study was exploratory in that we did not know which dimensions would be most important, and so all combinations were coded.

Practical refinements and elaborations

The major source of confusion in attributional coding is when it is not clear whose perspective is being coded. The simplest case is when our interest is in the speaker, and so each of the dimensions will be applied from the speaker's perspective. In this case be very clear that when Jane says 'the house is a mess because John is untidy' the cause (although it is an 'internal' kind of thing) is coded as external because it is external to Jane.

There is also confusion in the attribution literature because it is not always clear whether it is the cause or the outcome that is being coded, or maybe the connection between them. Think of the example, 'I failed the exam because I could not spot the questions in advance'. The cause, which relied on spotting questions, was not under this person's control. But the outcome might well have been if they believed another factor was the amount of revision they had done. Look again at the five definitions of the dimensions above. There is a progression from coding the cause in the first three, to coding the whole attribution for whether it indicates something *personal* about the individual, and then to whether the outcome was *controllable*. This is the strategy that we have found most useful, but for some purposes you might want to code the internality of the outcome, or the controllability of the cause. The only thing that is essential is that you define precisely which part of the statement you are coding with each dimension, and say what you have done in your report.

Content coding

Each attributional statement is coded in relation to its content. The most basic form is to code whether the outcome was positive, neutral or negative. Attribution theory claims that there is an essential distinction here – an attributional style which is unproductive when applied to negative outcomes may have quite different significance when applied to positive events.

In most research it will also be useful to code some aspect of the attribution. In abusive families we may want to know whether the outcome was an abuse incident so that the causes associated with such incidents can be grouped and examined. When a child has a chronic illness we might classify causes as the illness/medical treatment/action by the child, etc. Each classification gives the possibility of grouping the data in new ways. For example we could group all the attributions in which causes were medical treatments and see whether those which had a negative outcome showed the parents as having more, or less, control than those with a positive outcome. In the present study we constructed a quite elaborate index to cover some sixty definitions of values that were operated by the respondents. Then there were further categories to identify which media and broadcasting station were being discussed, to subdivide listeners and to record whether there was an indication of approval/ disapproval, or a description of taking action such as tuning in to a station. What we are doing here is using the extracted attributions as a way of getting essential material from the interview into a standard form, and then con- structing a content analysis on the statements.

The analysis

Once the attributions have been extracted and coded they can be processed to identify significant patterns. Because all of the information (apart from the

original statements) has been recorded numerically, it is easy to enter tl
into a computer statistics package in order to explore it. As indicated, \
looking for consistent tendencies which appear in the data, so we need a
method which allows us to explore freely. The most general-purpose package
for this work is SPSS – Statistical Package for the Social Sciences. In fact
any system that works out cross-tabulations will do the job, but SPSS makes
it easy to include the verbatim text along with the numerical codings and this
has real advantages.

The next stage is of repeated cycling through the data. Grounded theory
methodology specifies repeated interviews, but it is usually more practicable
to use a single interview to gather sufficiently comprehensive material for
repeated explorations. The cycling process allows patterns to be identified,
hypotheses to be formed, explored and tested and, eventually, the emergence
of strong underlying patterns. Certain of the patterns, taken together, amount
to a mapping of the underlying structure of the values and intentions of the
respondents.

The interpretation

Once the strongest patterns have been identified they need to be interpreted.
In fact, as a grounded theory approach the two parts of the process are
interdependent. There is a continuous cycling round the data finding patterns,
making tentative interpretations of them, and following up hypotheses about
other patterns that might help in understanding them. Many tendencies will
be found that are not especially interesting. For example, finding that 90 per
cent of causes are internal to the agent is (if you think about it) rather obvious.
Agents tend to be taking action (internal) or causing events by their nature.
However, finding that the cause is internal to the speaker more often for
unstable specific causes than for stable global ones may lead to some
interesting conjectures which can then be explored further in the data. One
might investigate whether the tendency only applies in certain contexts (as
indicated by a component of the content coding) or whether it is specific to
positive or negative statements. As hypotheses are developed, explored and
refined through the relationships between different aspects of the coding, they
can eventually be related back to the original attributional statements. The
coding tendencies which define the aspect of interest can be used to specify
the statements which are the clearest exemplars of that aspect and these can
be selectively printed so that the verbatim attributional accounts provide a
final check on the meaning. Note that by this stage the reflexivity of the
method is moving towards using the respondents' accounts to allow meanings
to be negotiated and conveyed between researcher and the recipient of the
research report.

An idea of the interplay between the attributional dimensions, the content coding and the attributional statements may be deduced from the kinds of results created by this process in the BBC study.

THE FINDINGS

We found strong tendencies to use particular patterns of attributional dimension in relation to particular types of statement. One important tendency was to use stable and global statements when referring to aspects of a broadcaster of which the speaker approved or disapproved. A different pattern, of global, sometimes personal, and controllable dimensions was used in relation to the decision of whether or not to listen. On inspection of the relevant statements, these two forms were quite distinct. The first tended to refer to intrinsic aspects of the station; the second, in its purest form, related to the impact that listening had on the life of the listener. We came to call the first component of the audience perception *Intrinsic* and the second component *Empowering*.

From the way these groups of statements operated it was clear that a station would need to be perceived positively in both respects to achieve an effective presence in terms of positive perception, consistent use, and audience loyalty. To be valued for intrinsic quality, but not to offer empowerment will mean that the broadcaster is admired and respected but not listened to. Empowerment without intrinsic value means that the station is used but not respected or valued and so will be readily discarded. For an international broadcaster with a mission to positively represent the home culture, it is essential to be rated highly on both intrinsic and empowering aspects. We have summarised the combination of the two sets of values as *Effective quality*. The next task was to determine the components of effective quality, and to identify how they operated.

Within the analysis, it was possible to identify, and scale, the values which contributed to perceptions of intrinsic value and empowerment. Those values that contributed to both aspects were selected, and the coding of statements making up each value was intensively analysed to determine which values operated similarly in attributional terms, and so could be grouped together. From this stage of the analysis emerged six *Core values* which accounted for the majority of variation in the data. These core values then became the basis for subsequent analyses.

The data from six different countries, independently analysed, consistently generated the same six core values. There were, however, substantial variations in the relative weights of components of the values, and in the relative significance of the values in contributing to effective quality. The six core values are listed in Table 10.1. It is important to recognise that what we are offering here are summary labels and definitions which best capture the range of meaning of each value. The words we have chosen will rarely if ever have been used by the respondents.

Table 10.1 The six core values of international broadcasting

Distinctive	has a recognisable style and a clear and acceptable identity
Functional	does the essential aspects of the job well. Includes professionalism and production values
Informative	effectively transmits the important information
Credible	can be trusted to be objective and accurate
Interesting	presents intrinsically interesting material in an engaging form
Empathetic	understands and respects the values of the local culture and works to make its material accessible

Establishing the nature of a core value

If we take the example of the core value 'empathetic' in Ankara, Delhi and
Warsaw, this comprised the four closely related values of 'accessible',
'knowledgeable', 'loyal' and 'sympathetic'. *Accessible* covers a range of
things, from ease of understanding the style, vocabulary, language and
accents used to the ease with which the station can be found on the dial. In
all three locations, a broadcaster's ability to demonstrate *knowledge* and
understanding of personal and local concerns was a widely used component
of the core value. *Sympathy* for the local language, culture and politics is
closely linked to respect for listeners' concerns which audiences take as
evidence of the broadcaster's sympathy. In Ankara, a sense of a broadcaster's
long-standing sympathy and knowledge, together with a commitment to
accessibility came together as *loyalty*.

The three strongest components of the core value 'empathetic' were
sympathy, accessibility, and knowledgeability. The relative strengths of the
contributing values in each location are indicated in Figure 10.1. This figure
not only indicates differences in how the values relate to each other in each

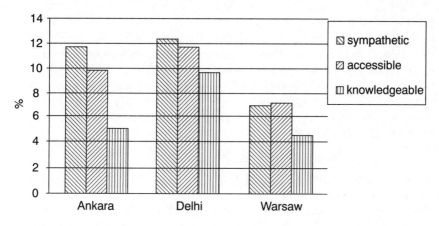

Figure 10.1 Major components of the core value 'empathetic' in three countries

country, but also that the core value of empathy was less important in Warsaw than in the other two locations.

Each core value is evaluated in terms of its relative strength on a variety of indicators. Some of these derive from how frequently components of the value were present in causal attributions, others derived from the tendency for the attributions to fall into certain significant patterns. Because the data consist of large numbers of coded statements it is possible to assign relative weights to these different aspects. In particular, the two essential components of 'intrinsic' and 'empowering' are weighted separately for each core value, in terms of salience in the discussion (from frequency of reference) and attributional power (from the factor by which the specified attributional pattern exceeds the statistically expected level).

The six core values, and the relative weighting attached to each aspect of each of them, constitutes a mathematical model of effective quality. The data within each location are used to quantify the components of the model so that each aspect of the audience perception of effective quality can be independently specified. The model can then be used in two ways:

1 To provide weightings on each core value with which quantitatively derived measures of satisfaction with a given station can be combined. Summing across the values then provides an overall performance indicator.
2 To make comparisons across stations, across countries, or through repeated sampling in the same country over time. The various parameters available, recorded separately for each core value, allow a detailed exploration of differences in performance as they arise.

Producing a score for effective quality

Now that the core values for listeners to international broadcasters have been established in a particular area, we can see the extent to which listeners to particular stations feel that these values are met. This is done by devising agree/disagree statements reflecting both the approval and listening dimensions of each of the six core values, and running these on quantitative surveys in the target area. The same statements are put to listeners to the BBC and two other international stations and respondents answer on a five-point scale. Here are some statements designed for use in a survey in Abidjan. The statements are repeated, with names amended, for listeners to Radio France International (RFI) and Voice of America (VOA).

Core value 'functional' – intrinsic:

I can rely on the BBC to bring the news that is important as soon as it happens.

Core value 'functional' – empowering:

The BBC gives the news which I will not hear about on our own stations.

Core value 'empathetic' – intrinsic:

The BBC understands what life is like for people living in Ivory Coast.

Core value 'empathetic' – empowering:

Listening to the BBC helps me to find out more about the things I am interested in.

In each country the relative significance of each component was used to ensure that it was the most important contributor to the values that made up the substance of the questions. For example, when constructing survey questions for the core value 'empathetic', the Ankara analysis showed that the strongest intrinsic value contributing to empathy was 'sympathy', while the strongest empowering component was 'knowledgeable'. To construct the survey questions we printed out a listing of all of the statements from Ankara which were coded for the value of sympathy, selected for the attributional pattern which defines intrinsic. We could then judge how this aspect of empathy was talked about and construct a question with appropriate wording. This process was repeated for each aspect of each core value. Finally, the proposed questions are passed back to the interviewer who had extracted the attributions in the original language. This person checked that the survey items covered the most important concerns of the respondents, and then translated them, again using the original material as a guide to the most appropriate wording. The minimum set would be twelve questions (intrinsic and empowering for each of six core values) which could be rated on a Likert scale of 'agree' to 'disagree' by respondents.

Once a survey has been run the data, which show how well each station is judged to perform on each core value, can be entered back into a model derived from the earlier analysis. Each aspect of each core value is weighted, so that the satisfaction with a particular value has an impact on the overall score in proportion to its importance to the audience. This process allows direct comparisons between countries while allowing use of those specific values that are most relevant for each country independently.

CONCLUSION

The research is reported in this chapter to support three claims. First that current developments in thinking about the research process provide a foundation for intensive and rigorous qualitative research which is capable of capturing much of the richness of human functioning. Second that an attributionally based analysis of the verbal content of interviews can generate a clear account of people's value systems, which attribution theory can then interpret. Third, that this kind of qualitative research can provide sound and usable findings in its own right and also be a secure foundation for quantitative surveys.

More broadly, the research method combining systemic interviewing with attributional analysis has been shown to confound the most damning criticism made of psychological research: that it often has no practical impact (Barlow *et al.*, 1984; Robson 1993). The research for the BBC World Service which has been used as an illustration in this chapter is just one of a wide and varied range of applications of systemic interviewing and attributional analysis which have been used by many of Britain's largest companies.

The BBC have been sufficiently encouraged by their evaluation of this methodology to fund a continuation of the research in ten further locations during the next two years.

NOTE

* I am grateful to Allen Cooper, Manager of International Broadcasting Audience Research at the BBC World Service, and to his staff, especially Colin Wilding, for their support for this research and for their significant contributions to its development.

REFERENCES

Barlow, D.H., Hayes, S. C. and Nelson, R. O. (1984) *The Scientist Practitioner: Research and accountability in clinical and educational settings*, Oxford: Pergamon.
Bertalanffy, L. von (1962) *General System Theory*, New York: Braziller.
Costain Schou, K. and Hewison, J. (1994) 'Issues of interpretive methodology: the utility and scope of grounded theory in contextual research', *Human Systems*, 4: 3–26.
Dey, I. (1993) *Qualitative Data Analysis: A user friendly guide for social scientists*, London: Routledge.
Gergen, K. J. (1992) 'Social constructionism in question', *Human Systems*, 2: 163–182.
Heider, F. (1958) *The Psychology of Interpersonal Relations*, New York: Wiley.
Henwood, K.L. and Pidgeon, N.F. (1992) 'Qualitative research and psychological theorizing', *British Journal of Psychology*, 83: 97–111.
Johnson, D.J. (1989) 'Open ended warfare: cybernetic nirvana or information graveyard?', Proceedings of the Market Research Society Annual Conference.
Lincoln, Y.S. and Guba, E.G. (1985) *Naturalistic Inquiry*, Newbury Park: Sage.
Pearce, B. (1989) *Communication and the Human Condition*, Illinois: Southern Illinois University Press.
Potter, J. and Wetherell, M. (1987) *Discourse and Social Psychology: Beyond attitudes and behaviour*, London: Sage.
Rae, J.P. (1989) 'Explanations and communicative constraints in naturally occurring discourse', unpublished PhD thesis, University of Leeds.
Reason, P. and Rowan, J. (1981) *Human Inquiry: A sourcebook of new paradigm research*, Chichester: Wiley.
Robson, C. (1993) *Real World Research*, Oxford: Blackwell.
Ryan, M. (1986) 'Implications from the "old" and the "new" physics for studying buyer behaviour', in D. Brinberg and R. Lutz (eds) *Perspective on Methodology in Consumer Research*, New York: Springer-Verlag.

Schank, R. and Abelson, R. (1977) *Scripts, Plans, Goals, and Understanding*, Hillsdale, N.J.: Erlbaum.

Segal, L. (1986) *The Dream of Reality: Heinz Von Foerster's constructivism*, New York: Norton.

Steier, F. (1991) *Research and Reflexivity*, London: Sage.

Stratton, P. (1992) 'Selling constructionism to market research', *Human Systems*, 3: 253–273.

Stratton, P. (1995) 'Attributional coding of interview data', in N. Hayes (ed.) *An Introduction to Qualitative Methods*, London: Routledge.

Stratton, P.M., Heard, D.H., Hanks, H.G., Munton, A.G., Brewin, C.R. and Davidson, C. (1986) 'Coding causal beliefs in natural discourse', *British Journal of Social Psychology*, 25: 299–313.

Stratton, P.M., Munton, A.G., Hanks, H.G.I., Heard, D.H. and Davidson, C. (1988) *Leeds Attributional Coding System (LACS) Manual*, Leeds: LFTRC.

Strauss, A.L. and Corbin, J. (1990) *Basics of Qualitative Research: Grounded theory procedures and techniques*, Newbury Park: Sage.

Watzlawick, P., Beavin, J.H. and Jackson, D.D. (1967) *Pragmatics of Human Communication*, New York: Norton.

Chapter 11

Constructing and deconstructing childhood

Images of children and charity appeals

Erica Burman

In this chapter I will be drawing on ideas and concepts drawn from deconstruction and poststructuralist theory to interrogate some of the meanings and investments of contemporary childhood. The analysis will be focused on a particular corpus of texts, namely images of children in charity appeals, as expressing key aspects of the contemporary cultural–political organisation of childhood. The theoretical and methodological approach I use here is a form of discourse analysis, where key categories are treated as indices or symptoms of particular histories and relationships (Burman and Parker 1993; Parker 1992). I use the term 'text' here to include both images and the written commentary accompanying them, and treat these as a window into the tissue of meanings they reflect and mobilise. As Goffman (1979) pointed out, material produced for advertising, albeit in this case charitable advertising, provides a rich source of culturally available meanings precisely by virtue of its elliptical and idealised nature.

THEORETICAL BACKGROUND: CONSTRUCTING CHILDHOOD

Historical studies of childhood suggest that the current discourse of childhood as innocent, spontaneous and in need of nurturance and protection is a modern construction (Ariès 1962; James and Prout 1990; Stainton Rogers and Stainton Rogers 1992). But practices of regulation police the contours of the natural, growing child. Hendrick (1990) discusses the emergence of 'the schooled child' and 'the family child' as indices of the importance accorded to psychological technologies of classification, while Hoyles (1989) has analysed how treating the child as innocent and unknowing has disenfranchised children's political resistance. On this score, both Boyden and Hudson (1985) and Ennew and Milne (1989) point out how the legal position of 'minor' functions, in the name of protection and dependence, to *deny* rights to children.

In terms of the role of psychology within these discourses, as a result of the 'psychological complex' (Rose 1985), the set of social practices such as health visiting, community nursing and social work that draw upon psychological stories of relationships and child development, children function as a key site of state intervention and regulation in families. In particular, these practices pathologise working-class mothers (Walkerdine and Lucey 1989). The psychological models on offer also recycle and scientise culturally gendered stereotypes within both their content and structure. In terms of cultural associations, the active, playing, discovering child of developmental psychology is a boy (Burman 1995a). This gendering of competence has implications for the differential evaluation of girls' and boys' educational achievement, with good, hardworking girl pupils seen as less clever (Walkerdine *et al.*, 1989).

CHILDREN AS COMMODITIES

Cultural significations around childhood have long been mobilised for commercial purposes. By virtue of their 'need' for socialisation and en-culturation, children are regarded as closer to nature. The naturalness connoted by childhood is used to sell health and beauty products. But the association with nature reflects the tendency, evident also in psychological approaches, to abstract children from their social (familial, cultural, histor-ical) locations. Further, psychological models of childhood as a period of shaping and preparation have been taken up by banks and insurance com-panies to add an explicit financial dimension to notions of protection, security and investment (as in the Abbey National slogan 'Growing, growing, gone'), while cars are marketed to restore past senses of power and pleasure ('Remember that feeling of total control?', Peugeot, 1992) or to ensure them for our children ('All life's journeys should be unforgettable', Rover, 1992).

Given the dynamic and reciprocal relation between psychology and social practices, popular cultural imagery of children can therefore be analysed both as a resource informing psychological models, *and* as a reflection of them. While the focus here is on the broader themes indicated by these representa-tions, elsewhere I analyse the role of psychology as recirculating and legitimating these social meanings (Burman 1994a; Burman 1995a). If, as Holland (1992) suggests, representations of children offer a displaced arena in which to explore themes of powerlessness and dependency, then loss and vulnerability can be safely expressed through children who are designated appropriate recipients of our 'help'. It is at this point that presuppositions of developmental psychology and the cultural practices it reflects and informs meet up with those of international aid and development policies. Charity advertisements offer a useful corpus of texts to explore how children function in the psychic economy of the very material economy of international aid. I will therefore be treating aid advertisements as exemplars, not only of ideologies of childhood but as reproducing more general discourses of First–Third World relations informing international aid and development policies. In this I will move from texts of advertisements, to analyse the practices of charity organisations (and accounts of those practices) and articulate these with assumptions underlying international aid policies.

ANALYSING AID ADS

Charitable and aid organisations for Third World development are forced to grapple with the tensions between fund-raising and education, since, as a reflection of the cultural chauvinism pandered to by the mass media, and as lamented by the charities themselves (e.g. Black 1992), disaster imagery forms a major source of the available cultural representations of the Third World (Graham and Lynn 1989). Images of children enlist our help, and the child becomes the vehicle or voice through whom the general appeal is made. It has been widely noted that children function within aid ads as the quintessential recipients, and, since parents or other adults are usually literally invisible, it is only by implication that the paternal feelings mobilised are extended to their families or communities. In this sense:

'An irony of the aid imagery, then, is that however accurate the picture, an appeal on behalf of the children may necessarily be *against* the community of which they are part, rather than on that community's behalf.'
(Holland 1992: 157)

The injunction to give to the poor and needy therefore maps onto the adult capacity to provide for children, which in the case of images of Third World children also reinscribes Western privilege (Reeves 1988). The tendency to depict children alone to emphasise their need not only reflects the general abstraction of childhood from cultural practices, but both locates the children as safely distant and renders their parents or communities as neglectful or inadequate in failing to meet their needs. Correspondingly, it is through being infantilised by sharing the position of their children that these gain legitimate access to 'our' 'help'. A related consequence of the dependence on the individual starving child as the general idiom for hunger is that the circumstances that give rise to famine and poverty remain unexplored. As Frederick Forsythe, a reporter who disobeyed BBC orders so as to stay and cover the war in Biafra, wrote:

'People who couldn't fathom the political complexities of the war could easily grasp the wrong in a picture of a child dying of starvation.'
(quoted in Harrison and Palmer 1986: 33)

In summary so far, then, advertising builds on a general tendency for representations of children to be divorced from cultural and historical practices. Childhood is set apart from the social relations of production and exchange, and invested with a set of meanings to promote consumption. Hence the generalisation of aid advertising from the particular (child) to the general (adult population) participates in the cultural economy of power and exchange relations. The depiction of children in aid ads thus reinscribes a series of overdeterminations: first the general representation of the child as innocent victim renders her worthy of aid; second the cultural abstraction of children from social practices fosters a depoliticisation of the circumstances giving rise to the crisis.

CHILDREN AND AID: THEORISING THE CON-TEXT

Before introducing the texts, a prior and necessary analytic step is to theorise more precisely the context in which such material is generated. What conditions prompt the emergence of this text, and what is the field of possible alternatives? Just as the set of conventions governing the representation of children has its history, so too does the relation between images of children and charity campaigns. These are as subject to fluctuations in policy, public awareness and technological developments as any other aspect of the media. Relevant sources for these questions are accounts of the history and functioning of charities (Black 1992; Burnell 1991), of the role of media coverage in specific 'disasters' (Harrison and Palmer 1986; Sorenson 1991), and analyses of the process and politics of international aid (Gill 1986; Harper in press; Sachs 1992). At this point we can note seven factors.

1 There is a particular history of charitable activity that needs to be taken into account in any analysis. Most British charities have their origins in nineteenth-century Christian philanthropic activity. We might therefore anticipate that discourses of charity will be linked with the role this is accorded within specific religious practices.
2 The emergence of the child as the signifier of need has its own history too, with Oxfam in 1949 portraying a photo of a distressed child and inviting specific sums of money 'to help one stricken family' (Black 1992: 35). The 1961 famine in the (then) Congo 'burnt the image of the starving African child onto the collective British conscience' (Black 1992: 63), and these images have become identified with aid interventions (see also Burman 1994c).
3 Any adequate analysis also should address the mutual relation of dependence that exists between the aid organisations and the mass media, of which the activity of buying advertising space (pioneered by Oxfam in 1946) is merely one small part. While the media constitute the gatekeepers of public awareness, equally news reporters have relied upon aid field-workers for information about and access to the disasters.
4 The changing impact and role of different mass media is related to technological developments and associated economic conditions in which they function. Gill (1986) and Harrison and Palmer (1986) discuss how newspaper reports broke the news of the horror of the Ethiopian famine in 1973, but it was television coverage that brought the 1984 famine in

Ethiopia into our homes. This shift in medium not only reflects changing viewing and reading habits but also arises from technological changes in the production of news coverage, such as cutbacks in the funding of overseas reporters and increasing dependence on international press agencies using satellite communication. Hence it took a documentary made by a team of investigative journalists primed by aid workers to break news of the 1984 Ethiopian famine. In addition to the dangers to journalists of covering war zones, and of the corresponding selection of what is available to be reported as news, therefore, these changes are vital in theorising the constraints and constitutive processes in the production of the available array of images of the Third World.

5 Public reaction to media coverage has come to lead state and organisational responses to Third World needs. It was the press coverage of the Ethiopia famine which prompted the spate of fund-raising events, such as Liveaid, Sportaid, and the telethons. Public pressure, as mobilised through these, has prompted some government gestures (such as 'Operation Irma') towards aid.

6 In this context, the texts that form the basis of this analysis can be introduced. I am going to focus on an 'opportunity sample' of advertisements in newspapers, on hoardings, or accompanying my bank statement or bills within a time period spanning mid-1991 to January 1994. My interest lies in assessing readily available representations of Third World children, and for my analysis I draw upon material aspects of my position as a cultural participant of a Western industrialised country (a middle-class professional participant) from which to generate these readings. I reflect more on this process at the end of this chapter.

7 Now we need to theorise the parameters of the textual space. The main texts I analyse are what are known as 'the 20 double', that is the double columned charity ad that regularly appears on the bottom right-hand corner of the front page of national newspapers, and sometimes inside too. In terms of possible substitutions in this slot, it alternates with ads for investment and savings accounts, on learning a language, how to extend your memory, travel offers, and for the Labour Party.

POSITIONS OF IDENTIFICATION

A discourse analysis of charity advertisements should not only identify focal elements, but should also highlight agencies and their relations. If children are privileged discursive objects in these texts, then what other positions are elaborated for donors and recipients?

What 'we' can do

The adverts elaborate a set of distinct subject positions for 'us' and 'them'. This splitting produces different domains of action and reaction. What 'we', as donors, can do is offer help or sponsorship. We are exhorted to 'stop the genocide' by a variety of miracles, gifts and acts of restoration, with the iconography of rescue by representatives of a technological society exemplified by doctors, nurses and aid workers bearing handpumps and plastic shelters.

What 'we' get out of it

The adverts tell us what 'we' get out of 'helping'. This includes the invitation to 'experience the joy of sponsorship' (ActionAid), to echo the statement 'I want to give the gift of life', to 'make a real difference to people's lives' (Oxfam) or simply express how 'I want to help' (Oxfam). At seasonal times we are endowed with the capacity to 'Bring joy to the children of the World. Together, we can put a stop to suffering' (ANBS). The positions set out for 'us' confirm our adult status in the us–them polarity through our capacity to give.

Juxtapositions

An alternative strategy uses juxtapositions or 'guilt by comparison' (Holland 1992). The focus here shifts from the appalling image alone to construct an address to the position of the reader which both emphasises our privilege, and how a donation of relative insignificance to 'us' can achieve so much for 'them'. Instances include 'do you really need 50p more than she does?' (ActionAid); 'life is cheap' (ActionAid); '£15 can intoxicate you for a night or inoculate her for life' (ActionAid); '20 degrees minus. This is the kind of Xmas 2.7 million former Yugoslavs have to look forward to' (Oxfam). Themes of competition mix with shame as in 'don't be left out' (skip lunch, Save the Children). Shock and shame figure within leaflets distributed door to door or available in charity shops, as in Oxfam's instructions for measuring child malnutrition. In some cases the ads address common responses of apathy, of being overwhelmed and indifference: 'Please don't look away' (ActionAid); 'With so much poverty in the world where on earth do you start?' (ActionAid); 'This won't stop the child next door screaming. Sending £25 will' (NSPCC).

DISCOURSES

Starving children

What is being suggested if 'only you can help' (Adopt a Granny)? And who are 'they' whom 'we' are invited to 'help'? What relationships are set up? What explanations are invoked, and how are 'we' positioned in them? As exemplars of common humanity, children are abstracted from particular cultural and historical locations at the price of absolution from responsibility for their plight. 'We' are positioned as surrogate parents, a move which constitutes 'them', the rest of the peoples the hungry child represents and connotes, as neglectful. Children are generally depicted alone; fathers are absent and mothers, where they appear, are rendered into a child-like dependency through their helpless state. An alternative approach recasts the donor–recipient relationship, as in Oxfam's logo 'project partners'. But even here the newspaper ads in general circulation contrast with more detailed literature for the committed reader.

Images of starving children, as the idiom of hunger generally, are all too prevalent in the texts (UNICEF, Concern, Care). They convey qualities of dependence, passivity and illness that aim to solicit care, as in UNICEF's 'for as long as the children need us we'll be there: you *can* help save children's lives in Somalia'. But these appalling images, together with the text that generalises from one child or family to a whole region, or even to the more general category of 'the poor' can incur costs:

> [T]hese pictured children may well have sacrificed the indulgence childhood demands. Without the flattery offered by the appealing image they may arouse adult sadism without deflecting it and confirm a contempt for those many parts of the world which seem unable to help their own.
>
> (Holland 1992: 154)

Self-reliance

The predication of compassion on the representation of humble and submissive recipients makes it difficult for aid organisations to highlight project partners' own activities for reconstruction. Such information is deemed to complicate the fund-eliciting reaction of pity. Nevertheless, in response to criticisms, an alternative discourse of self-reliance is elaborated within the aid ads. Examples include 'if you sponsor Shomita no one will have to sponsor her children' (ActionAid); 'The last thing we want to give Jalib is food' (ActionAid); 'She was sponsored when she was six. Now she teaches sixty' (ActionAid); 'Sometimes the burden of the Third World is not what it appears to be' (Intermediate Technology). But while this seemingly more positive approach emphasises the commitment and resourcefulness of Third World children (and their families) to helping themselves, hidden within this is a tacit assumption of conditionality: that 'we' are only prepared to 'help' if giving now means we won't have to give later. But in the effort of overcoming the previous model of passivity the message of self-reliance seems to protest too much: 'Wateraid encourages people to take responsibility for their own lives.' But the question that this begs is surely: didn't they take responsibility for their own lives before circumstances of famine or poverty positioned them as lacking in the resources necessary to effect the changes in their lives? The difficulties around this discourse of self-reliance are a broader reflection of the current aid philosophy of 'sustainable development' which fails to consider whether the projects were developed in response to people's requirements as they have defined them, or as defined by Northern 'experts', and results in projects which either fail or produce only short-term and superficial change (Morris 1992; Pottier 1993).

Helping

Helping others to help themselves can turn out to be a variant of, rather than a corrective to, the more prevalent discourse of helping, with its attendant subject positions. Indeed the philosophy of helping embodied in charitable activity has a long history of linking support with threat and power. In general terms, the definition of help is now planned according to institutional and professional definitions of need, and as such is conditional. As those who struggle to claim state benefits in this country well know, to be the recipient of aid is to be subject to the gaze of the helper. This relationship of surveillance is reflected in a trivial and benign form in ads which offer sponsors regular bulletins on how their lucky sponsee is progressing, but it is also indicative of the more general structure of development aid. Who do we help when we help? What motivations prompt the urge to give? The Christian origins of charity are more linked to saving one's own soul than saving another's skin. This, Gronemeyer (1992) argues, has found its modern, secular form in the philosophy of improvement and in the drive to ward off death by greater material security. In bestowing help we confirm our own standards, and heterogeneity of cultural practices is reduced to homogeneity. Similarly, the positions of giving, teaching and caring formulated within the ads set up positions of passive recipients, of ignorant pupils, and of ill victims.

In terms of their function as bearers of images of the Third World and development issues, the problem with charity ads is that they confound concepts of 'need' and 'neediness'. At issue here is the question of who decides. Undoubtedly, in most of the appeals that appear in newspaper columns there can be little dispute about immediate need. Acts of restoration of the kinds 'we' are empowered to provide are represented as repairing or restoring the recipient to their prior state. The representation of their 'cry for help', that is representing need through assuming the voice of the recipient, ostensibly positions them as definer of their need. But in terms of the policies that guide 'development', the identification of 'neediness' 'is much more the result of a comparison with a foreign normality, which is effectively declared to be obligatory. One becomes needy on account of a diagnosis – I decide when you are needy' (Gronemeyer 1992: 66).

Participation

Charity therefore sets up subject positions of 'us' and 'them', where the help 'we' offer 'them' is on 'our' own terms. The current move to focus on the participation of those who receive the aid (from donor–recipient to project partners), while apparently an improvement from the portrayal of passive, helpless recipients, does not always resolve the problems. The discourse of participation, with its roots in theories of conscientisation and empowerment, adopted by non-governmental organisations, has now entered international development policies. While the more radical empowerment approaches still carry paternalistic presumptions of having the ability to confer power, as a kind of 'conscientization from without' (Rahnema 1992: 125) (thereby in danger of disempowering those they seek to empower), in its mainstream institutional form, participation has been criticised as offering a more insidious form of neo-colonialism combined with a centralisation of state power over local peoples through their enlistment into the development narrative. No longer perceived as a threat, participation has become a politically attractive slogan that raises funds. Self-help becomes the euphemism for passing on the costs of compulsory structural adjustment programmes to the poor through credit loan schemes which deepen the cycle of debt (Rahnema 1992).

Population

A recent addition to the charity ad discourse is the theme of population. Population Concern's text reads: 'For the first time in four years Saba is not pregnant' (Population Concern). The rhetoric here is of access to birth control as a basic human right. But nested within this seemingly incontrovertible proposition is a set of assumptions about poor people's responsibility for their own poverty, and, further, that the fertility rates of peoples of the Third World endanger not only the financial well-being of those individuals and their countries but pose an ecological threat to the whole world. The text continues: 'This rapid rise [of the birth rate] is compounding the crisis of poverty and the environment in developing countries.' This theme reflects the current centrality of policies on family planning and population management to development programmes. While in 1959 Eisenhower considered birth control a private matter beyond state intervention, by 1969 Nixon was committed to family planning which was taken up by Bush in 1973 as the population problem. The management of fertility is now a central component of the allocation of international aid and development money (Duden 1992).

Short-term solutions

In depicting need, the imperative to make an emotional impact in order to elicit funds does not encourage analysis of how these circumstances came about. In particular, the focus within charity appeals (perhaps inevitably in the case of emergencies) on crisis intervention militates against developing analyses about how or why 'developing countries' have been 'de-developed', or what it is they lack or lag behind on (reproducing the developmental deficit model) and why poor people are poor. Simple and short-term (and easily fundable) measures are presented as complete technological fixes for complex problems. One of these is surgery: 'The £15 miracle' (Sight Savers). As well as conducting miracles 'we' can provide solutions ('There is a solution. Wateraid and you', 1992). Perhaps currently the most vaunted quick techno-logical solution in the child-saving industry is oral rehydration therapy (ORT), the sachets of sugar and salt that, reconstituted with sterile water, can ward off dehydration in people weakened and ill from diarrhoeal infections. These are presented as 'Saving lives with salt and sugar' (Save the Children), 'The solution he's drinking could save his life. And it only costs 10p' (Save the Children). Because no other factors are mentioned, it is all too easy for responsibility for structural poverty and de-development to devolve onto the impoverished people themselves. The focus on finite simple devices, however attractive, also maintains the illusion that the West possesses the scientific expertise to dispense with death and disease. Assumptions such as these make it hard to talk about long-term development or explanations for inequalities such as Oxfam's 'Poverty rules and it's not OK', since these pale into distant abstraction compared to these technological fixes.

One world

The discourse of 'one world' makes its appearance within the charity ads as 'a world family' (Plan International UK). This would seem to convey a sense of solidarity and collective reponsibility for shared problems. But what this slides over is the asymmetry of First–Third World relations which are far from the cosy image of familial togetherness. The change depicted within charity ads, no doubt driven by disasters and emergencies, is largely concerned with restoring basic needs, with Third World children's survival counterposed with First World children's development. But this focus on immediate response and gain leaves us with no analysis of how or why this situation came about. Moreover, the claim that we are 'changing the world one child at a time' (Plan International UK) presents an individualistic and voluntaristic model of change that dispenses with the primary international (including financial) organisations that have the means to effect, or impede, real change, and with whom the responsibility should lie.

METHODOLOGICAL REFLECTIONS

Some comments are in order about the status and limits of this analysis.

Authorial intention and the practice of discourse analysis

There is a general perception that analysing texts is an activity which problematises the truth claims of the content described. While discourse analysis does challenge the facticity of texts by focusing on their historical and discursive construction (Burman 1991), this does not necessarily entail a derogation of the practices it comments upon. Hence the analysis undertaken here does not deride the activity of giving charity, nor the activities of the charity organisations. Rather what I am arguing is that charity campaigns, as highly crafted, strategic interventions, offer a rich, and arguably a primary, resource for widely circulating representations of 'developing' countries. As such they occupy the semantic space which links popular representations of the Third World with more technical presuppositions of governmental development policy. Further, the literature I have drawn upon for this analysis is in the main drawn from debates within those charities and NGOs in which these are the key issues of concern (Black 1992; Coulter 1989; Nyoni 1988/9; Reeves and Hammond 1988). Indeed it is these questions that generate tensions between the audio-visual, communication, education and the fund-raising departments of such organisations.

Danger of reproducing those meanings

It could be argued that the analysis here reproduces precisely the images and assumptions that it critiques by virtue of making this commentary. This is a real danger, and discourse analysts need to be aware of the ways the verbal and visual material they analyse gains new life from such activity. However, the process of reading and interpreting is itself a process, an activity, and the narrative context within which these assumptions are rearticulated wards off or constrains this. But, in taking seriously the productivity of the text, and the constructive activity of reading, I cannot claim absolute authorial control of the readings made of my readings. This ethical problem can itself be topicalised, in that the activity of commenting upon aid ads reproduces precisely the dilemmas posed for the aid organisations themselves. In this sense, problems of analysing and generating readings can themselves become a resource for the analysis.

Role of reflexivity

Theorising the role of analyst, as within discourses rather than outside them, wards off any moves towards complacent ironical readings. While it may be tempting to regard already existing text (as in media material) as separate, with the analyst positioned as less complicit or participative within the text than in, say, interview material, this relies on an inadequate theorising of the activity of analysis. It is necessary for the analyst to participate in the practices s/he comments upon in order to generate readings (Smith 1990). We have to access our knowledge as culturally competent members in order to identify and interpret the discourses (see also Burman 1994c).

Material context of production

It is clearly inadequate to analyse images/texts outside the material context of their production (cf. Barker 1990). On this point I have tried to map out something of the political events and technological developments that have shaped the strategies for charity appeals that we see today. Further investigation of the charity market would be relevant, exploring how the advertising activity of this highly competitive sector is regulated by a monthly publication, *The Charity Aid Examiner*, of 48–54 pages published in London. Its circulation is confined to motivated subscribers at £170 per issue. According to the publishers, this provides detailed analyses of those charities who spend more than 1 per cent of the total sum spent by all charities in the national papers each month, and calculates the overall amount spent each day in each publication. It functions as the measure of the financial success and health of the various charities, as well as indicating which forms of ads are regarded as most successful.

Intra-textual metacommentary and subversion

The identification of the '20 double' slot as a 'charity space' constitutes this as a discursive object which can become the site for subversion of the genre. So we have ads which assume the form and voice of charity appeals for the South, including Southern children, as in the appeal to 'Adopt a whale', or 'Tropical forest for sale', or 'S.O.S. Save our skins', this last accompanying the oil tanker disaster off the Shetland Islands in January 1993. The child rescue and sponsorship genre has been imported even more explicitly in the current (1994) dolphin and whale protection slogan of 'Adopt this baby!'. Similarly, the routine substitutions of charity ads with investment and bank accounts is used by the charities themselves as a means to attract attention in more covert ways. Hence an ad that looks like it offers tax-saving or investment advice to avoid state seizure of assets as death duties turns a message to make a will into an opportunity to give money to the Third World, as in the Children's Society ('Making a will') and Christian Aid ('Make a will. Make a difference', 'Will your only legacy be upset, confusion and paperwork?') ads.

Parameters of variation

There are various dimensions of variation that I have not addressed in this account, but would be necessary to develop it further. First, in the analysis above I have not made temporal distinctions, but there are clear seasonal variations that govern frequency and style of aid ads (notably at Christmas). Second, the analysis is general, rather than linked to specific events. It therefore does not take account of changes in advertising strategy or address differences arising from the perceived severity of the crisis. Third, my sample of texts was drawn from a range of charities. It could be argued that this blurs important distinctions between agency style and politics of representation. While my analytic questions concerned assessing the general range of meanings and positions elaborated within aid ads, and I was unwilling to make invidious comparisons for these purposes, clearly a more systematic study would need to differentiate between agencies.

Insider accounts

Following on from this, it should be clear that any adequate analysis of images produced by charities should be informed by accounts of the image producers. Aid workers engage daily with the tensions between fund-raising and programming. Most major charities, especially those concerned with Third World issues, do have image guidelines which specify non-patronising and non-objectifying codes of representation (e.g. Save the Children 1991). The assumptions underlying the process of producing a text, as well as its finished form, call for study, and some such ethnographic work is being conducted (Ennew 1993). So, for example, a creative designer in the publicity department of one organisation told me that, in designing a 'double 20' ad slot, the criteria used included being eye-catching, appealing, that a definite emotion should be portrayed (the child should look happy if immunised, sad if starving, etc.), and that harrowing images could be used if they were accurate.

CONCLUSION

The starting point for my focus on the representation of children was that the category childhood is not simply located temporally or chronologically prior to adulthood, but is rather constituted in relation to it. To import a psycho-analytic inflection, childhood and adulthood function in a dynamic relation of mutual projection and displacement (Burman 1994b). While this conceptual framework refers to representations and conceptualisations of childhood and adulthood, rather than specific adults and children, I have indicated some material consequences arising from the dominant discourses of childhood mobilised in these texts for children and adults the world over. So while I have been concerned with a specific set of texts, I have illustrated how these reflect broader discourses that structure relations of power central to the current world order, that is, the relationships between 'over'-developed and so-called 'developing' countries. General methodological questions and practices have been addressed through the focus on the topic of aid advertisements, and psychological theory was identified as reflecting and informing the cultural resources informing the narratives of culture, childhood and adulthood they elaborate. In particular, the commitment to universalised, abstracted and homogeneous models of development was shown to reinscribe Western and masculine assumptions which, through the attachment to a romantic, nostalgic concept of childhood, globalises the Western cultural models and inadvertently imposes them on Third World children, families and cultures. As psychologists we should be sensitive and critical of the resonances between psychological and economic models, overdetermined in the language of 'development' (Burman 1995b). More than this, we can also treat the categories structuring our psychological models as resources for cultural analysis. Like the real children and communities they render marginal, criminal or invisible, dominant constructions of childhood emerge as far from innocent in the production and reproduction of prevailing structures of authority.

REFERENCES

Ariès, P. (1962) *Centuries of Childhood*, London: Cape.
Barker, M. (1990) *Comics: Power, ideology and the critics*, Manchester: Manchester University Press.
Black, M. (1992) *A Cause for Our Times: Oxfam, the first fifty years*, Oxford: Oxfam.
Boyden, J. and Hudson, A. (1985) *Children: Rights and responsibilities*, London: Minority Rights Group.
Burman, E. (1991) 'What discourse is not', *Philosophical Psychology*, 4, 3: 325–342.
Burman, E. (1994a) 'Poor children: charity appeals and ideologies of childhood', *Changes*, 12, 1: 29–36.
Burman, E. (1994b) *Deconstructing Developmental Psychology*, London: Routledge.
Burman, E. (1994c) 'Innocents abroad: projecting Western fantasies of childhood in the iconography of emergencies', *Disasters: Journal of Disaster Studies and Management*, 18, 3: 238–253.
Burman, E. (1994d) 'Interviewing', in P. Banister, E. Burman, I. Parker, M. Taylor and C. Tindall (eds) *Qualitative Methods in Psychology*, Milton Keynes: Open University Press.
Burman, E. (1995a) 'What is it? Masculinity and femininity in the cultural representation of childhood', in C. Kitzinger and S. Wilkinson (eds) *Feminism and Discourse*, London: Sage.
Burman, E. (1995b) 'The abnormal distribution of development', *Gender, Place and Culture*, 2, 1: 21–36.
Burman, E. and Parker, I. (eds) (1993) *Discourse Analytic Research: Repertoires and readings of texts in action*, London: Routledge.
Burnell, P. (1991) *Charity, Politics and the Third World*, London: Harvester Wheatsheaf.
Coulter, P. (1989) 'Pretty as a picture', *New Internationalist*, April: 10–12.
Duden, B. (1992) 'Population', in W. Sachs (ed.) *The Development Dictionary*, London: Zed Press.
Ennew, J. (1993) 'NGO's "policies" for children', paper for the Joint Seminar of The Open University and Development Studies Institute, 'Children, NGOs and the State', London School of Economics, July.
Ennew, J. and Milne, B. (1989) *The Next Generation: Lives of Third World children*, London: Zed Press.
Gill, P. (1986) *A Year in the Death of Africa*, London: Paladin.
Goffman, E. (1979) *Gender Advertisements*, London: Macmillan.

Graham, J. and Lynn, S. (1989) 'Mud huts and flints: children's images of the Third World', *Education*, 3–13, June: 29–32.

Gronemeyer, M. (1992) 'Helping', in W. Sachs (ed.) *The Development Dictionary*, London: Zed Press.

Harper, D. (in press) 'New frameworks for the research into explanations of poverty', *British Journal of Social Psychology*.

Harrison, P. and Palmer, R. (1986) *News Out of Africa*, London: Hilary Shipman.

Hart, A. (1988) 'Images of the Third World', in M. Reeves and J. Hammond (eds) *Looking Beyond the Frame: Racism, representation and resistance*, Oxford; Third World First.

Hendrick, H. (1990) 'Constructions and reconstructions of British childhood: an interpretive survey, 1800 to the present day', in A. James and A. Prout (eds) *Constructing and Reconstructing Childhood*, Basingstoke: Falmer Press.

Holland, P. (1992) *What is a Child? Popular images of childhood*, London: Pandora Press.

Hoyles, M. (1989) *The Politics of Childhood*, London: Journeyman.

James, A. and Prout, A. (eds) (1990) *Constructing and Reconstructing Childhood*, Basingstoke: Falmer Press.

Morris, P. (1992) *The Despairing Developer*, London: I.B. Tauris.

Nyoni, S. (1988/9) 'Images of poverty', *Poverty*: 6–10.

Parker, I. (1992) *Discourse Dynamics*, London: Routledge.

Pottier, J. (ed.) (1993) *Practising Development: Social science perspectives*, London: Routledge.

Rahnema, M. (1992) 'Participation', in W. Sachs (ed.) *The Development Dictionary*, London: Zed Press.

Reeves, M. (1988) 'The politics of charity', in M. Reeves and J. Hammond (eds) *Looking Beyond the Frame: Racism, representation and resistance*, Oxford: Third World First.

Rose, N. (1985) *The Psychological Complex: Psychology, politics and society in England 1869–1939*, London: Routledge & Kegan Paul.

Sachs, W. (ed.) (1992) *The Development Dictionary: A guide to knowledge as power*, London: Zed Press.

Save the Children (1991) *Focus on Images*, London: Save the Children.

Smith, D. (1990) *Texts, Facts and Femininity: Exploring the relations of ruling*, London: Routledge.

Sorenson, J. (1991) 'Mass media and discourse on famine in the Horn of Africa', *Discourse and Society*, 2, 2: 223–242.

Stainton Rogers, R. and Stainton Rogers, W. (1992) *Stories of Childhood: Shifting agendas of child concern*, Brighton: Harvester Wheatsheaf.

Walkerdine, V. and Lucey, H. (1989) *Democracy in the Kitchen: Regulating mothers and socialising daughters*, London: Virago.

Walkerdine, V. and the Girls and Mathematics Unit (1989) *Counting Girls Out*, London: Virago.

Chapter 12

Discursive complexes in material culture

Ian Parker

In this chapter a discourse analytic reading of an item of material culture is undertaken using psychoanalytic notions to elaborate 'discursive complexes'. The position of the researcher as subject is a crucial element in psycho-analytic readings of texts, and so the chapter opens with theoretical reflections upon the role of method in the version of discourse analysis presented here. The empirical part of the paper is designed to illustrate how forms of psychodynamic subjectivity circulate through culture and are then re-pres-ented to the reader. The discussion explores implications of the approach for qualitative research in psychology.

The text from the back of a tube of children's toothpaste would appear, at first sight, to be a both innocent and trivial fragment of contemporary commonsense. 'Commonsense' is usually a good deal less innocuous than it pretends to be, however, and it replays taken-for-granted descriptions of, and prescriptions for, what it is to be an acceptable member of a culture. Of the many varieties of discourse analysis inside and outside psychology, the form influenced by poststructuralist debates has been most useful in unravelling the webs of ideology that inhere in popular culture (and in psychology). Discourse analysis here deconstructs, with the help of Foucault's (1975, 1976) observations on modern subjectivity, the intimate link between lan-guage and power in 'commonsense' (Parker 1992). What seems trivial can be seen as symptomatic of patterns of regulation, and the toothpaste text in question can now no longer be read with an innocent eye. An examination of culture, that which is usually taken to be exterior to the subject as researcher, could be a simple elaboration of discourses as sets of statements which construct objects, but it is now also necessary to enter analytic space, that which is interior to the subjectivity of the researcher. This move, which is ostensibly reductive, apparently individualist, is actually a move deeper into culture itself.

A Foucauldian discourse analytic reading of this toothpaste text (Banister, Burman, Parker, Taylor and Tindall 1994) makes a number of assumptions about the nature of language as well as the positions set up for subjects as actors in the text and as addressees of the 'messages'. These assumptions (*and* the messages) carry with them culturally prescribed understandings about the nature of subjectivity in the circumambient culture. In this chapter we can go further to explore the way in which the assumptions in turn entail some employment of psychoanalytic categories. Although Foucault (1976) himself was concerned with psychoanalysis as a form of confession, psychoanalytic notions also underpin images of the body as compliant with, and resistant to, language in his work. Foucault (1969) anticipates discussions of variation, function and construction in discourse analysis in social psychology (Potter and Wetherell 1987), and points toward the elaboration of these aspects of language in psychoanalytic terms. Let us take these three assumptions about the nature of discourse in turn, and follow through that analytic dynamic.

A first assumption concerns *variation*. The assumption is that the host of connotations that dance on each pinpoint of the text are all relayed, at some level, to the reader. While all the varieties of meaning could simply be seen as conveyed to the reader at a 'non-conscious' level, in a realm of processing 'outside awareness', specific psychoanalytic notions of representation are required to account for how the meanings operate alongside and against one another. The multiple semiotics of the packet and written instructions are seen as 'overdetermined' (that is, arising from many different patterns of meaning at one and the same time). The space for one meaning does not prohibit another from functioning, and the meanings do not necessarily operate upon the reader sequentially. The text, like the unconscious, is seen as knowing no time nor logical contradiction, in the sense that variation, as illogical contradiction, reigns as a *condition* for what we take to be coherence (as we fix one meaning and disregard the others that are necessary to give it a particular context and form). It matters to us, of course, that the meanings in the text flood into the subject whether they know it or whether or not they want that to happen, and any discourse analytic reading of texts is to some extent therapeutic.

A second assumption concerns *function*, and the way that the text produces certain effects upon a reader. Once we break from seeing function as the deliberate exercise of 'interests', we move into the realm of the unconscious, and of unconscious meanings addressing and catching the reader's unconscious. The experience of the reader as addressee is transformed in the process of reading such that they are locked in some way into the discursive structure of the text. One way of conceptualising this, following Althusser's (1971) account of the work of ideology, is to say that the reader is 'interpellated', or hailed by the text, and that any response to the text, whether that response indicates agreement with the message, or resistance to the claims the text is making about the nature of the reader and prescriptions for action being formulated for them, is conditioned by this interpellation. A good way of describing this process is to employ the notion of 'subject position', with the reader being seen as positioned as a form of subject at different points in the text. Again, the view that we bring to the analysis concerning overdetermination of meaning in the text allows us to see multiple subject positions as formed *simultaneously* and in contradiction to one another. The positions that are constituted for the addressee may be complementary on occasion, but language also routinely disrupts our sense of self, and we anxiously and perpetually smooth it over to keep ourselves together. Psychoanalytic discourse analysis opens the contradictions in subject positions, and so too the contradictions in the subject caught in the text.

The third assumption concerns the *construction* of the meaning in the text as a relatively enduring semantic structure that 'holds' the reader in position. While there is undoubtedly the reconstruction of sense moment by moment on the different occasions the text is read, there are also *patterns* of meaning, the discourses as sets of statements that constitute objects, that return to the reader. These patterns are relayed in the wider culture that hosts the text and the reader, and replayed as the organised tacit conditions for sense that makes it possible for the text to work. The kinds of reader or 'subject' constituted in the culture (subjects schooled in talk of the unconscious, infantile sexuality and suchlike) come to the text prepared to read particular constellations of signs (keywords, turns of phrase, and allusions to what is 'other' to the text) that have been fabricated as part of the underlying commonsense of the culture (Parker 1993). Here it is useful to read the culture alongside the text as composed of 'discursive complexes' which relay meaning and specify subject positions. The step that we take into an analysis of discourse as a patterned field of signification as well as an accomplishment of individual speakers then leads us to take seriously cultural resources that individuals draw upon to fashion themselves as competent selves. Psychoanalysis is a potent element in the discourse of selfhood in Western culture, and so discourse analysis should itself draw upon that resource in the research process.

METHOD

Three aspects of psychoanalytic method as it pertains to discourse research can be identified, and these will be employed during the analysis of text in question in this chapter.

The first concerns the sensitivity of the researcher, and the ways in which the subjective resources of the reader are brought to bear on the material. These resources are structured, in the process of a psychoanalytic reading, by transference (what is brought to the unconscious relationship the reader has to the text by the text, and its host culture) and counter-transference (what is brought to the text by the reader, and the culture they inhabit). The subjectivity of the reader is mobilised by this dual relationship and gives rise to certain responses (which emerge in the course of the reading) and inhibitions (which obscure a relationship with the intersubjective field that constitutes a text within a symbolic community). It is easier, of course, to display and reflect upon responses than it is to do so with inhibitions, but the analysis can attempt to keep present to attention the ways in which 'absences' and 'otherness' to the text is systematically structured. The symptomatic reading that results will take the form of systematic speculation around the points where the text does not make 'sense'.

The second aspect concerns the form of the reading, and the ways in which psychoanalytic concepts are brought to bear on the text to open up the semantic (and so, also, discursively constituted psychic) mechanisms that organise it. Psychoanalysis is treated here as a methodological vocabulary which is deployed to restructure the text in terms that render unconscious defences and libidinal forces meaningful as linguistic patterns. The aim here is not to uncover such defences or forces in the 'author' of the text (though an imagined author may be produced at some point to facilitate the reading), but to focus on the patterns in the text, in the relationship it provokes with the reader and in the relationship it reproduces (as mediator) between the reader and culture (and so wider systems of discourse). At each point of focus psychoanalytic vocabulary reframes and elaborates what may be going on. In the case of the patterns in the text psychoanalytic terms can be kept at a distance (as if they simply existed in the material), but the relationship between the text and reader and the relationship it re-marks between the reader and the culture *includes* us (and the overall analytic frame is again that of transference and counter-transference).

The third aspect concerns the way forms of culture are represented in the text, and in particular the way in which psychoanalytic culture is transmitted in discourse (directly or indirectly, deliberately or unintentionally). A reading of culture as a meshwork of discourses which can be analytically decomposed needs to be connected here with a cultural history of the different forms of subjectivity (and the emphasis for these purposes is on psychoanalytic subjectivity) that are constituted for readers now. Psychoanalytic notions which thread through Western twentieth-century culture are located in the text here as 'discursive complexes' which simultaneously carry discourses and elaborate sets of subject positions for actors in the text and for readers of the text. Discursive complexes are patterns of meaning that systematically form objects and subjects, but their internal structure derives from psycho-analytic discourse. Notions of childhood 'complex', the 'ego' and the 'unconscious' together with the panoply of strategies that one may use to reflect upon these objects ('acting out', 'repetition', 'working through', etc.) circulate as elements of self-understanding in Western culture. A psycho-analytic discourse reading does not treat these notions as given, but looks to the ways in which texts reproduce such categories, and reproduce subjects who can make sense of the texts that hold them.

THE TEXT

The back of the toothpaste tube contains, in blue type, the following instructions:

DIRECTIONS FOR USE
Choose a children's brush that has a small head and add a pea-sized amount of Punch & Judy toothpaste. To teach your child to clean teeth, stand behind and place your hand under the child's chin to tilt head back and see mouth. Brush both sides of teeth as well as tops. Brush after breakfast and last thing at night. Supervise the brushing of your child's teeth until the age of eight. If your child is taking fluoride treatment, seek professional advice concerning daily intake.

Contains 0.8 per cent Sodium Monofluorophosphate

The tube is small, like other tubes of toothpaste for children, and white. The front of the tube has, in large red letters with blue shadow, the legend 'PUNCH & JUDY TOOTHPASTE'. The manufacturer's name ('Maws') is above in silhouette on a blue background, and there is a line below, in red, which reads, 'Children's Toothpaste with *Fluoride*'. A border of red strawberries (with blue leaves) circles each end of the tube, and eight more strawberries are dotted around on the front. There is a picture on the front of the tube, and again next to instructions, of the head of Punch smiling and holding a red toothbrush in his mouth. He wears a blue ruff around his neck and a red frill around his one visible hand (which holds the brush).

ANALYSIS

A preliminary analysis (Banister, Burman, Parker, Taylor and Tindall 1994), following methodological steps outlined in Parker (1992) which trace the clusters of objects, subjects and social relationships that are specified in the text, concluded with an outline of four discourses. These were: *'rationalist'* – in which the ability to follow procedures ('directions for use') requires choices of implement and judgement of amount ('small head' and 'pea-sized amount') and is predicated on recognition of appropriate authority in health care (following 'directions' and seeking 'professional advice'); *'familial'* – in which ownership ('your child') runs alongside supervision and continuous care (the assumption that the child is present each breakfast and 'last thing at night') and is framed by the image of bad parenting (the figure of 'Punch & Judy'); *'developmental–educational'* – in which the teaching of the child (parental activity) precedes supervision (the child's still tutored but self-governed activity) and then reaches an identifiable stage as a developmental milestone (the 'age of eight'); and *'medical'* – in which the process of using the toothpaste is necessarily linked to hygiene (brushing after meals),

professional supervision ('fluoride treatment') and the specification of inges-
tion and chemical composition of substances ('daily intake', '0.8 per cent
Sodium Monofluorophosphate').

An essential part of discourse analysis is the production of a 'critical
distance' between the reader and the text so that one is able to ask what
collections of relationships and theories of self must obtain for this material
to make sense. That step back can go as far as to throw into question the
material conditions that would be necessary for the text to 'work'. There are,
for example, background assumptions about the nature of memory and the
activity of teethcleaning as a private activity for which tutoring (through the
medium of the text) is appropriate, and the text operates as a practice in a
world of toothbrushes, running water and electric light (to see the teeth last
thing at night). The psychoanalytic construction, function and variation in the
text can also be approached through exploring the conditions of possibility
for these notions to work in this culture as conditions of possibility for
psychoanalysis itself. One can ask how such aspects of the world (privatised
hygiene, personalised advice and self-regulation) also incite forms of behaviour, experience and reflection that are amenable to psychotherapeutic,
psychoanalytic talk. Two further methodological points of focus can be
illustrated here.

The first concerns 'feeling', forms of inchoate response to the text which
cannot be tied one to one to terms or phrases. Psychoanalysis is centrally
concerned with the organisation of affect, and the analysis of meaning, which
discourse analysis is capable of addressing, needs now to be supplemented
with an analysis of the 'drives' in the text. This is not to say that actual
libidinal forces pulsate through the text, but that meanings are structured such
that they operate as dynamic, and then for the reader as psychodynamic,
forces. The case in point here is how one would be able to capture the *violence*
in the text. An activity is represented here in which the child is physically
restrained while a cleaning implement is inserted in the mouth. There is
powerful affect running alongside meaning, and it is helpful to attend to our
'emotional response' to the text, to images in the text here as varieties of
affect produced in discourse. The violence is distributed around certain
oppositions, which are then mapped onto subjects (the parent and the child)
specified in the text.

The second methodological point of focus concerns the elaboration of
oppositions, and their particular relationship to domination and compliance
(and to force and resistance). It is useful to attend to forms of splitting in the
text, with the production of oppositions which can be read deconstructively
to open up the text as a cultural practice, for to open the text up in this way
reveals the operations of power that privilege certain practices. This point
extends a 'deconstructive' reading of texts (Parker 1988). In this case the pair
'adult–child' is mapped onto 'reality–pleasure' (ensuring hygiene versus
enjoying the taste), 'knowledge–naivety' (following instructions versus

being supervised) and 'work–play' (teaching the task versus consuming jolly toothpaste), and – this is where the violence is reproduced – onto the opposition 'active–passive'. The activity and passivity in the text are also replayed in the relationship of the text to reader, with the recipient of advice subordinate to the addressor (as subject supposed to know) and professional (in alliance with the addressor).

These considerations are now of assistance in building upon the initial description of the four discourses to produce a psychoanalytic reading, and thus to the elaboration of 'discursive complexes'. Discursive complexes as, simultaneously, forms of discourse and relays of psychoanalytic subjectivity can be used as analytic devices to connect the material in the text with broader cultural patterns. Discursive complexes take the form of psychoanalytic concepts, but should be understood as socially constructed, symbolically maintained, not as reflections of individual psychic states (though it will indeed be the case that an individual 'subjected' to such symbolic material is constituted as a 'psychoanalytic subject' for whom such a mode of interpretation will then make sense).

THE OEDIPAL TRIANGLE

Although the Oedipus complex is so important in psychoanalysis, Freud declined to call it a 'complex' until 1910, fourteen years after he first puzzled over the fraught connection the infant has with the first love object (in Western nuclear families, usually the mother) and then with the first threat (usually the father, as the third term in the relationship). The image of the oedipal triangle structures the internal psychic economy of the infant, and as a discursive form it both structures and disrupts the opposition in this text between 'adult' and 'child'. The repression of gender as a category in this text, marked by the absence of gendered possessive pronouns ('to clean teeth', 'sides of teeth'), also raises a question about the gender of each of the participants in the scene enacted here. Gender is absent in cultural conditions which are saturated by gender. Why? And why should the relationship between addressee and infant ('your child') be violent, violating?

The clue which solves both questions is the motif of Punch and Judy, and that motif is relayed into the text by the figure of Punch. Punch and Judy function here as exemplars of aberrant abusive parents, and Punch alone operates in a double position as representative of the Law (the third term with the stick, which in this case is also the toothbrush which he holds in his mouth) and as violator of the Law (with the stick as the weapon with which he batters the child and Judy). Žižek (1991), employing psychoanalytic theory, has pointed out that the Law always produces excess, supplementary unlawful violence as a condition for the Law to function. A supplement father in the Punch and Judy narrative, the policeman, then enforces the Law as good parental figure, and a further splitting in the narrative produces the crocodile (who traditionally, it can be noted, has big white teeth) as the excess of violence which threatens all three in the triangle. The 'adult–child' couple, then, is overlaid by a particular affective shape which is given by the discursive complex of the oedipal triangle, and it is then possible to account for the splitting between the activities of (health) care in the text and the (regulative) violence of the text as a screen for that which is excluded (Oedipus).

THE REALITY PRINCIPLE

In the Punch and Judy narrative which both frames the activity specified in this text and functions as a warning as to the characteristics of parents who would fail to follow these instructions, Punch is the figure who shouts 'That's the way to do it!'. Punch initiates the infant and the audience (of children) into a form of violent (ir)rationality, a surplus of enjoyment in the puppet narrative which is also, for the battered baby, and Judy, beyond the pleasure principle. The discursive complex of the reality principle is useful here to capture the opposition 'reality–pleasure' that underpins this text. Mouth hygiene is on the side of reality, and enjoyment of the taste on the side of pleasure, but the opposition carries much more besides. The opposition comes all the closer to psychoanalytic notions of reality (the social) and pleasure (the body) when it is mapped onto other oppositions that are operating in this material. In this discursive complex, the irrational and the rational are also mapped onto the relationship between the body and language.

The untutored child is physically restrained, and the body is moved into positions that will facilitate the eventual supervision (as a moment of transition between the pleasure of the infant and the reality of the adult world) and then self-governance of the child (after 8) who is able to 'clean teeth'. While the child's body is physically positioned, the adult (the addressee) is positioned as a rational subject through language. The adult is constituted as a being who can be addressed through language (in this case, written instructions), and the relationship with authority (the addressor, as 'subject supposed to know', the imaginary author of the instructions) is symbolically mediated. The seeking of 'professional advice' will also be carried out through the medium of language. In this opposition, then, the body is irrational (to be tutored), child, and the mind is rational (to be addressed), adult. The opposition also encourages a particular commonsense 'theoretical' reflection – that which one finds in Althusser's (1971) attempt to produce a psychoanalytic account of ideology for example – on the way in which one is inducted into society as a physical practice, something that can be set in contrast to the ways in which one then reflects upon society as a linguistic achievement.

ENIGMATIC SIGNIFIERS

The opposition between the adult and the child also carries a contrast between knowledge and naivety, in which one member of the pair is able to follow instructions, and the other follows the route to knowledge through supervision from ignorance. The naivety of the child is also important to psychoanalysis, which adds a paradoxical twist to images of childhood innocence. For while the child is seen as outside the social order, innocent of the nature of reality (and following the pleasure principle) it is in its nature (also following the pleasure principle) to be driven to know. What the child experiences of sexuality, for example, is not yet linked with what it is possible to know, and what it is possible to know of sexuality as adult knowledge will both articulate and transform what the child once experienced. The paradox of the innocent child surrounded by, and affected by, adult mysteries which it cannot yet comprehend can be grasped, picking up a term used by the analyst Laplanche (1979), through the discursive complex of 'enigmatic signifiers'.

In this text, however, apart from questions of sexuality (obscured and operative through the absence of gender), there are questions of power and violence; that which is incomprehensible to the child (as physical restraint) will be rendered meaningful as the child reaches a certain developmental point. Here the penetration of the child's body (their mouth) is linked to a form of knowledge (and the practice of a form of knowledge). The description here is technical, positions the child as an object, and the parent maintains the child as if they were a mechanism (which then, at some developmental point, becomes sentient). Reading the text through the figure of enigmatic signifiers also throws further light on the riddle of the 'violence' of the text. The activity of brushing the interior of the mouth after restraining the head is a scene in which an adult with power gazes upon and acts upon the child. There is then a resonance between objectification of the child (as innocent object with the wish to become subject) and accounts of objectification in pornography. The fluoride is also marked as an object to be inserted, as 'intake', as a substance to be placed into the child, and the toothbrush functions metaphorically as a 'speculum' (a device for observing the interior of the body and producing knowledge) constituting the space (the mouth, the tutored child) from which discourse will one day emerge.

SITES OF RESISTANCE

It would be possible to provide a quasi-Foucauldian reading of the text as a sealed world in which processes of regulation and surveillance constitute all the limits and interior space of what it is possible to do and know. However, the opposition 'work–play', the contrast between the teaching of the task and the consumption of the jolly toothpaste, opens a space for manoeuvre, a space that a psychoanalytic reading should exploit. There is a carnivalesque resistance in the form of Punch and Judy. Rather like the anarchic vision of 'schizophrenia' in Deleuze and Guattari's (1977) *Anti-Oedipus*, Punch and Judy are provoked as a condition of the text, and to work efficiently to support the text as instruction they must be limited, bounded, contained, so that their subversive potential cannot be realised. They are produced to the limit (and to regulate the limits) of what is rational (against the irrational). The text is part of a machinery of desire (and, for Deleuze and Guattari, of capitalism); it incites play to sell a commodity and then turns that into work to reproduce the relations of power that make such commodities possible.

What makes it possible for this text to work is that the child (and the reader positioned as a child, in identification with the child, as they buy the text) is lured into the scene. The subjugation and training of the child is facilitated by the images of play, and the reader is drawn into the text as a player with power, but not in command of the apparatus of power (that is, the powerful subject is also subject to the power). However, a Foucauldian account of power is always also an account of resistance, and to speak of a discursive complex of 'sites of resistance' allows us to elaborate how that resistance may operate in the psychic economy of readers. The very process of luring the child (and adult identified as child) into the text provokes the fantasy of disruption, the transformation of the supervision scene into play. Punch, for example, is the Law *and* the disruptor of the Law, and at the very moment that he exercises the Law to the full he throws it into question. This reading of the text also throws it into question, and psychoanalysis, as a theory of resistance, opens a space from which we may think against the text, mark ourselves as different to the subject positions it creates for us and within us.

DISCUSSION

Some further consideration should now be given to method, and in particular to the cultural location of psychoanalysis as a lens through which to view subjectivity and as a vocabulary by means of which a reading of a text can be articulated. It would be possible to argue (as many psychoanalytic practitioners and theorists do) that psychoanalysis provides a vivid insight into the psychic economy of the paraphernalia of material culture because it accurately addresses the internal forces and relations of the individual human subjects that produce (or write) and consume (or read) it. No such claim is being made here; if anything, the opposite is being suggested. For research subjectivity and psychoanalytic structures are seen in this chapter as *constituted* by the culture they inhabit. That is, transference, counter-transference, defence mechanisms and libidinal forces are themselves seen as semantic forms which circulate through 'discursive complexes'. In this case, therefore, the reading of a text which is ostensibly so apparently innocent of the unconscious has to be 're-read' as it is reconstituted as a piece of material in a psychoanalytic culture.

This chapter has employed psychoanalytic notions in the broadest sense to elaborate a discourse analytic reading. Although there has been reference to particular theories within the Freudian and post-Freudian tradition, my concern has been with the most general culturally available analytic images of the family, rationality, curiosity and resistance. The Lacanian tradition as been particularly useful in this reading, with the work of Althusser (1971), Deleuze and Guattari (1977), Laplanche (1977) and Žižek (1991) throwing light on the work of ideology, resistance, knowledge and power. It is important to note that the ways we can reflect on the operations of this text as researchers are also conditioned by the very forms of discourse that inhabit the text. Here, then, we should be aware of assumptions in the Lacanian tradition that frame our interpretation. In the case of the infant being inducted physically into language and the adult reproducing that practice through the medium of language, for example, we should take care to see this as an *account* of ideology, not necessarily as an accurate explication of its nature. This theoretical, and psychoanalytic, reflection is expressed, among other places, in Althusser's (1971) writing which counterposes the induction of the subject into ideology as a practice (of 'ideological state apparatuses' such as the school) to the theoretical practice and scientific reflection upon ideology as conducted through the symbolic order. Similar points could be made about the specific cultural location of Deleuze and Guattari's celebration of 'schizophrenia' as resistance, Laplanche's description of the child puzzling over adult sensual knowledge and Žižek's view of the Law as always provoking its hideous reverse.

The analytic device of the 'discursive complex' is used to provide a more thoroughly embedded notion of subject position than that offered by, for example, Davies and Harré (1990). The position taken by the subject is not adopted moment by moment as an individual engages with the material, but is discursively given to the reader. This does not mean that the reader is passive, but that certain conditions of possibility for the text also permit certain relationships to be formed within the text and, from within other texts, towards and against it. The engagement with any text is always an engagement from within discourse, and the task of a discourse analytic reading is to engage in a way that lays bare the work of ideology and the plays of power, the unravelling of ideology and the spaces of resistance (Parker 1992).

In the research process the subject positions, and general issues of activity and passivity in the text, are compounded by the process of reading as the struggle for mastery over the text. Different forms of identification are produced in the text, as actors in the text operate as exemplars of subject positions that can be adopted or refused. The analysis has adopted a subject position (of researcher) which also speaks about what is excluded (repressed), and an active position is taken in relation to regions of the symbolic order that are usually closed. The subject position of the researcher can then also be drawn out using psychoanalytic theory. There are risks. In this case the gaze of the psy-complex (the array of theories and practices that comprise the discipline of academic and professional psychology) is reproduced in the activity of the parent regulating, through the supervisory gaze, the child. The developmental–educational discourse that runs through the text is interwoven with images of the rational individual, the family and medicine, and this cluster of discourses reinforces the power of psychology as a 'regime of truth' (Banister *et al.* 1994). The researcher using psychoanalytic theory as described in this chapter now gazes upon the text, and upon the parent and child, in a metaposition that is actually still of a piece with the activities of the psy-complex. The regulation of children is a condition for the psy-complex, and it is important to remember that it is also a condition for psychoanalysis (and now for us) as part of (and other of) the psy-complex.

ACKNOWLEDGEMENTS

I would like to thank Erica Burman for help with versions of this chapter.

REFERENCES

Althusser, L. (1971) *Lenin and Philosophy, and other essays*, London: New Left Books.
Banister, P., Burman, E., Parker, I., Taylor, M. and Tindall, C. (1994) *Qualitative Methods in Psychology: A Research Guide*, Milton Keynes: Open University Press.
Davies, B. and Harré, R. (1990) 'Positioning: the discursive production of selves', *Journal for the Theory of Social Behaviour*, 20, 1: 43–63.
Deleuze, G. and Guattari, F. (1977) *Anti-Oedipus: Capitalism and schizophrenia*, New York: Viking.
Foucault, M. (1969/1972) *The Archaeology of Knowledge*, London: Tavistock.
Foucault, M. (1975/1977) *Discipline and Punish*, London: Allen Lane.
Foucault, M. (1976/1981) *The History of Sexuality: Volume One, An Introduction*, Harmondsworth: Pelican.
Laplanche, J. (1977/1979) *New Foundations for Psychoanalysis*, Oxford: Blackwell.
Parker, I. (1988) 'Deconstructing accounts', in C. Antaki (ed.) *Analysing Everyday Explanation: A casebook of methods*, London: Sage.
Parker, I. (1992) *Discourse Dynamics: Critical analysis for social and individual psychology*, London: Routledge.
Parker, I. (1993) 'Social constructionist psychoanalysis and the real', in B. Kaplan, L. Mos, H. Stam and W. Thorngate (eds) *Recent Trends in Theoretical Psychology (Vol. III)*, New York: Springer-Verlag.
Potter, J. and Wetherell, M. (1987) *Discourse and Social Psychology: Beyond attitudes and behaviour*, London: Sage.
Žižek, S. (1991) *For They Know Not What They Do: Enjoyment as a political factor*, London: Verso.

Part III

Controlled investigations

Preface

The chapters in this section highlight some important features of controlled investigations. These include demand characteristics, stimulus isolation, predictive and descriptive research strategies in the use of qualitative methods, the interactive process of conducting controlled investigations and the importance of intuition, the value of case studies, and the use of multiple measures. Collectively, the chapters show the ingenuity required for undertaking controlled investigations in psychology.

Chapter 13 on 'Methodological issues in hypnosis' shows the importance of recognising that subjects in psychological investigations are actively cognising participants eager to please the investigator. In designing experiments in psychology the author considers that we must always be aware of the possibility that the phenomena we are measuring may be as much a product of our procedures as something measured by them. Research into hypnosis has shown that non-hypnotic subjects are just as likely to perform anti-social acts when instructed to do so as subjects given an hypnotic induction procedure. While these studies cannot demonstrate that hypnosis is not a special state, they suggest that one does not need to invoke the concept of an hypnotic state to explain many of the facts attributed to hypnosis. Similarly, while hypnosis can be useful in the treatment of a number of complaints including insomnia, skin complaints, dental stress, etc., hypnotic techniques may involve a variety of factors that are not unique to hypnosis that might account for the improvements. These include social support, relaxation, social compliance, etc., and illustrate the difficulties associated with isolating the specific aspects of a complex stimulus responsible for the effects.

Chapter 14 on 'Qualitative methods in cognitive psychology' summarises two studies which illustrate contrasting yet equally important research strategies. One study illustrates an explanatory research strategy which aims to assess the predictive validity of alternative explanations of choice behaviour, and where the conditions under which decisions were made were carefully controlled. Another study illustrates a descriptive research strategy where the goal was to describe behaviour and cognition in the real world in order to develop and construct theories, rather than to empirically distinguish between alternatives. The descriptive study involved constructing a diary which gave subjects the opportunity to truly express themselves yet contain sufficient structure and standardisation so that the data could be usefully and meaningfully analysed by content analysis. The controlled study involved respondents making decisions and speaking aloud their thoughts under different conditions for a problem. The authors note that many qualitative methods, especially when applied to real world cognition, have the potential to produce very large amounts of data, which may well be interesting, but extremely difficult to reduce to manageable levels; and that an important issue concerns the 'fit' between the research aim and the method of data collection. Cross validation with behavioural evidence is also advocated to check the validity of inferences from self-reports.

Chapter 15 on 'Remembering in a social context' advocates that only through the systematic application of experimental and analytic techniques involving tight control over as many relevant factors as possible will understanding advance in the study of collaborative recall. The chapter illustrates how investigation in this area can involve the use of several control groups. It also shows how new methodological issues inevitably crop up as research proceeds, and illustrates the creative thinking involved in tackling these issues. The chapter shows that a whole series of different experiments failed to support the original intuitive hypothesis that two people are better than one at remembering a shared experience. The studies, however, have found conditions under which pairs of people do generate new memories, which has led to the new intuition that it is the psychological circumstances surrounding learning that help to determine the subsequent emergence of new memories in pairs. As such, the studies have led to the investigation of topics and aspects not originally conceived, and demonstrate the interactive process of controlled research with the importance of an intuitive understanding of phenomena.

Chapter 16 on 'The case study method in cognitive neuropsychology' notes the recent increase in research into the effects of brain injury on cognitive performance, where the precise nature of different impairments in selected patients are studied and compared with research on appropriately matched normal control groups of non-brain damaged individuals. The author considers that many of the best known theories in contemporary cognitive psychology are as strongly supported by findings from individual case studies of clinical patients as they are by experiments that examine the performance of normal subjects under laboratory conditions. In the case of phonological dyslexia, for instance, where there is a dissociation between the ability to read words and non-words, this is exactly what would be predicted on the basis of the dual route model of reading. Interestingly, the author notes that cases of phonological dyslexia have only been reported in the literature since the dual route model became popular; which is perhaps illustrative of the important influence which a theory can have. In turn, the author considers that theories of cognitive performance which can accommodate data from brain injured patients as well as data from normal subjects are likely to increase substantially in importance.

Chapter 17 on 'Methods and techniques for assessing written communication' provides a series of pointers and guidelines from research which can be used as aids to improve the writing and readability of texts and instructions. Research shows that simple methods of giving a rough measure of the readability of texts can be devised, and some measures are outlined which can be useful for assessing research instruments and documents. The chapter makes several points on experimental approaches to the evaluation of features of text, and the advantage is noted of using several measures. The chapter is directly relevant to undertaking research into written communication and to improving the communication of research results.

Chapter 13

Methodological issues in hypnosis

Graham F. Wagstaff

HYPNOSIS, PSYCHOLOGY AND METHODOLOGY

Considering the popular interest that the topic of hypnosis evokes, it is perhaps surprising that we find so little reference to it in mainstream psychology textbooks. In fact, the area of hypnosis has produced some of the most innovative experimental research designs in psychology and has also highlighted some methodological issues that have implications well beyond the realms of hypnosis. In this brief chapter I will attempt to provide a sketch of some of these issues.

THE STATE VERSUS NON-STATE DEBATE

Since the early days of hypnosis a fundamental controversy has existed between two opposing schools of thought; this is often referred to as the 'state versus non-state' debate (Fellows 1990; Lynn and Rhue 1991). In many respects the 'state' view of hypnosis represents the traditional view of hypnosis. It was once thought that hypnosis was a special sort of sleep or sleepwalking; indeed, the term 'hypnosis' itself derives from the Greek *hypnos*, or sleep, and some writers continue to refer to hypnotically suscept- ible individuals as 'somnambules'. But although some state theorists still attempt to relate phenomena of hypnosis and sleep (see, for example, Evans 1991), the idea that hypnosis is actually a form of sleep is now largely rejected. Nevertheless, most state theorists continue to argue that, funda- mentally, hypnosis is an altered state of consciousness or 'trance', usually brought about by certain induction rituals. It is also assumed that this state can vary in depth, such that the deeper or more 'hypnotised' one becomes the more one is likely to respond to hypnotic suggestions (for examples, see Barber 1991; Bowers 1983; Hilgard 1978, 1986; Nash 1991). Probably the most influential modern state theory is Hilgard's 'neo-dissociation theory' (Hilgard 1978, 1985, 1986, 1991).

Hilgard argues that there exist multiple systems of control that are not all conscious at the same time. Normally these cognitive systems are under the influence of a central control system, or 'executive ego', that controls and monitors the other systems. However, when a subject enters 'hypnosis', much of this overall control is given up to the hypnotist who can thereby control the subsidiary systems by giving instructions or suggestions. As a result, the 'hypnotised' subject may experience motor movements as involuntary, and experience distortions of memory and perception, such as amnesia, positive and negative hallucinations, and analgesia. To illustrate the operation of hypnotic dissociation Hilgard frequently refers to what he calls the 'hidden observer' phenomenon. To demonstrate this, subjects are 'hypnotised' and given the following instruction: 'When I place my hand on your shoulder, I shall be able to talk to a hidden part of you that knows things are going on in your body, things that are unknown to the part of you to which I am now talking. The part to which I am talking will not know what you are telling me or even that you are talking.' (Knox, Morgan and Hilgard 1974: 842). Using this procedure, Hilgard and his supporters claim that they can demonstrate the existence of dissociated cognitive sub-systems during hypnosis.

In contrast, modern supporters of the non-state view reject the traditional notion of hypnosis as an altered state of consciousness (see for example, Barber 1969; Coe and Sarbin 1991; Sarbin and Coe 1972; Spanos 1982, 1986, 1991; Spanos and Chaves 1989; Wagstaff 1981, 1986, 1991). Non-state theorists contend that various hypnotic phenomena are more readily explicable in terms of interactions between more mundane psychological processes such as imagination, relaxation, role-enactment, compliance, conformity, attention, attitudes and expectancies. Non-state theorists see hypnosis as primarily a strategic role-enactment. In other words, 'susceptible' hypnotic subjects enact the role of a 'hypnotised' person as defined by cultural expectations and cues provided by the immediate situation. The degree to which they take on the role also depends on whether they possess appropriate attitudes (for example, whether they are worried about loss of control, or being manipulated). This role-enactment is largely accomplished by the use of deliberate strategies aimed to make hypnotic suggestions come about. For example, to experience a suggestion for arm lowering ('your arm is getting heavier') subjects may try to imagine weights attached to their arms, and to experience hypnotic 'amnesia' ('you will find it difficult to remember what has happened') subjects may deliberately distract themselves from the target items during the recall period. However, according to some state theorists, much hypnotic behaviour may also include 'behavioural compliance', or 'acting out suggestions' without the appropriate subjective experiences (see for example, Spanos 1991, 1992; Wagstaff 1981, 1991). In effect then, to non-state theorists, terms such as 'hypnosis' and 'hypnotic' are simply labels that refer to situations defined by participants or observers as such (because, for example, the situations contain what are called 'hypnotic induction' rituals); they do not refer to the existence of some kind of special state or process.

Thus we have two apparently opposing theoretical views. How do we decide between the two?

THE LOGIC OF CONTROL GROUPS IN HYPNOSIS RESEARCH

Hypnosis research usually involves the administration of an induction procedure, which typically involves suggestions for sleep and relaxation, followed by a set of further suggestions, such as arm lowering ('your arm is getting heavier'), arm levitation ('your arm is getting lighter'), hand clasp ('you cannot separate your hands'), hallucinations ('there is a cat in your lap'), and amnesia ('you will find it difficult to remember what has happened'). When presented together with induction, these latter suggestions are termed 'hypnotic' suggestions, and collections of such items have been used to form a number of standardised scales to measure hypnotic susceptibility (for a summary, see Bowers 1983). However, the suggestions can also be given without induction, in which case they are termed 'non-hypnotic' or 'waking' suggestions. Most hypnosis research has therefore involved comparisons between hypnotic subjects, that is, subjects who have been given an hypnotic induction procedure, and non-hypnotic control subjects who have been given various instructions.

One of the most frequently used control groups in hypnosis research has been the simulating group (Orne 1959, 1971, 1979; Wagstaff and Benson 1987). In the 'real-simulator' design, hypnotic subjects ('reals') are compared to a group of subjects who are instructed to fake or simulate hypnosis; simulators are told that this is relatively easy to do, but are not told how to do it. Often pre-tests are given so that only subjects who score low on tests of hypnotic susceptibility are selected as simulators; the rationale being that, according to state theorists, highly hypnotically susceptible simulators may accidentally fall into a 'state' during simulation. This, however, presents its own problems, as the reals and simulators then come from different populations. Another popular control is the 'task-motivational group' (Barber 1969). Task motivated subjects are told to try hard to imagine or experience suggested effects, but they are given no induction procedures.

The logic behind such control groups in hypnosis research is that if hypnotic subjects respond differently to controls, then one might assume that hypnosis involves some special element, such as a special state, and cannot be accounted for in terms of the more mundane concepts advanced by non-state theorists. On the other hand, if the hypnotic subjects behave no differently from non-hypnotic controls, then there is no necessity to invoke the concept of a special state or trance to explain the behaviour of the hypnotic subjects. It can be noted, however, that some writers have emphasised that the finding of no difference between hypnotic and control subjects does not in itself indicate that there is no such thing as an hypnotic state; hypnotic and control subjects may be behaving in the same way, but for different reasons (Bowers 1983; Bowers and Davidson 1991). In response to this problem, a number of other designs have evolved; but as we shall see, these have had their problems too.

PHYSIOLOGICAL CORRELATES OF HYPNOSIS

If hypnosis is a special state, perhaps it has some identifying physiological characteristics. An important issue in research into the physiological effects of hypnosis is that of specifying appropriate instructions for the non-hypnotic control subjects. Hypnotic procedures typically include a number of instructions that have obvious physiological consequences independently of any assumption about the existence of an hypnotic state. For example, there are often fairly definable patterns of physiological responses related to fairly mundane activities such as eye closure, relaxation, concentration, and attention, all of which may be involved in the behaviour of hypnotic subjects. It is important, therefore, to ensure that controls are appropriately instructed regarding these activities. The physiological responses of a person seated, relaxing, and concentrating with eyes closed may be markedly different from someone alert and simply staring round the room, yet have nothing to do with 'hypnosis' per se.

The evidence suggests that the subject who is responsive to hypnotic suggestions is not asleep or sleepwalking (Barber, Spanos and Chaves 1974). Nevertheless, hypnotic subjects often display the physiological concomitants of being relaxed. This is not surprising given that most standard induction rituals involve instructions for relaxation. However, the issue obviously arises as to whether hypnosis is in fact simply a state of relaxation. Edmonston (1991) has argued that hypnosis *is* just a state of relaxation. However, contrary to this proposal, some researchers have found that relaxation is not necessary to produce hypnotic effects. In fact, hypnotically susceptible subjects are just as responsive to suggestions when involved in strenuous activities such as pedalling an exercise bike. This has been termed 'alert' hypnosis (Banyai and Hilgard, 1976; Malott 1984). Nevertheless, in reply, Edmonston (1991) has continued to argue that the state of hypnosis is actually relaxation on the grounds that one can still be relaxed (cognitively) even when engaged in physical activity. Athletes, for instance, often report that they perform best when 'relaxed'. However, if we accept this reply, we are left with the difficulty (so far unresolved) of finding a set of definable physiological correlates that will relate traditional 'relaxed' and 'alert' hypnosis.

Particular problems in assessing physiological correlates of hypnosis arise when subjects classified as highly susceptible to hypnosis (highs) are compared with subjects, given identical instructions, who are classed as not susceptible to hypnosis (lows). Subjects who are classified as 'lows' can illustrate what is known as a 'negative subject effect' (Jones and Spanos 1982); that is, lows, because they do not wish to give the appearance of being susceptible to hypnosis, may actually reject or perform counter to the suggestions given to them. Consequently, lows may respond differently not only from highs given hypnotic induction, but also from independent non-hypnotic controls. Thus, for example, the physiological responses of highs given hypnotic suggestions to attend to, or ignore, a stimulus may not differ from non-hypnotic controls given similar suggestions outside the context of hypnosis, but the responses of *both* groups may differ from those of lows who deliberately ignore the suggestions or do the opposite of what is suggested.

Appropriately instructed independent control subjects are therefore essential for meaningful research in this area, and there now seems to be fairly wide agreement amongst researchers of both state and non-state persuasion that, when appropriate controls are applied, there is no definitive evidence for a unique physiological correlate of 'hypnosis' (Davies 1988; Sarbin and Slagle 1979; Jones and Flynn 1989; Spanos 1982; Wagstaff 1981). However, the search continues (see, for example, Gruzelier 1988).

HYPNOSIS AND THE ENHANCEMENT OF PERFORMANCE

The idea that hypnosis enables one to transcend normal performance has been seen by some as evidence itself for the existence of a special hypnotic state. However, research in this area has also drawn attention to the fact that many of the apparently 'extraordinary' feats attributed to hypnosis are extraordinary simply because observers are unaware of the capacities of the average motivated individual. Thus 'extraordinary' feats, such as eating a raw onion whilst (successfully) acting as though the onion were an apple, or being suspended between two chairs whilst supporting the weight of a person, are easily accomplished by most people. Indeed, most people are quite able to perform the apparently transcendent feats in stage demonstrations of hypnosis without any attempt to employ an hypnotic induction procedure (Barber 1969; Barber, Spanos and Chaves 1974). The message here is obvious; before accepting *any* piece of hypnotic behaviour as extraordinary, try testing a control group. But care is needed.

Much early laboratory research in the area of performance enhancement was flawed by the use of within-subjects experimental designs in which subjects act as their own controls (i.e. the same subjects are tested in both hypnotic and non-hypnotic situations). Often in such situations subjects manifest what has been termed a 'holding back' effect in the non-hypnotic control situation; that is, they underperform in the control trials so that their performance appears 'boosted' in the hypnotic trials (Wagstaff 1981). Consequently, the most appropriate design for testing claims of hypnotic transcendence is an independent group design, in which the hypnotic and control subjects are assigned to different groups (Barber 1969). When appropriate controls are applied, such as the use of independent task-motivated controls and simulators, there seems to be no evidence that hypnotic subjects perform better than controls on a wide range of tasks including appearing deaf, blind and colour blind, acting like a child and recalling events from childhood, lifting weights and other athletic tasks, and showing improvements in eyesight (Barber 1969; Barber, Spanos and Chaves 1974; Jacobs and Gotthelf 1986; Jones and Flynn 1989: Wagstaff 1981).

Although the idea that hypnosis enables people to transcend non-hypnotic performance is now generally rejected by both state and non-state theorists, the dissociationist view of hypnosis still appears to give credence to some phenomena which, in any other psychological context, would very likely be treated with considerable scepticism. For instance, one of the most dramatic hypnotic effects is the alleged 'negative hallucination'; i.e. in response to suggestion hypnotic subjects will fail to see someone or something, such as a person or chair, set before their eyes. The assumption made by dissociationists is that, although the material is not seen by the 'aware' part of the mind, it is somehow 'seen' by another part of the mind, outside awareness. If true, this interpretation is fascinating, for it seems to defy any mainstream psychological theory of perception. What psychological mechanism could (excluding strategies such as looking away, or closing one's eyes) possibly allow us to selectively block out a huge area of the visual field? Without such an explanation, it is difficult to offer a non-state explanation other than that of behavioural compliance; subjects are pretending that they cannot see something which is actually as clear as day to them (Wagstaff 1981, 1991). Indeed, some recent work using an experimental design developed by Spanos and his associates seems strongly to support the view that compliance may be a significant component in this effect (Spanos 1992). In one study they gave subjects a negative hallucination suggestion that they would not see a number '8' that was presented clearly in front of them. Some subjects subsequently claimed they had seen nothing. These same subjects were then told that 'reals', unlike 'fakers', *do* see the number for a short period, but then it fades. Having been given this information, virtually all of these subjects confirmed they *had* seen the number. However, this does not necessarily settle the issue; an ardent state theorist could still conceivably argue that these kinds of instructions can, in themselves, act as suggestions to release or not release the information that has been 'seen' by, and stored in, different 'parts' of consciousness.

Similar problems occur with other examples which, on first consideration, might indicate the operation of compliance. For instance Barber, Spanos and Chaves (1974) report that when, having received a suggestion for hypnotic deafness, subjects were asked 'Can you hear me?', a number reported 'No I can't.' A non-state theorist could reasonably argue these subjects were 'caught out'; but a dissociationist might argue it was 'another part of consciousness' speaking.

Also related to the view that hypnosis can evoke unusual behaviours are claims that hypnosis can impel people to commit self-injurious and anti-social acts of which they would not normally be capable. A few early experiments did seem to confirm that 'hypnotised' persons can be made to perform acts that are immoral or harmful, either to themselves or others; such acts have included indecent exposure, picking up a dangerous snake, throwing acid at the experimenter, minor thefts, and verbal attacks (Wagstaff 1989, 1991, 1993). However, a number of reviewers of these studies have concluded that the notion of an hypnotic state is not necessary to explain the results. Instead they can be explained primarily in terms of subjects a) wanting to help the hypnotist/experimenter, b) thinking their actions were actually safe, and/or c) making assumptions that someone else would take responsibility for the consequences of the acts (Barber 1969; Coe, Kobayashi and Howard 1972, 1973; Orne and Evans 1965; Udolf 1983).

For example, early studies by Rowland (1939) and Young (1952) found that a majority of 'deeply hypnotised' subjects would attempt to pick up a dangerous snake and throw acid at the experimenter; subjects generally refused to do this in the 'waking' state. However, Orne and Evans (1965) found that both hypnotic subjects *and* non-hypnotic subjects would attempt to pick up a dangerous snake, plunge their hands into a beaker of concentrated nitric acid, and throw the acid at the experimenter, when given emphatic suggestions to do so. Of significance in this study was the finding that whereas five out of six subjects carried out the acts when 'hypnotised', only two of the same subjects carried out the acts when not 'hypnotised'. However, *all* six non-hypnotic simulators carried out the tasks. This again illustrates well the problem of using only within-subjects designs in hypnosis research.

Further studies have shown that non-hypnotic subjects are just as likely as (and sometimes slightly more likely than) hypnotic subjects to perform a variety of anti-social or repugnant acts that have included mutilating the bible, cutting up the national flag, making a homosexual approach, and even heroin dealing (Coe, Kobayashi and Howard 1973; Levitt *et al.* 1975; O'Brien and Rabuck 1976). Although some have argued that most subjects are only likely to engage in what appear to be dangerous anti-social activities if they perceive from the design and procedures of the study that the situation is 'safe' (Orne and Holland 1968: Mixon 1974), other research indicates that this is not necessarily the case (Calverley and Barber 1965; Sheridan and King 1972).

Many of the results presented in this section fit in with a large amount of other evidence that indicates that subjects, regardless of whether 'hypnotised' or not, are highly motivated to respond to the demands of the particular context, which include pleasing the experimenter or authority figure and making the experiment 'work' (Orne 1962, 1970; Milgram 1974; Wagstaff 1981, 1986, 1991). And whilst none of the methodologies employed in these studies could ever conclusively demonstrate that hypnosis is *not* a special state, the results do seem to suggest that one does not need to invoke the concept of an hypnotic state to explain many of the feats attributed to hypnosis.

HYPNOSIS AND MEMORY

Hypnosis has been linked with a number of memory phenomena. The last two decades have seen a growing interest by the police in the use of hypnosis for 'refreshing' memory. However, early research in this area was again flawed because of the use of same-subjects designs, or the fact that insufficient attention was paid to motivating the control groups. Another problem was that sometimes attention was only paid to the amount of correct information produced without regard to general accuracy (the proportion of correct to incorrect information). It is possible that an hypnotic subject may produce more correct responses simply by using a more lax criterion for report; i.e. guessing and producing more incorrect as well as correct information (Wagstaff 1984).

Despite a few highly disputed studies, there is now a fairly overwhelming body of experimental evidence to indicate that, when appropriate independent control measures are applied, hypnotic procedures do not improve the accuracy of memory (including memories of childhood) to a level above that achievable in a motivated non-hypnotic condition. When differences sometimes do occur between hypnotic and motivated non-hypnotic groups they tend to exist because the hypnotic groups are reporting more false positive errors; that is, hypnotic subjects claim they can remember or express more confidence in things and events which were not present (for reviews see Anderton 1986; Barber 1965; Smith 1983; Wagstaff 1984, 1989, 1993). However, the extent to which hypnotically induced inaccuracies reflect genuine irreversible memory distortions or simply reporting biases is a matter of contention (Laurence and Perry 1983; McCann and Sheehan 1987; Orne et al. 1984; Spanos and McLean 1986). Finding a paradigm that will definitively settle this issue has proved difficult. For instance, whilst a procedure that involves confronting 'confabulators' with the original information can apparently successfully reverse 'pseudomemories', it could be argued that such a procedure in itself simply presents an extra suggestion and/ or operates to 'release' the original memories from another dissociated part of consciousness. One of the more successful designs, therefore, has been that of Murray, Cross and Whipple (1992) who found that both hypnotic and non-hypnotic false memory reports could be reduced by offering subjects financial incentives for accurate report.

Even more contentious is the phenomenon of hypnotic amnesia. Typically hypnotic amnesia is demonstrated by presenting the hypnotic subject with some material followed by a suggestion that, either during or after the hypnosis session, he or she will find it difficult to remember this material until given a reversal signal. Standard measures of hypnotic amnesia are, as one might expect, easy to simulate, and consequently researchers have looked for some rather more subtle measures of amnesia. According to some, one such measure is 'source amnesia' (Evans 1979). It has been argued that, after a session of hypnosis, some 'reals' will sometimes recall novel information given to them whilst they were 'hypnotised', but they will be unable to say how they came by this information. Simulators, however, tend not to do this. This kind of comparison highlights one of the major problems with the real–simulator design. Simulators are typically told to behave like 'excellent' hypnotic subjects. When they do this the result is often an 'overplay effect'. That is, simulators behave as if 'extremely hypnotised', consequently (just like some, but not all, of the 'reals') they display *total* amnesia for both the information and the source, so source amnesia is impossible (Wagstaff 1981). What is necessary, therefore, is a control group instructed to show *partial* amnesia; and there is now evidence to suggest that, when such controls are applied, non-hypnotic subjects will indeed display 'source amnesia' (Coe 1989).

Another much disputed amnesia effect is that of 'disorganised retrieval' (Evans and Kihlstrom 1973; Kihlstrom and Wilson 1984). It has been argued by some that if one selects hypnotic subjects who are 'partially amnesic' (i.e. remember a few items), these subjects tend to remember the few items that they do remember in a disorganised fashion (not in serial order, and not in semantic clusters). This is unlike 'normal' memory, and simulators tend not to show this effect. However, as simulators tend to manifest *total* amnesia, they never actually get the chance to show disorganisation in recall. Accordingly, non-state theorists have used different controls; and, in line with the non-state position, similar disorganisation effects have been shown by non-hypnotic subjects who have been instructed simply to 'pretend to forget', or 'attend away' from the material (Spanos 1986; Wagstaff 1977b, 1982; Wagstaff and Carroll 1987).

But if hypnotic amnesia is indeed, as non-state theorists describe it, a deliberate, strategic act to fail to remember (for example, by holding back information, or attending away from the material) then one might expect that if subjects are explicitly instructed to tell the truth and try hard to remember, hypnotic amnesia should be easily 'breached'. Some have found that hypnotic amnesia cannot be breached by such methods (Kihlstrom *et al.* 1980), however, Coe (1989) has reported that amnesia can be breached, but only after subjects are asked to be honest, rigged up to a lie detector, and shown a videotape of their performance. Nevertheless, state theorists might reasonably argue that Coe's collection of procedures might themselves act as 'amnesia reversal cues', and the onus remains on non-state theorists to explain why hypnotic amnesia is so difficult to breach using non-hypnotic methods.

Non-state theorists have suggested that the reason why hypnotic amnesia is so difficult to breach is that some subjects may have such an investment in displaying amnesia that they would 'lose face' if they started to remember simply as a result of instructions to be honest or to try to remember. Consequently, for amnesia to be breached, subjects need to be able to recall without 'losing face'. Accordingly, Spanos, Radtke and Bertrand (1985) used a design in which 'amnesic' subjects were told that the 'forgotten' material was located in 'hidden parts' of the mind. This procedure successfully breached amnesia. But again, because dissociationists argue that in the cases of reversible hypnotic amnesia the material really *is* hidden in other parts of the mind, the results still remain open to a dissociationist interpretation. Possibly more persuasive, therefore, for the non-state position is a study by Wagstaff (1977a) in which subjects were given an amnesia suggestion, but, *before* being asked to recall, they were given an opportunity to say they were role-playing rather than in a 'trance'. When this procedure was used, amnesia seemed to disappear completely, even with subjects who claimed they were not just role-playing .

POST-HYPNOTIC RESPONDING AND TRANCE-LOGIC

If hypnosis is a deliberate role-enactment, rather than an involuntary response, one might expect hypnotic responding to cease when the hypnotist is no longer present. Apparently contrary to this view, Orne, Sheehan and Evans (1968) found that some hypnotic subjects continued to respond to a post-hypnotic suggestion (to touch their foreheads on hearing the word 'experiment') even when the hypnotist was not present; whereas simulators stopped responding in the absence of the hypnotist. One problem with the design of this study, however, was that the post-hypnotic response was tested by someone obviously known to the experimenter. Thus whilst a non-response would have been perfectly compatible with the role of a simulator who, as part of the same experiment, had been explicitly instructed to simulate, it would not have been with the role of a 'hypnotised' individual (Wagstaff 1981). To assess this interpretation Spanos *et al.* (1987) tested for post-hypnotic responding using someone who ostensibly had nothing whatsoever to do with the experiment. Using this design they found that post-hypnotic responses disappeared entirely.

Further problems with the interpretation of 'real–simulator' comparisons have emerged with investigations into a set of hypnotic phenomena that have been collectively labelled 'trance-logic'. This term was devised by Orne (1959, 1979) to refer to the observation that, unlike simulators, some 'hypnotised' individuals appear to be able to tolerate illogical inconsistencies. For instance, if instructed a) to look at a person, and b) to see (hallucinate) that person standing in a different place, simulators tend to report a single hallucinated image. However, some hypnotic subjects may report seeing *both* the image of an hallucinated person, and the actual person; this has been labelled the 'double-hallucination response'. Also, simulators tend to report opaque hallucinations, whereas some hypnotic subjects may report seeing 'transparent' hallucinations. And when responding to suggestions for age regression, some hypnotic subjects may say they feel like both a child *and* an adult ('duality'), and correctly write a complex sentence that no child could write ('incongruous writing'), whereas simulators will tend to say they felt like a child all of the time, and write a complex sentence incorrectly (Orne 1959; Nogrady *et al.* 1983; de Groot and Gwynn 1989). Although attempts to replicate real–simulator differences on the so-called 'double-hallucination' response have been unsuccessful, other 'trance-logical' phenomena have been replicated (de Groot and Gwynn 1989).

These phenomena may, however, again reflect a limitation of the real–simulator design. It could be argued that, acting as 'excellent' hypnotic subjects, simulators may again simply be overplaying their role. *Some* 'excellent' hypnotic subjects *do* behave like the simulators, but not all. So perhaps these other 'trance-logical' hypnotic subjects are simply exercising their imaginations, or offering less complete or extreme responses (Wagstaff 1981). To test this view some researchers have used control groups who have been instructed to *imagine* rather than fake the various effects, or have been given equivalent instructions without hypnotic induction. Such groups have successfully reproduced the 'trance-logic' effects (Spanos 1986: de Groot and Gwynn 1989). Nevertheless, of course, the problem remains that, just because the effects can be replicated by appropriately instructed controls, it does not necessarily follow that hypnotic subjects are behaving in the same way for the same reasons.

CLINICAL HYPNOSIS

The issue of whether hypnosis is or is not most appropriately described as an altered state is often confused with that of whether hypnotic techniques can have therapeutic benefits. Although non-state theorists would argue that some of the therapeutic benefits of hypnosis have been exaggerated (see for example, Wagstaff 1981: Johnson 1989; Stam 1989), few would deny that what are described as hypnotic procedures can be remarkably successful in the treatment of a number of complaints, including insomnia, obesity, mild phobias, smoking, skin complaints and dental stress, especially when compared with no treatment at all (Heap and Dryden 1991: Wadden and Anderton 1982). In such cases the question is not so much does hypnosis 'work', but compared to what, and why? Hypnotic techniques usually involve a variety of factors that are not unique to hypnosis and that might account for improvements without the necessity of postulating the intervention of an 'hypnotic state'. Such factors include social support, relaxation, covert modelling, placebo effects and even social compliance (Wadden and Anderton 1982; Wagstaff 1981, 1987).

Unfortunately, controlled clinical trials in this area have not yet been sufficiently rigorous to enable any firm conclusions to be drawn as to whether the notion of an hypnotic state is necessary or even useful in accounting for symptom improvement following hypnotic procedures. One obvious ingredient of any trial must be some measure of the patient's *beliefs* about the efficacy of the treatment (Johnson 1989). For example, Wagstaff and Royce (1994) found that an hypnotic procedure to cure nailbiting outperformed a non-hypnotic procedure, but the best predictor of outcome improvement was not the presence or absence of hypnotic induction (or 'hypnosis'), but the patient's beliefs about the efficacy of the procedures (success did, however, also significantly correlate with subjects' verbal reports of how 'hypnotised' they felt). However, this study was an exception; rarely are such beliefs actually measured and included as an experimental variable.

HYPNOTIC ANALGESIA

To many people it is the ability of hypnotic subjects to endure or eliminate surgical pain that demonstrates most clearly the validity of the 'hypnotic state'; to argue that people can endure surgery with little or no distress would seem to be inexplicable in terms of non-state perspectives. However, non-state theorists contend that it is possible to explain this phenomenon without invoking the concept of an hypnotic state. They point out, for example, that cases of surgery using hypnosis are comparatively rare, and that procedures for hypnotic analgesia usually involve a variety of non-specific coping strategies that are potent pain relievers; these include suggestions for pain relief (numbness, coldness, etc.), relaxation and distraction, and pre-operative preparation to alleviate fear and anxiety (Barber, Spanos and Chaves 1974; Chaves 1989). Nevertheless, whilst state theorists do not deny that these factors may be influential, they deny that non-hypnotic factors can account entirely for profound hypnotic analgesia. Hilgard, for example, argues that hypnotic analgesia involves two components, non-hypnotic factors, such as those just mentioned, and a specific hypnotic dissociative process, whereby pain is dissociated from awareness (Hilgard and Hilgard 1983; Hilgard 1986; see also, Bowers 1983). As it is obviously difficult to conduct controlled experiments on surgical pain to test these ideas, researchers have turned to laboratory methods to study hypnotic analgesia.

In laboratory studies, usually the pain inducing procedure involves placing the subject's arm in ice water, or using a pressure stimulus. Both methods can induce severe pain without any permanent damage. One would think that an obvious method for testing the validity of reports of hypnotic analgesia would be to use physiological measures associated with pain. However, the interpretation of studies employing this method has proved difficult. For instance, some studies have found that, although hypnotic subjects do report reduced sensations of pain following suggestions for analgesia, the physiological concomitants of pain (such as increased heart rate and blood pressure) appear to contradict these reports. This might suggest that some hypnotic subjects report less pain than they actually feel (Wagstaff 1981). A number of state theorists, however, believe that this finding can be explained in terms of dissociation.

To demonstrate this they have applied their 'hidden-observer' procedure outlined earlier, whereby during the hypnosis session the experimenter attempts to contact another 'part' of consciousness. Some researchers have found that although the 'hypnotised' subject will often report a decrease in pain in response to a noxious stimulus, the 'hidden observer', allegedly representing a dissociated part of consciousness, reports pain as 'normal' (Bowers 1983; Hilgard 1986). This finding has been used to support the idea that during hypnotic analgesia pain is 'felt' outside awareness, and thus explains the apparent contradiction between verbal reports and physiological indices. Non-state theorists, however, suggest that two other factors may be involved in this effect, both of which represent subjects' attempts to accord with experimental demands. First the hypnotic subject may simply be exhibiting compliance and reporting in the 'hidden-observer' condition what he or she *really* feels (pain), and second the subject may be using pain coping strategies in the 'normal' hypnosis condition, but switching away from these in the 'hidden-observer' condition. In support of the non-state view there is a variety of evidence to indicate that non-hypnotic pain reducing strategies are as effective as hypnotic ones (Spanos 1986, 1989). However, the problem still arises that, although the responses of hypnotic and non-hypnotic subjects may be similar, the processes that give rise to those responses may be different (Bowers and Davidson 1991).

Importantly, although simulators can readily imitate analgesia, Nogrady *et al.* (1983) found that simulators do not seem to produce the classic 'hidden-observer' effect (i.e. their simulated 'hidden observers' do not report more pain than the 'hypnotised' part). Instead, when given hidden-observer instructions, simulators' hidden observers continued to report analgesia. It can be noted, however, that some 'good' hypnotic subjects also continue to report analgesia during the hidden-observer condition, so the possibility arises that the response of simulators in this respect may simply reflect their view of the conservative response of an 'excellent' subject (the simulator 'overplay effect' yet again).

In an attempt to overcome these problems Spanos and his associates have evolved some paradigms that do not simply involve a comparison of hypnotic subjects with non-hypnotic controls, and have come up with results that seem to support the non-state view. For example, they have used experimental instructions that imply that the same, less or greater pain will be felt during the hidden-observer condition, and have found that the 'hidden observers' of hypnotic subjects respond accordingly. Also, they have found that, if subjected to a painful stimulus, hypnotic subjects will subsequently report having experienced analgesia, or not, depending on whether the experimental instructions imply that they were, or were not, 'hypnotised' at the time when they were receiving the stimulus (Spanos 1986, 1989; Spanos *et al.* 1990). Such results seem to suggest that reports of hypnotic analgesia may represent a mixture of 'real' effects, due to pain coping strategies, and response bias effects, that arise as subjects attempt to play the experimental role.

State theorists, however, vigorously oppose this interpretation. Not only do they assert that hypnotic analgesia *is* more effective than non-hypnotic analgesia, but that during hypnotic analgesia there is evidence of true dissociation (Bowers and Davidson 1991). For example, Bowers and Davidson (1991) report some unpublished findings that during hypnotic analgesia hypnotic subjects can perform well on a competing ('dissociated') cognitive task, whereas non-hypnotic subjects perform less well on the competing cognitive task. This result, however, apparently contradicts other results that indicate that hypnotic subjects do *not* perform better, in fact they can be *worse* than controls at competing tasks (Wagstaff 1981).

These issues clearly remain unresolved; however, if nothing else, the fact that different laboratories should produce different results perhaps attests to the importance of experimental demands in shaping subjects' responses.

TRAINING THE INSUSCEPTIBLE

If, as non-state theorists claim, hypnotic responding results from a set of appropriate attitudes and expectations, and the adoption of a number of role strategies, then perhaps an ultimate test would be to see whether it is possible to train someone, previously hypnotically insusceptible, to become susceptible. And, indeed, some of the most interesting recent developments in hypnosis research have revolved around attempts by non-state theorists to train subjects to become hypnotically susceptible. Using techniques to inculcate in subjects those attitudes, expectancies and strategies that non-state theorists believe are responsible for producing hypnotic effects, some researchers have claimed considerable success in turning low susceptibles into high susceptibles (Bertrand 1989; Spanos 1991). Critics of this work, however, claim that the gains are short lived and that training procedures are producing compliance rather than true hypnotic responding (Bates *et al.* 1988; Bowers and Davidson 1991). Both criticisms have been disputed, but if, as Wagstaff (1981, 1986, 1991) and Spanos (1992) suggest, compliance *is* an important element in much hypnotic responding, then perhaps it is debatable whether the latter point should be viewed entirely as a criticism.

CONCLUSION

Although the central controversy in hypnosis seems to remain unresolved, experimental studies of hypnosis have clearly taught us two important methodological lessons that are deceptively simple. First, we must never underestimate the capacities of ordinary people. No matter how extraordinary a piece of behaviour may seem, never assume that control subjects could not, or would not, do it'. Second we must be constantly aware of the fact that subjects in psychology experiments are active cognising participants, not passive automata. This is hardly a new idea, but if hypnosis research is anything to go by, it is worth repeating. As Pierce commented nearly a century ago:

> It is to the highest degree probable that the subject's . . . general attitude of mind is that of ready complacency and a cheerful willingness to assist the investigator in every possible way by reporting to him those very things that he is most eager to find, and that the very questions of the experimenter . . . suggest the shade of reply expected.

(Quoted in Orne 1962: 472)

In designing experiments, therefore, we must always be aware of the possibility that the phenomena we are measuring may be as much *products* of our procedures as they are something measured *by* them.

REFERENCES

Anderton, C.H. (1986) 'The forensic use of hypnosis', in F.A. De Piano and H.C. Salzberg (eds) *Clinical Applications of Hypnosis*, Norwood, N.J.: Ablex.

Banyai, E.I. and Hilgard, E.R. (1976) 'A comparison of active alert hypnotic induction and traditional relaxation induction', *Journal of Abnormal Psychology*, 85: 218–224.

Barber, J. (1991) 'The locksmith model: accessing hypnotic responsiveness', in S.J. Lynn and J.W. Rhue (eds) *Theories of Hypnosis: Current models and perspectives*, New York: Guilford.

Barber, T.X. (1965) 'The effects of "hypnosis" on learning and recall: a methodological critique', *Journal of Abnormal Psychology*, 21, 19–25.

Barber, T.X. (1969) *Hypnosis: A scientific approach*, New York: Van Nostrand.

Barber, T.X., Spanos, N.P. and Chaves, J.F. (1974) *Hypnotism, Imagination and Human Potentialities*, New York: Pergamon.

Bates, B.L., Miller, R.J., Cross, H.J. and Brigham, T.A. (1988) 'Modifying hypnotic suggestibility with the Carleton Skills Training Program', *Journal of Personality and Social Psychology*, 55: 120–127.

Bertrand, L.D. (1989) 'The assessment and modification of hypnotic susceptibility', in N.P. Spanos and J.F. Chaves (eds) *Hypnosis: The cognitive-behavioral perspective*, Buffalo, N.Y.: Prometheus.

Bowers, K.S. (1983) *Hypnosis for the Seriously Curious*, New York: Norton.

Bowers, K.S. and Davidson, T.M. (1991) 'A neodissociative critique of Spanos's social psychological model of hypnosis', in S.J. Lynn and J.W. Rhue (eds) *Theories of Hypnosis: Current models and perspectives*, New York: Guilford.

Calverley, D.S. and Barber, T.X. (1965) '"Hypnosis" and antisocial behavior: an experimental evaluation', cited by T.X. Barber (1969), *Hypnosis: A scientific approach*, New York: Van Nostrand.

Chaves, J.F. (1989) 'Hypnotic control of clinical pain', in N.P. Spanos and J.F. Chaves (eds) *Hypnosis: The cognitive-behavioral perspective*, Buffalo, N.Y.: Prometheus.

Coe, W.C. (1989) 'Posthypnotic amnesia: theory and research', in N.P. Spanos and

J.F. Chaves (eds) *Hypnosis: The cognitive-behavioural perspective*, Buffalo, N.Y.: Prometheus.

Coe, W.C. and Sarbin, T.R. (1991) 'Role theory: hypnosis from a dramaturgical and narrational perspective', in S.J. Lynn, and J.W. Rhue, (eds) *Theories of Hypnosis: Current models and perspectives*, New York: Guilford.

Coe, W.C., Kobayashi, K. and Howard, M.L. (1972) 'An approach toward isolating factors that influence antisocial conduct in hypnosis', *International Journal of Clinical and Experimental Hypnosis*, 20: 118–131.

Coe, W.C., Kobayashi, K. and Howard, M.L. (1973) 'Experimental and ethical problems of evaluating the influence of hypnosis in antisocial conduct', *Journal of Abnormal Psychology*, 82: 476–482.

Coe, W.C. (1989) 'Posthypnotic amnesia: Theory and research', in Spanos, N.P. and Chaves, J.F. (eds) *Hypnosis: The Cognitive Behavioural Perspective*, Buffalo, N.Y.: Prometheus, 110–148.

Davies, P. (1988) 'Some considerations of the physiological effects of hypnosis', in M. Heap (ed.) *Hypnosis: Current clinical, experimental and forensic practices*, London: Croom Helm.

de Groot, H.P. and Gwynn, M.I. (1989) 'Trance logic, duality and hidden observer responding', in N.P. Spanos and J.F. Chaves (eds) *Hypnosis: The cognitive-behavioral perspective*, Buffalo, N.Y.: Prometheus.

Edmonston, W.E. (1991) 'Anesis', in S.J. Lynn and J.W. Rhue (eds) *Theories of Hypnosis: Current models and perspectives*, New York: Guilford.

Evans, F.J. (1979) 'Contextual forgetting: post-hypnotic source amnesia', *Journal of Abnormal Psychology*, 88: 556–563.

Evans, F.J. (1991) 'Hypnotizability: individual differences in dissociation and the flexible control of psychological processes', in S.J. Lynn and J.W. Rhue (eds) *Theories of Hypnosis: Current models and perspectives*, New York: Guilford.

Evans, F.J. and Kihlstrom, J.F. (1973) 'Post-hypnotic amnesia as disrupted retrieval', *Journal of Abnormal Psychology*, 82: 317–323.

Fellows, B.J. (1990) 'Current theories of hypnosis: a critical review', *British Journal of Experimental and Clinical Hypnosis*, 7: 81–92.

Gruzelier, J. (1988) 'The neuropsychology of hypnosis', in M. Heap (ed.) *Hypnosis: Current clinical, experimental and forensic practices*, London: Croom Helm.

Heap, M. and Dryden, W. (1991) *Hypnotherapy: A handbook*, Milton Keynes: Open University Press.

Hilgard, E.R. (1978) 'States of consciousness in hypnosis: divisions or levels?', in F.H. Frankel and H.S. Zamansky (eds) *Hypnosis at its Bicentennial: Selected papers*, New York: Plenum.

Hilgard, E.R. (1985) 'Conscious and unconscious processes in hypnosis', in D. Waxman, P.C. Misra, M. Gibson and M.A. Basker (eds) *Modern Trends in Hypnosis*, New York: Plenum.

Hilgard, E.R. (1986) *Divided Consciousness: Multiple controls in human thought and action*, New York: Wiley.

Hilgard, E.R. (1991) 'A neodissociation interpretation of hypnosis', in S.J. Lynn and J.W. Rhue (eds) *Theories of Hypnosis: Current models and perspectives*, New York: Guilford.

Hilgard, E.R. and Hilgard, J.R. (1983) *Hypnosis in the Relief of Pain*, Los Altos, Calif.: William Kaufmann.

Jacobs, S. and Gotthelf, C. (1986) 'Effects of hypnosis on physical and athletic performance', in F.A. De Piano and H.C. Salzberg (eds) *Clinical Applications of Hypnosis*, Norwood, N.J.: Ablex.

Johnson, R.F.Q. (1989) 'Hypnosis, suggestion and dermatological changes: a consideration of the production and diminution of dermatological entities', in N.P. Spanos and J.F. Chaves (eds) *Hypnosis: The cognitive-behavioral perspective*, Buffalo, N.Y.: Prometheus.

Jones, W.J. and Flynn, D.M. (1989) 'Methodological and theoretical considerations in the study of "hypnotic" effects in perception', in N.P. Spanos and J.F. Chaves (eds) *Hypnosis: The cognitive-behavioral perspective*, Buffalo, N.Y.: Prometheus.

Jones, B. and Spanos, N.P. (1982) 'Suggestions for altered auditory sensitivity, the negative subject effect and hypnotic susceptibility: A signal detection analysis', *Journal of Personality and Social Psychology*, 43: 637–647.

Kihlstrom, J.F. and Wilson, L. (1984) 'Temporal organization of recall during posthypnotic amnesia', *Journal of Abnormal Psychology*, 93: 200–208.

Kihlstrom, J.F., Evans, F.J., Orne, E.C. and Orne, M.T. (1980) 'Attempting to breach posthypnotic amnesia', *Journal of Abnormal Psychology*, 89: 603–616.

Knox, J.V., Morgan, A.H. and Hilgard, E.R. (1974) 'Pain and suffering in ischemia: the paradox of hypnotically suggested anesthesia as contradicted by reports from the "hidden-observer"', *Archives of General Psychiatry*, 30: 840–847.

Laurence, J.-R. and Perry, C. (1983) 'Hypnotically created memory among highly hypnotizable subjects', *Science*, 222: 523–524.

Levitt, R.E., Aronoff, G., Morgan, C.D., Overley, T.M. and Parrish, M.J. (1975) 'Testing the coercive power of hypnosis: committing objectionable acts', *International Journal of Clinical and Experimental Hypnosis*, 23: 59–67.

Lynn, S.J. and Rhue, J.W. (eds) (1991) *Theories of Hypnosis: Current models and perspectives*, New York: Guilford.

Malott, J.M. (1984) 'Active-alert hypnosis: replication and extension of previous research', *Journal of Abnormal Psychology*, 93: 246–249.

McCann, T.E. and Sheehan, P.W. (1987) 'The breaching of pseudomemory under hypnotic instruction: implications for original memory retrieval', *British Journal of Experimental and Clinical Hypnosis*, 4: 101–108.

Milgram, S. (1974) *Obedience to Authority*, London: Tavistock.

Mixon, P. (1974) 'Instead of deception', in M. Armistead (ed.) *Reconstructing Social Psychology*, Harmondsworth: Penguin.

Murray, G.J., Cross, H.J. and Whipple, J. (1992) 'Hypnotically created pseudo-memories: further investigation into the "memory distortion or response bias" question', *Journal of Abnormal Psychology*, 101: 75–77.

Nash, M.R. (1991) 'Hypnosis as a special case of psychological regression', in S.J. Lynn and J.W. Rhue (eds) *Theories of Hypnosis: Current models and perspectives*, New York: Guilford.

Nogrady, H., McConkey, K.M., Laurence, J.R. and Perry, C. (1983) 'Dissociation, duality, and demand characteristics in hypnosis', *Journal of Abnormal Psychology*, 92: 223–235.

O'Brien, R.M. and Rabuck, S.J. (1976) 'Experimentally produced self-repugnant behavior as a function of hypnosis and waking suggestion: a pilot study', *American Journal of Clinical Hypnosis*, 18: 272–276.

Orne, M.T. (1959) 'The nature of hypnosis: artifact and essence', *Journal of Abnormal Psychology*, 58: 277–299.

Orne, M.T. (1962) 'On the social psychology of the psychological experiment: with particular reference to demand characteristics and their implications', *American Psychologist*, 17: 776–783.

Orne, M.T. (1970) 'Hypnosis, motivation and the ecological validity of the psychological experiment', in W.J. Arnold and M.M. Page (eds) *Nebraska Symposium on Motivation*, Lincoln, Nebraska: Nebraska Press.

Orne, M.T. (1971) 'The simulation of hypnosis: why, how, and what it means', *International Journal of Clinical and Experimental Hypnosis*, 19: 183–210.

Orne, M.T. (1979) 'On the simulating subject as quasi-control group in hypnosis research: what, why and how?', in E. Fromm and R.E. Shor (eds) *Hypnosis: Research developments and perspectives*, New York: Aldine.

Orne, M.T. and Evans, F.J. (1965) 'Social control in the psychological experiment: antisocial behaviour and hypnosis', *Journal of Personality and Social Psychology*, 1: 189–200.

Orne, M.T. and Holland, C.C. (1968) 'On the ecological validity of laboratory deceptions', *International Journal of Psychiatry*, 6: 282–293.

Orne, M.T., Sheehan, P.W. and Evans, F.J. (1968) 'Occurrence of posthypnotic behavior outside the experimental setting', *Journal of Personality and Social Psychology*, 9: 189–196.

Orne, M.T., Soskis, D.A., Dinges, D.F. and Orne, E.C. (1984) 'Hypnotically induced testimony', in G.L. Wells and E.F. Loftus (eds) *Eyewitness Testimony: Psychological perspectives*, Cambridge: Cambridge University Press.

Rowland, L.W. (1939) 'Will hypnotised persons try to harm themselves or others?' *Journal of Abnormal and Social Psychology*, 34: 114–117.

Sarbin, T.R. and Coe, W.C. (1972) *Hypnosis: A social psychological analysis of influence communication*, New York: Holt, Rinehart & Winston.

Sarbin, T.R. and Slagle, R.W. (1979) 'Hypnosis and psychophysiological outcomes', in E. Fromm and R.E. Shor (eds) *Hypnosis: Developments in research and new perspectives*, 2nd edn, Chicago: Aldine.

Sheridan, C.L. and King, R.G. (1972) 'Obedience to authority with an authentic victim', *Proceedings, 80th Annual Convention APA*: 165–166.

Smith, M.C. (1983) 'Hypnotic memory enhancement of witnesses: does it work?', *Psychological Bulletin*, 94: 387–407.

Spanos, N.P. (1982) 'A social psychological approach to hypnotic behavior', in G. Weary and H.L. Mirels (eds) *Integrations of Clinical and Social Psychology*, Oxford: Oxford University Press.

Spanos, N.P. (1986) 'Hypnotic behavior: a social psychological interpretation of amnesia, analgesia, and "trance logic"', *The Behavioral and Brain Sciences*, 9: 449–502.

Spanos, N.P. (1989) 'Experimental research on hypnotic analgesia', in N.P. Spanos and J.F. Chaves (eds) *Hypnosis: The cognitive-behavioural perspective*, Buffalo, N.Y.: Prometheus.

Spanos, N.P. (1991) 'A sociocognitive approach to hypnosis', in S.J. Lynn and J.W. Rhue (eds) *Theories of Hypnosis: Current models and perspectives*, New York: Guilford.

Spanos, N.P. (1992) 'Compliance and reinterpretation in hypnotic responding', *Contemporary Hypnosis*, 9: 7–14.

Spanos, N.P. and McLean, J. (1986) 'Hypnotically created pseudomemories: memory distortions or reporting biases?', *British Journal of Experimental and Clinical Hypnosis*: 155–159.

Spanos, N.P. and Chaves, J.F. (eds) (1989) *Hypnosis: The cognitive-behavioral perspective*, Buffalo, N.Y.: Prometheus.

Spanos, N.P., Radtke, H.L. and Bertrand, L.D. (1985) 'Hypnotic amnesia as a strategic enactment: breaching amnesia in highly susceptible subjects', *Journal of Personality and Social Psychology*, 47: 1155–1169.

Spanos, N.P., Menary, E., Brett, P.J., Cross, W. and Ahmed, Q. (1987) 'Failure of posthypnotic responding to occur outside the experimental setting', *Journal of Abnormal Psychology*, 96: 52–57.

Spanos, N.P., Perlini, A.H., Patrick, L., Bell, S. and Gwynn, M.I. (1990) 'The role of compliance in hypnotic and non-hypnotic analgesia', *Journal of Research in Personality*, 24: 433–453.

Stam, H.J. (1989) 'From symptom to cure. Hypnotic interventions in cancer', in N.P. Spanos and J.F. Chaves (eds) *Hypnosis: The cognitive-behavioral perspective*, Buffalo, N.Y.: Prometheus.

Udolf, R. (1983) *Forensic Hypnosis: Psychological and legal aspects*, Lexington, Mass.: Lexington Books.

Wadden, T. and Anderton, C.H. (1982) 'The clinical use of hypnosis', *Psychological Bulletin*, 91: 215–243.

Wagstaff, G.F. (1977a) 'An experimental study of compliance and post-hypnotic amnesia', *British Journal of Social and Clinical Psychology*, 16: 225–228.

Wagstaff, G.F. (1977b) 'Post-hypnotic amnesia as disrupted retrieval: a role-playing paradigm', *Quarterly Journal of Experimental Psychology*, 29: 499–504.

Wagstaff, G.F. (1981) *Hypnosis, Compliance, and Belief*, Brighton: Harvester/ New York: St Martin's Press.

Wagstaff, G.F. (1982) 'Disorganized recall, suggested amnesia and compliance', *Psychological Reports*, 51: 1255–1258.

Wagstaff, G.F. (1984) 'The enhancement of witness memory by hypnosis: a review and methodological critique of the experimental literature', *British Journal of Experimental and Clinical Hypnosis*, 2: 3–12.

Wagstaff, G.F. (1986) 'Hypnosis as compliance and belief: a sociocognitive view', in P.L.N. Naish (ed.) *What is Hypnosis?*, Philadelphia: Open University Press.

Wagstaff, G.F. (1987) 'Hypnotic induction, hypnotherapy and the placebo effect', *British Journal of Experimental and Clinical Hypnosis*, 4: 168–170.

Wagstaff, G.F. (1989) 'Forensic aspects of hypnosis', in N.P. Spanos and J.F. Chaves (eds) *Hypnosis: The cognitive-behavioral perspective*, Buffalo, N.Y.: Prometheus.

Wagstaff, G.F. (1991) 'Compliance, belief and semantics in hypnosis: a nonstate, sociocognitive perspective', in S.J. Lynn and J.W. Rhue (eds) *Theories of Hypnosis: Current models and perspectives*, New York: Guilford.

Wagstaff, G.F. (1993) 'What expert witnesses can tell courts about hypnosis: a review of the association between hypnosis and the law', *Expert Evidence: The International Digest of Human Behaviour Science and Law*, 2: 60–70.

Wagstaff, G.F. and Benson, D. (1987) 'Exploring hypnotic processes with the cognitive simulator comparison group', *British Journal of Experimental and Clinical Hypnosis*, 4: 83–91.

Wagstaff, G.F. and Carroll, R. (1987) 'The cognitive simulation of hypnotic amnesia and disorganized retrieval', *Medical Science Research*, 15: 85–86.

Wagstaff, G.F. and Royce, C. (1994) 'Hypnosis and the treatment of nailbiting: a preliminary trial', *Contemporary Hypnosis*, 11, 9–13.

Young, P.C. (1952) 'Antisocial uses of hypnosis', in L.M. Le Cron (ed.) *Experimental Hypnosis*, 2nd edn, New York: Macmillan.

Chapter 14

Qualitative methods in cognitive psychology

Illustrations from decision process research and environmental cognition

Rob Ranyard and Janis Williamson

INTRODUCTION

In this chapter some of the main types of qualitative method used in cognitive psychology are described, together with three important criteria for their evaluation. Two illustrations are then presented in detail: (1) from environmental cognition, a diary study of errors in routefinding; and (2) from decision process research, a think-aloud study of multiattribute choice. These examples show how the difficulties of qualitative methods can be overcome to make available rich sources of data, often tapping into real world contexts.

The studies illustrate two contrasting yet equally important research strategies. The decision process study illustrates an *explanatory* research strategy which aims to assess the predictive validity of alternative process explanations of choice behaviour. In order to do this the conditions under which decisions were made had to be carefully controlled. The novel feature of the explanatory strategy adopted was that qualitative predictions about features of concurrent verbal reports were generated and tested, in addition to the usual choice predictions. In contrast, the routefinding study illustrated a *descriptive* research strategy. The goal was to describe behaviour and cognition in the real world. Thus, the emphasis was on descriptive and ecological validity, and the interpretation of evidence in terms of the most descriptively valid (and parsimonious) cognitive theory. The theoretical goal, then, was to develop and construct theories rather than to empirically distinguish between alternatives.

The chapter concludes with a discussion of two important issues: how the procedural rigour of qualitative methods can be improved, and how their validity can be assured. Finally, some suggestions for further reading are given.

TYPES OF QUALITATIVE DATA AND EVALUATIVE CRITERIA

Figure 14.1 lists the main types of qualitative data organised as a matrix defined by two important dimensions. Although it summarises the methods

Focus / Context	Inside (experience)	Outside (behaviour)
Controlled conditions	concurrent verbal reports (think aloud, probe, etc.) retrospective verbal reports	information acquisition data final judgements and choices
Real world	cognitive interviews diaries other accounts	eye witness reports naturalistic observation formal records of judgements and decisions

Figure 14.1 Basic dimensions of qualitative methods for decision process research

that have been used in decision process research, this simple taxonomy readily generalises to other fields, including environmental cognition.

The first dimension is whether the focus of the method is on the *inside* of the decision maker (DM), exploring experience, or on the *outside*, describing behaviour. This inside/outside dichotomy defines the columns of the matrix. The second dimension is whether the context of the study is under *controlled conditions*, often a laboratory experiment, or alternatively some naturally occurring, *real world* situation. This defines the rows of the matrix.

In basic decision making research the outside focus has been dominant with final judgements and choices traditionally regarded as primary data. Although the emergence of process-oriented research has resulted in a wider range of qualitative data being accepted, many researchers seem to prefer to stay within the top-right box of Figure 14.1, trusting, for example, information acquisition monitoring more than, say, think-aloud data. There are two main reasons for this. The first is the widespread mistrust of the validity of self-reports in general, and of reports of one's own cognitions in particular (e.g. Nisbett and Wilson 1977). Validity in this context means *descriptive validity*, the extent to which the results accurately describe underlying cognitions. Fortunately, the classic contribution to this debate by Ericsson and Simon (1980, 1984) persuaded many researchers that concurrent and retrospective verbal reports can be valid in certain situations, and they have increasingly been used. The second reason for the general 'top-right box' preference is because of the importance that has been attached to the main advantage of controlled conditions, namely, enabling empirical tests of the *predictive validity* of alternative theories to be carried out. Controlled experiments, however, are often weak with respect to *ecological validity*, meaning that the results may not generalise beyond the laboratory.

The importance of this problem has been increasingly recognised in various fields of cognition and this has led to the increased use of case studies and naturalistic experiments. It is in contexts such as these that qualitative methods come into their own. For example, case studies of real decisions, using interviews and the analysis of accounts by decision makers and other witnesses, have provided important insights into the decision process (e.g. Montgomery and Svenson 1989). Another interesting development has been the increased use of the diary method in studies covering diverse areas of everyday cognition (Kruysse 1992; Reason 1979; Reason and Lucas 1984; Terry 1988; Young, Hay and Ellis 1985). This technique is particularly suitable for tapping into naturally occurring behaviour, as subjects carry the diaries with them and record instances of the behaviour of interest whenever and wherever they happen. It is a self-report 'inside' method (Figure 14.1) where respondents are asked to monitor and report on their own behaviour, in contrast to an 'outside', naturalistic observation approach where the researcher collects objective data about some aspect of the subject's behaviour.

ILLUSTRATION 1: ENVIRONMENTAL COGNITION – ROUTE FINDING

The topic of environmental cognition encompasses contributions from diverse professional groups, most notably psychologists, sociologists, architects, geographers and town planners. Each of these groups have their own particular interests, but for cognitive psychologists the main concern is with the ways in which the external environment might be represented in the mind. This concern forms the main subject matter of the cognitive mapping literature; much research in this area has focused on looking at how children and adults develop understanding, knowledge and memory for their everyday environments (Siegel and White 1975; Matthews 1992). Other aspects of research include attempts to externalise the cognitive maps possessed by individuals; the aim here is to describe the nature of environmental representations, for example in terms of accuracy, distortions, effects of environmental features such as landmarks, intersections and so on (Byrne 1979, 1982; Sadalla and Staplin 1980; Chase and Chi 1981; Thorndyke and Hayes-Roth 1982). From studies such as these, and many others, much has come to be known about the development and nature of environmental representations.

However, little research has been undertaken to investigate the efficiency of everyday travel around the environment. Generally speaking people seem to function quite well within their everyday environment, in terms of navigation and routefinding, but anecdotal evidence also suggests that minor difficulties occur with some regularity. The research described in this section looks at naturally occurring lapses and errors in everyday routefinding, and employs the diary method of data collection.

Method

The aim was to construct a diary which would give subjects the opportunity to express themselves as fully and as freely as possible, but yet contain sufficient structure and standardisation that the data collected could be usefully and meaningfully analysed. In this particular study (see Williamson and Barrow 1994 for a full discussion), the diaries were structured in such a way that they allowed subjects to provide a free written description of the errors or lapses which occurred, and then to respond to a series of standardised questions about circumstances surrounding the error. Thus although individual descriptions of errors were very varied, much standardised information was also available for analysis. For example the information asked for in this diary study included:

- a brief description of the error
- the mode of travel (e.g. car, on foot)
- the type of location (city, country, suburbs)
- the familiarity of the environment (five point scale)
- a brief description of why the error had occurred

Subjects were asked to keep diaries over a four-week period. They were supplied with four diaries, each with enough space for ten error descriptions. Each diary was kept for a period of seven days; subjects returned each diary in person or by post on a prearranged day and began the next one. They were requested to return each diary at the appropriate time, even if they had no errors to report in a given week. This was to help with administration and record keeping on the part of the researcher. Subjects were given background information about the study and were shown an 'example error' to aid them in completion of their diaries. It was emphasised that they should record every error, no matter how trivial it seemed, and that they should record the details as soon as possible after the error occurred.

Forty-nine subjects took part in the study and produced 198 errors over the four-week period. Number of errors reported per subject ranged from 1 to 11, with a mean of 4.2. Initial analysis of the data concentrated on establishing some basic parameters of the error sample, in terms of percentage errors occurring while on foot, in a car, etc., locations of errors (indoor/outdoor), and familiarity of environment where errors took place. Errors made on foot account for half of the sample, whereas the vast majority of the rest occurred during car journeys. Although many errors occurred in unfamiliar environments (37 per cent), almost two-thirds occurred in environments which had been rated as at least moderately familiar, and in many cases very familiar.

Content analysis

The diaries were then analysed using content analysis. That is, the content of the subjects' description of each error and its possible cause was used to try to develop usable sets of categories of errors and their causes. There are many ways of conducting content analysis, with particular importance attached to the nature of the recording unit (Holsti 1969). In this study the whole of the subject's description was used as the recording unit.

Error descriptions varied enormously among subjects, in terms of length, detail, clarity of expression and insight. Because of these factors, classification of subjects' descriptions into a coherent set of errors and causes was not a straightforward task. During a preliminary reading of the data, notes were made about the types of error which seemed to be occurring, and these were formulated into a tentative category set. Both researchers carried out this process independently, and then during a discussion session the initial classification was refined further by amalgamating and reconceptualising some of the categories. Part of this process involved deciding explicitly on criteria for membership of a category. As far as possible, subjects' own wording was used in the naming of categories, again to try to minimise subjective bias. However for some categories the final name was chosen by the researchers to encapsulate as concisely and accurately as possible the error types they contained. Having derived an apparently usable set of categories, the two researchers then independently classified each description of the errors and their causes according to the criteria agreed. These independent classifications then had to be checked for inter-rater reliability. In this case the method used was a measure of percentage agreement between the two raters' classifications. This resulted in a high degree of reliability (at least 80 per cent) for each of the categories. Any disagreement between the raters over category membership was resolved by discussion and further reference to the relevant criteria.

The final categories of error types and their incidence within the sample are shown in Table 14.1, and error causes and their incidence in Table 14.2.

The data in these tables indicate that a useful pattern of the incidence of errors and their causes was able to be extracted from the large amount of written description which subjects had originally supplied. In all, nine types of error were identified, and four of these ('wrong turning', 'missed turning', 'route selection error' and 'misconception of location') accounted for almost three-quarters of the errors. Overall, more errors occurred in familiar than

Table 14.1 Overall percentage distribution of types of error, including breakdown for familiar and unfamiliar environments (N=198)

Type of Error	Overall percentage	Environment Familiar	Unfamiliar
1 Wrong turning	33	25	8
2 Missed turning	16	10	6
3 Route selection error	13	4	9
4 Misconception of location	10	7	3
5 Travelled to incorrect location	9	8	1
6 Premature exit	7	4	3
7 Return route error	5	2	3
8 Route exit failure	3	1	2
9 Miscellaneous	4	2	2

Table 14.2(a) Overall percentage distribution of causes of error, including breakdown for familiar and unfamiliar environments (N=151)

Reason	Overall percentage	Environment Familiar	Unfamiliar
1 Environmental cause	43	21	22
2 Inattention	28	21	7
3 Inadequate knowledge	19	6	13
4 Habit	7	7	0
5 Inadequate cognitive map	3	2	1

Table 14.2(b) Overall percentage distribution of environmental causes of error, including breakdown for familiar and unfamiliar environments (N=65)

Reason	Overall percentage	Environment Familiar	Unfamiliar
1 Inadequate signposting	31	8	23
2 Perceptual confusion	29	22	7
3 System complexity	16	8	8
4 Novel routes	12	6	6
5 Environment change	12	6	6

unfamiliar environments. Although this may seem contrary to what might be expected, people do spend a greater proportion of their lives in familiar surroundings, and so the opportunity for errors to occur there is correspondingly greater. The most commonly occurring types of error were wrong and missed turnings; both of these happened more frequently in familiar environments, and this finding was particularly marked in the case of wrong turnings. Both of these events are relatively trivial occurrences, in the sense that they should be fairly easily detected and corrected using some common environmental heuristic. The remaining categories of error occurred with less frequency, but nevertheless were quite evenly distributed across subjects' diaries. Considered together, the categories illustrate the variety of errors which seem to occur with some regularity during everyday travel. In terms of causes of error, not all subjects gave usable explanations for their errors, though a large majority did so. The first three categories of error shown in Table 14.2(a) ('environmental cause', 'inattention', and 'inadequate knowledge') together accounted for 90 per cent of the total. The largest proportion of errors (43 per cent) was attributed to environmental causes (further subdivided in Table 14.2(b)), and these occurred almost equally often in familiar and unfamiliar environments. In contrast, the majority of errors due to 'inattention' and all of those attributed to 'habit' occurred in familiar environments. Errors due to inadequate knowledge or planning were twice as likely to occur in unfamiliar as familiar environments. These patterns make sense, in that in familiar environments on well practised routes or routine journeys, less conscious attention is needed for route monitoring. Many of these errors appeared to be of the 'slip' variety as described by Reason (1979), where the attention deployed to the route monitoring task is spread too thinly to maintain smooth execution of the journey, or attentional resources are suddenly directed elsewhere, resulting in a lapse of attention for the route-finding task, and possibly leading to an error. In contrast, in an unfamiliar or unknown environment people are likely to be devoting much more conscious attention to the progress of their journey, and in this case lack of advance planning or appropriate knowledge are more likely to cause error.

Discussion: implications for theories of cognitive mapping

The aim of this research had been to develop some classification system for the incidence and type of errors and causes, and this was certainly achieved. Although no theoretical predictions were being tested, it is true to say that the findings support prevailing opinion within cognitive mapping literature, that although humans do not have an accurate map-like representation of the outside world in their minds, they nevertheless function impressively within the constraints of the representation they do have. Although these subjects appeared to make quite a few errors, the nature of these errors was often quite trivial and easily corrected, but more importantly, the causes of the errors are attributed to not paying enough attention, force of habit, or to some external cause in the environment rather than to a deficiency in the cognitive representation. This point leads to a cautionary note on the descriptive validity of the findings, to be discussed in a later section.

ILLUSTRATION 2: DECISION PROCESS RESEARCH

One of the important issues for contemporary decision process research is how mental representations affect final decisions. In connection with this,

Tversky and Kahneman (1981) began to develop a theory of mental, or psychological accounting to explain certain preference changes they had observed. As an example of this, consider their *Jacket and Calculator* problem (1981: 456):

> Imagine that you are about to purchase a jacket for $15 and a calculator for $125. The calculator salesman informs you that the calculator you wish to buy is on sale for $120 at the other branch of the store, located 20 minutes drive away. Would you make the trip to the other store?

Out of a sample of ninety-three college students given this hypothetical choice, only 29 per cent said they would make the trip. Notice that the calculator is quite expensive. Tversky and Kahneman gave a different sample of eighty-eight students a second version of the problem in which the calculator was cheaper ($15 or $10 at the other store) although the jacket was expensive ($125). This time, 68 per cent of the sample were prepared to make the trip. Thus, a $5 change in a high calculator price, when the jacket price was low, produced a majority 'no' choice, whereas a $5 change in a low calculator price, when the jacket price was high, produced a majority 'yes' choice.

This change in preference was interpreted by Tversky and Kahneman in terms of mental or psychological accounts, defined as frames of reference set up for specific consumer choices or transactions. Three levels of account were distinguished (see Kahneman and Tversky 1984: 347). *Minimal* accounts include only the differences between choice options and disregard the features they share. *Topical* accounts 'relate the consequences of possible choices to a reference level that is determined by the context within which the decision arises'. The context here is specified quite narrowly as the specific choice 'topic'. *Comprehensive* accounts include a wider range of outcomes and contextual factors. Tversky and Kahneman argued that many choice problems are framed at the level of the minimal or topical account. The topical account in particular was claimed to have an important role in framing. The change in preference they observed with the Jacket and Calculator problem was interpreted as evidence that people frame choices at this level. If the choice topic is assumed to be 'buying a calculator' then the $5 saving will be evaluated with respect to the calculator price, which is different in the two versions of the problem. However, the minimal account ($5) and the comprehensive account (the total shopping bill of $140) are invariant across the two versions. Therefore, it was argued, the change in preference must be due to the change in topical account.

Whilst accepting that topical accounts may play a key role, we became interested in the idea that comprehensive accounts also influence the decision process. We therefore carried out a further study of the Jacket and Calculator problem to test specific predictions arising from the mental account framework (Ranyard and Abdel-Nabi 1993). In the first study, we systematically varied the jacket price while keeping the calculator price the same. This is assumed to manipulate the comprehensive account while keeping the topical account constant. We found a small effect on choice, which confirmed our prediction. In a second, qualitative study (summarised below) we further tested our prediction that mental accounting at a more comprehensive level is involved in the choice process.

Method

Six written versions of the Jacket and Calculator problem were prepared using different combinations of calculator price, mode of travel (driving or walking to the other store) and jacket price (£30 or £130). Respondents indicated their choice and degree of preference, and in addition spoke aloud their thoughts as they did so. Forty-eight adult volunteers were recruited, who were paid for their participation in the whole study, which took about forty minutes on average.

The procedure for think-aloud studies recommended by Svenson (1989) was followed as closely as possible. Subjects were tested individually in a quiet room. They were given standardised written instructions about the first part of the study, which consisted of two hypothetical consumer choice problems. The second one was the Jacket and Calculator problem, and the first was a practice item to familiarise them with the think-aloud procedure. Subjects were instructed to take as much time as they needed to come to a decision, and to think aloud while working on the problem, i.e. to say out loud everything they were thinking as they thought it, no matter how insignificant or embarrassing it might seem. To encourage spontaneity, they were told that if they were silent for more than a few seconds (in practice 5 seconds) they would be prompted with the request 'please tell me what you are thinking'. Any problems that arose during the practice task, such as excessive hesitancy or reluctance to think aloud, were discussed before they attempted the second problem. Subject and experimenter sat back-to-back, in order to preclude any unintentional feedback being given.

Analysis of verbal protocols

The verbal protocols were transcribed verbatim, except for sections in which respondents read aloud the presented scenario. This was indicated in the transcription, along with specific prompts and clarifications given by the experimenter. A global coding scheme was devised in which the whole protocol produced by each respondent was coded into one of the following mutually exclusive categories. Examples of verbal protocols assigned to each category are shown in Table 14.4.

1 *Unclear account (U).* Insufficient information in the protocol to indicate the mental account used as a frame of reference.

2 *Minimal account (M)*. Referring to the differences between the alternatives only, i.e. the 20 minutes travelling time, or the £5 calculator price difference, but not the broader accounts defined below. Elaborations which developed the evaluation of these differences were coded as part of the minimal account (e.g. travelling 20 minutes was inconvenient because it would also involve a 20 minute return journey; £5 would be worth saving if you didn't have much money, etc.)

3 *Topical account (T)*. In addition to referring to differences between the alternatives, calculator prices or the context of buying a calculator are referred to as part of the evaluation. Incidental mentions of calculator prices are not sufficient for allocation to this category. If the broader contexts defined below were also mentioned, the protocol was coded as below.

4 *Comprehensive account (C)*. In addition to referring to differences between the alternatives, broader contexts other than the calculator purchase topic are included in the evaluation. In particular, the whole cost of things bought, context of jacket and calculator purchases, the context of 'going shopping' for these things were considered to be part of a comprehensive account. Also, a broader temporal context for the 20 minutes difference was defined as a comprehensive account, e.g. putting the 20 minutes in the context of a morning out shopping, or a lunch break from work.

These categories can be thought of as forming an ordinal scale of accounts, from low to high in 'comprehensiveness', in the order they were described above. When assigning verbal protocols to these categories, coders may be unable to decide between adjacent ones because of ambiguity. A coding rule was devised to cover this, whereby the protocol is assigned to the lower level of account in cases of doubt, because this involves making fewer inferences about what the respondent means to say.

Both authors independently assigned the protocols to account categories using the above definitions and coding rule. Good initial agreement was obtained on all categories. On Cohen's measure of agreement between chance level and complete agreement, a value of kappa = 0.75 was obtained (Siegel and Castellan 1988). Disagreements were resolved by discussion. In some cases, it was decided that one coder had made an error, and this was corrected. In the remaining cases, where there was some ambiguity in the protocol, the coding rule was used to determine the final assignment. The frequencies of final assignments are shown in Table 14.3 split by jacket price conditions, with the overall frequencies shown in the final column. This shows that just over half the protocols were coded as *minimal*, a quarter as *comprehensive*, and less than 15 per cent as *topical*. Table 14.3 also shows that the frequencies of account were somewhat different depending on the jacket price: more verbal protocols were classified as topical or comprehensive in the versions with the higher jacket price.

Table 14.3 Frequencies of protocols in each account category, split by jacket price conditions

Type of account	Jacket price		Total
	£30	£130	
Unclear	3	1	4
Minimal	16	9	25
Topical	2	5	7
Comprehensive	3	9	12
Total	24	24	48

Table 14.4 Examples of verbal protocols coded as minimal, topical and comprehensive mental accounts

---

MINIMAL ACCOUNT – (CALC £15/JACKET £130/WALK)

Yes, I would make the trip to the store because what I'd be thinking is that if I could save £5 for the calculator, it is worth walking 20 minutes away. Do I believe the assistant?. . . My preference would be strong, I think, because it would be worth walking 20 minutes to save £5.

TOPICAL ACCOUNT – (CALC £15/JACKET £130/DRIVE)

Yes, I would make the trip to the store. My preference is strong. The reason for that is because for the calculator to be bought at £10 rather than £15, the travelling distance outweighs the actual cost. I think I said that right.

COMPREHENSIVE ACCOUNT – (CALC £15/JACKET £130/WALK)

If I was buying both I must have quite a lot of money, especially at that price, so I think I would say 'No'. I might not believe him anyway. Being as I have just read something where I'm on a beach it makes me feel that I'm still on holiday and in that case I might risk a 20 minute walk but I think I'd settle on 'No'. How strong is your preference? I would say it's quite strong, so I'll tick very strong. Really because of the small price of the calculator in comparison to the jacket. If you are going to buy a jacket for £130, then £5 off a calculator isn't much money, is it? But I don't think I would buy a jacket for £130 anyway. It would be a very rare event.

Discussion: implications for decision process research

Overall, the think-aloud study supports the psychological validity of the notion of mental accounts at different levels of comprehensiveness. About 90 per cent of verbal protocols were coded into the three levels of minimal, topical and comprehensive account. One would have expected, from Tversky and Kahneman's (1981) analysis, that most of them would have been in the topical category. However, this was the least frequent of the three, with minimal accounts playing a more prominent role than expected.

Nevertheless, positive evidence of more comprehensive framing was evident in nearly 40 per cent of protocols. The protocols showed how evaluations of advantages were contingent on the level of account adopted. A number of ways of evaluating the £5 advantage were evident. Some references were to its absolute value, how useful £5 might be and so on, while others related it to current wealth or to topical or comprehensive accounts as defined earlier. For example, the subject who referred to the £5 saving as a third off the calculator price was clearly evaluating it with reference to a topical account. Similarly, alternative ways of evaluating the 20 minutes difference in travelling were also evident.

METHODOLOGICAL ISSUES

Practical matters

Many qualitative methods, especially when applied to real world cognition, have the potential to produce very large amounts of data which may well be interesting, but extremely difficult to reduce to manageable levels and make any sense of; awareness of this possibility and careful consideration in the development of materials and procedures can help allay these potential difficulties. One very important issue concerns the 'fit' between the research aim and the method of data collection. It is advisable to design the subject's task to reflect as closely as possible what you want to know. So, for example, in the routefinding diary study, in addition to the written description of the error and its cause which were obviously the main focus of interest, subjects were also asked to supply a limited amount of other standardised information, which it was felt might have some bearing on the errors reported. In the event, not all the data collected was used, and with hindsight less information might perhaps have been asked for. A small-scale pilot study can often be useful, in order to evaluate the amount of information you are likely to generate, and adjustments can then be made to the final version of the data collection instrument. This can help to avoid being swamped by so much data that analysis becomes unnecessarily time consuming and arduous.

Content analysis

Content analysis was used in both examples of research reported here. In the diary study, subjects' reports on their errors and causes were analysed, whereas in the decision-making study, subjects' think-aloud protocols as they made their choices were analysed. One advantage of using whole descriptions as the coding unit relates to the data quantity issue discussed above; it makes it easier to cope with large volumes of written or spoken information.

Content analysis, in common with many qualitative methods is necessarily a subjective process, and so in order to guard against possible researcher bias is best undertaken by at least two people, who initially work independently of each other. In many cases, it is also useful for one of these people to be unaware of the nature or direction of any hypotheses being tested, as there can be a tendency, however unintentional, of seeing what you want to see in the data, and disregarding that which doesn't fit expectations (Robson 1993). The process of developing the category system will obviously be influenced by the nature of the data, the subtlety of the coding system required, and by the requirements of any hypotheses being investigated. However, even taking these factors into account the general aim should probably be to achieve a list of categories which are exhaustive (i.e. account for all the data), mutually exclusive (i.e. membership of one category precludes membership of any others), and manageable in size. (However, see Scherl and Smithson (1987) for a discussion of less rigid coding methods.) Essentially a balance is required between accounting for the data in a concise and consistent manner, and also including the subtleties within the rich data source being used.

The studies reported here represent two different applications of content analysis. In the routefinding study, the aim of the data analysis was to provide a *description* of the nature and incidence of a naturally occurring phenomenon, and so, congruent with a grounded theory approach (Henwood and Pidgeon 1992), there were no prior expectations as to the pattern of the data, and no specific hypotheses being tested. In contrast the content analysis reported in the decision-making study was driven by specific theoretical expectations and predictions. In this study, therefore, categories were already defined before content analysis began, whereas in the former study the derivation of categories was completely driven by the patterns which existed naturally within the data. In both cases, the technique proved to be a valuable tool in handling potentially difficult data.

ISSUES OF VALIDITY

Descriptive validity

Both of our illustrations used self-report data, which is naturally subjective, relying as it does on the subject to interpret and report events and experiences as accurately and truthfully as possible. Clearly, evidence such as this must be interpreted with the realisation that it may contain certain inaccuracies or biases (Morris 1984). Part of the error attribution data in the diary study provides an example of this problem. It was found that environmental causes as a whole were the most frequently cited reasons for error. This finding needs to be interpreted with care: subjects may have a tendency to blame their error on an external cause such as the lack of signposts, rather than a cognitive cause such as lack of attention. As observed earlier, some, perhaps most, cognitive researchers avoid such problems by deciding that only behavioural evidence is admissible. This chapter has set out an alternative research strategy, one which capitalises on the richness and informativeness of self-reports while at the same time guarding against errors of omission and commission. Safeguards of two main kinds are important. First, as the two illustrations have shown, rigorous methodological procedures can reduce the likelihood of descriptive inaccuracies. Second, comparisons between self-reports and alternative, behavioural evidence are necessary. In the decision process study, concordance was found between the mental account inferred from self-reports and the final choices of the subjects who produced them. Also, an independent, choice-only study was carried out to investigate the patterns of choice predicted by mental account representations (Ranyard and Abdel-Nabi 1993). In the routefinding research, a follow-up study is under way to investigate, using standardised psychometric instruments, the cognitive abilities of those who report frequent routefinding errors. These examples of cross-validation with behavioural evidence (also known as 'triangulation') all serve to check the descriptive validity of inferences from self-reports.

Predictive and ecological validity

The inevitable drawback of explanatory studies is the lowering of ecological validity which arises from controlling conditions. In the case of the Jacket and Calculator study, the task can be criticised as being a somewhat contrived consumer choice problem, not to mention a purely hypothetical one. The defence against this criticism is that researchers have to pay the price of lower ecological validity if they want to test a theory's predictive validity; however, the task presented to subjects has *sufficient* ecological validity to justify generalisations to real world contexts (in this case, actual consumer choices). If this argument is to be convincing, researchers should always try to make their controlled conditions as realistic as possible. In spite of the reservations which may exist over the use of qualitative self-report methods the studies presented in this chapter convincingly demonstrate the worth of these particular techniques.

FURTHER READING

Robson (1993) has recently produced a very useful guide to real world research methods which includes helpful discussions of content analysis and other approaches to qualitative analysis. Other useful sources on the issues discussed in this chapter are the classic methodological texts by Ericsson and Simon (1984) and Holsti (1969). The volume edited by Harris and Morris (1984) contains several papers using an ecological approach to memory and cognition which also provide useful advice on practical and theoretical matters. Finally, readers interested in learning more about decision process research will find the recent texts by Montgomery and Svenson (1989) and Payne, Bettman and Johnson (1993) most informative.

REFERENCES

Byrne, R. (1979) 'Memory for urban geography', *Quarterly Journal of Experimental Psychology*, 31: 147–154.

Byrne, R. (1982) 'Geographical knowledge and orientation', in A. Ellis (ed.) *Normality and Pathology in Cognitive Function*, London: Academic Press.

Chase, W. and Chi, M. (1981) 'Cognitive skill: implications for spatial skill in large scale environments', in J. Harvey (ed.) *Cognition, Social Behaviour and the Environment*, New Jersey: Lawrence Erlbaum Associates.

Ericsson, K. and Simon, H. (1980) 'Verbal reports as data', *Psychological Review*, 87: 215–251.

Ericsson, K. and Simon, H. (1984) *Protocol Analysis*, Cambridge, Mass.: MIT Press.

Harris, J. and Morris, P. (1984) *Everyday Memory, Actions and Absentmindedness*, London: Academic Press.

Henwood, K. and Pidgeon, N. (1992) 'Qualitative research and psychological theorizing', *British Journal of Psychology*, 83: 97–111.

Holsti, O. (1969) *Content Analysis for the Social Sciences and Humanities*, Reading, MA: Addison-Wesley.

Kahneman, D. and Tversky, A. (1984) 'Choices, values and frames', *American Psychologist*, 39: 341–350.

Kruysse, H. (1992) 'How slips result in traffic conflicts and accidents', *Applied Cognitive Psychology*, 6: 607–618.

Matthews, M. (1992) *Making Sense of Place: Children's understanding of large scale environments*, Hemel Hempstead: Harvester Wheatsheaf.

Montgomery, H. and Svenson, O. (1989) *Process and Structure in Human Decision Making*, Chichester: Wiley.

Morris, P. (1984) 'The validity of subjective reports on memory', in J. Harris and P. Morris (eds) *Everyday Memory, Actions and Absentmindedness*, London: Academic Press.

Nisbett, R. and Wilson, T. (1977) 'Telling more than we can know: verbal reports on mental processes', *Psychological Review*, 84: 231–259.

Payne, J.W., Bettman, J.R. and Johnson, E.J. (1993) *The Adaptive Decision Maker*, Cambridge: Cambridge University Press.

Ranyard, R. and Abdel-Nabi, D. (1993) 'Mental accounting and the process of multiattribute choice', *Acta Psychologica*, 84: 161–177.

Reason, J. (1979) 'Actions not as planned: the price of automatization', in G. Underwood and R. Stevens (eds), *Aspects of Consciousness, Psychological Issues*, Vol. 1, London: Academic Press.

Reason, J. and Lucas, D. (1984) 'Using cognitive diaries to investigate naturally occurring memory blocks', in J. Harris and P. Morris (eds), *Everyday Memory, Actions and Absentmindedness*, London: Academic Press.

Robson, C. (1993) *Real World Research*, Oxford: Blackwell.

Sadalla, E. and Staplin, L. (1980) 'The perception of traversed distance: intersections', *Environment and Behaviour*, 11: 33–70.

Scherl, L. and Smithson, M. (1987) 'A new dimension to content analysis: exploring relationships among thematic categories', *Quality and Quantity*, 21: 199–208.

Siegel, S. and Castellan, N. (1988) *Nonparametric Statistics for the Social Sciences*, 2nd edn, McGraw-Hill International Edition.

Siegel, A. and White, S. (1975) 'Development of spatial representations of large scale environments', in H.W. Reese (ed.) *Advances in Child Development and Behaviour*, Vol. 10, New York: Academic Press.

Svenson, O. (1989) 'Eliciting and analysing verbal protocols in process studies of judgement and decision making', in H. Montgomery and O. Svenson (eds) *Process and Structure in Human Decision Making*, Chichester: Wiley.

Terry, W. (1988) 'Everyday forgetting: data from a diary study', *Psychological Reports*, 62: 299–303.

Thorndyke, P. and Hayes-Roth, B. (1982) 'Differences in spatial knowledge acquired from maps and navigation', *Cognitive Psychology*, 14: 560–589.

Tversky, A. and Kahneman, D. (1981) 'The framing of decisions and the psychology of choice', *Science*, 211: 453–458.

Young, A., Hay, D. and Ellis, A. (1985) 'The faces that launched a thousand slips: everyday difficulties and errors in recognising people', *British Journal of Psychology*, 76: 495–523.

Williamson, J. and Barrow, C.J. (1994) 'Errors in everyday routefinding: a classification of types and possible causes', *Applied Cognitive Psychology*, 8: 513–524.

Chapter 15

Remembering in a social context

Experimental methods for the evaluation of collaborative recall

Peter R. Meudell

Two things seem necessary for good research. First a lasting problem that is of genuine interest (at least to the individual and hopefully to the rest of the scientific community) and second a method that is sensitive enough to open up facets of the problem to public gaze.

SPECIFICATION OF A PROBLEM

The research to be reported in this chapter started more or less from intuition. No work is entirely without precedent, however, and in part the genesis of the ideas that follow stemmed from work by Geoffrey Stephenson in the 1980s (e.g. Stephenson and Wagner 1989), although its roots are also to be found much earlier in Bartlett's famous work on memory (Bartlett 1932).

We have concentrated on the *social* aspects of memory that involve two people talking over a mutually experienced event. What I have in mind are the following types of social interactions involving memory:

1 after seeing a film you might discuss aspects of the plot with a friend who also saw it: you might have failed to follow certain parts and thus be seeking clarification or you may just enjoy 'reliving' the experiences with another person;
2 after attending a conference you might talk over a paper that was presented with a colleague – 'did Dr X mean this when he said that or did he mean something else?';
3 in a family, you might revive memories of many aspects of your own, your partner's or children's lives and shared experiences; this kind of 'memory chat' is often triggered by looking over old photographs.

What kinds of questions might be asked about these situations involving collaborative recall? Here are some that immediately spring to mind:

1 Are two people better than one at remembering a shared experience?
2 Do two people generate new memories not available to either member of the pair on their own?

3 Does a person's confidence in what they recall change as a result of discussing it with another individual?

4 Does the relationship between the people matter as to how well they remember – do partners do better than strangers, for example?

5 In a more or less stable partnership, is one member given the role of mnemonic leader whose view about past events is, ultimately, adopted by the pair?

6 Is there a gender difference in the type or extent of contributions that people make to shared recall?

7 What are the processes by which people shape an agreed account of a past event from their separate memories?

8 Does the agreed account have characteristic distortions and biases?

9 Do pairs of people introduce more false positive errors in their joint recall than do individuals?

10 Just how frequently do people engage in, and what are the triggering factors of, conversations involving memory?

We (Meudell, Hitch and Kirby 1992) decided that we would begin our work in this area by examining the first two questions in the above list – namely, do two people outperform one solitary individual when remembering a common experience and do two people in some way cross cue each other so as to produce new or 'emergent' memories not accessible to either member of the pair?

METHODOLOGICAL FACTORS

There are a number of ways in which these types of question could be answered. One attack is to look at what people say to each other when talking over their memories and to try and make sense of 'what is going on' in the interaction. This discursive approach has no concern for whether the information collaborating people generate is accurate or not: the methodology is interested in the *processes* of the social interaction and the concern is about the ways in which what are seen to be *arbitrary* realities are constructed (see Edwards, Potter and Middleton 1992). As Edwards *et al.* put it, discourse analysis – as the approach is termed – focuses on 'how everyday *versions* of events (including persons, things, states of affairs) are *constructed* and *occasioned* in talk and text' (emphasis in original).

Obviously, given the focus of this chapter, it goes without saying that how people talk to others about their memories is felt to be a topic worthy of systematic investigation. However, whether discourse analysis is the appropriate vehicle to understand and answer the various questions listed above is open to debate. As Baddeley (1992) has queried of the discourse analytic method: 'Does everyone who analyses the same material come up with the same answer? If not how do they decide which is the better answer?' This inherent potential for idiosyncratic interpretation combined with lack of control and absence of replicability means the method is not one that is likely to provide lasting insights into the social context in which memories take place. Further, even if these methodological problems could be overcome, it is not obvious that the conclusions that might be reached could have much generality; that is, it is far from clear how an analysis of the discussion of two particular individuals about a particular experience can yield much that would apply to other people in other situations talking over other memories. Nevertheless, whilst the method may be weak, the issues raised by discourse theorists and the human circumstances involving memory that they investigate are potentially intriguing. Thus the concern for how memories are *used* rather than how they are encoded, represented and retrieved is interesting – it is, however, open to a more systematic attack than discourse theory appears to provide.

In contrast to the above, our approach has been entirely experimental and we wish to argue that only through the systematic application of experimental and analytic techniques involving tight control over as many relevant factors as possible will understanding advance in this area.

A straightforward experimental design

A simple experimental design that might appear to directly attack the two selected questions is straightforward to propose. People are exposed to material that they are requested to learn and then, at a later stage, the collaborative recall performance of pairs of people is compared with that of individuals. Whilst this procedure will certainly answer whether two people can recall more than one, it cannot answer the question of whether collaborating pairs generate new information that neither member of the pair on their own could remember. This is so for the following reason.

Assume that the representations in memory of an event can be thought of as a list of features, dimensions or aspects and that we label these aspects a,b,c and so on. On a test of memory, an individual might thus recall x,y,z aspects about the event. When two people collaborate, one might remember r,s,x and the other t,x,y. When they come together we thus predict, all other things being equal, that this pair would remember r,s,t,x,y,z. The pair would thus outperform the individuals merely by virtue of the fact that what they individually remember is somewhat different and, accordingly, their pooled recall is higher than most individuals.

Compare the above with the following situation. Two people collaborate over their memory for a shared experience and one recalls r,s,x and the other remembers t,x. However, as a result of discussion and reflection (and thus mutual cross cuing) they might also correctly recall aspects a and b of the original event. That is, the total recall of this pair is r,s,t,x,a,b – six features in all but, in this case, two emergent memories have appeared as a result of the social interaction. Total recall is higher than for an individual partly because of the fact that people recall different aspects of events, but also because the social interaction is facilitatory and makes accessible otherwise inaccessible memories.

In these hypothetical examples, we of course know what people have recalled. In terms of an actual experiment, however, all we would know is that an individual alone recalled x,y,z and a pair recalled r,s,t,x,a,b. We could therefore certainly say that pairs recalled more than individuals but, since we could not know which memories were separately contributed and which emerged through the processes of cross cuing, we would not know whether pairs actually produced any new information or not. What is needed therefore is an experiment which enables us to know, not only what a pair finally recalls, but also what the individual people within the pair actually contributed. If we knew that we would then be in a position to discover whether any novel memories, inaccessible to either member of the pair, had emerged.

An inferential solution?

Pursuing the simple design of directly comparing pairs' recall with that of individuals, the perceptive reader might have divined that there is a potential solution to the problem of ascertaining precisely which recalled items (if any) in collaborative remembering are new to both members of the pair. This solution involves a prediction of what *should* be recalled by pairs on the basis of what individuals *can* remember. That is, call the probability of recall of any item by an individual A $P(i|A)$ and the probability of recall of the same item by a collaborating pair AB $P(i|AB)$. Then, by simple probability theory:

$$P(i|AB) = P(i|A) + P(i|B) - P(i|A \text{ and } B)$$

where $P(i|A \text{ and } B)$ is the probability that both A and B could recall the same item. Thus $P(i|AB)$ is predicted, all other things being equal, to reflect the separate and independent contributions when two people collaborate. In concrete terms, if A recalls a,b,c and B recalls a,b,x,y,z then the pair should be predicted to remember a,b,c,x,y,z. – i.e.

Total for A and B = A's recall + B's recall – shared recall

Now, the *observed* $P(i|AB)$ derived via experiment from collaborating pairs can be compared directly with that predicted on the basis of individual recall data. If the observed value of $P(i|AB)$ is greater than that predicted on the basis of individual recalls then this must result from the pair generating new memories that could not be predicted from individual recalls.

Whilst the logic of this is impeccable, unfortunately it might not work in practice. This is so since pairs might not completely pool their memories in the way the statistics might suggest. That is, whilst person A might theoretically be able to recall a,b,c if tested in isolation and, similarly, person B might recall a,b,x,y,z on their own, when they come together they may (perhaps through social 'inhibition' or 'process loss' – see Steiner 1972) only recall a,b,x,y. They 'lose' items c,z. If, in addition, they do indeed generate new information r,s then their total recall would be a,b,x,y,r,s – exactly as predicted by the statistical independence model but where new information has been generated and has more or less been compensated for by 'process loss'.

This approach is thus unduly conservative. If the observed value of P(i|AB) is greater than the predicted value then this clearly demonstrates the facilitatory effects of recalling in pairs. However, if the observed value of P(i|AB) is equal to or less than the predicted value of P(i|AB) it does not follow that new information was not generated by the pair. In fact, many have shown (e.g. Stephenson, Brandstatter and Wagner 1983) that, whilst pairs do recall more than individuals, the observed values of P(i|AB) are less than those predicted on the basis of individual performance – in other words pairs do perform better than individuals but they do so in a sub-optimal way.

A more sensitive design

It is apparent from the foregoing that to find out whether new memories emerge in pairs we need a knowledge of what an individual recalling in a pair could have recalled on their own. This has led us to use a sequential design where everybody recalls initially on their own (so we then know what particular memories are available and accessible to them). We then test the people in pairs and, since we know what each could recall as an individual, we can readily identify whether any new memories are produced by the pair.

This sequential design will not suffice in isolation, however, since forming pairs for recall on the second occasion is completely confounded by the fact that we are asking people to remember twice. Perhaps an individual re-membering on a second occasion might recall new information that was not recalled on the first test (see Roediger and Payne 1982; Wheeler and Roediger 1992). In our sequential design, therefore, new information might emerge in pairs not because of the facilitatory effects of social interaction but because both members are recalling for a *second* time. The obvious control is thus to ask some people to recall initially as individuals and, later, recall the same information once more on their own. We have called the people who remember twice on their own 'reminiscence controls', and only if the amount of new information is greater in pairs than in reminiscence controls could the facilitatory effects of social interaction on memory be claimed. Figure 15.1 shows in a schematic way the design that we have used.

Even this design is not sufficient to ensure that all the methodological factors are covered. Another problem is that, in the design, everyone has to recall twice. It is therefore possible that the initial recall in some way stifles, on second recall, the generation of new memories in pairs. One mechanism that might be at work is that, on the second test, people tend to recall their

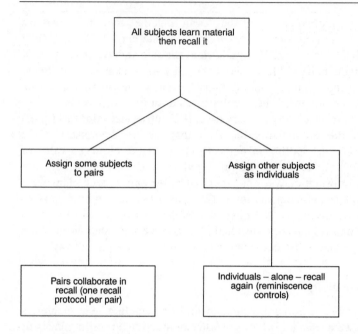

Figure 15.1 Schematic representation of the fundamental sequential design used in the experiments of Meudell *et al.* (1992)

first recalls and do not try to 'relive' the original experience. If this were true new memories might not emerge in pairs as a result of the nature of the paradigm adopted.

This is a perfectly reasonable speculation but, once again, there is a clear experimental way around the problem. The solution is to form a third group of people (group one being people who recall twice on their own and group two being people who form pairs for second recall after recalling on their own initially). This new group would recall only once, in pairs and at the same time as the other groups are making their second recalls. In this third group, of course, we cannot know what new items have been generated. However, if recalling initially does somehow affect second recall and specifically inhibits the generation of new memories, then group three (who only recall once) should outperform group two in terms of total recall performance.

Measures of memory

What kinds of aspect of memory performance can be measured in this experimental situation? Although I have flagged that two measures are of particular interest – namely the total amount recalled and the presence of new

PERSON A ALONE will recall:

- correct items UNIQUE to A
- correct items that B also recalls
- intrusion errors that are unique to A
- intrusion errors that are identical to B's

PERSON B ALONE will recall:

- correct items UNIQUE to B
- correct items that A also recalls
- intrusion errors that are unique to B
- intrusion errors that are identical to A's

JOINTLY A and B might then recall:

- some of A's uniquely correct items
- some of B's uniquely correct items
- some of the correct items recalled by A and B
- new items that neither A nor B initially recalled

- some of A's unique intrusion errors
- some of B's unique intrusion errors
- some intrusion errors that A and B both made
- new intrusion errors made by the pair

It follows that JOINTLY A and B might fail to produce in their recall:

- some of A's correct items
- some of B's correct items
- some correct items produced by both A and B

- some of A's intrusion errors
- some of B's intrusion errors
- some intrusion errors produced by both A and B

Figure 15.2 The categories of recalls that people might produce when recalling initially on their own and then as a pair

information in pairs not available to either individual alone – there are, because of the sequential nature of the design, a large number of other measures that can be derived. These are illustrated in Figure 15.2.

It is apparent that the complete outcome of what is in truth a relatively simple design is, in fact, rather rich in information. We have not yet had the opportunity to investigate all these aspects of collaborative memory perform-ance but it should be clear that the total correct recalls by pairs and the number of new items that might be produced are but the tip of an iceberg of potential measures. Incorrect responses as well as correct ones are a feature of collaborative as well as individual recall.

A brief comment on the psychological processes involved in this col-laborative situation might be in order at this point. Although our research has not yet reached the point where we can report on the mechanisms by which items come to be accepted or disregarded by pairs, one likely candidate is the confidence with which a person believes that an item that he or she can recall is a genuine memory. The basis for any one person's confidence in a particular memory will be based upon two factors – one cognitive and the other related to personality. First, for any individual, a particular memory may be more or less well represented in memory and so the attachment of high or low confidence is appropriate. Second, as a result of individual differences some people may be inherently more confident than others in their memories even though (if it could be measured) they might have identical amounts of mnemonic information at their disposal.

As far as *individuals* recalling twice are concerned, the situation with respect to the range of measures of memory that can be derived is much simpler, as Figure 15.3 shows.

PERSON C on first test might recall

- correct items
- intrusion errors

PERSON C on second test might recall

- some of the items that were correct on first test
- new correct items

- some of the same intrusion errors from first test
- new intrusions

It also follows that on second test PERSON C might fail to recall:

- some items that were correct on first test
- some first trial intrusions

Figure 15.3 The categories of responses that an individual recalling material on two separate occasions could produce

Of course, when evaluating pairs' performances on second recall, any comparisons must be made in relation to how individuals perform on their second recall. Thus, for example, whether pairs tend to produce many new intrusion errors depends upon a comparison with the number produced by individuals on second test.

RELEVANT EXPERIMENTAL WORK

It would be sterile in the extreme merely to sketch methodological factors and a consideration of some of the outcomes of the experiments that have already been run will help to put flesh on the bones of the design. Accordingly, I shall briefly review some of our completed studies in this section.

However, as will become apparent, new methodological issues inevitably crop up as the research proceeds.

Experiments varying learning material

The first experiment we ran (Meudell *et al.* 1992) involved people remembering unrelated lists of words. In this study we found that pairs of people outperformed individuals (as we did in all the subsequent studies) but, somewhat to our surprise, the amount of new information that emerged on second test was *identical* for individuals and pairs. Thus, contrary to our intuitions, social interaction did not facilitate the emergence of new memories.

Our first thought about this result was that the negative outcome must have occurred because of some unconsidered factor in our design. We decided that, given that we believed the basic framework was fundamentally satisfactory and sensitive to the emergence of new memories, the problem must lie with the material we were asking people to remember. After all, what can people talk about in this collaborative situation? Person A might recall the word 'dog' and Person B might remember 'chair' and perhaps that is all they can contribute. New memories do not emerge because people cannot provide enough in the way of 'chat' to cross cue each other to facilitate the retrieval of otherwise inaccessible memories.

As a result, our next experiment used rich stimulus material (a 10 minute clip from a Hollywood movie) as material to remember. Memory was assessed by means of a questionnaire (the items on the questionnaire were open ended but the answers were quite unambiguous so that performance could be scored readily). However, once again, no new memories emerged in pairs.

Reluctant to abandon the idea that pairs of people were somehow able to facilitate new memories, our next step was to argue that it was not so much rich information in the stimulus that mattered but rather the richness of the representation in memory that determined whether cross cuing took place and thus whether new memories appeared. To this end we asked people to look at photographs of faces. Some people saw famous faces (e.g. Margaret Thatcher) and others saw unknown faces. Each face had the name written underneath and the task was to recall the names of the faces. We argued that, if cross cuing took place, it should be more effective with famous faces than with unknown ones. That is, for a famous face, Person A might remember that 'wasn't one of them that female prime minister' and this might act as a very effective cue for person B (who otherwise might not have recalled the name). In contrast, what could be said that might be especially helpful about a face about which people knew next to nothing? Probably very little and so new memories might not emerge.

The results of this experiment were also quite clear. Although for both pairs and individuals, famous face names were better remembered than unfamous ones, pairs of people recalling famous names did *not* generate more new names on second test than did individual controls.

Since we have used unstructured material (unrelated words), structured material (a film clip), familiar material (famous faces) and unfamiliar material (unknown faces), we doubt whether the absence of new information in pairs is an effect of the type of information that we have asked people to remember. Either there is no phenomenon or we have still missed something critical in the execution of the studies.

Tulving and Pearlstone (1966) have carried out an experiment which seems singularly pertinent to this last anxiety. Tulving and Pearlstone presented experimental subjects with lists of words but the words were all exemplars of a number of semantic categories. Occasionally, some subjects failed to recall any exemplars from a category but then, if provided a category cue by the experimenter ('there were some fruits'), individuals would retrieve items from the unrecalled category. Tulving and Pearlstone interpreted their results in terms of the distinction between the availability of information in memory and its accessibility or retrievability. They argued that the extra items were available in memory but were inaccessible until the category label was provided to cue retrieval. However, since the experimenter gave the subjects cues, the situation can equally be seen as one involving social processes in memory – one person (the experimenter) provides a cue to another (an experimental subject) who then elicits additional new information not available to the individual on their own. A clearer demonstration of one form of cross cuing facilitating retrieval in social situations would be harder to devise. We therefore decided to directly investigate this phenomenon within our paradigm.

If people are initially required to remember categorised word lists on their own and then come together to recall as collaborating pairs then, hypothetically, cross cuing might arise through the following mechanism. Person 'A' might initially fail to recall any items from a particular category but Person 'B' might so do. When the pair collaborate, Person 'B' would recall some exemplars from the category that Person 'A' had not recalled thus – potentially – 'triggering' retrieval by 'A' of items not previously accessible to either 'A' or 'B'. In fact, we have shown (Meudell, Hitch and Boyle 1995) that this does not happen. Once more, no more new information is generated in pairs (where the opportunity for cross cuing is expressly manipulated) than by individuals.

Our explanation for this result is that, in the original Tulving and Pearlstone experiment, the experimenter provided an explicit category cue. In contrast, in the social setting investigated by Meudell, Hitch and Boyle (1995) it seems probable that individuals might simply have produced exemplars and their partners had to *infer* category membership. Thus, for example, whilst being explicitly *told* 'there were some names of fruits in the list' might help a subject's retrieval in the manner of Tulving and Pearlstone, hearing the word 'banana' merely spoken by a collaborating partner might not necessarily provoke the idea 'fruits' and might conceivably induce ideas relating to 'exotic places', 'curved objects', 'yellow things' and the like. In short, the lack of specificity of another person's recalled exemplars might militate against the possibility of cross cuing taking place.

Variations in types of processing during learning

Next we wondered if what mattered for the emergence of cross cuing was the mental perspective that people had when they viewed events. Perhaps those who had the same or different perspectives might somehow 'spark' each other off so as to generate new memories.

One experiment in the Meudell *et al.* (1992) series used words as materials to remember and we used two orienting tasks during learning. Some people estimated, for each word, how large the depicted object was in relation to a mouse; other people estimated the price of the depicted objects. On second recall we then combined people with the same or different perspectives. It made no difference whatsoever – the amount of new information generated by pairs on second test was unaffected by whether members of the pair had the same or different orienting tasks during learning and, furthermore, neither type of pair produced more new memories than individual controls.

Concerned that our material and, perhaps, our perspectives, were not very meaningful, we have subsequently run another experiment where people saw a video clip of a presenter showing the viewer around someone's house. We asked people to imagine they were interior designers or burglars whilst viewing (Meudell, Hitch and Dunkerly 1995). Pairs were again brought together with the same or with different viewing perspectives. However, even in this relatively realistic setting, no new information emerged in pairs compared to individual controls.

Variations in type of collective and individual response

One methodological criticism that can be made of all the work so far summarised is that it involves an all or none response – people can either recall an item or they cannot. Perhaps the great benefit of social collaboration in memory might come not from gaining new items in a quite discreet way but, with a *graded* response, somehow being able to get *closer* to the truth of what happened.

To investigate this notion we asked, adopting the usual fundamental design, people to give the date on which a well-known public event occurred (Meudell 1995). What we imagined was that as individuals, person A might say that an event (which actually took place in 1982) occurred in 1984 and that person B might say it happened in 1986. When they came together they might get closer to the real date – they might agree on 1983, for example. This could happen through the way in which memories are thought to be dated through 'landmarks' (Friedman 1993). That is, events are often dated by reference to other public and personal incidents whose times of occurrence are more or less known. In theory, the dovetailing of the separate knowledge bases of two people might facilitate dating in this way. However, this could not happen for individuals on second test since they would not have the benefit of access to another person's temporal knowledge base. The results showed, however, mutual discussion involving the sharing of information about dates and times did not appear to allow pairs to get closer to the true dates of events. In fact, people merely seemed to average their separate responses so that, in the example above, the pair would come out with a collective date of 1985 for the event. Since this is better for one person but worse for the other, this is hardly evidence for the facilitation of memory by social interaction. However, there was a (non-significant) trend for pairs to produce more accurate memories than individuals and furthermore, this graded test of memory (for time) relates to context memory and not content memory. More work is clearly needed and a graded test of content memory may be informative in this respect.

Variations in motivation and knowledge of one's partner

In all the studies so far reported, it could be argued that however meaningful the stimuli are to our subjects they might not be intrinsically interesting and that social facilitation of memory only occurs when people are thoroughly motivated to discuss their memories. Furthermore, our experimental procedures have arbitrarily 'thrown' together pairs of people who tend not to know each other especially well (typically students from the same academic year). Perhaps cross cuing can only realistically occur when people are well known to each other.

Putting these two factors together we (Meudell 1994) sampled our subject panel for husbands and wives who both had a strong, enduring and long interest in the soap opera *Coronation Street*. Following our usual paradigm, all recalled alone initially and then some recalled as a pair, whilst some recalled individually on both occasions. The test was in two parts on both recalls – the first test was a questionnaire about events in the *Street* and the second required people to identify photographs of characters from the history of the soap.

Even in this situation with high motivation and extensive knowledge of their collaborator, no more new information emerged in pairs on second recall (for either events or faces) compared to that shown by individual controls. It would appear that neither high motivation nor close relationship with one's partner is sufficient to ensure the emergence of otherwise inaccessible memories in pairs.

CONCLUSIONS

The major problem with the above work is that all the experiments have proved negative. Since it is impossible to prove the negative case, this is clearly cause for concern. Specifically, in relation to methodology, the obvious suspicion might be that the paradigm employed is not sensitive enough to detect the phenomena and/or there is a fundamental flaw in the set-up. It seems unlikely that there is a problem with the repeated testing aspect of the design since we have run the control condition where pairs are tested only once (at the same time as the second test for experimental pairs) and there is no difference in total recall performance between these two groups. If the design lacks sensitivity then, necessarily, the phenomenon must be small and thus conceivably might not be of major practical significance.

In fact, recent work in our laboratories has found conditions under which pairs of people *do* generate new memories. These conditions are, of course, critical to our approach to the social context of memory and seem to relate to the circumstances prevailing when learning is taking place. From a methodological perspective, however, the point to be made is that our sequential design can, *in principle*, demonstrate that pairs of people can generate new information. It is thus our present intuition that it is the psychological circumstances surrounding learning that help to determine the subsequent emergence of new memories in pairs and that explanations linked to artefacts involving methodological factors are unlikely to be correct.

REFERENCES

Baddeley, A. (1992) 'Is memory all talk?', *The Psychologist*, 10: 447–448.

Bartlett, F. C. (1932) *Remembering*, Cambridge: Cambridge University Press.

Edwards, D., Potter, J. and Middleton, D. (1992) 'Toward a discursive psychology of remembering', *The Psychologist*, 10: 441–446.

Friedman, W. J. (1993) 'Memory for the time of past events', *Psychological Bulletin*, 113: 44–66.

Meudell, P. R. (1994) 'Memories of *Coronation Street*: do people cross cue each other so as to produce new memories?', paper presented to the *British Psychological Society*, Brighton.

Meudell, P. R. (1995) 'Do people cross cue each other so as to generate new information and produce more accurate memories?', in H. C. Foot (ed.) *Proceedings of the International Conference on Group and Interactive Learning*, Ashurst: Computational Mechanics Publications.

Meudell, P. R., Hitch, G. J. and Kirby, P. (1992) 'Are two heads better than one? Experimental investigations of the social facilitation of memory', *Applied Cognitive Psychology*, 6: 525–543.

Meudell, P. R., Hitch, G. J. and Boyle, M. M. (1995) 'Collaboration in recall: do pairs of people cross cue each other to produce new memories?', *Quarterly Journal of Experimental Psychology*, 45A: 141–152.

Meudell, P. R., Hitch, G. J. and Dunkerly, J. (1995) 'Sharing memories with the same or different perspectives', in preparation.

Neisser, U. (1978) 'Memory: what are the important questions?', in M.M. Gruneberg, P.E. Morris and R.N. Sykes (eds) *Practical Aspects of Memory*, London: Academic Press.

Roediger, H.L.I.I.I. and Payne, D. G. (1982) 'Hypermnesia: the role of repeated testing', *Journal of Experimental Psychology: Learning, Memory and Cognition*, 8: 66–72.

Steiner, I. D. (1972) *Group Processes and Productivity*, San Diego, California: Academic Press.

Stephenson, G. M. and Wagner, W. (1989) 'Origins of the misplaced confidence effect in collaborative recall', *Applied Cognitive Psychology*, 3: 227–236.

Stephenson, G. M., Brandstatter, H. and Wagner, W. (1983) 'An experimental study of social performance and delay on the testimonial validity of story recall', *European Journal of Social Psychology*, 13: 175–191.

Tulving, E., and Pearlstone, Z. (1966) 'Availability versus accessibility of information in memory for words', *Journal of Verbal Learning and Verbal Behavior*, 5: 381–391.

Wheeler, M. A. and Roediger, H.L.I.I.I. (1992) 'Disparate effects of repeated testing: reconciling Ballard's (1913) and Bartlett's (1932) results', *Psychological Science*, 3: 240–245.

Chapter 16

The case study method in cognitive neuropsychology

J.R. Hanley

INTRODUCTION

Over the past twenty years, the number of cognitive psychologists, particularly on this side of the Atlantic, who spend at least part of their time conducting case studies of patients who have suffered brain injury has increased quite dramatically. Underlying this upsurge of interest in the effects of brain injury on cognitive performance has been the appreciation that considerable progress can be made in understanding the way in which the cognitive system is organised if one examines the precise nature of the different impairments from which carefully selected patients suffer.

Cognitive neuropsychology, just like connectionist modelling, is an *approach* to cognitive psychology rather than an *area* of cognitive psychology. It is therefore not a part of the discipline that any cognitive psychologist can afford to ignore. Someone whose main research interests are concerned with, for instance, the way in which humans parse syntactically ambiguous sentences might, quite reasonably, decide to pay relatively little attention to recent developments in work on, say, face recognition. They would be ill advised, however, to ignore recent cognitive neuropsychological studies of patients whose ability to understand language has been impaired by brain injury. Many of the best known theories in contemporary cognitive psychology are as strongly supported by findings from individual case studies of clinical patients as they are by experiments that examine the performance of normal subjects under laboratory conditions. Such theories include the dual route model of reading (Coltheart, Curtis, Atkins and Haller 1993), the working memory model (Baddeley 1992) and sequential stage models of face processing (Young and Bruce 1991). Indeed, it is hard to think of any area of the subject in which cognitive neuropsychology has yet to make an impact.

Nevertheless, cognitive neuropsychology does embody a set of beliefs, and depends upon a set of theoretical assumptions that are easily misunderstood, and which may not even be familiar to many recent psychology graduates. Moreover some of these assumptions differ from those of traditional neuropsychology even though, I will argue, they are not necessarily incompatible with those of either mainstream cognitive psychology or those of connectionist modelling. The purpose of this chapter, therefore, is to present an introduction to the history, philosophy, methodology and research techniques that lie behind recent work in cognitive neuropsychology.

AIMS OF COGNITIVE NEUROPSYCHOLOGY

It is generally accepted (e.g. Ellis and Young 1988) that work in cognitive neuropsychology has two related goals. The first of these is relevant to the fact that, in recent years, cognitive psychologists have attempted to extend the domain of their theorising to phenomena which exist outside as well as within their experimental laboratories. The question, therefore, is whether cognitive psychology can provide an adequate account of the way in which cognitive performance can break down as a result of brain injury.

If the brain were a mechanism in which all aspects of cognitive activity were performed equally by all of its components, then injury might be expected to make the brain *generally* less efficient at cognitive processing. Although such a scenario is conceivable in principle, it does not seem to fit the available evidence. On the contrary, the effects of brain injury can often be very selective; patients can show very striking *dissociations* between cognitive tasks on which they perform as well as normal subjects and tasks at which they are severely impaired.

There have been some striking examples of this in the literature for an extremely long time. For instance, Dejerine reported a patient in 1893 who was no longer able to read words following a stroke. Despite this, he remained able to produce and understand spoken language at a satisfactory level. In addition, his ability to write and spell was preserved. In most cases of acquired dyslexia, the reading impairment is not absolute, with some aspects of reading skill being preserved. In phonological dyslexia (e.g. Patterson 1982) for instance, there is a dissociation between the ability to read familiar words (e.g. blast), which is preserved, and the ability to read nonwords (e.g. blasp), which is severely impaired.

The issue for cognitive psychologists is whether the distinction between the areas of impairment and the areas of preserved function make sense in terms of any existing theory. In the case of phonological dyslexia, for instance, a dissociation between the ability to read words and nonwords is exactly what would be predicted on the basis of the dual route model of reading (Coltheart *et al.* 1993). In this respect, it is interesting to note that cases of phonological dyslexia have only been reported in the literature since the dual route model became popular. The influence and importance of any theory that is able to accommodate data from brain injured patients as well as data from normal subjects is likely to increase substantially as a consequence.

Slightly more controversially, cognitive neuropsychologists also believe that any theory that is incompatible with data from cognitive neuropsychology is seriously weakened. It is not acceptable to maintain that a particular theory is relevant only to one restricted domain of empirical observation such as data from traditional laboratory experiments. For instance, if it wishes to avoid rejection, any theory of face identification which states that names of familiar people are stored alongside other facts that we know about people, such as their occupation, must come up with an explanation of why anomic patients can frequently recall people's occupations but not their names (e.g. Flude, Ellis and Kay 1989). Similarly, Coltheart *et al.* (1993) argue that the inability of the reading model put forward by Seidenberg and McClelland (1989) to simulate phonological dyslexia represents a major weakness with the model despite the elegant way in which it can handle data from tasks such as speeded naming of words by normal subjects.

Theories thus develop or wither in the face of data from brain injured patients. In addition, new theories have sprung up in areas such as the psychology of spelling and writing which traditional psychological data had previously been quite unable to penetrate (Ellis 1988). It is the potential power of cognitive neuropsychology to influence so dramatically current theorising that undoubtedly accounts for its current popularity.

DISSOCIATIONS AND MODULARITY

What evidence from dissociations seems to indicate is that the brain has a *modular* structure, with different cognitive functions being carried out by separate *specialist* processors. Thus, Dejerine's case suggested that to some extent the areas that are responsible for the perception of spoken language are separate from those involved in written word perception. More interestingly, it suggested that the mechanisms that are responsible for spelling are in some respects distinct from those involved in reading.

Of course there is nothing unique about cognitive neuropsychology in the way that it uses evidence from dissociations to argue for the existence of functionally distinct subsystems. For example, Tulving, Schacter and Stark (1982) demonstrated that performance on a test of implicit memory (word fragment completion) by normal subjects can be relatively unaffected by the length of the retention interval, unlike performance on tests of explicit memory which declines rapidly over time. Tulving and his colleagues have argued that evidence such as this is best explained in terms of there being separate memory systems responsible for performance on tests of implicit and explicit memory. In fact, such data fits very neatly with neuropsychological research on amnesic patients who perform poorly on tests of explicit memory but within the normal range on tests of word fragment completion (Warrington and Weiskrantz 1970).

The *extent* to which the cognitive system is modular is, of course, a matter of debate amongst cognitive neuropsychologists. For example, in the area of face recognition, the issue of whether there is a module specific to faces that is distinct from modules involved in other forms of visual recognition is particularly interesting at present. It is now well established that patients can lose the ability to recognise once familiar faces following brain injury without losing the ability to recognise people from their name or voice. However, some argue that the problem in 'prosopagnosia' reflects a lower level configural processing deficit (Farah 1991; Levine and Calvanio 1989), and will therefore impair not just face processing, but all types of visual recognition that require configural processing. In opposition to this, many would claim that the ability of some prosopagnosic patients to perform well on indirect tests of face recognition (see Young, Hellawell and de Haan 1988) makes such an account unlikely. Damasio and his colleagues (Damasio, Tranel and Damasio 1990) have claimed that 'patients with face agnosia are also impaired in the recognition of other unique stimuli – houses, cars, pets, articles of clothing . . . patients with face agnosia fail to recognise an exemplar as a unique individual'. However, McNeil and Warrington's (1993) recent striking example of a prosopagnosic farmer who was able to recognise the faces of familiar sheep but not humans suggests, on the contrary, that the recognition problem can be very selective indeed.

Papers that report dissociations between impaired performance on one task and preserved performance on another task by a particular patient are extremely common amongst cognitive neuropsychological case studies. Nevertheless, single dissociations do suffer from an important potential problem. If a patient performs well on one task but badly on another, it is quite conceivable under certain circumstances that the same impaired module is responsible for performance on both tasks. It may well be the case that one task is simply more difficult than the other. The impaired module may be able to cope with the easier task but be unable to meet the demands of the more difficult task. Such an interpretation can be effectively ruled out by means of a double dissociation.

A classic example of a double dissociation in cognitive neuropsychology is between performance on short-term memory tasks such as immediate serial recall, and performance on tests of long-term memory. When an amnesic patient is asked to recall a list of items a few minutes after it has been presented, performance is likely to be at floor level, suggesting a long-term memory impairment (e.g. Milner 1966). By contrast, their memory span (the number of items that they are able to repeat back in order immediately following presentation) may be unimpaired, suggesting that short-term memory is normal. Evidence that this dissociation does not simply occur because serial recall is an easier task comes from patients with short-term memory impairments who are not amnesic (e.g. Warrington and Shallice 1969). Such a patient might perform well on tests of long-term memory such as recalling a word list after half an hour despite having a memory span of only one or two items. This is consistent with the view that performance on tests of short-term memory are to some extent subserved by modules that are separate from those required for tests of long-term memory. Although it must be acknowledged that double dissociations do not absolutely *prove* the existence of separate modules (for details, see Dunn and Kirsner 1988), it is accepted that double dissociations nevertheless provide strong grounds for believing that separate modules may exist.

Exactly what it means for a component of the cognitive system to be a module is also a source of controversy. In his important book, entitled the *Modularity of Mind*, Fodor (1983) outlined a set of features which, he believes, apply to modular systems. The two of these that would be probably be most widely accepted by cognitive neuropsychologists are the claims that modules are domain specific and that they are cognitively impenetrable. Domain specificity means that a module will only respond to one type of input. As we have seen, the module that recognises objects will not, it appears, successfully identify a face. Cognitive impenetrability means that the operation of a module cannot be influenced by higher level cognitive processing. For example, only to a limited extent is our ability to recognise a word, Fodor argues, influenced by the context in which that word appears. On the other hand, Fodor's claim that the modular structure of the brain is innately determined is much less plausible. As Ellis and Young (1988) point out, it is difficult to see how the modules responsible for reading and writing could be innately predetermined given the relatively recent development of literacy in the history of the human race.

When considering the modular structure of the cognitive system, it is also important to consider a distinction made by Sherry and Schacter (1987) between *stores* which differ in terms of the type of information that they contain (e.g. faces, objects, words, etc.) and *systems* which differ in terms of their rules of operation (i.e. how they encode, retain or retrieve information). The principles by which these stores operate might be the same even though the different stores may represent information in 'neurologically distinct places'. Sherry and Schacter believe that multiple memory *systems*, by contrast, only exist when 'each module has its own acquisition, retention and retrieval processes and that the rules of operation of these processes differ across modules'. In these terms, cognitive neuropsychologists would probably accept that most of the modules that they are describing should be referred to as stores rather than systems. In the case of face recognition, for instance, despite the strong evidence that exists for modularity, there is little evidence that the faces module operates according to different principles from those which govern, say, object recognition (Bruce and Young 1986).

HISTORY AND PHILOSOPHY

Today's generation of cognitive neuropsychologists are certainly not the first group of researchers to have developed models with a modular structure on the basis of data from single case studies of brain injured patients. Over a hundred years ago, neurologists such as Lichtheim (1885) and Wernicke (1874) were creating elaborate flow diagrams which bear many striking similarities to those found in contemporary textbooks on cognitive neuropsychology.

Within approximately fifty years, however, as a result of the writings of people such as Head (1926), the influence of the 'diagram makers' had waned considerably. Head himself, for example, argued that 'superficially' different types of language impairment reflected general intellectual difficulties brought about by brain injury rather than impairment to distinct modular structures. Viewed from today's perspective, Head's views may seem somewhat crude and obscure. As McCarthy and Warrington (1990) point out, however, his criticisms of the diagram makers were complemented by Lashley's (1929) influential 'mass action' view of the role of neurons in the cortex.

One of the main reasons why the work of the early cognitive neuropsychologists in the nineteenth century lost its influence was that theories of cognitive function became confused with theories of anatomical localisation. A particular module became identified with a particular area of the brain. This unfortunately (and inappropriately) meant that the functional components of the models became vulnerable to criticism when the theorising about the anatomical localisation of the individual modules was disconfirmed as a result of post-mortem investigations. Today, however, the emergence of the philosophy of mind that is known as *Functionalism* (Fodor 1981) means that theorising about psychological organisation and anatomical location can be disentangled.

Of course, it must be the case that different cognitive modules occupy anatomically distinct areas of the brain if damage to the brain can detrimentally affect the activity of one module but not another. Consistent with this, advocates of Functionalism are firmly committed to the view that mental states are brain states, and so are happy to accept the identity theory of the relationship between the mind and the brain. However, mental states are seen as being *emergent* functional properties of brain states; mental states are brain states seen at a particular level of abstraction. It is possible to understand how the brain works in purely functional terms without worrying about physiological data. One can therefore talk about the brain, and about the effects of brain injury, without using the vocabulary of neurology, physiology or anatomy at all. Today nobody should seriously doubt the academic legitimacy of postulating the existence of a particular functional module within the brain without concern about that module's anatomical location.

GROUP STUDIES

As we have seen, cognitive neuropsychologists generally prefer to study patients as individual cases. Traditionally, however, work in neuropsychology has tended to study patients within groups. Frequently, a particular 'syndrome' is identified (e.g. amnesics, dyslexics, aphasics, frontal lobe patients, etc.) and patients are initially classified in terms of the syndrome into which they apparently fall. Once a number of 'similar' patients have been identified, they are then examined as a group, and the mean score obtained by the group on the one or more tests might be compared with the scores obtained by an appropriate control group.

Cognitive neuropsychologists, however, are worried about the basis for assigning subjects to groups. How does the experimenter know that they are examining patients with the same functional impairments? Perhaps the use of averaging in group studies disguises important differences. Perhaps some of the symptoms that co-occur in a syndrome such as Broca's aphasia co-occur for functionally uninteresting anatomical reasons rather than for functionally important psychological reasons. That is, a set of symptoms may co-occur, not because they all have the same underlying cause, but because a set of distinct modules occupy locations that are physically close to one another in the brain. Cognitive neuropsychologists therefore prefer single case studies. Each patient is seen as a separate 'experiment' of nature that psychological theory must be able to account for (Ellis 1987). There is no prior allocation of subjects to some putative syndrome or symptom complex.

This is not to say that the group study has no role in cognitive neuropsychology. The single case study has proved particularly useful in enabling us to fragment the cognitive system into distinct modules on the basis of dissociations and double dissociations. A single case methodology is not ideally suited to the discovery of *associations*, however. For instance, if a theorist wishes to claim that phonological short-term memory plays a key role in the learning of new vocabulary, then the demonstration that a patient with poor memory span cannot learn previously unfamiliar Russian words (Baddeley, Papagno and Vallar 1988) is interesting but far from decisive. One's confidence that phonological short-term memory does indeed play this role will increase in line with the number of observed short-term memory patients that perform in a similar fashion. However, a theorist must always be prepared for the possibility that just one case who fails to demonstrate the association can disprove the claim, regardless of the number of seemingly confirming cases they have discovered.

Group studies are also of value if individual patients can be assigned to groups on the basis of some set of objective physical criteria, as is the case with Parkinson's disease, for instance. If one wishes to investigate the cognitive impairments associated with Parkinson's disease, then it seems quite reasonable to investigate the performance of a large group of patients. Nevertheless, even if the mean performance of the patient group falls below that of controls the investigator must pay attention to outliers. The performance of any subject(s) from within the patient group who score well on the test in question must be accounted for if the claim that the disease is the primary cause of the cognitive impairment is to be established.

POTENTIAL PROBLEMS

Although case studies reporting a patient's cognitive impairments have been part of the literature for many years, a number of them have unfortunately been carried out by people untrained in the techniques of behavioural measurement. Consequently, some of them have relied on anecdotal evidence rather than data from appropriately designed psychological tests, and have not compared the patient's performance with that of appropriately matched control groups. In recent years, techniques have become more sophisticated. For example, in the area of face processing, the sophisticated testing procedures used by Young and his associates (de Haan, Young and Newcombe 1991; Ellis, Young and Critchley 1989; Hanley, Young and Pearson 1989) to investigate impairments of familiar face identification represent a major advance over earlier studies which relied heavily on the impression that the patient gave to the clinician or to relatives. The remainder of this section outlines some of the potential pitfalls in designing a case study. For further information about succesful case study techniques, see Shallice (1979).

If one wishes to establish a dissociation between performance by a patient on two types of cognitive task, then it is vital that potentially confounding factors are eliminated. One of the points that Shallice makes is that if testing continues over several sessions, then performance on the critical test(s) on which the subject performs poorly should be replicated. There is always the danger that a patient is showing good performance on tests administered in the later sessions not because of any theoretically interesting dissociation, but because the patient has recovered!

Another potential problem is the nature of the task demands. For example, a patient may perform badly on a particular test simply because they failed to understand the task that they were being asked to perform, or because they simply lacked the ability to perform the motor response that the task requires. It is therefore crucial that evidence of poor performance is supported by the results of a number of different tests in which the task requirements are *varied* as much as possible. It is also important that the task demands of the tests on which the subject performs well and the tests that the subject performs poorly are as *closely matched* as possible. A very neat example of this was provided by Parry, Young, Saul and Moss (1991), in which three different types of face processing impairment (of familar face identification, of facial expression recognition, and of unfamiliar face matching) were all investigated by tests which required simple forced choice recognition decisions to pairs of faces.

Another potential problem concerns the nature of the control subjects. It is typical for a case study to include performance by a patient on certain standardised tests for which control data is already available. Generally, the patient will also be tested on several other experimental tasks, specially designed for the purposes of the case study, for which control data is not already available. Clearly, control data must be collected for the new tests using subjects who are as closely matched as possible with the patient in terms of age, sex, years of education and type of employment. However, to establish a dissociation, it is not optimal to use specially matched control subjects on tests which the subject does badly, and to rely on pre-existing control data for tests which the subject performs 'within the normal range'. There is always the danger that the new control subjects are a more able set of individuals than the pre-existing control subjects. Should this be the case, then any observed 'dissociation' may in reality reflect differences in the ability of the two control samples rather than a difference in the way that the patient performs on the tests they have been given. Consequently, the same matched controls should be used on all of the critical tests that establish the dissociation, including standardised tests.

The definition of normal performance is a potential problem that is less easy to resolve. It is generally accepted that a patient is showing impaired performance on a particular test if their score falls at least two standard deviations below the mean score of normal controls. However, nobody should be convinced by a 'dissociation' when normal performance is assumed if the patient scores, say, 1.8 standard deviations below the mean of the control subjects on a different test.

One of the main safeguards against false data in science is the opportunity to attempt to replicate whatever experiment one wishes. Unfortunately, however, replication of a case study with a particular patient is not always possible. If different results are obtained, it may be that the patient's condition has improved/deteriorated since the original study was performed. It is certainly not possible to 'disprove' or fail to replicate the results of a case study by conducting the same set of experiments on a different patient. If different results are obtained, then the original study may indeed be flawed. However, it may also be the case that the two patients tested differed in important ways. Hopefully any poorly conducted or fraudulent case studies with aberrant results can eventually be isolated from the rest of the literature if they continue to stand out over a long period of time.

The success of cognitive neuropsychology also relies on the assumption that the patient's cognitive system was organised in the same way as that of normal people prior to the brain injury. It also assumes that no new modules develop to take the place of the injured ones. There is no way of proving that this is the case. However, as Ellis and Young (1988) point out, all scientific methodologies, including the case study technique in cognitive neuropsychology, appear to rely on certain untestable assumptions that must either be accepted a priori or rejected. The proof of the pudding is in the eating. If data from case studies fits well with data from normal subjects and with data from other areas of cognitive science then everything is fine. If the assumptions are false then there is hardly likely to be any genuine progress and cognitive neuropsychology will ultimately grind to a halt.

It should also be pointed out that recent developments in connectionist modelling do not pose any kind of threat to cognitive neuropsychology. Although many connectionist models employ the concept of memory representations being distributed across a large number of processing units, these models are not necessarily in conflict with the concept of modularity. For example, the brain can be seen as comprising a large number of discrete modules, in each of which information is represented in the form of distributed representations. It seems that the two approaches can profitably interact as is the case with Plaut and Shallice's (1993) recent attempt to explain Deep Dyslexia in terms of a distributed connectionist model. Deep Dyslexia has proved particularly difficult to account for in satisfactory terms using standard flow diagrams. When 'functional lesions' (reducing the number of units in particular areas of the model) were made to Plaut and Shallice's model, many of the symptoms associated with Deep Dyslexia emerged in a straightforward way. Since cognitive neuropsychology has been successful primarily in establishing the identity of some of the different modules, connectionism can perhaps help us to understand more precisely the computational principles by which individual modules operate. Today the advocates of mass action have become our friends instead of our enemies.

FURTHER READING

Those wishing to find out more about cognitive neuropsychology are fortunate that three excellent texts (Ellis and Young 1988; McCarthy and Warrington 1990; Shallice 1988) have been published in recent years. As will be evident to those who are familiar with them, this chapter owes a great deal to all three. The book by Ellis and Young is particularly recommended for the novice. Those wishing to read more about Functionalism are referred to Hanley (1991) in the first instance.

REFERENCES

Baddeley, A.D. (1992) 'Is working memory working?', *Quarterly Journal of Experimental Psychology*, 44A: 1–31.

Baddeley, A.D., Papagno, C. and Vallar, G. (1988) 'When long-term learning depends on short-term storage', *Journal of Memory and Language*, 27: 586–595.

Bruce, V. and Young, A. (1986) 'Understanding face recognition', *British Journal of Psychology*, 77: 305–327.

Coltheart, M., Curtis, B., Atkins, P. and Haller, M. (1993) 'Models of reading aloud: dual-route and parallel-distributed processing approaches', *Psychological Review*, 100: 589–608.

Damasio, A.R., Tranel, D. and Damasio, H. (1990) 'Face agnosia and the neural substrates of memory', *Annual Review of Neuroscience*, 13: 89–109.

de Haan, E.H.F., Young, A. and Newcombe, F. (1991) 'A dissociation between the sense of familiarity and access to semantic information concerning familiar people', *European Journal of Cognitive Psychology*, 3: 51–67.

Dejerine, J. (1892) 'Contribution à l'étude anatomo-pathologique et clinique des différentes variétés de cécité verbale', *Compte Rendu hebdomadaire des sciences et mémoires de la société de biologie*, 4: 61–90.

Dunn, J.C. and Kirsner, K. (1988) 'Discovering functionally independent mental processes: the principle of reversed association', *Psychological Review*, 95: 91–101.

Ellis, A.W. (1987) 'Intimations of modularity, or, the modularity of mind', in M. Coltheart, G. Job, R. Sartori (eds) *The Cognitive Neuropsychology of Language*, London: Lawrence Erlbaum.

Ellis, A.W. (1988) 'Normal writing processes and peripheral acquired dysgraphias', *Language and Cognitive Processes*, 3: 99–127.

Ellis, A.W. and Young, A.W. (1988) *Human Cognitive Neuropsychology*, London: Lawrence Erlbaum.

Ellis, A.W., Young, A.W. and Critchley, E.M.R. (1989) 'Loss of memory for people following temporal lobe damage', *Brain*, 112: 1469–1483.

Farah, M.J. (1991) 'Patterns of co-occurrence among the associative agnosias: implications for visual object representation', *Cognitive Neuropsychology*, 8: 1–19.

Flude, B.M., Ellis, A.W. and Kay, J. (1989) 'Face processing and name retrieval in an anomic aphasic: names are stored separately from semantic information about familiar people', *Brain and Cognition*, 20: 439–462.

Fodor, J.A. (1981) 'The mind–body problem', *Scientific American*, 244: 114–123.

Fodor, J.A. (1983) *The Modularity of Mind*, Cambridge, Mass.: MIT Press.

Hanley, J.R. (1991) 'Cognitive neuropsychology and the philosophy of mind', in R. Tallis and H. Robinson (eds) *The Pursuit of Mind*, Manchester: Carcanet Press.

Hanley, J.R., Young, A.W. and Pearson, N.A. (1989) 'Defective recognition of familiar people', *Cognitive Neuropsychology*, 6: 179–210.

Head, H. (1926) *Aphasia and Kindred Disorders of Speech*, Cambridge: Cambridge University Press.

Lashley, K. (1929) *Brain Mechanisms and Intelligence*, Chicago, Ill.: University of Chicago Press.

Levine, D.M. and Calvanio, R. (1989) 'Prosopagnosia: a deficit in configural processing', *Brain and Cognition*, 10: 149–170.

Lichtheim, L. (1885) 'On aphasia', *Brain*, 7: 433–484.

McCarthy, R.A. and Warrington, E.K. (1990) *Cognitive Neuropsychology: A clinical introduction*, London: Academic Press.

McNeil, J.E. and Warrington, E.K. (1993) 'Prosopagnosia: a face specific disorder', *Quarterly Journal of Experimental Psychology*, 46A: 1–10.

Milner, B. (1966) 'Amnesia following operation on the temporal lobes', in C.W.M. Whitty and O.L. Zangwill (eds) *Amnesia*, London: Butterworths.

Parry, F.M., Young, A.W., Saul, J.S. and Moss, A. (1991) 'Dissociable face processing impairments after brain injury', *Journal of Clinical and Experimental Neuropsychology*, 13: 545–558.

Patterson, K. (1982) 'The relation between phonological coding and reading: further neuropsychological observations', in A.W. Ellis (ed.) *Normality and Pathology in Cognitive Function*, London: Academic Press.

Plaut, D. and Shallice, T. (1993) 'Deep dyslexia: a case study of connectionist neuropsychology', *Cognitive Neuropsychology*, 10: 377–500.

Seidenberg, M.S. and McClelland, J.L. (1989) 'A distributed developmental model of word recognition and naming', *Psychological Review*, 96: 523–568.

Shallice, T. (1979) 'Case study approach in neuropsychological research', *Journal of Clinical Neuropsychology*, 1: 183–211.

Shallice, T. (1988) *From Neuropsychology to Mental Structure*, New York: Cambridge University Press.

Sherry, D.F. and Schacter, D.L. (1987) 'The evolution of multiple memory systems', *Psychological Review*, 94: 439–454.

Tulving, E., Schacter, D.L. and Stark, H.A. (1982) 'Priming effects in word fragment completion are independent of recognition memory', *Journal of Experimental Psychology: Learning, Memory and Cognition*, 8: 336–342.

Warrington, E.K. and Shallice, T. (1969) 'The selective impairment of auditory short-term memory', *Brain*, 92: 885–896.

Warrington, E.K. and Weiskrantz, L. (1970) 'Amnesic syndrome: consolidation or retrieval', *Nature*, 228: 628–630.

Wernicke, C. (1874) *Der Aphasiche Symptomencomplex*, Breslau: Cohn and Weigart.

Young, A.W. and Bruce, V. (1991) 'Perceptual categories and the computation of "grandmother"', *European Journal of Cognitive Psychology*, 3: 5–49.

Young, A.W., Hellawell, D. and de Haan, E.H.F. (1988) 'Cross-domain semantic priming in normal subjects and a prosopagnosic patient', *Quarterly Journal of Experimental Psychology*, 40A: 561–580.

Chapter 17

Will these instructions do? Methods and techniques for assessing written communication

James Hartley

How much text have you read this week? And how much have you written? Psychology students read and write a great deal. And the kinds of things that they write vary widely. Some items are dashed off without much thought – letters home, reminder notes, etc. Some require more painstaking effort – an assessed essay, instructions for participants in an experiment, a poster for a group presentation, and perhaps the final discussion chapter of a thesis.

Yet all of these different kinds of writing have one thing in common. Any piece of text is written for a particular audience or reader. And, I suppose, the more we know about our audience – and the more frequently we've done the task – the easier it will be. (This is presumably one of the difficulties in writing a thesis. Most of us only write one, and we do not often write text fearing that what we have to say might be severely criticised.)

There is a large research literature on the topic of writing, and I do not propose to review it here. (I have listed the main references at the end of this chapter in an annotated bibliography.) My purpose in writing this chapter is:

1 to indicate those areas of this research that might be useful to students in their work; and
2 to describe some of the methods and techniques that psychologists use to assess the quality and effectiveness of different kinds of text.

In this chapter I shall suggest that there are four different – but overlapping – areas of research in this connection. These entail research on:

1 how to write clearly;
2 how to revise, or improve other people's texts;
3 how to present the text effectively (whether on paper or on a computer screen) and
4 how to evaluate the success of one's accomplishments in the three areas above.

The first two areas of research are concerned with the *language* of the text, the third with its *layout*, and the fourth with *evaluation*.

HOW TO WRITE CLEARLY

Numerous people – psychologists, authors, editors – have offered guidelines on how to write clearly. (See the bibliography.) There are some difficulties with such guidelines for, usually, they are too general. Some people think, for example, that it is not very helpful to be told 'Write short, unambiguous, sentences'. First of all, you are not told how to do it. Next, some variability in sentence length seems to be desirable. And then, if the guidelines get more explicit, it is easy enough to think of exceptions to the rule.

Nonetheless, I happen to think that guidelines can be useful. Guidelines need not be followed slavishly, and they can serve as a checklist and as a reminder of issues that perhaps should be considered. Appendix 17.1 lists some guidelines for clear writing that students might find useful.

Today, of course, it is possible that a student will be writing with a word-processing package that provides a lot of editorial help. In effect these packages provide automated guidelines that can be systematically applied. Such computer programs are useful for doing the donkey work of editing, but unfortunately they are unable to tell you anything about the content of your prose: they cannot, for example, tell you whether or not your choice of example is a good one.

The nature of writing

It is commonplace, in articles about the nature of writing, to divide the processes of writing into three main, overlapping, stages: *planning* – thinking about the content of the text, and its organisation; *writing* – putting down one's thoughts on paper – or on screen; and *editing* – re-thinking and re-planning, as well as correcting spelling errors and the like. Skilled writers move constantly to and fro between these stages when writing.

Some researchers have suggested that in order to improve one's writing skills it is helpful to separate out these three stages – and the sub-stages that they in turn entail – whilst writing. Thus researchers suggest that in the *planning* stage you should map out the broad issues involved that you wish to cover and the sequence in which you will eventually put them. In the *writing* stage some suggest that you should write as quickly as you can, without paying a great deal of attention to punctuation and spelling, or even completing sentences. *Editing* can follow later, and this stage too can be subdivided. For example, you might edit first for content, then for grammar and style, and finally check the references. Working with word-processors has made this much easier to do.

Although using word-processors has changed the way that people write (for example, it is harder to talk of writing separate drafts any more) the basic processes that people use remain much the same. People still plan, write and edit, although perhaps in different proportions than before. This means that some of the findings obtained in earlier studies are still applicable today. In one such study, carried out in 1988, Alan Branthwaite and I used a questionnaire to collect data from eighty-eight highly productive British academic psychologists. (I regret that limitations of space prevent me from describing how we defined 'productive'!) The conclusions that we reached, in terms of giving advice for the less productive academics and for students, are listed in Table 17.1.

Table 17.1 The characteristic strategies of productive writers in psychology

Most productive writers in psychology:

1 Make a rough plan (which they don't necessarily stick to).
2 Complete sections one at a time. (However, they do not necessarily do them in order.)
3 Use a word-processor.
4 Find quiet conditions in which to write and, if possible, write in the same place (or places).
5 Set goals and targets for themselves to achieve.
6 Write frequently – doing small sections at a time – rather than write in long 'binge sessions'.
7 Get colleagues and friends to comment on early drafts.
8 Often collaborate with long-standing colleagues and trusted friends.

Source: Hartley and Branthwaite (1989)

HOW TO REVISE TEXT

Suppose you have completed the first draft – or your first attempt – of the introductory section to a project or a thesis, what might you do to improve it? Or suppose that a friend gives you a copy of his or her first draft, and asks you to comment on it. What do you do? And is what you do the same in both situations?

The research on revision suggests that expert writers revise differently than novices. Expert writers attend to more global problems (e.g. re-sequencing the content, and rewriting larger chunks of text) than do novices. Expert writers are better than novices at detecting problems in their texts, and experts are better at deciding what to do about such problems once they have detected them. However, even experts find it harder to detect problems in their own texts than to detect them in other people's. Thus the research on revision suggests that it is probably easier to revise someone else's text than it is to revise your own. One reason for this appears to be that you are too close to your own text, and too involved. What has become a commonplace for you can still be very difficult for a reader seeing it for the first time.

Appendix 17.2 lists some guidelines for revising text that I once prepared for secondary school children working in pairs. Again, I hope that these guidelines may be helpful for readers of this chapter. They suggest, as indicated above, that editing is not a simple matter, that it can be subdivided into different components, and that these can be worked on separately.

Finally, I should note in this section that most people see editing as being concerned with editing only *the wording* of the text. I want to argue here, and in more detail below, that editing should also be concerned with making sure that the presentation of all the information, be it text or tabular, is meaningful and consistent.

HOW TO PRESENT TEXT EFFECTIVELY

I have long argued – and I hope demonstrated – in my research that the layout of the text on the page (or on the screen) is of vital importance in helping people to comprehend it. Limitations of space prevent me from rehearsing my arguments here in full, but the basic points are:

1 The layout (of text, tables, captions, etc.) needs to be clear and consistent on every page. The reader should never have to wonder where to go to next.
2 One way to achieve this is to plan in advance the amount of line-spacing that one is going to allow between the elements in the text, both vertically and horizontally.

In text of the kind you are reading now there is, typically, more space above a heading than there is below it, but this amount of space may sometimes vary from page to page. The text itself is probably set with a straight left- and right-hand margin (or set *justified* as it is technically called). This is achieved by varying the spacing between the words – and sometimes between the letters – as well as by using hyphenation. New paragraphs are probably denoted by indentation.

In text of this kind this choice of settings probably does not matter very much. The text has a relatively straightforward structure, and you are a skilled and sophisticated reader with years of practice. Imagine, however, that you are a less able reader, presented with text that has a more complicated structure. Imagine, for example, you are a 6-year-old confronted with a primary school mathematics textbook.

With more complicated text settings I want to suggest that you might consider further the vertical and the horizontal settings of the text. Vertically you might like to start each new sentence within a paragraph on a new line, and to use a line-space to signify the start of a new paragraph. Horizontally, you might like to use *unjustified* text, where the space between each word is regular and consistent leading to a ragged right-hand margin, and you might like to consider where you will start and end each line. You could use indentation to show substructure, and you could stop at syntactic points on each line (e.g. following a colon, comma or a full stop) in order to be able to keep together meaningful groupings in the text. One rule you might use, for example, could be: 'Never end a line with the first word of a new sentence'.

Figure 17.1 shows a 'before' and 'after' version of a piece of text where some of these ideas about vertical and horizontal spacing have been applied. The reader will find many other illustrations in my textbook (Hartley 1994). Similar arguments can be applied to the design of tabular materials. So, if you are writing instructions for participants to follow in an experiment, or materials for participants to use, or perhaps a poster for a conference presentation, please consider some of these issues. (Appendix 17.3 lists guidelines for designing posters advocated by the British Psychological Society.)

Original layout

Instructions
On each of the following two pages you will find an abstract taken from a journal article. Words have been left out of the abstracts and blanks have been put in their place. Your task is to decide what word has been left out of each blank and to write that word in the space provided. Reading the whole abstract first may help you to decide what word goes in each blank. Please write only one word in each blank, try to fill in every blank, but skip blanks if you wish.

Revised layout

Instructions
On each of the following two pages you will find an abstract taken from a journal article.
Words have been left out of the abstracts and blanks have been put in their place.
Your task is to decide what word has been left out of each blank and to write that word in the space provided.

Reading the whole abstract first may help you to decide what word goes in each blank.

Please:
 write only one word in each blank,
 try to fill in every blank, but
 skip blanks if you wish.

Figure 17.1 The effects of structured spacing on the appearance of text

HOW TO EVALUATE TEXT

Psychologists use a variety of tools and procedures for evaluating text. Some are appropriate for evaluating someone else's text, some are appropriate for evaluating your own text, and some, of course, are appropriate for both purposes. Similarly, some measures are used by writers before they finalise their text, some are used after it has been produced, and some are used in both situations.

Perhaps the most common question asked about a piece of text is how suitable or appropriate it is for its intended readers. Sometimes, when the readership is well known, it is relatively easy to arrive at an answer. However, if the text is to be used by multiple users for a variety of purposes, then the task becomes more difficult. Several measures can be used to evaluate the suitability of an intended text for its readers. Let us consider some of them in turn.

Readability formulae

Readability formulae can be applied to text in order to predict the age at which readers, on average, will have the necessary reading skills and abilities to understand it. Most readability formulae, in fact, are not as accurate at predicting this as one might think, but the figures that they provide do give a rough guide. Furthermore, if one wishes to compare different texts, or different versions of the same text, then one can get a good idea of their relative difficulty.

There are several readability formulae available, and many of them have now been computerised so that they can accompany word-processing packages. However, the basic principles underlying the different formulae are much the same. Typically formulae combine, with a constant, two main measures in order to predict reading age. These two main measures are:

1 the average length of the sentences in sections of the text; and
2 the average length of the words in these sections.

Some formulae are quite complex to calculate by hand, but others are much simpler. One of the simplest, the Gunning Fog Index, is as follows:

- Take a sample of 100 words.
- Calculate the average number of words per sentence in this sample. (Sometimes you may need to go beyond the 100 words to make this number realistic.)
- Count the number of words with three or more syllables in the sample.
- Add the average number of words per sentence to the total number of words with three or more syllables.
- Multiply the result by 0.4.
- Repeat the procedure with additional samples from the text.
- Average the results.

The answer that one gets is the reading grade level as used in US schools. (Grade 1 = 6 years old; Grade 2 = 7 years old, etc.) You need to add five to this number to obtain an equivalent British reading age (if you think British and American children are similar). You might like to try this formula on chapters in this book. (You should find for this chapter that the predicted British reading age level is around 16 to 18 years old.)

Today, with the advent of word-processing packages, it is easier to apply more complex formulae. For example, the word-processing system that I used to produce this text contained three readability formulae. For this chapter as a whole the results were as follows:

Formula	British reading age
Flesch	18.3
Flesch–Kincaid	16.3
Gunning	19.3

It can be seen that the predictions from the three formulae vary quite a bit, but that they are in line with that from the Fog Index described above.

The basic idea underlying readability formulae is that the longer the sentences and the more difficult the vocabulary, then the more difficult the text will be. Clearly such a notion, whilst generally sensible, has its limitations. Some technical abbreviations are short (e.g. 'DNA') but difficult for people who have not heard of them. Some words are long, but because of their frequent use, become quite familiar (e.g. 'postgraduate'). The order of the words, the sentences and the paragraphs is not taken into account by the formulae, and nor are the effects of other devices used to aid comprehension (such as the typographical layout and the presence of illustrative materials). Also, most importantly, the readers' motivation and prior knowledge are not assessed.

A readability formula then provides a *rough* guide to text difficulty. If the score goes off the scale (as is often the case with government documents) then clearly the text is too difficult for most readers. One of the main advantages, however, of a readability formula is that it can be applied to a text without having to consult readers. Almost all other measures of text difficulty require readers to participate. One such measure is the *cloze procedure*.

The cloze procedure

With this measure samples of the text are presented to readers with, say, every sixth word missing, and the readers are required to fill in the missing gaps. Technically speaking, if every sixth word is deleted then six versions should be presented, with the gaps starting from a different point following the first sentence – which is usually given in full. However, it is more common _____ prepare one version, and perhaps _____ to focus the gaps on _____ words. Whatever the procedure, the _____ are scored either (a) by _____ accepting as correct those responses _____ directly match what the original _____ actually said, or (b) by _____ these together with acceptable synonyms. Since the two scoring methods correlate highly, it is more objective to use the tougher measure of matching exact words. (In the case above these were: 'to', 'even', 'important', 'passages', 'only', 'that', 'author' and 'accepting'.)

Readers' scores are improved by having more words between the gaps, by varying the length of the gap to match that of the missing words, by providing dashes to match the number of missing letters in each word, and by providing the reader with the first of the missing letters. These additional clues may be useful to consider using if you are working with less able readers.

These minor variations in format do not, however, affect the main purpose of this measure, which is to assess the reader's comprehension of the text and, by inference, its difficulty. The cloze procedure has an added advantage over readability formulae in that it can be used to assess the effects of the presence of other features (such as underlining or illustrations) on the comprehension of the text.

Readers' judgements

A rather different but useful measure of text difficulty is to ask readers to judge this feature for themselves. One simple procedure is to ask readers to circle on the text those sentences or words that they think readers *less knowledgeable than themselves* will find difficult. In my experience if you ask readers to point out difficulties for *others* then they are much more forthcoming than if you ask them to point out their own difficulties.

Readers' preferences

Another way to use readers to evaluate two or more texts is to ask them to say which ones they prefer, or to tell you which features they like in one text and not in another. Readers have clear views about what they like in texts, and how they expect texts to perform. So first impressions might colour attitudes to a text. A text that looks dull, dense and turgid is not going to encourage one to read it.

Preference measures, in my view, provide additional information which other measures cannot give. They can tell you whether a revised text is preferred to an original, whether readers see no difference, or whether people prefer the original even though (in your eyes) it is not as effective. However, preference measures can have some unexpected complexities: judgements need to be with reference to a particular base-line, and there is a tendency for people rating two texts, say, out of 10, to give them marks of 6 and 8!

Experimental tests

The measures described above can be carried out relatively informally. Some researchers, however, may wish to carry out more formal experimental

---

Exercise 1

Together with a colleague, inspect the research posters on display in your department (or at a conference).

Rate each one for clarity.

Determine why certain posters get high ratings and certain ones get low ratings.

Exercise 2

In your next research seminar, observe carefully the overhead transparencies used by the speaker.

Determine what factors make them easy/difficult to read.

Consider what extra difficulties there might be for people who are visually impaired.

Exercise 3

Take the overhead transparencies you have prepared for your next talk and put them on display.

Go to the back of the room and judge their legibility.

Consider what you might do if you find yourself speaking in a much larger room.

---

comparisons, and to use more precise measuring instruments. Some people, for instance, might be interested in measuring reading speed, or the ease with which readers can find information, or the readers' degrees of understanding, or how successfully readers can use the document to follow its instructions, etc. Some techniques might be quite precise – e.g. involving the use of eye-movement recording devices – and some might require finely tuned statistical procedures to tease out significant interacting variables.

Over the last ten years or so my colleagues and I have used a variety of measures (and combinations of them) to evaluate experimentally various features of instructional text. Some of these measures have proved more appropriate than others in different circumstances. Thus oral reading measures (where the reader reads out loud) can give detailed information about specific parts of the text that create difficulties; search tasks can evaluate the layout of highly structured text (such as bibliographies, directories, and hypertext); comprehension measures can evaluate the effectiveness of continuous prose; and readability and preference measures can provide additional information.

Experimental evaluations of text require one to start off with a specific problem, to prepare a variety of solutions to it, to select the ones that seem most plausible, and then to evaluate their success by using a battery of appropriate measures. Such evaluations are limited because:

1 it is not possible to evaluate and compare every possible solution to a problem;
2 the methods that we have at our disposal for evaluation in this area tend to be somewhat limited;
3 readers who know that they are taking part in an experiment may behave differently from normal; and
4 different measures have their own in-built assumptions. (For example, many measures seem to assume that the reader starts at the beginning of a piece of text and reads it through steadily until the end.)

Nonetheless, experimental comparisons can provide evidence that is valuable in evaluating the effectiveness of different textual features, and this is particularly the case when several measures are used to obtain the data. Readers who would like to see an illustration of this approach might like to read a paper of mine (Hartley 1994) where I describe how I used preference measures, the Flesch readability formula and the cloze procedure to examine the readability of original and revised journal abstracts. In this paper the combined evidence from the three measures was more convincing than the evidence would have been if only one measure had been used.

Cyclical testing and revising

Often we may not be interested so much in making *comparisons* between texts as in using the methods available to help us *improve* a text. One of the most useful approaches here involves cyclical testing and revising. This approach requires testing a text with appropriate readers, revising it on the basis of the results obtained, testing it again with another set of readers, revising it again and so on, until the text achieves its objectives.

A good example of this type of approach is provided in an article by Waller (1984) that is described in my textbook. Waller shows how he and his colleagues used this procedure to improve a form produced by the Department of Health and Social Security. Initially about 75 per cent of these forms were completed unsatisfactorily. This meant that forms had to be sent back for clarification, or the respondents followed up in one way or another, at a very high cost. Waller describes how the form was redesigned, tested, redesigned again, and so on, through four versions. Following these procedures the error rate was reduced to 25 per cent. After further revisions, the error rate is now estimated to be about 20 per cent. This has led to massive savings for the government department concerned.

Cost-effectiveness

A rather different kind of measure involves making estimates of the cost-effectiveness of new versions of a piece of text. In my own experiments I have sometimes shown reductions in the costs of production, without any loss in comprehension, and sometimes improvements in comprehension for a slight increase in cost. It is important to note that badly designed documents have hidden costs. They provide unnecessary difficulties for readers, they lead to errors, and they convey the wrong impression of the originator. In my view, it is more cost-effective to produce a (relatively) expensive document that works than it is to produce a (relatively) cheap one that doesn't.

CONCLUSIONS

Generally speaking I have wanted to argue in this chapter that writing is not difficult. We do it all the time in many different contexts. It is the particular context that sometimes makes the task seem difficult. However, if one keeps to the notion of communicating to a reader, separating out the different sub-skills, and using a word-processor to facilitate planning, writing and editing, then the task need not be so alarming. Much of what has been said in this chapter is commonsense, and inwardly we know most of it already. The exercises listed on p. 271 are designed to reinforce this point. The trick is to put into practice what we already know!

APPENDIX 17.1

Guidelines for clear writing

1 *Use simple wording*
Short, familiar words are easier to understand than are technical terms which mean the same thing. Thus it is probably better to write something like 'We cannot assume from the start . . .' than it is to say 'We cannot assume, a priori, . . .'

2 *Avoid over-using abbreviations*
Many psychologists abbreviate technical terms: e.g. STM and LTM. Text which is full of abbreviations can look off-putting. Furthermore, if the abbreviations are unfamiliar it is easy to forget what they stand for. (I suggest you examine your computer centre literature for typical examples.)

3 *Vary sentence lengths*
Short sentences are easier to understand than long ones. Long sentences overload the memory system. Short sentences do not. However, some variation in sentence length is appropriate as otherwise the text gets 'choppy'.

As a rule of thumb, sentences less than twenty words are probably fine. Sentences 20–30 words long are probably satisfactory. Sentences 30–40 words long are suspect, and sentences with over forty words in them will probably benefit from rewriting. (The average sentence length of the text in this chapter is, according to my word-processing package, 22 words long.)

It does not necessarily follow that short sentences are always clear. Many short sentences can turn out to be ambiguous.

4 *Use short paragraphs*

Other things being equal it would seem that short paragraphs are easier to read than long ones. However, as with the suggestion about short sentences, some variation in paragraph length is probably desirable. Nonetheless, it is probably better to err on the side of short paragraphs rather than long ones.

5 *Use active tenses if possible*

Generally speaking, text is usually easier to understand when writers use the active rather than the passive voice. Compare the active form, 'We find that the psychologists are more variable than the sociologists' with the passive form, 'For the psychologists, as compared with the sociologists, greater variation is found'. My word-processing package seems to suggest (sorry *suggests*) that I use a lot of passive constructions.

6 *Avoid negatives*

Text is clearer when writers avoid negatives, especially double or treble ones. Negatives can be confusing. I once saw, for example, a label fixed to a lathe in a school workshop which read, 'This machine is dangerous: it is not to be used only by the teacher'. Negative qualifications *can* be used, however, for particular emphasis, and for correcting misconceptions. Double negatives in imperatives (e.g. 'Do not . . . unless . . .') are sometimes easier to understand than single ones.

7 *Place sequences in order*

There are many ways of sequencing text but, whichever way you choose, the presentation needs to be in order. Procedures are perhaps best described in the order in which they must take place. For example, instead of saying, 'Before the machine is switched on, the lid must be closed and the powder placed in the compartment', it would be better to say, 'Place the powder in the compartment and close the lid before switching on the machine.'

Numbers or *bullets* can be used to make a series of points within a paragraph. Thus one might rewrite the sentence, 'Four devices to help the reader are skeleton outlines for each chapter, headings in the text, a concluding summary and a comprehensive index' as follows:

Four devices which help the reader are:

- skeleton outlines for each chapter;
- headings in the text;
- a concluding summary; and
- a comprehensive index.

It is probably best to use *numbers* when there is an order, or sequence in the points being made. *Bullets* are more appropriate when each point is of equal value.

8 Use devices to make the organisational structure clear

Writers can use several devices to help clarify the structure and the sequence of text. *Introductory, interim* and *end summaries* can be helpful.

Headings in text label the sections so that writers and readers know where they are and where they are going. Headings help the reader to scan, select and retrieve material, as well as to recall it. Headings can be written in the form of statements or in the form of questions. *Numbering* the headings (and indeed the paragraphs) can also be helpful, although sometimes the numbering of paragraphs can get overdone.

A rather different way of making text organisation more explicit is to use verbal *signals*. Signals are non-content words that serve to emphasise the structure or the organisation of the passage. Words and phrases such as *however*, or *on the other hand* signal to the reader that some form of comparison is to be made. Similarly words and phrases like *firstly, three reasons for this are, a better example, however, might be* signal the structure of the argument, and comparisons with subsections. Likewise, words and phrases such as *therefore, as a result*, signal causal relationships. Studies have shown that such signals help readers to grasp the underlying structure of an author's argument.

9 When in difficulty . . .

Finally, if you are finding it difficult to explain something, think of how you would explain it to someone else. Think of what you would say, and then write it down. Then polish this – using the procedures outlined in Appendix 17.2.

APPENDIX 17.2

Some guidelines for revising text.

1 Read the text through asking yourself:
- What is the writer trying to do?
- Who is the text for?

2 Read the text through again, but this time ask yourself:
- What changes do I need to make to help the writer?
- How can I make the text clearer?
- What changes do I need to make to help the reader?
- How can I make the text easier to follow?

3 To make these changes you may need:
- to make big or **global** changes (e.g. rewrite sections yourself); or

- to make small or minor **text** changes (e.g. change slightly the original text).

You will need to decide whether you are going to focus first on global changes or first on text changes.

4 **Global** changes you might like to consider in turn are:
- resequencing parts of the text;
- rewriting sections in your own words;
- adding examples;
- changing the writer's examples for better ones;
- deleting parts that seem confusing.

5 **Text** changes you might like to consider in turn are:
- using simpler wording;
- using shorter sentences;
- using shorter paragraphs;
- using active rather than passive tenses;
- substituting positives for negatives;
- writing sequences in order;
- spacing numbered sequences or lists down the page (as here).

6 Keep reading your revised text through from start to finish to see if you want to make any more global and text changes.

7 Finally repeat this whole procedure some time after making your initial revisions (say 24 hours) and do it without looking back at the original text.

APPENDIX 17.3

B.P.S. Guidelines for the preparation of posters.

1 The poster board surface is usually 120 cm high and 180 cm wide.
2 Prepare for the top of your poster a display label indicating: (i) the title of your paper, (ii) the author(s), and their affiliation.
3 Bear in mind that your poster will be viewed from distances of 1 to 2 metres. The lettering for the title should be at least 2.5 cm high, and preferably printed in a bold typeface. The lettering for the text should be at least 1 cm high. (Remember that well-spaced text is easier to read than text 'set solid'.)
4 Use capital letters only where necessary. Lower case letters are easier to read.
5 You need to get your point across in less than 60 seconds. The average poster reader spends less time than this per poster. Therefore, reduce the amount of text and enlarge what you show.
6 Use short, descriptive titles.
7 It helps if you can indicate (by numbers, letters or arrows) a sequence to

be followed in studying your material. (Ideally it helps if the text follows the normal reading sequence.)

8 Use figures and pictures. Tables are more difficult to comprehend.

9 Your poster should be self-explanatory, but you should be available to supplement and discuss particular points raised by enquiry. The poster session potentially provides a more intimate forum for informal discussion than the standard paper presentation, but this becomes difficult if you are obliged to devote most of your time to clarifying your poster for a succession of visitors.

10 You should have a number of copies of your paper available for distribution to interested persons. (Make sure that they contain your name and address, and the date and place of the presentation.)

11 Please do not write or paint on the poster boards.

Guidelines reprinted (and slightly adapted) from the B.P.S. Guidelines For Poster Displays, July, 1992. *Reprinted with permission of the B.P.S.*

ANNOTATED BIBLIOGRAPHY

Books/papers on how to write clearly, etc.

Berger, A. A. (1993) *Improving Writing Skills*, Newbury Park, Calif.: Sage.
  A short, readable book for academics and postgraduates, with advice on how to write memos, letters, reports and proposals.
Day, R. A. (1989) *How to Write and Publish a Scientific Paper*, 3rd edn, Cambridge: Cambridge University Press.
  This is one of the most readable of books of this type. In addition to chapters on how to write a paper, there are succinct accounts of how to present a poster paper, how to write a book review and, indeed, how to write a thesis.

Reviews of research on writing

Hartley, J. (ed.) (1992) *Technology and Writing*, London: Jessica Kingsley.
  After an introductory review of the research on writing, this text includes papers on computers and writing in educational settings, work with readers with special needs, writing *for* computers – as opposed to writing *with* them – and future directions for computer-aided writing.
Hayes, J. R. and Flower, L.S. (1986) 'Writing research and the writer', *American Psychologist*, 41, 10: 1106–1113.
  This classic paper reviews research leading to, and research arising from, Hayes and Flower's influential model of the writing process.

Books/papers on academic writers

Chandler, D. (1995) *The Experience of Writing*, Oxford: Intellect Books.
  This is a stimulating account of the different writing styles of academics. Of particular interest are the distinctions drawn between those who plan a lot, and

revise a little ('planners') and those who plan a little, and revise a good deal ('discoverers').

Hartley, J. and Branthwaite, A. (1989) 'The psychologist as wordsmith: a questionnaire study of the writing strategies of productive British psychologists', *Higher Education*, 18: 423–452.

This paper uses cluster analyses to see if there are groups of productive academic psychologists with different writing styles. The analyses suggest that these writers can be distinguished in terms of their approach ('thinkers' versus 'doers') and in terms of their feelings ('anxious' versus 'enthusiastic'). Some prescriptions for improving productivity are provided.

A text on layout and design

Hartley, J. (1994) *Designing Instructional Text*, 3rd edn, London: Kogan Page.

This text develops the argument that the spatial arrangement of a text profoundly affects how one understands it. There are illustrated chapters on this theme, as well as chapters on how to write and revise text, and how to evaluate design decisions. Also included are chapters on writing text for older and/or visually impaired readers.

Books/papers on the design of tables, graphs and posters

Briscoe, M. H. (1990) *A Researcher's Guide to Scientific and Medical Illustrations*, New York: Springer Verlag.

This text gives practical advice on the design of tables, graphs, slides and posters.

Hartley, J. (1991) 'Tabling information', *American Psychologist*, 46, 6: 655–656.

This brief paper examines sources of difficulties for readers provided by poorly designed tables.

Kosslyn, S.M. (1994) *Elements of Graph Design*, New York: Freeman.

Here a notable psychologist explains step by step how to create clear graphics together with explanations for particular decisions.

Waller, R. (1984) 'Designing a government form: a case history', *Information Design Journal*, 4: 36–57.

This paper presents a good account of cyclical revision and testing.

Woolsey, D. J. (1989) 'Combatting poster fatigue: how to use visual manner and analysis to effect better visual communications', *Trends in Neuroscience*, 12, 9: 325–332.

This is one of the most detailed treatments of the design of posters that I am aware of.

Papers on evaluating text

Hartley, J. (1996) 'Is this chapter any use? Methods for evaluating text', in J. R. Wilson and E. N. Corlett (eds.) *Evaluation of Human Work: A Practical Ergonomics Methodology*, 2nd edn, London: Taylor and Francis.

This chapter in this textbook covers much the same material as this present one, but it is more detailed and contains over seventy references.

Hartley, J. (1994) 'Three ways to improve the clarity of journal abstracts', *British Journal of Educational Psychology*, 64, 2: 331–342.

This paper shows how combining methods of evaluation provides a clearer picture than does using one method alone. It also suggests how psychology journal abstracts can be improved.

Schriver, K. A. (1989) 'Evaluating text quality: the continuum from text-focused to

reader-focused methods', *I.E.E.E. Transactions on Professional Communication*, 32, 4: 238–255.
This paper considers many more methods of evaluating text than are considered in this chapter. A distinction is drawn between text-focused, expert-focused and reader-focused approaches to evaluation. This paper has 150 references.

Index